PORTUGAL
AND
SPAIN

THE BRITANNICA GUIDE TO COUNTRIES OF THE EUROPEAN UNION

PORTUGAL
AND
SPAIN

EDITED BY MICHAEL RAY, ASSISTANT EDITOR, GEOGRAPHY

Britannica
Educational Publishing

IN ASSOCIATION WITH

ROSEN
EDUCATIONAL SERVICES

Published in 2014 by Britannica Educational Publishing
(a trademark of Encyclopædia Britannica, Inc.)
in association with Rosen Educational Services, LLC
29 East 21st Street, New York, NY 10010.

Distributed exclusively by Rosen Educational Services.
For a listing of additional Britannica Educational Publishing titles, call toll free (800) 237-9932.

First Edition

Britannica Educational Publishing
J.E. Luebering: Director, Core Reference Group
Adam Augustyn: Assistant Manager, Core Reference Group
Marilyn L. Barton: Senior Coordinator, Production Control
Steven Bosco: Director, Editorial Technologies
Lisa S. Braucher: Senior Producer and Data Editor
Yvette Charboneau: Senior Copy Editor
Kathy Nakamura: Manager, Media Acquisition
Michael Ray, Assistant Editor, Geography

Rosen Educational Services
Jeanne Nagle: Senior Editor
Nelson Sá: Art Director
Cindy Reiman: Photography Manager
Brian Garvey: Designer, Cover Design
Introduction by Richard Barrington

Library of Congress Cataloging-in-Publication Data

Portugal and Spain/edited by Michael Ray.
    pages cm.—(The Britannica guide to countries of the European Union)
"In association with Britannica Educational Publishing, Rosen Educational Services."
Includes bibliographical references and index.
ISBN 978-1-61530-967-2 (library binding)
1. Portugal—Juvenile literature. 2. Spain—Juvenile literature. 3. European Union—
Portugal—Juvenile literature. 4. European Union—Spain—Juvenile literture. I. Ray, Michael
(Michael J.), 1973- editor.
DP517.P628 2014
946—dc23
                                                                        2013011119

Manufactured in the United States of America

On the cover: *(background)* The façade of one of two skyscrapers that form the Kio Towers,
known as the Gate of Europe, in Madrid, Spain. *(Lower left foreground)* A portion of a
monument to Spanish politician José Calvo Sotelo, whose murder in 1936 led to the start of
the Spanish Civil War. *Jerónimo Alba/age fotostock/Getty Images (tower), Hisham Ibrahi/
Photographer's Choice/Getty Images (monument)*

Cover, p. iii (map and stars), back cover, multiple interior pages (stars) © iStockphoto.
com/pop_jop; cover, multiple interior pages (background graphic) Mina De La O/Digital
Vision/Getty Images

CONTENTS

67

78

89

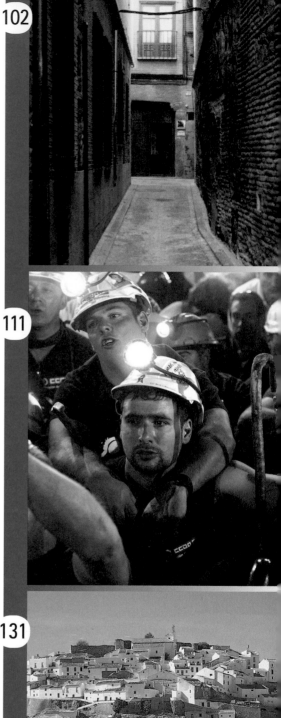

102

111

131

189

201

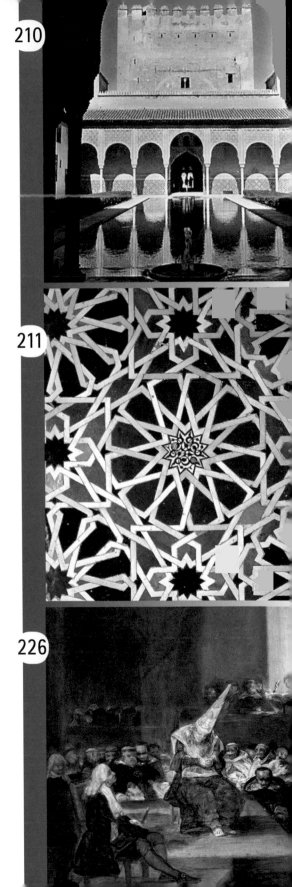

210

211

226

232

237

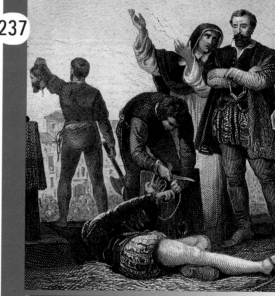

296

Map featuring Portugal and Spain. Nicholas Belton/E+/Getty Images

Given the location of neighbouring Portugal and Spain, and the noteworthy seafaring traditions of both, it is easy to see how these countries have been able to exert great influence over the world at large. Nestled on the Iberian Peninsula, at the southwestern edge of the European continent, Portugal and Spain were in a unique position to explore new lands. Adventurers from the peninsula set sail southward to Africa and west to the Americas, spreading the culture of their respective homelands along the way through colonization and territorial claims.

This book offers a twofold study of each country. In-depth analysis of the state of Portugal and Spain today details the language, traditions, and cultures of each nation—elements shared by hundreds of millions of people the world over in countries that have been touched by Iberian exploration and conquest through the ages. Additionally, comprehensive Portuguese and Spanish histories reveal how such widespread influence came about in the first place.

Portugal is the smaller of the two nations, but it is strategically well-positioned, taking up most of the western coast of the Iberian Peninsula. Its geography and climate encompass both northern European and Mediterranean elements, with cold, mountainous country dominating the north and interior of Portugal, while the south is made up of warm plains and coastal regions.

Despite the diverse landscape, the country's population is homogeneous: almost 90 percent of the people are Roman Catholic, and virtually all speak Portuguese as their first language—which, while similar to Spanish, is a distinct language that has evolved differently from the language of Portugal's Iberian neighbours.

As is the case with other countries of the European Union, Portugal has experienced periods of economic instability through the centuries. Some of its more recent growing pains can be better understood by considering that the country only emerged from authoritarian rule in the mid-1970s, and spent much of the next two decades establishing democratic and free-market institutions. Meanwhile, the Portuguese population has been experiencing another important transition, away from living in rural areas and toward a more urban lifestyle.

These recent challenges are just the latest episodes in a history rife with changing fortunes. In its earliest years, Portugal was the target of a series of foreign settlements and invasions. By the time the Romans gained control in the second century BCE, Celtic, Phoenician, and Carthaginian settlers had already established a foothold in the region. The Romans, in turn, were followed by Germanic and Muslim invaders. Subsequently, from the 10th century through the late 14th century, control of Portugal changed hands among a variety of competing local factions. During this period, however, a national identity and some semblance of a royal succession began to emerge, coalescing into the house of Aviz. Under this dynasty, which ruled in Portugal beginning in 1383, the country's independence from foreign rulers was secure, and its leadership stabilized.

From then on, Portugal looked to extend its reach outward to new lands. A central figure during this period of exploration was a Portuguese prince, Henry the Navigator. In the 15th century, Henry encouraged the study of navigation and increasingly ambitious missions of exploration. In time, those explorations would turn to conquest and empire-building. These exploits saw Portugal establish control of key trading routes and outposts in Africa, Asia, and South America.

The rule of the house of Aviz came to an end in 1580, when Portugal was occupied by Philip II of Spain. There followed 60 years of union with Spain under Philip and two successors, but this situation came to an abrupt end in 1640. With assistance from France (a nemesis of Spain's at the time), Portugal built a strong independence movement that drove out the Spaniards and installed a Portuguese duke, John IV, as king.

The 18th century saw Portugal profit greatly from the mining of precious metals and diamonds in Brazil, as well as from trade with England. Close ties with England were to play an even bigger role in the early 19th century, when the British were instrumental in repelling a series of invasions of Portugal by Napoleon. These invasions left the Portuguese monarchy in a weakened condition, and the royal family was forced to spend more than a decade in exile in Brazil. Portugal's economic conditions steadily worsened, and in 1910 the monarchy was overthrown in favor of a republic that proved to be highly unstable. After a turbulent period of rapidly changing governments, a military coup took control of the country in 1926. Portugal became a dictatorship until 1974, when another military coup overthrew the existing government. What followed was a brief chaotic political period that included flirtations with socialism and communism as the country divested itself of the remnants of its colonial empire. Gradually, Portugal evolved toward an increasingly democratic form of government.

Portugal's experience in the late 20th century was similar to that of other European countries. It emerged from totalitarian control with the hope of democracy, but also with the ongoing challenge of establishing an orderly economy and institutional structure that could thrive under a freer system. The same type of transition was experienced at around the same time by Portugal's neighbour, Spain.

Roughly five times the size of Portugal, Spain also is geographically more varied than its neighbouring country, with snow-capped mountains, deserts, broad plateaus, and agricultural expanses that include sunny citrus farms. The country is also culturally diverse, which in part is due to the wide range of foreign settlers and invaders who have passed through the region through the ages. This cultural diversity is reflected in the range of regional dialects in Spain. In addition to the official Castilian language, Catalan, Galacian, and Euskera are spoken in specific areas. Religion offers a common thread among this diversity; Roman Catholicism is the dominant faith throughout the country.

The Mediterranean climate of Spain's beaches and an abundance of striking architecture make the country a favorite tourist destination. Every year the number of visitors to Spain exceeds the resident population of the country, making tourism a key economic component. Spain's cultural life is another reason so many tourists visit the country each year. The Spanish have a passion for good food and wine, as well as for the arts. Spaniards have made their mark on the world stage in artistic fields such as literature, with writers including Miguel de Cervantes and painters such as Pablo Picasso, who tops an impressive list of famous Spanish artists.

Despite the monetary support received from tourism, Spain's economy has faced a number of challenges. In addition to a transition from dictatorship to democracy in the late 20th century, the government has granted a great deal of autonomy to Spain's 17 different official regions, which can be an impediment to coordinating national economic programs. Another economic challenge is the time-honored custom of businesses taking long breaks, which can last anywhere from two to five hours, in the middle of the afternoon.

Both Spain's cultural assets and its economic challenges can be seen as products of its history, which certainly does not lack for variety and drama. Like Portugal, Spain's early history saw the introduction of people from a variety of places throughout Europe and North Africa. In particular, Romans, Visigoths, and Muslims all had periods of dominance in Spain. After a long struggle for control, Christian Spaniards began to take back territory from Muslim rulers in the 11th and 12th centuries. The country remained largely divided into a number of different states until the major provinces of Aragon and Castile were united by the marriage of King Ferdinand and Queen Isabella in the late 15th century, which joined much of the eastern and western portions of Spain. Yet consolidating control over this combined kingdom remained a challenge. By working systematically together, Ferdinand and Isabella succeeded in bringing a powerful class of nobility in line, thus advancing Spain's progression toward being a unified country—though the populations of Castile and Aragon remained very different from one another.

Unfortunately, Ferdinand and Isabella were also responsible for one of the most notorious episodes in European history, the Spanish Inquisition. Spain had long had a significant Jewish population, but throughout the Middle Ages tensions between this minority and the Catholic majority had grown. Building on the divisive sentiment rampant throughout the country, the Roman Catholic Church in Spain instituted a court of inquisition, designed to ferret out supposed heretics, thereby wresting wealth and power from Jews who had converted to Catholicism, who were highly suspect at the time. In the process the Jewish population of Spain was diminished through executions, exiles, and forced conversions. At around the same time, Ferdinand and Isabella also reduced Muslim influence in southern Spain through a combination of military conquest, forced conversions, and expulsions.

Retaking the southern province of Granada from the Muslims gave Spain a perfect geographic launching point for naval exploration. This is yet another significant and often controversial legacy of the reign of Ferdinand and Isabella. They famously backed the 1492 expedition by Christopher Columbus that led to discoveries in the New World. In later years, the establishment of colonies in North and South America would lead to violent conflicts with other European colonial powers, as well as the often brutal repression of the native populations of those lands. Spanish exploration and colonization also were instrumental in shaping the modern cultures of Central and South America through the introduction of Christianity and the Spanish language.

While Spain was expanding its territories overseas, its reach in Europe was extended when the royal succession following Ferdinand intertwined with the powerful Hapsburgs, who ruled large portions of Europe. The union embroiled Spain in a series of wars with other European powers and the Ottoman Empire. These wars, and especially the destruction of the Spanish Armada in an attempted attack on England, helped weaken Spain financially, militarily, and politically—a pattern of decline that would continue for over a century under the Hapsburg dynasty. Spain would be further weakened by a war over the royal succession at the start of the 18th century that marked the start of the Bourbon dynasty, which linked Spain to France.

Beginning with a revolution in 1868, Spain would see its system of government go through a long series of political change that had the country governed by monarchy, republics, and dictatorship. The country's internal upheaval was a factor in the loss of its colonial possessions, which at one point had extended throughout much of the Americas and all the way to the Philippines in the Pacific. The loss of these territories came sometimes to foreign rivals and sometimes to local independence movements; between the two, the 20th century saw a Spain that was a far cry from the global power it had once been.

With the 1975 death of the dictator Francisco Franco, who had seized power in 1939 with help from Nazi Germany, the monarchy was restored in Spain in the form of King Juan Carlos, a descendent of the Bourbon line. Juan Carlos promptly instituted democratic reforms, making the country a constitutional monarchy in which the king's role was largely ceremonial. Spain has seen some periods of economic growth as a democracy. It has joined the European Union, and participates in the unified European currency, the euro. However, Spain was especially hard-hit by the 2008 economic downturn, and the Spanish government was forced to impose increasingly austere budgets as it struggled to rebuild the country's shattered banking sector.

Modern Spain and Portugal have continuing economic problems, but their influence on the world cannot be denied. This influence is not simply a matter of history; prominent examples of its lasting effects are seen to this day. In 2013, the Roman Catholic Church chose as its new pope an archbishop from Argentina, a country that owes its language and important aspects of its culture to Spain. Brazil won the rights to host soccer's World Cup in 2014 and the Summer Olympics in 2016, bringing these global events to a land where the dominant language is Portuguese. Since Portugal and Spain each have left an imprint on the world that can still be seen so widely and so clearly today, the history behind those imprints is well worth exploring in the pages of this book.

CHAPTER 1

PORTUGAL: THE LAND AND ITS PEOPLE

Portugal occupies the Atlantic coast of the Iberian Peninsula in southwestern Europe. Once continental Europe's greatest power, Portugal shares commonalities—geographic and cultural—with the countries of both northern Europe and the Mediterranean. Its cold, rocky northern coast and mountainous interior are sparsely settled, scenic, and wild, while the country's south, the Algarve, is warm and fertile. The rugged Estrela Mountains (Serra da Estrela, or "Star Mountain Range"), which lie between the Tagus and Mondego rivers, contain the country's highest point.

Portugal occupies one-sixth of the Iberian Peninsula at Europe's southwestern perimeter. To its north and east is Spain, which makes up the rest of the peninsula; to the south and the west is the Atlantic Ocean; and to the west and southwest lie the Azores (Açores) and the Madeira Islands, which are part of metropolitan Portugal. Portugal is not a large country, but it offers a great diversity of physical geography, ranging from low-lying coasts and plains to the Estrela Mountains, which rise to nearly 6,500 feet (2,000 metres) at the country's highest point.

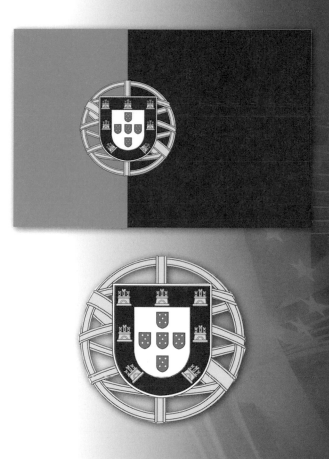

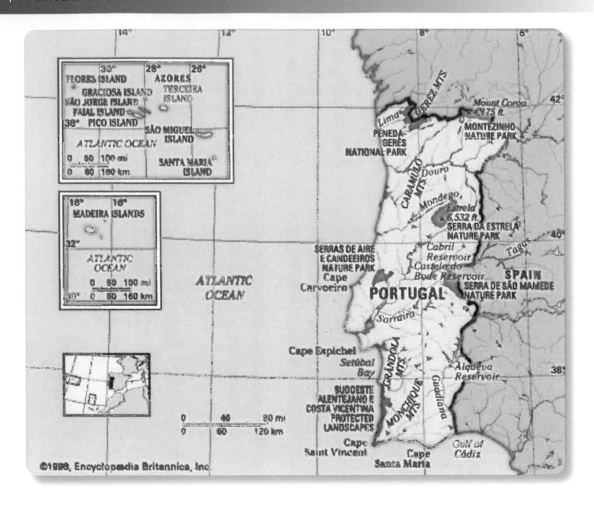

With Spanish Galicia, northern Portugal comprises the mountainous border of the Meseta (the block of ancient rock that forms the core of the Iberian Peninsula); southern Portugal also contains extensive areas of limestone and other sedimentary strata, mostly plateaus or plains. Other physical features link Portugal with Spain: its major rivers—Douro, Tagus (Rio Tejo), Guadiana—rise in the central Meseta before draining west (or, in the case of the Guadiana, south) to the Atlantic, while the proximity of the Meseta affects the climate and increases the rainfall of the northern Portuguese interior, contributing to that region's verdant vegetation. Southern Portugal, however, is predominantly Mediterranean both in vegetation and in climate. Despite Portugal's remarkable scenic diversity, the essence of its relief and underlying geology can be described under three headings: the north, the northern interior, and the south. The old coastal provinces of Beira Litoral and Estremadura are transitional in cultural landscape, vegetation, and climate but southern in relief and geology.

In order to discuss Portugal's physiographic regions, however, it is necessary to consider the provincial divisions of the country that no longer exist as administrative entities but that survive as important geographical designations. Although superseded by several planning regions and districts that now organize Portugal, six provinces have traditionally divided the country since the Middle Ages (though these never served as administrative units): Minho, located between the Minho and Douro rivers; Trás-os-Montes, bounded by Spain (north and east), by the gorges of the Douro River (south), and by the mountains (west); Beira, extending from the Douro River in the north to the Tagus in the southeast and from the border with Spain to the Atlantic Ocean; Estremadura, containing Lisbon; the Alentejo, covering south-central Portugal; and the Algarve, in southern Portugal. From 1933 to 1959, mainland Portugal also was officially further divided into 11 new provinces that were created

Historic provinces of Portugal.

LISBON

Once a remote outpost on what was thought to be the farthest edge of the known world, Lisbon established itself as a centre of operations for Portuguese exploration by the 15th century. The city centre was destroyed by an earthquake in 1755 but was rebuilt by the marquês de Pombal. This seagirt city of multicoloured houses and elegant parks and gardens is no longer the capital of a vast overseas empire. It has been reconstructed as a bustling modern metropolis. In fact, Lisbon was designated a European City of Culture in 1994 and in 1998 hosted the World's Fair (Expo '98), which sparked the city's biggest renewal project since the rebuilding that followed the 1755 earthquake, including the construction of the combined road-rail Vasco da Gama Bridge and other extensive upgrades of the city's transportation infrastructure. The fair also was the primary catalyst for the construction along the Tagus River of an oceanarium, marinas, hotels, commercial complexes, and entertainment venues.

Despite modernization, Lisbon in many ways retains the air of a 19th-century city. The *varinas* (fish vendors) who roam the streets dressed in long black skirts still carry their wares in baskets on their heads. Vessels tie up at quays where the clang of trolley cars blends with ships' horns. At dawn, fishing boats deposit their catch for noisy auction with Lisbon shop owners, while the fish vendors wait to fill the baskets they peddle through the streets. Farther inland, the fish market gives way to the equally colourful and clamorous fruit and vegetable market. Lisbon's port also maintains an intimacy with its city that was common in the days before steam. Amid the freighters, warships, cruise liners, and ferryboats, a picturesque note is struck by the *fragatas* of Phoenician origin; these crescent-shaped boats with their striking black hulls and pink sails still perform most of the harbour's lighterage.

The general outlines of the city remain as they have for hundreds of years. Lisbon is still a city of balconies and vistas. Some of the most striking of the latter can be seen from the *miradouros*, the terraces maintained by the municipality on seven of its hillsides. (Many Lisboetas, as the people of Lisbon are known, profess their city to have seven traditional hills, like Rome.) For centuries Lisboetas have discussed the symptoms of an affliction they believe to be endemic in their city: *saudade* ("melancholy"), a state of anxiety tempered by fatalism that is said to be reflected in *fado* ("fate"), the melodic but deeply emotional folk songs that can still be heard in specific restaurants, mainly in the historic quarters of Alfama and Bairro Alto.

A residential tower over the Vasco da Gama shopping centre in the Expo area of Lisbon. Pedro Moura Pinheiro

on a geographic and economic basis: the Algarve, the Alto (Upper) Alentejo, the Baixo (Lower) Alentejo, Beira Alta (Upper Beira), Beira Baixa (Lower Beira), Beira Litoral, Douro Litoral, Estremadura, Minho, Ribatejo, and Trás-os-Montes e Alto (Upper) Douro.

RELIEF

Less than one-eighth of Portugal rises above 2,300 feet (700 metres). Most of the country's mountains are north of the Tagus River, which flows northeast to southwest and divides the country. North of the Tagus, more than nine-tenths of the land rises above 1,300 feet (400 metres); in the south, only one range, São Mamede, surpasses 3,200 feet (1,000 metres).

NORTH

In the northwest the mountains of the Minho province, surmounted by the Larouco Mountains, which rise to 5,010 feet (1,527 metres), form an amphitheatre facing the Atlantic Ocean. The area is composed of metamorphic rocks (crystalline schists, slates, and quartzites) and intrusive or granitic rocks, marked by fault lines that give rise to hot springs. Rolling plateaus and deeply entrenched streams characterize the relatively fertile granitic regions; the schist outcrops offer poor soils. Between the ridges, rivers such as the Lima and the Cávado flow through deep gorges or in flat-floored valleys. The narrow coastal strip is backed by hills that rise steeply to 1,000 to 2,000 feet (300 to 600 metres).

NORTHERN INTERIOR

Beyond the mountains of the Minho is Trás-os-Montes, which is bordered on two sides by Spain. In the region south of the Douro, which is also the western extension of the Spanish Meseta, are Beira Alta and Beira Baixa.

In the north of the northern interior region are high plateaus (*terra fria* ["cold country"]) at 2,000 to 2,600 feet (600 to 800 metres) that are heavily faulted and composed largely of ancient Precambrian rock (more than 540 million years old), such as granites, schists, and slates. They form a rolling topography. The rivers follow lines of structural weakness and run northwest-southeast. After rejuvenation in the past 5 million years, they now flow in deep valleys and canyons that reach depths of as much as 1,600 feet (500 metres) below sea level. The singular monadnock of the Nogueira Mountains rises to 4,330 feet (1,320 metres) above the general plateau level.

A similar pattern of relief and geology is found south of the Douro, but the sheltered valleys of dark-coloured schists trap the heat of a Mediterranean climate, creating a *terra quente* ("hot country"). The high Beiras plain is bounded on the northwest by the Caramulo (3,527 feet [1,075 metres]) and Montemuro mountains (4,531 feet [1,381 metres]) and their foothills; the plain is flanked to the south and southeast by the granite and schist escarpment of the Estrela Mountains, which, together with the lower Guardunha Mountains (4,026 feet [1,227 metres]), represent the continuation in Portugal of the Central Sierras of Spain. Between the two ridges, the Guarda plateau has an average elevation of 3,000 feet (900 metres). The mountain chain extends southwestward to the Açor (4,652 feet [1,418 metres]) and Lousã mountains (3,953 feet [1,205 metres]). Farther south the eroded plateau of Beira Baixa drops from an elevation of 1,600 feet (500 metres) to 700 feet (200 metres) toward the Tagus River. It merges almost imperceptibly into the highlands of the Alto Alentejo.

SOUTH

Some three-fifths of Portugal's land below 1,300 feet (400 metres) is found in the south. From the lower Douro to Lisbon and the lower Tagus, the plains—mainly Triassic sandstones—of the old western provinces of Beira Litoral and Estremadura descend to low-lying, sometimes marshy coasts. Shifting sands and dunes have been stabilized since the 19th century, but lagoons and salt marshes still characterize the river mouths (e.g., Aveiro Lagoon at the mouth of the Vouga River).

Inland, east and south of Leiria, Jurassic limestones interspersed with large areas of slightly younger Cretaceous sandstones and conglomerates have been eroded into rolling sandy hills and steep calcareous escarpments. Ancient volcanic activity has left basalt plateaus.

Between the Tagus and the Guadiana, the Alto Alentejo is a continuation of the Spanish tablelands—a series of plateaus, either crystalline (Paleozoic Cambrian and Silurian schists), at 600 to 1,300 feet (180 to 400 metres) with poor soils except where outcrops of diorite have weathered into rich black soils, or limestone, with piedmont springs at their foot. North of Beja, in the Baixo Alentejo, ridges of quartz and marble oriented northwest-southeast account for a monotonously undulating relief between 300 and 600 feet (90 and 180 metres). This terminates in the east with the schistose Caldeirão Mountains (1,893 feet [577 metres]). Sheltered by the mountains from northern climatic influences are the more extensive scarps and hills of the Algarve. These are composed of limestones and sandstones of the Mesozoic Era. The Monchique Mountains, a dissected massif of intrusive igneous rock (syenite), rise to 2,959 feet (902 metres) at Mount Foia.

THE MADEIRA ISLANDS

The Madeira archipelago includes eight volcanic islands in the Atlantic, 600 miles (1,000 km) southwest of the mainland. Only two of these, Madeira and Porto Santo, are inhabited. Madeira forms an asymmetrical mountainous hump in mid-ocean, rising to 6,109 feet (1,862 metres) in the interior, falling more steeply in the north. Thick layers of basalt alternating with beds of ash and scoriae create a stepped relief that has been deeply dissected into gorges and canyons. The

AZORES

The Azores are an archipelago and *região autónoma* (autonomous region) of Portugal, lying in the North Atlantic Ocean roughly 1,000 miles (1,600 km) west of mainland Portugal. The archipelago includes nine major islands. The Azores are divided into three widely separated island groups: the eastern group, consisting of São Miguel, Santa Maria, and the Formigas islets; the central group, consisting of Faial, Pico, São Jorge, Terceira, and Graciosa; and the northwestern group, consisting of Flores and Corvo. The capital is Ponta Delgada on São Miguel.

The nearest continental land is Cape Roca, Portugal, which lies 875 miles (1,400 km) east of Santa Maria. Thus, the Azores are farther from mainland Europe than are any other eastern Atlantic islands. Rising from the ocean atop the Mid-Atlantic Ridge, they are in effect a major mountain range. The islands rise steeply from shores lined with rock and pebble debris (scree, or talus) to heights reaching 7,713 feet (2,351 metres) on Pico. Their unstable geologic nature is indicated by numerous earthquakes and volcanic eruptions. In 1522 the town of Vila Franca do Campo, then capital of São Miguel, was buried during a massive convulsion, and as recently as 1957–58 the Capelinhos eruption enlarged Faial Island. Indeed, many island houses are constructed of building blocks made of basalt. Deep craters (calderas) as well as lakes are a dramatic feature of the islands. On São Miguel Island the volcanic heat on the shores of Lake Furnas, a popular picnic spot, is sufficient for cooking.

(continued on next page)

Farm on the northern coast of São Jorge Island, Azores. © Tony Arruza/Bruce Coleman Inc.

(continued from previous page)

The Azores have a subtropical climate with high humidity. An abundant flora of European and Mediterranean origins is found there, and mixed forests still cover many of the islands' hillsides. Intensive agriculture produces cereals (wheat and corn [maize]), vegetables, and fruit (including pineapples and wine grapes). A high-quality cured cheese is made at São Jorge. Among the other principal products of the Azores are various dairy products, fish, pineapples, tea, and wine. A free trade zone has been set up on Santa Maria Island. The scenic beauty of the islands draws visitors in increasing numbers. One of the prime tourist activities is whale watching (whaling ceased in 1984). Some 20 species of cetaceans can viewed.

The inhabitants of the Azores are mostly of Portuguese origin and predominantly Roman Catholic. A high density of population and limited economic opportunities provoked extensive emigration, mainly to the United States and Canada, from the end of the 19th century well into the 20th century and has not entirely ceased. The islands' isolation has diminished and communications have considerably improved. Every island has an airport or airstrip. The principal seaports are Angra do Heroísmo (or Angra), Ponta Delgada, and Horta. Lajes and Santa Maria became important air bases and centres of communication between the United States and Europe during World War II; since 1951, by agreement with Portugal, the United States has maintained a NATO air base on Lajes. Before the development of weather satellites, meteorological data compiled and transmitted from the Azores was essential to European weather forecasting.

cratorial Curral das Freiras is about 2,265 feet (690 metres) deep. Paul da Serra is a bleak high-level plateau. The eastern tip of Madeira, like the uninhabited Desertas Islands, is sandy. The island of Porto Santo is low-lying and flat.

DRAINAGE

All of Portugal's main rivers flow from Spain over the edge of the Meseta in a series of defiles (narrow gorges), and their usefulness, either for navigation or as routeways for roads and railways, is thus limited. The longest river crossing Portugal, the Douro, which extends some 200 miles (300 km) in the country, has been made navigable from near Porto to the Spanish frontier. In its upper reaches, the Douro riverbed drops 16 feet (5 metres) per mile in gorges 90 to 160 feet (30 to 50 metres) deep, a navigability problem resolved by locks built into five dams, including one that is 115 feet (35 metres) high. The longest river wholly in the country is the 137-mile (220-km) Mondego River, which rises in the Estrela Mountains. Other mainly Portuguese rivers include the Vouga, Sado, and Zêzere (a tributary of the Tagus). Like the Mondego, all are navigable for short distances. Rich silt land (*campo*) in the lower Tagus valley is the result of regular flooding, which is especially severe when strong southerly gales drive high seas up the estuary. The Guadiana, which flows south into the Gulf of Cádiz, forms part of the frontier with Spain, as does the Minho in the north.

Portugal has more than 500 miles (800 km) of coastline, four-fifths of which faces westward. Except at the mouths of the larger rivers, there are few major indentations or natural harbours; the most important are those of Lisbon, on the Tagus, and Setúbal, on the Sado. The entrance to the Tagus is a long, narrow deepwater channel opening out into a broad expanse of inland water. Other harbours depend on the protection of headlands (e.g., the artificial harbours of Leixões and Sines).

SOILS

Most of Portugal's soils are arid, acidic, and sandy, though in the north the soil often is rocky. Except for parts of northern Portugal that receive significant precipitation and along the country's primary rivers, which deposit fertile alluvium, the soils are not suitable for intensive agricultural production. In the central and southern parts of the country, the soils are generally poor and incapable of significant agricultural production without extensive irrigation schemes.

CLIMATE

Climate, through its effect on vegetation, divides Portugal. As in Spain, three sets of influences are involved: Atlantic, continental (Mesetan), and Mediterranean. The Atlantic climate predominates overall, putting most of the country into the humid zone of the Iberian Peninsula; this is especially true in the northwest, where the climate is mild and rainy. Summer temperatures near sea level may average up to 76 °F (24 °C) but are rather lower at exposed higher elevations. Winter temperatures average 37 to 40 °F (3 to 4 °C) but tend to be milder south of the Douro. Annual rainfall averages more than 40 inches (1,000 mm).

In the extreme northwest, much of the Minho receives 40 to 80 inches (1,000 to 2,000 mm) of precipitation, with more than 100 inches (2,500 mm) falling on mountain slopes. Inland, lee slopes are arid, receiving at most 20 inches (500 mm), much of which is lost through high evaporation rates. In the interior, continental influences increase the duration of the summer drought to more than a month and intensify winter severity. High-pressure conditions from the Spanish Meseta or from Siberian anticyclones bring very cold temperatures. The Alentejo can experience both acute winter cold and extreme summer heat. In the highest areas of the Estrela Mountains and northern ranges, temperatures drop to 32 °F (0 °C), and snow remains on the summits for several months. In the south, where the Azores high-pressure system prevails in summer, the period of drought lengthens to two months or more. Temperatures average about 75 °F (24 °C) in summer and 50 °F (10 °C) in winter. Mean annual precipitation is slightly more than 20 inches (500 mm) along the coast and a bit higher in the mountains of the Algarve. Nevertheless, there is considerable climatic variability from one year to the next.

Mediterranean, Saharan, and oceanic influences produce seasonal precipitation, occasional dry winds, and thermal equability, respectively, in the Madeiras. Climate varies markedly with altitude. In the Azores the anticyclone dominates, though conditions can be highly variable. Rainfall, for example, is irregular both in annual total and in regime: Horta (on Faial Island) may have more than 40 inches (1,000 mm) a year or may suffer severe drought.

PLANT AND ANIMAL LIFE

Portugal's vegetation is a mixture of Atlantic, or European, and Mediterranean (with some African) species. Overall, the former accounts for some two-thirds of species, but the regional distribution is revealing. North of the Mondego valley, nearly three-fifths of the plants are European species (some seven-eighths in the northern interior), and only one-fourth are Mediterranean; in the south the proportions are three-tenths and nearly one-half, respectively. One-third are foreign species, introduced in periods of colonization.

Millennia of human activity have left Portugal with only one-fourth of its area under woodland; the remainder of the country features two types of Mediterranean scrublands—called maquis and *matorral*, or steppe. Mixed deciduous trees are confined to the north and northern interior, where the landscapes of the Minho are lush and green except for the

Vineyards and olive groves in the upper Douro River valley of the Trás-os-Montes area, Portugal. Eric Carle/Shostal Associates

heaths (*mato*) of the Cambrian schists. These carry erica, heather, cistus, and bracken. The original oak climax (with *Quercus robur* as the dominant species) has been largely replaced by maritime pine with some cork oak and extensive plantations of eucalyptus. Olives extended into the north in Roman times but are now generally limited to elevations below 1,200 feet (400 metres); inland, where the summer drought is longer, they can be found in some areas with elevations as high as 2,200 feet (700 metres). In the Douro valley, juniper scrub has been replaced by vineyards.

The thickest forests in Portugal are found in the traditional province of Beira, where cultivation is limited to less than one-fourth of the area. Pines prevail in the north, chestnut groves on the granites, and ericas on the dense maquis. The elevational succession of vegetation is strongly marked on the Estrela Mountains, where a zone of Pyrenean oak extends above the pedunculated oaks, chestnuts, and pines to 5,500 feet (1,700 metres), while southern slopes are covered with a maquis of cistus and tree heath. The central ridge marks the southern limit of deciduous oak, which is thereafter replaced by *Q. lusitanica* (Portuguese oak). Heat-loving stone pines mix with maritime pines.

In the south the Alentejo still has extensive *matorral* and *charneca*, uncultivated land dominated by cistus or groves of cork oak, often managed in estates, and holm oak. Most of the Algarve landscape is dominated by the vine and by trees typical of Mediterranean arboriculture—olive, fig, almond, and carob.

The rich vegetation of both Madeira and the Azores has been Europeanized. The climate encourages year-round growth of a considerable variety of flora. A wealth of ferns, mosses, heaths (especially tree heaths), and junipers reflects the influence of grazing and human activities on these islands. About 100 plants are peculiar to Madeira, either as indigenous or as highly individualized varieties. Only Madeira has much woodland, most of it the result of reforestation (e.g., of poplar, pine, and eucalyptus). Two-thirds of Madeira is a conservation area; its Laurel Forest (Laurisilva) was designated a UNESCO World Heritage site in 1999.

Parks, reserves, and other protected areas covering more than 5 percent of the mainland have been declared from the far north of Portugal (Peneda-Gerês and Montesinho) to the extreme south (Formosa River), from the east (Malcata Mountains and Guadiana valley) to the west (Berlengas Islands, Sintra), and in several areas of natural beauty in between. Since the mid-1980s, environmental concerns and ecological associations have grown slowly but steadily. In 1990, as part of an effort to expand protection of the environment, the government established an environment ministry.

The fauna of Portugal is a mixture of European and North African types. As in Spain, the wild goat, wild pig, and deer can be found in the countryside. The wolf survives in the remote parts of the far north and northeast, and the lynx inhabits the Malcata Mountains. The fox, rabbit, and Iberian hare are ubiquitous. Birdlife is rich because the peninsula lies on the winter migration route of western and central European species. Hunting zones cover nearly one-third of Portugal. In the Azores, only the smaller mammals are found— such as the rabbit, weasel, ferret, rat (brown and black), and mouse as well as various types of bats. Game birds include woodcock, red partridge, quail, and snipe. The highly endangered Mediterranean monk seal is native to Madeira's Desertas Islands, which were designated a nature reserve in 1990. Some 40 species of birds breed there, including the Madeira laurel pigeon and the Zino's petrel. The variety of beetles (nearly 700 species, many indigenous) and moths (more than 100 species, about one-fourth of which are peculiar to the Madeiras) is remarkable.

Fish are plentiful in the Atlantic waters of mainland Portugal, especially the European sardine. Crustaceans are common on the northern rocky coasts, and clams and oysters are raised in the Algarve. Larger fish (tunny, bonito) as well as mullet are caught off the Azores and the Madeira Islands.

ETHNIC GROUPS AND LANGUAGES

Although western Iberia has been occupied for a long time, relatively few human remains of the Paleolithic Period (Old Stone Age) have been found. Neolithic Period (New Stone Age) and Bronze Age discoveries are more common, among them many dolmens (stone monuments). Some of the earliest permanent settlements were the northern *castros*, hill villages first built by Neolithic farmers who began clearing the forests. Incoming peoples—Phoenicians, Greeks, and Celts—intermingled with the settled

PORTUGUESE LANGUAGE

Portuguese is a Romance language spoken in Portugal, Brazil, and Portuguese colonial and formerly colonial territories. Galician, spoken in northwestern Spain, is a dialect of Portuguese. Written materials in Portuguese date from a property agreement of the late 12th century, and literary works appeared in the 13th and 14th centuries. In 2008 the Portuguese parliament passed an act mandating the use of a standardized orthography based on Brazilian forms.

Standard Portuguese is based on the dialect of Lisbon. Dialectal variation within the country is not great, but Brazilian Portuguese varies from European Portuguese in several respects, including several sound changes and some differences in verb conjugation and syntax; for example, object pronouns occur before the verb in Brazilian Portuguese, as in Spanish, but after the verb in standard Portuguese. The four major dialect groups of Portuguese are Northern Portuguese, or Galician, Central Portuguese, Southern Portuguese (including the dialect of Lisbon), and Insular Portuguese (including Brazilian and Madeiran). Portuguese is often mutually intelligible with Spanish despite differences in phonology, grammar, and vocabulary.

Typical of the Portuguese sound system is the use of nasal vowels, indicated in the orthography by *m* or *n* following the vowel (e.g., *sim* "yes," *bem* "well") or by the use of a tilde (-) over the vowel (*mão* "hand," *nação* "nation"). In grammar its verb system is quite different from that of Spanish. Portuguese has a conjugated or personal infinitive and a future subjunctive and uses the verb *ter* (Latin *tenere*, Spanish *tener* "to have, to hold") as an auxiliary verb instead of *haver* (Latin *habere*, Spanish *haber* "to have"; in Spanish used only as an auxiliary verb).

inhabitants, and Celticized natives occupied the fortified castros. For two centuries these were centres of resistance to the Roman legions. Subsequently the Romans, Suebi, Visigoths, Moors, and Jews exerted influence on the territory. Portugal's location at the western extremity of Europe made it a gathering place for invaders by land, and its long coastline invited settlement by seafarers.

More than nine-tenths of the country's population are ethnic Portuguese, and there are also small numbers of Brazilians, Han Chinese, and people from Portugal's former colonial possessions in Africa and Asia. Ethnic Marranos (descendants of Jews who converted to Christianity but who secretly continued to practice Judaism) constitute about 1 percent of the population, and the country's Roma (Gypsy) population lives primarily in the Algarve. Language is an extremely common bond: Portuguese is the first language of nearly the entire population.

RELIGION

More than ninth-tenths of Portugal's citizens are Roman Catholic. Regular attendance at mass, however, has declined in the cities and larger towns, particularly in the south. Less than 2 percent of the population is Protestant, with Anglicans and Methodists the oldest and largest denominations. In the late 20th century, fundamentalist and Evangelical churches grew in popularity, though the number

Staircase leading to the church of Bom Jesus do Monte, a Catholic sanctuary and pilgrimage site in Braga, Portugal. Porterfield-Chickering/ Photo Researchers

of their adherents remained quite small. The Jewish population of Portugal is also tiny, as Jews were forced to convert or emigrate during the Inquisition in the late 15th century.

SETTLEMENT PATTERNS

The landscapes of mainland Portugal are the result of human activity since prehistoric times. Inhabited caves and rock shelters, some with rock art (e.g., in Escoural), indicate occupation during the Upper Paleolithic Period. The discovery of 20,000-year-old engravings in the Côa River valley led to the opening in 1996 of an archaeological park of prehistoric rock art. Most of the later Neolithic megalithic monuments and rock-cut tombs are found in west-central Portugal or south of the Tagus. Known sites of early metal-using (Copper Age [Chalcolithic Period] and Bronze Age) people are concentrated in the drier portions of Portugal. Only from the Early Iron Age onward does the whole of Portugal appear to have been equally densely occupied, although the area lying between Braga and the Gerez (Gerês) valley is singularly rich in Roman remains.

Many of Portugal's urban centres date from Roman times. Settlements developed on lower ground around native fortified hilltop *castros* in northern Portugal. The harbour at Lisbon had been used by the Carthaginians, but it was the Romans who enlarged the site into a strategically located administrative centre for the province of Lusitania. Lisbon continued as a Visigothic stronghold. Indeed, fortification is the keynote for most of Portugal's settlement history. The Middle Ages and the Reconquista (Reconquest) left fortified, usually hilltop towns throughout the country but especially toward the Spanish frontier in the south (e.g., Santarém, Tomar, Évora, Portalegre, Estremoz, Beja, Castelo Branco, Abrantes, and Monsanto). Other small towns grew from Cistercian colonization on the Estremadura coast (e.g., the abbey at Alcobaça and granges at Alvominha, Cós, Maiorga, Salir do Porto, and Turquel). New towns were created later for a variety of reasons, including

proximity to mineral springs (Caldas da Rainha) or important fortresses (Leiria and Viana do Castelo). Along the coasts the fortunes of port settlements were as unstable as the shifting sands that blocked their harbours, and most modern ports are of relatively recent origin (e.g., Faro, in the south, and Olhão, an 18th-century fishing settlement).

The pattern of rural settlement also reflects both historical and physical factors. The *bocage* (hedgerow country: fields surrounded by woodlands) of the Minho is associated with a dense distribution of individual holdings on granite that drops to a thin scatter in areas of schist. Most buildings are of two stories with an outside staircase. Nucleated settlement, formerly associated with communal farming systems, is characteristic of the Trás-os-Montes and the pastoral districts of Beira Alta. In Estremadura, traditional farmsteads consist of a number of single-storied buildings. In the formerly feudal south, estate labourers and tenants were housed centrally in long barracklike buildings grouped around montes (courtyards), whose origins date from Arab and even Roman times. The waterwheels and fig-drying floors associated with the dispersed farmsteads of arboriculture districts in the Algarve are another Arab legacy. Neither the Madeiras nor the Azores were occupied before the start of colonization by the Portuguese in the 16th century.

Today the population distribution within Portugal reveals striking contrasts between the more densely populated north and the more sparsely populated south. A number of rural areas have suffered considerable population losses, resulting in economic and social depression, particularly in parts of the north, the Alentejo, and southern inland areas. The coastal zones between Braga and Setúbal, with their low-lying plains and urban development, have attracted a large proportion of the population. Few places outside the industrial areas of Lisbon, Setúbal, and Porto are able to absorb their own working populations. Areas such as the Minho and parts of the coastal plains are seriously overpopulated. Overall, about two-thirds of Portugal's population live in urban areas.

In the main, rural settlement is dispersed, with inhabitants living in small villages under a system of open-field farming. Beira Litoral and Estremadura have settlements varying between dispersed and clustered farmsteads. In the Aveiro district, clusters of farmsteads and other dwellings are strung along roads in strips, often of considerable length and density. Fishing, one of the earliest enterprises of the Portuguese, still plays an important role in coastal communities. Owing in part to the rigours and hazards of this and certain other traditionally male occupations, as well as intensive waves of largely male emigration, women have substantially outnumbered men in the Portuguese population since the first modern census in 1864 (a previous census had been carried out in 1527).

DEMOGRAPHIC TRENDS

The decolonization process that took place after the Revolution of the Carnations (April 25, 1974) inevitably had demographic repercussions on metropolitan Portugal because of the large number of people (mostly Portuguese) who left the former overseas provinces. Some one million refugees, most of whom came from Angola in part because of the civil

TOMAR

Tomar is a city and *concelho* ("municipality") in central Portugal, on the Nabão River, a tributary of the Zêzere, northeast of Lisbon. The city contains the 12th-century castle of the Knights Templar and the convent of the Order of Christ (Ordem de Cristo; founded 1314), which played an important part in the voyages of discovery; these were designated a UNESCO World Heritage site in 1983. Other notable architectural examples include a 16th-century church built in the Manueline style (a mixture of Moorish and florid Gothic) by João de Castilho, and the Renaissance church of Our Lady of the Immaculate Conception (Nossa Senhora da Conceição; 1579). The ruined palace of Henry the Navigator was restored in the 16th century. Tomar is an agricultural trade centre (olive oil, wine, fruits, and vegetables), and tourism is important.

Portuguese cities and towns, the effect of which was a high unemployment rate that continued for the next decade.

Portugal has one of the highest rates of emigration in Europe. Before 1960 most of its émigrés went to Brazil and a few other Latin American countries. The population underwent its only decline in the modern period during the 1960s, when two external developments coincided: severe labour shortages in industrialized western Europe induced an outflow of Portuguese workers, and Portugal's efforts to suppress the liberation movements in its African colonies prompted thousands of young men to emigrate illegally in order to avoid conscription. From Madeira and the Azores too, emigration was a continuing pattern—from the Azores mainly to the United States and from Madeira mainly to South America.

Life expectancy in Portugal is high in comparison with the rest of the world, but it is slightly lower than most other countries in western Europe. Birth rates are about half the world average; death rates are slightly higher than the world average. At the beginning of the 21st century, population growth was slow, and it was anticipated to begin a slight decline.

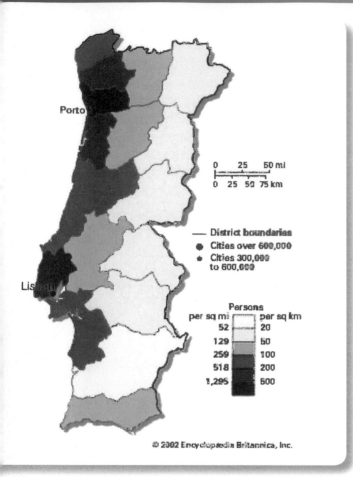

Population density of Portugal. Encyclopaedia Britannica, Inc.

war between the liberation movements, settled in Portugal. The majority of the repatriates (*retornados*) crowded into

CHAPTER 2

THE PORTUGUESE ECONOMY

Portugal was the world's richest country when its colonial empire in Asia, Africa, and South America was at its peak. Because this wealth was not used to develop domestic industrial infrastructure, however, Portugal gradually became one of western Europe's poorest countries in the 19th and 20th centuries. From the mid-1970s, after the Portuguese revolution, the country's economy was disconnected from Portugal's remaining overseas possessions in Africa and reoriented toward Europe. In 1986 Portugal joined the European Economic Community (ultimately succeeded by the European Union [EU]), spurring strong and steady economic growth. Similar to those of other western European countries, Portugal's economy is now dominated by services; manufacturing constitutes a significant share of output, while agricultural output is relatively minor, accounting for less than 3 percent of output. In the early 21st century, economic growth had improved living standards dramatically, raised incomes, and reduced unemployment. In addition, since Portugal's accession to the EU, large inflows of structural funds, private capital, and direct investment have fostered and sustained development. Portugal was one of the countries hardest hit by the euro-zone debt crisis that erupted in 2009, however, and a raft of government measures proved ineffective at halting the country's economic meltdown. In 2011 the EU and the International Monetary Fund authorized a €78 billion (about $116 billion) bailout package for Portugal, contingent on the adoption of strict austerity guidelines.

AGRICULTURE, FORESTRY, AND FISHING

Crop yields and animal productivity in Portugal are well below the EU average because of low agricultural investment, minimal mechanization, little use of fertilizers, and the fragmented land-tenure system. The main crops grown in Portugal are cereals (wheat, barley, corn [maize], and rice), potatoes, grapes (for wine), olives, and tomatoes. Since 1999, Portuguese farmers have planted genetically modified corn. Portugal is among the world's largest exporters of tomato paste, and is a leading exporter of wines. Port and muscatel, both dessert wines, are among Portugal's most famous varieties of wine.

In mainland Portugal, where there are nearly 50 demarcated wine regions, viticulture is a dominant activity; many people also work in the industry on the island of Madeira, where investment in vinification techniques has sustained the renown of Madeira wines. Newer crops include sunflowers, and Portugal also produces large quantities of fruits (oranges and apples). The country's agricultural exports help offset the cost of imported wheat and meat. Nearly one-third of Portugal's land area is used for agriculture.

Small farms predominate, particularly in the north, where they are too small and made up of too many dispersed holdings to allow integrated farming and rational crop rotation. In the south (except for the Algarve region) before 1975, intensive

Vineyards in the Minho area, Portugal. G. Mairani

cultivation was prevented by the system of *latifúndios*, or large estates, which were owned by absentee landlords who had no interest in making capital investment in machinery, fertilizers, and other items that would increase productivity. After the 1974 revolution, agrarian reforms were implemented south of the Tagus, where about 3.2 million acres (1.3 million hectares) of land in large holdings were expropriated (with compensation) and nationalized. The policy was aimed at, among other things, destroying the *latifúndio* system, changing the tenancy system, handing uncultivated land back to the people, abolishing quitrent (rent paid by peasants to use royal or state-owned land or property), increasing the irrigated area, introducing new crops,

PORT

Port is a sweet, fortified, usually red wine of considerable renown from the Douro region of northern Portugal. It is named for the town of Oporto, where it is aged and bottled. The term "port" is also used to describe any of several similar fortified wines produced elsewhere. The region of true port production is strictly delimited by Portuguese law. The soil and grapes, and the skill of Oporto vintners in blending, produce wines of remarkable character, with types running through a series of flavours. Vintage port, the finest, is not blended; but harvests deemed worthy to produce it are rare. The full richness of the port taste is found in dark vintage and vintage character ports; these types are taken from the cask after two or three years and complete their aging in the bottle. Vintage character port is a blend of best wines, sometimes called crusted port because, as with vintage port, it forms a crust within the bottle. Ruby port is a blend of younger wines. Tawny port is blended and matures in cask, changing its colour.

Peculiar to the vinification of port is a large dosage of brandy given to the still fermenting must, by which the character of the wine is greatly changed. Much time is needed for the maturing of ports; in 1950, for example, 1912 port was still excellent. There is some white port, usually made from white grapes, but it is not of equal distinction. The name port has been appropriated by certain wines of other countries, sometimes not aged, often not from the same grapes.

intensifying the output of fodder and cereals, and developing livestock. A large part of the nationalized land was turned over to collective and cooperative production units. The hasty transition, however, precipitated political tension and a decline in the agricultural output of the Alentejo region. The land redistribution policy was reversed after 1976, as succeeding governments sought to encourage modernization and higher productivity by a return to private ownership. Agricultural subsidies were made available, though not all farmers took advantage of them. The Alqueva Dam—criticized for its destruction of a significant amount of rock art and rare fauna and flora, including some one million trees—began operations in 2002 and provides irrigation to southern Portugal.

Sheep, pigs, and cattle are among the country's leading livestock. Beef cattle, dairying, and wool production contribute to Portugal's economy, though their relative importance varies by region.

About two-fifths of Portugal is wooded, and the majority of its forests are privately owned (among the highest proportions in Europe). Most of the mountainous areas are well suited to forestry, and the demand for forest products has prompted considerable reforestation efforts since the last quarter of the 19th century in areas where crop yields are low and where erosion tends to be severe. The pulp and paper industry contributes

Stripped cork oak trees in the Alentejo area, Portugal. Josef Muench

significantly to the economy. Portugal is a leading producer of cork, which has become a significant export. Eucalyptus plantations cover about one-seventh of forest land, and pine is also important.

Portugal's long coastline and the abundance of fish in the surrounding waters have favoured the development of the fishing industry. Among some 70 varieties are sardines, horse mackerel, and hake caught near the coasts, tuna from the Azores, scabbard fish from Madeira, and codfish from the North Atlantic, which together make a large contribution to food supplies. The fishing industry, facing intense international competition and disadvantaged by small, old boats, suffered a severe decline in the mid-1980s. With funds from the EU for new fishing vessels, a program for renovation, new EU agreements and bilateral accords, and the establishment of seaport training schools, the fishing industry revived in the 1990s, and its products are exported all over the world. The Port of Leixões in the north, Peniche and Setúbal in the west, and Portimão and Olhão in the Algarve are among the main fishery centres. Compared with other coastal European countries (e.g., Norway and Denmark), however, catches are relatively small, and the fishing industry is unable to meet domestic need; about one-fourth of the fish consumed in Portugal is imported, mainly from Iceland (stockfish), Norway (dried cod), and Russia (sardines). Oysters, sea bream, sea bass, and trout are reared in tidal estuaries.

RESOURCES AND POWER

Tungsten, tin, chromium, and other alloy metals are mined in commercial quantities, and most of the tungsten is exported. Ornamental and industrial rocks, especially marble, have become a substantial export. Coal mined at Moncorvo supplies the national steelworks. Copper is extracted at the extensive Neves Corvo mine, and since 1989 Portugal has exported large quantities of copper concentrates. Other products range from granite to mineral water, and the country has large uranium reserves.

Portugal imports about four-fifths of its energy supplies; it depends heavily on the importation of petroleum and petroleum products as well as coal, which accounts for about 25 percent of the country's electricity production. (Domestic production of coal has increased since the mid-1980s, but the coal is of fairly low quality.) A natural gas pipeline from North Africa was completed in 1997. Nearly one-fifth of Portugal's electricity is provided by hydropower, and a smaller proportion comes from thermal energy.

In the early 21st century, Portugal increased its use of alternative energy sources. A large wind farm—the largest in Europe at the time it was built—opened in 2008 in northern Portugal, and one of the world's largest photovoltaic farms (which use solar panels to generate electricity) is near the town of Moura in southeastern Portugal. The country also has experimented with wave-power technology.

MANUFACTURING

About four-fifths of Portugal's industrial capacity is concentrated around Lisbon and Setúbal in the south and Porto, Braga, and Aveiro in the north. Lisbon and Setúbal support oil refining, chemical industries, cement processing, automobile manufacturing and assembly, electronics manufacture, wood-pulp and cork production, and fish and beverage processing. Light industry prevails in the north. Textiles, footwear, furniture, wine, and processed foods are produced in Porto. Aveiro is a centre for wood pulp and wood products, and Braga specializes in clothing, cutlery, and electronics. Fuel and energy production is important at Sines, a deepwater port about 90 miles (150 km) south of Lisbon, and Coimbra and Leira are notable for the production of plastic molds and machine tools.

In 1975 (after the revolution) Portugal's heavy industry, basic industries (e.g., cement and petrochemical processing, shipbuilding, generation of electricity), and even some light industries were nationalized. However, in the late 1980s these industries underwent privatization, which has had far-reaching effects. Nearly all public enterprises were privatized, some in tranches, providing the central government with large revenues. Private domestic firms handle the traditional labour-intensive light industries and construction, and subsidiaries of multinational corporations dominate the more technologically advanced industries such as electronics manufacture, automobile manufacture and assembly, and pharmaceutical production.

FINANCE

Portugal's currency was formerly the escudo, which had replaced the real in 1911 after the overthrow of the monarchy the previous year. However, after meeting the EU's convergence criteria, Portugal adopted the euro, the EU's single currency, in 1999. In 2002 the euro replaced the escudo as Portugal's sole currency.

Like the manufacturing sector, the banking and insurance industries were nationalized in the mid-1970s. Beginning in the 1980s, however, these sectors were liberalized and reprivatized. By the beginning of the 21st century, with full liberalization long established, financial markets had been extensively modernized and insurance companies and banks privatized. Caixa Geral de Depósitos, Portugal's largest bank, was an exception. New banks and brokerage houses were established and a wide range of financial instruments created. During the 1990s there was significant consolidation of the banking sector, and now only a handful of major groups dominate the market. Leading commercial banks, involved in securities, have established investment companies. Spanish banks are also important within Portugal. The Portuguese banking system was badly shaken by the euro-zone crisis, and in 2012 undercapitalized banks were forced to accept bailout funds that originated with the International Monetary Fund and the EU.

Portuguese bond and stock markets operate on a par with other European and world markets. Trading activity has expanded, and Portuguese bonds appear in globally recognized indices. In 2000 the Lisbon exchange merged with the exchange in Porto. The Lisbon exchange handles spot transactions, while Porto is a futures and options exchange. In 2001 the Lisbon exchange became a member of Euronext, the first fully integrated cross-border equities market, which in 2006 merged with the New York Stock Exchange; the Lisbon exchange also formed an alliance with the Brazilian Securities, Commodities and Futures Exchange, a leading Latin American exchange.

TRADE

For a relatively small country, Portugal has a large foreign trade. Total imports (primarily food and beverages, wheat, crude oil, machinery, automobiles, and raw materials) generally have far outpaced total exports. Among Portugal's chief exports are automobiles and transport components, machine tools, textiles, clothing, footwear, paper pulp, wine, cork, plastic molds, and tomato paste. EU countries are Portugal's principal trading partners, accounting for four-fifths of exports and three-fourths of imports. Major trading partners include Spain, Germany, France, Italy, and the United Kingdom. Trade with Portugal's former colonial possessions in Africa has declined to a small fraction of the total, but trade has increased with Latin America, especially Brazil. Brazil's size and historical and linguistic relationship have made it attractive for investments from major Portuguese companies. Portugal's trade deficit has traditionally been financed by emigrant worker remittances and income from tourism.

SERVICES

The service sector is extremely important to Portugal's economy, accounting for more than three-fifths of total output. Tourism has surged to become a major industry, and millions of people visit Portugal annually. Notable tourist destinations include Lisbon, the Algarve, and the Douro valley. Visitors from France,

Germany, Spain, and the United Kingdom make up the bulk of tourists.

LABOUR AND TAXATION

Employment in Portugal is fairly diversified. More than half of all workers are employed in services, while one-eighth work in the primary sector, including agriculture and mining. Manufacturing, construction, and the public utilities employ about one-quarter of workers.

Workers have the right to be represented, and there are several hundred trade unions and two trade union federations. One federation, the Intersindical, grew from communist roots. Formed in 1970 and reorganized in 1974, it has more than 100 affiliated organizations. The other major federation is the União Geral dos Trabalhadores (UGT; General Union of Workers), which developed out of the socialist movement. Although no official statistics exist, it is estimated that about 30 percent of workers belong to a union. The overall rate of unionization declined from the 1970s, when a system was implemented allowing workers to forgo payment of union membership dues.

Taxation, at about one-third to two-fifths of gross domestic product, is relatively low in comparison with that of many other western European countries. Individual income tax rates are progressive, varying considerably depending upon an individual's level of income. Corporate taxes and the value-added tax provide a significant source of revenue for the government. Consumption taxes account for about one-third of total tax revenue, compared with about one-tenth for corporate taxes and one-fifth for individual income taxes. Payroll and social security taxes constitute about one-third of total tax revenue.

TRANSPORTATION AND TELECOMMUNICATIONS

Several of Portugal's main roads date to ancient times. Transport and communications were seriously neglected for much of the 20th century, but, beginning late in the century, there was a concerted effort backed by massive funding from the EU to remedy the situation. As a result, the total road network has been extended. A four-lane *auto-estrada* (superhighway) connects Lisbon to Porto, the capital of the north. A motorway links Lisbon with Madrid, and there is a four-lane highway from Lisbon to the Algarve. Expressways reach the largest towns and extend to the border and ports. Secondary roads link the towns with almost every part of the interior. The 10.7-mile (17.2-km) Vasco da Gama Bridge, the second bridge in Lisbon to span the Tagus River, was completed early in 1998. However, the bridge has not totally relieved traffic congestion, prompting consideration of building either a new bridge or a tunnel to cross the Tagus.

The Portuguese railway system has been improved, and the enterprise Rede Ferroviária Nacional (REFER) was established in 1997 to manage it. In the 1990s and early 21st century, Lisbon's metro system was extended outside the city limits with the addition of several new stations. Among them was the Gare do Oriente, a main station located in the Parque das Nações (Park of Nations), on land east of the city centre, that was designed by renowned architect Santiago Calatrava. Porto also has developed a light rail system, parts of which run underground. Lisbon's 25th of April Bridge, once Europe's longest suspension bridge, has been adapted to include a railway line.

Portugal's main international airport is Lisbon's Portela Airport. There are also international airports in Faro and Porto, and airports in Madeira and the Azores receive flights from international destinations. Small airports for domestic flights are located near several other cities. The country's flagship airline is TAP Portugal. There are several other Portuguese airlines, and the country is also served by numerous international carriers that provide both passenger and cargo services.

Portugal's ports have received considerable investment to improve and expand their ability to handle cargo and containers and to provide other services. Major Portuguese ports include Lisbon, the Port of Leixões (serving Porto), Setúbal, and Sines. The northern Douro is now navigable. River transport includes both pleasure cruisers and commercial barges.

Advances in technology and telecommunications have speeded the transformation of Portugal's finance and business sector. Historically, the extension of fixed telephone lines in Portugal was slow; as a result, many individuals have adopted cellular phones, making Portugal among Europe's leaders in per capita mobile phone use (by the end of the first decade of the 21st century the country had 1.4 mobile phone subscriptions per person). The cellular phone market is intensely competitive. Portugal has implemented reforms in its telecommunications sector that favoured liberalization and privatization. Internet use grew dramatically in the late 1990s and early 21st century, though computer use in Portugal remained low compared with that of most other EU countries.

CHAPTER 3

PORTUGUESE GOVERNMENT AND SOCIETY

Portugal has been a republic since the overthrow of King Manuel II and the house of Bragança in 1910. From 1910 to 1926, the era of Portugal's First Republic, a parliamentary democracy was established, though monarchists attempted to overthrow it, and factions quickly arose among republicans. In 1926 a bloodless military coup overthrew the republic, replacing it with an authoritarian government. In 1932 António de Oliveira Salazar established a corporative dictatorship—the so-called Nuevo Estado (New State)—that lasted until 1974, four years after Salazar's death. During the dictatorship, democratic-like institutions existed but were merely a facade, stacked with supporters of Salazar; political freedoms were suppressed, sometimes ruthlessly. Since the Revolution of the Carnations on April 25, 1974, Portugal has had a democratic republic. Its postrevolutionary constitution, first adopted in 1976 and modified several times since, established a semipresidential system whereby executive power was divided between a president and a prime minister. The constitution was revised in 1982, when ideological elements were minimized, and again in 1989, when the way was paved for privatization and a transition to a free-market economy.

Portugal's chief of state is the president, who is directly elected by universal suffrage for a five-year term and may be elected to only two consecutive terms. The president is responsible for guaranteeing Portugal's independence and national unity. Presidential duties also include serving as chief commander of the armed forces, appointing and dismissing the prime minister (who must be able to command majority support in the legislature), appointing and dismissing other members of the government at the proposal of the prime minister, sending messages to parliament and convening or dissolving it as necessary, and setting the dates of elections after consultation with the Council of State.

The constitution designates the Council of Ministers, the cabinet, as Portugal's chief policy-making body. The cabinet consists of the prime minister, who presides over its meetings, the ministers of government departments, and some secretaries of state (ministers without portfolios). The prime minister is simultaneously responsible to the president (regarding the overall functioning of governmental institutions) and to parliament (regarding the content of public policy). The prime minister directs, coordinates, and implements government policy. By tradition the prime minister is the head of the civil service.

The parliament comprises the unicameral Assembly of the Republic, which has 230 deputies. Its duties include debating and voting upon legislation, authorizing the government to raise revenues, and approving the laws passed by the legislatures of the autonomous regions. The parliament may also dismiss the government by rejecting a vote of confidence requested by the government or by passing a motion of censure against the government.

LOCAL GOVERNMENT

Portugal has three tiers of government below the national level. The lowest tier comprises the parishes (*freguesias*), of which there are about 4,000. Each parish has a directly elected assembly (*assembleia de freguesia*), which appoints its own executive body, the parish board (*junta de freguesia*). The second tier consists of the municipalities (*concelhos*), which number some 300. Municipalities include rural and urban areas within their territorial limits. Each municipality has a municipal assembly (*assembleia municipal*), made up of the presidents of the boards of the constituent parishes and an equal number plus one of directly elected members; a municipal chamber (*câmara municipal*), which is the executive of the municipality; and a municipal council (*conselho municipal*), a consultative organ through which the views of social, cultural, professional, and economic organizations within the municipality are transmitted to the municipal chamber. Above the municipalities are 18 districts (*distritos*)—20 including Madeira and the Azores—each with an appointed civil governor.

The constitution of 1976 called for the establishment of administrative regions (*regiões administrativas*), and the government created plans to subdivide the country, but by the early 21st century such a scheme had yet to be implemented (and had been rejected in a national referendum in 1998). Nevertheless, to simplify the implementation and administration of EU programs, the government devised a system consisting of five regions for the mainland: North (Norte), Central (Centro), Lisbon and the Tagus Valley (Lisboa e Vale do Tejo), the Alentejo, and the Algarve. The archipelagoes of Madeira and the Azores are autonomous regions (*regiãos autónomas*), a special status granted in the 1976 constitution, in recognition of their geographic, economic, social, and

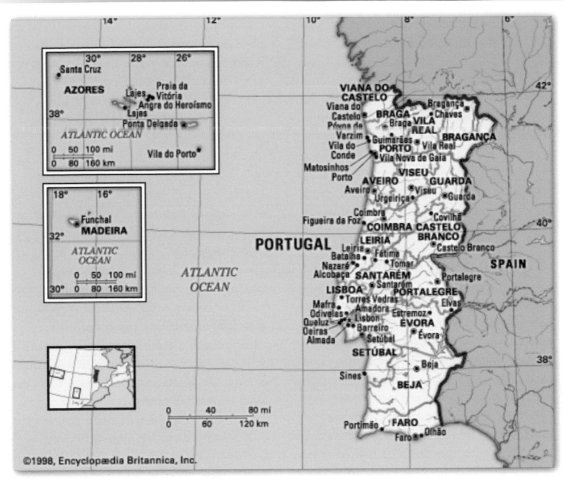

©1998, Encyclopædia Britannica, Inc.

cultural uniqueness and their historical aspirations for greater independence. Each autonomous region has its own government (cabinet and president), legislature (regional assembly), and administration.

JUSTICE

Portugal's judiciary is formally independent of the executive and legislative branches. The country is divided into several dozen judicial circuits, above which there are four regional districts. The highest judicial organ is the Supreme Tribunal of Justice. There is also a Constitutional Tribunal, which has 13 justices appointed by parliament and which rules on the constitutionality of laws. A jury system was introduced with the 1976 constitution.

The role of the military as the watchdog of the 1974 revolution and the subsequent transition to democracy was enshrined by the 1976 constitution in the Council of the Revolution. A constitutional committee operated in conjunction with the Council of the Revolution, which determined the constitutionality of legislation. Revisions made to the constitution in 1982 abolished the Council of the Revolution and the constitutional committee and replaced them with a Council of State and the Constitutional Tribunal. Members of the Council of State are the president of the republic (who presides over the council), the president of the parliament, the prime minister, the president of the Constitutional Tribunal, the attorney general, the presidents of the governments of the autonomous regions, certain former presidents of the republic, five persons appointed by the president, and five persons selected by the Assembly of the Republic.

POLITICAL PROCESS

All citizens at least age 18 are eligible to vote. Voters directly elect the president, who serves a five-year term, and members of the Assembly of the Republic. Elections to the Assembly of the Republic must occur at least once every four years; seats are apportioned to parties (voters cast ballots for party lists rather than for individual candidates) on the basis of proportional representation in multiseat constituencies. Although Portugal utilizes a proportional system, two parties are dominant: the centre-left Socialist Party (Partido Socialista) and the centre-right Social Democratic Party (Partido Social Democrata). There are also several minor parties, including the conservative Popular Party (Partido Popular) and communist and ecologist parties. Voters (including EU citizens living in Portugal) also elect deputies to the European Parliament, the EU's legislative body. Women, who were first granted the right to vote in Portugal in 1931 (though the franchise then was limited to women with university degrees or secondary-school

qualifications), have made great strides in postrevolutionary Portugal, regularly constituting about one-quarter of the members of the Assembly of the Republic.

SECURITY

The Portuguese military is commanded by the president, who also appoints the chiefs of staff. Formerly, military service was compulsory, but conscription was eliminated in the early 21st century. The armed forces consist of an army, an air force, and a navy. Before passage of the National Defense Law in 1982, the military had veto power over legislation affecting it, including expenditures and international agreements. Portugal was a founding member of the North Atlantic Treaty Organization in 1949, and it is also a member of the Western European Union, which serves to coordinate European defense and security policies.

The Portuguese police are divided into four categories. The Public Security Police (Polícia de Segurança Pública; PSP) and the Republican National Guard (Guarda Nacional Republicana; GNR) are under the control of the Ministry of Internal Administration. The GNR includes the road police and has jurisdiction over rural areas. The PSP patrols urban areas and directs city traffic. The Fiscal Guard (Guarda Fiscal), which is stationed at frontier crossings and points of entry and is responsible for collecting import duties and investigating smuggling and other violations of border regulations, is under the supervision of the Ministry of Finance. There is also a judicial police force, the

Polícia Judiciária. The crime rate in Portugal is low, and the decriminalization of virtually all drugs in 2001 made Portugal a test case for law enforcement agencies around the world. With rates of addiction down and rehabilitation programs replacing incarceration, the Portuguese experiment was widely heralded as a bold response to a pressing public health issue.

HEALTH AND WELFARE

The Portuguese welfare system is composed of several types of institutions that insure workers against sickness, disability, and old age and provide for the payment of pensions and family allowances. Compulsory insurance is provided by employers in most sectors of business and industry; employees also pay into the fund. Trade-union provident funds and welfare funds for other employees provide assistance for most categories of workers, and there are voluntary mutual assistance associations and provident institutions for the military forces and civil servants. Many large companies maintain their own welfare and sickness benefit programs and pensions for their employees.

Portugal has both public and private hospitals. Major hospitals are generally located in the main district capitals, and other hospitals are found in smaller centres. There are also several hundred other health centres. Charity hospitals (*santas casas da misericórdia*), which were first founded in 1498 when the Irmandade da Misericórdia (Fraternity of Mercy) was formed in Lisbon by Leonor de Lencastre, the widow of King John II, are funded by a national lottery and play an important social role, especially among the elderly. Special institutions include a cancer hospital and research unit in Lisbon, a school of tropical medicine, and a modern rehabilitation centre for people with disabilities near Lisbon. The health care system was long undermined by inefficiency, funding shortfalls, and a shortage of doctors, though, beginning in the 1990s, the government began to address the system's endemic problems. A major reform of the health care system was undertaken in 2002 with the goal of reducing costs and increasing efficiency. Key challenges for Portugal's national health service in the 21st century included balancing the needs of an aging populace with the costs associated with providing the necessary care.

HOUSING

Article 65 of Portugal's constitution proclaims that all citizens have a right to "a dwelling of adequate size satisfying standards of hygiene and comfort and preserving personal and family privacy." It further requires the government to establish housing policies that are "based on urban planning that secures the existence of an adequate network of transport and social facilities" and to create a "system of rents compatible with family incomes and of individual ownership of dwellings." Nevertheless, particularly in urban areas, Portugal has suffered from substandard housing and severe housing shortages. Dwelling size is small by European standards. However, the rate of home ownership is fairly high, some two-thirds of dwellings being owner-occupied (a marked increase from 1970, when only about half were owner-occupied), and comparatively few owner-occupied homes carry mortgages (though the proportion of mortgages has increased as home ownership has grown). In rural areas the situation was no better, and many places were not electrified until the 1990s. During the 1980s, shantytowns consisting of several hundred thousand dwellings (many of which were unsafe) were constructed on the outskirts of metropolitan areas, particularly Lisbon and Porto. The government began to address poor housing conditions in the 1990s, when it adopted measures to increase and improve the housing stock for less-affluent people. Overall, property values are high, and some of the most desirable apartments are those in residential blocks built in the riverside area east of Lisbon that was cleared in the late 1990s for the World's Fair (Expo '98).

EDUCATION

Early education for children aged 3 to 6 is available for free, and schooling is compulsory between the ages of 6 and 18. Education has become a high priority of government funding, particularly since the late 1980s, when a study found that one-fifth of the population over age 15 was illiterate. By the beginning of the 21st century, the literacy rate exceeded 90 percent, and nearly every child was enrolled in school; however, failure rates remain high, and child labour, prevalent especially in the north, has not yet been eliminated. Private schools supplement the state schools, which provide free education for the majority of people. There are several public and private universities, including the long-established University of Coimbra (originally founded in Lisbon in 1290, relocated permanently to Coimbra in 1537), the University of Lisbon (founded 1911), the Technical University of Lisbon (founded 1930), the University of Porto (founded 1911), and the Portuguese Catholic University (founded in 1968 in Lisbon). There are also technical institutes, nursing and technical health schools, military academies, and several specialized schools for subjects such as the sciences and hotel management.

UNIVERSITY OF LISBON

The University of Lisbon is a coeducational state institution of higher learning in Lisbon. The modern university, restored in 1911, traces its history, together with that of the University of Coimbra, to the medieval University of Lisbon founded in 1288. King Dinis of Portugal endowed a *studium generale*, a place of study accepting scholars from all over Europe and conferring a recognized degree. The university subsequently was moved several times to Coimbra and back to Lisbon. It remained in Lisbon from 1377 to 1537, when it again migrated, this time permanently, to Coimbra.

In 1911 the present sister university was founded in Lisbon. Modern faculties include science, letters, law, pharmacy, medicine, and psychology and educational science.

CHAPTER 4

PORTUGUESE CULTURAL LIFE

Portuguese culture is based on a past that dates from prehistoric times into the eras of Roman and Moorish invasion. All have left their traces in a rich legacy of archaeological remains, including prehistoric cave paintings at Escoural, the Roman township of Conimbriga, the Roman temple (known as the Temple of Diana) in Évora, and the typical Moorish architecture of such southern towns as Olhão and Tavira.

There have been considerable efforts to conserve architecture and art across the country, especially religious artifacts, palaces, and the several distinctive styles of *casas portuguesa,* or modest homes. Preservation has led to the declaration of the city centres of Évora, Sintra, Porto, and, in the Azores, Angra do Heroísmo as UNESCO World Heritage sites.

DAILY LIFE AND SOCIAL CUSTOMS

Despite certain affinities with the neighbouring Spaniards, the Portuguese have their own distinctive way of life. The geographic variety of the country has evoked different responses, but there is less regionalism than in Spain. Moreover, lifestyles have altered radically as rural populations have declined

Angra do Heroísmo, Terceira Island, Azores. Walter Imber

and cities and their suburbs have expanded. Urban centres provide a range of entertainment, and fairs and markets are highlights of social gatherings. A long tradition of dancing and singing continues among the Portuguese. Nearly every village has its own *terreiro*, or dance floor, usually constructed of concrete, though in some places it is still made of beaten earth. Each region has its own style of dances and songs; most traditional songs are of a slower rhythm than those in Spain. Small accordions and *gaitas*, or bagpipes, are among a considerable range of instruments that accompany dances, and Portuguese guitars (and sometimes violas) accompany the fado, a song form that epitomizes *saudade*—the yearning, romantic aspect of the Portuguese character. Regional dances, which include the *vira, chula, corridinho, tirana,* and fandango, often reflect the courting and matrimonial traditions of the area. Much has been done to preserve these and other folk expressions as tourist attractions.

National dress is still seen in the northern Minho province at weddings and other festivals. Traditional garments such as the red and green stocking cap of the Alentejo cattleman still exist, and the *samarra* (a short jacket with a collar of fox fur) and *cifões* (the equestrian's leather chaps) survive. Rustic plows and wooden carts drawn by oxen or mules are still used by small farmers (though in the perennial battle against forest fires, shepherds who guard their flocks in forest areas have been supplied with mobile phones). The wearing of black for protracted periods of mourning is common, especially in the villages.

Access to supermarkets has transformed eating habits in cities and urban areas. In the countryside the staple diet is one of fish, vegetables, and fruit. Although Portugal's waters abound with fresh fish, the dried salted codfish known as *bacalhau,* now often imported, is considered the national dish. A seafood stew known as *cataplana* (for the hammered copper clamshell-style vessel in which it is cooked) is ubiquitous throughout the country. In many areas meat is seldom eaten, although the Alentejo region is known for its pork and Trás-os-Montes for cured meats. *Cozido a portuguesa,* a stew made with meats and vegetables, is a popular dish. Breads, cakes, and sweets—the last one a legacy of Moorish occupation—take a variety of forms, with many regional specialties. Portugal is well known for its wide variety of cheeses. Wine is the ubiquitous table beverage. In the north the wine of choice is often the red version of the so-called green wine, or *vinho verde,* usually preferred as a lightly sparkling white wine. Perhaps the most famous Portuguese export is the fortified wine called port, named after the town of Porto, where it has been bottled for centuries. Distinguished mainly for notable vintages, port is also enjoyed as ruby, tawny, and dry white varieties.

Portugal has a wide variety of regional fairs, many of which are combined with

FADO

Fado is a type of Portuguese singing, traditionally associated with pubs and cafés, that is renowned for its expressive and profoundly melancholic character. The singer of fado (literally, "fate") speaks to the often harsh realities of everyday life, sometimes with a sense of resignation, sometimes with the hope of resolution. The song is performed by either a female or a male vocalist, typically to the accompaniment of one or two *guitarras* (10- or 12-string guitars), one or two *violas* (6-string guitars), and perhaps also a *viola baixo* (a small 8-string bass *viola*). Most of the repertoire follows a duple metre (usually with four beats to a measure), with a text arranged in quatrains or in any of several other common Portuguese poetic forms. Inevitably enriched with an array of emotive bodily gestures and facial expressions, fado aims—and indeed, is required—to evoke a penetrating sense of *saudade* (roughly, "yearning").

There are two distinct styles of fado, the older of which is associated with the city of Lisbon and the younger with the north-central Portuguese city of Coimbra. The Lisbon style emerged in the first half of the 19th century in the city's Alfama district, a socially and economically marginalized area that was a nexus of Iberian, South American (particularly Brazilian), and African peoples and traditions. A diverse array of dance traditions circulated within this milieu, including the Afro-Brazilian *lundum*; the Brazilian *fado* (distinct from the song genre that bears the same name); the *fofa*, which was common both in Portugal and in Brazil; and the Spanish *fandango*. Also popular at the time was the modinha, a type of Portuguese and Brazilian art song that often was accompanied by the guitar. The musics of these dance traditions merged with the *modinha*, ultimately giving birth to fado.

The second style of fado developed roughly from the 1870s to the 1890s in the university city of Coimbra. In contrast to the Lisbon style, which sprang from a sidelined segment of society, appealed to working-class audiences, and included many female performers, the Coimbra style (also called *canção de Coimbra*, "songs of Coimbra") was generally a product and a pastime of the privileged classes, and it was typically performed by men. Cultivated in cafés by college students and university faculty, the new fado drew from the city's deep literary tradition, as well as from bel canto singing and diverse musical styles brought by students from various regions of Portugal. A further difference between the Coimbra and Lisbon styles was the manner in which they addressed the hardships of everyday life: the fado of Coimbra inspired hope, while that of Lisbon suggested surrender. Other distinctive features of the Coimbra style included a lack of improvisation (performances were solidly rehearsed) and the elevation of the *guitarras* and *violas* to a position of prominence from what had been an essentially accompanimental role. Indeed, the Coimbra tradition generated a separate, instrumental repertoire for guitar.

Since the late 19th century both styles of fado have continued to develop, gaining audiences well beyond the tavern and café. In the late 1890s and the early decades of the 20th century, fado found a place on the vaudeville stage, and in the 1920s and '30s Coimbra *fadistas*

Edmundo de Bettancourt and Lucos Junot were instrumental in expanding the music's listenership. In the late 1930s Alfama native Amália Rodrigues appeared on the scene. Renowned for her passionate performances, Rodrigues pushed the Lisbon style in new directions, incorporating Spanish and Mexican rhythms and tapping contemporary poets for her lyrics.

The late 20th century brought an ebb in fado's popularity, but by the early 21st century there was renewed interest in the music. Many artists, including Carlos do Carmo, Cristina Branco, and Mariza, had begun to expand the traditional guitar accompaniment to include piano, violin, accordion, and other instruments, while other *fadistas* followed in the footsteps of Alfonso, exploring new ways to blend fado with other popular genres.

religious festivals. Religious customs in this Roman Catholic country still include, in the north, the burning of the yule log in the atrium of the village church at Christmas so that the poor may warm themselves. Twice annually (May and October) large numbers of the faithful make a pilgrimage to the shrine of Fátima, where three children reported that they had received messages from the Virgin Mary. All Saints' Day festivals (November 1), especially in Lisbon and Porto, draw large crowds. Among the secular holidays are Liberty Day (April 25), which marks the Revolution of the Carnations of 1974 and is accompanied by parades and various cultural events; Portugal Day (June 10), which commemorates the death of 16th-century soldier-poet Luís de Camões; and Republic Day (October 5), which celebrates the overthrow of the monarchy and the establishment of the republic in 1910.

FÁTIMA

The village and sanctuary of Fátima is located in central Portugal, on the tableland of Cova da Iria, 18 miles (29 km) southeast of Leiria. Fátima was named for a 12th-century Moorish princess and since 1917 has been one of the greatest Marian shrines in the world, visited by thousands of pilgrims annually. On May 13, 1917, and in each subsequent month until October of that year, three young peasant children, Lucia dos Santos and her cousins Francisco and Jacinta Marto, reportedly saw a woman who identified herself as the Lady of the Rosary. On October 13, a crowd (generally estimated at about 70,000) gathered at Fátima witnessed a "miraculous solar phenomenon" immediately after the lady had appeared to the children. After initial opposition, the Bishop of Leiria on October 13, 1930, accepted the children's visions as the appearance of the Virgin Mary; in the same year papal indulgences were granted to pilgrims. The content of the devotion includes frequent recitation of the rosary and devotion to the Immaculate Heart of the Blessed Virgin Mary.

The first national pilgrimage to Fátima took place in 1927, and the basilica was begun in 1928 and consecrated in 1953. With a tower 213 feet (65 metres) high, surmounted by a large bronze crown and a crystal cross, it is flanked by hospitals and retreat houses and faces a vast square in which is the little Chapel of the Apparitions. Numerous cures have been reported, though publicity has not been sought. On the 50th anniversary of the first vision, May 13, 1967, a crowd of pilgrims, estimated to number one million, gathered at Fátima to hear Pope Paul VI say mass and pray for peace.

At the end of the 20th century there was growing speculation concerning the three messages the Virgin Mary was said to have revealed to the peasant children in 1917. While two of the messages had been disclosed in the 1940s—commonly interpreted as the prediction of the end of World War I and the start of World War II and the rise and fall of communism—the third had been kept secret by the Vatican, giving rise to numerous theories. In May 2000 it was finally announced that the third message was the Virgin Mary's vision of the 1981 assassination attempt on Pope John Paul II. The news came during a beatification ceremony for Francisco and Jacinta Marto.

THE ARTS

Throughout the centuries Portugal's arts have been enriched by foreign influences, including those of the Flemish, French, and Italian peoples. The voyages of the Portuguese explorers, such as Ferdinand Magellan, who was the first to circumnavigate the globe, and Vasco da Gama, who pioneered an eastern route to Asia around the Cape of Good Hope (the first European to sail around the cape was another Portuguese navigator, Bartolomeu Dias, in 1488), opened the country to Asian influences, and the revelation of Brazil's wealth of gold and jewels fed the Baroque flame in decoration.

LITERATURE

The literature of Portugal is distinguished by a wealth and variety of lyric poetry, which has characterized it from the beginning of the Portuguese language, after the Roman occupation; by its wealth of historical writing documenting Portugal's rulers, conquests, and expansion; by the moral and allegorical Renaissance drama of Gil Vicente; by *Os Lusíadas* (*The Lusiads*), the 16th-century national epic of Luís de Camões; by the 19th-century realist novels of José Maria de Eça de Queirós; by Fernando Pessoa's poetry and prose of the 20th century; by a substantial number of female writers; and by a resurgence of poetry and the novel in the 1970s, which culminated in José Saramago's winning the Nobel Prize for Literature in 1998.

The Portuguese language became synthesized in the 12th century, when a lyrical quality was outstanding in both poetry and prose. With *Os Lusíadas* (1572; *The Lusiads*), Camões first gave expression to the nation's epic genius, and the 20th-century poet Fernando Pessoa, writing under numerous pseudonyms, introduced a Modernist European

JOSÉ SARAMAGO

The Portuguese novelist and man of letters José Saramago (born November 16, 1922, Azinhaga, Portugal—died June 18, 2010, Lanzarote, Canary Islands, Spain) was awarded the Nobel Prize for Literature in 1998. The son of rural labourers, Saramago grew up in great poverty in Lisbon. After holding a series of jobs as mechanic and metalworker, Saramago began working in a Lisbon publishing firm and eventually became a journalist and translator. He joined the Portuguese Communist Party in 1969, published several volumes of poems, and served as editor of a Lisbon newspaper in 1974–75 during the cultural thaw that followed the overthrow of the dictatorship of António Salazar. An anticommunist backlash followed in which Saramago lost his position, and in his 50s he began writing the novels that would eventually establish his international reputation.

One of Saramago's most important novels is *Memorial do convento* (1982; "Memoirs of the Convent"; Eng. trans. *Baltasar and Blimunda*). With 18th-century Portugal (during the Inquisition) as a backdrop, it chronicles the efforts of a handicapped war veteran and his lover to flee their situation by using a flying machine powered by human will. Saramago alternates this allegorical fantasy with grimly realistic descriptions of the construction of the Mafra Convent by thousands of labourers pressed into service by King John V. Another ambitious novel, *O ano da morte de Ricardo Reis* (1984; *The Year of the Death of Ricardo Reis*), juxtaposes the romantic involvements of its narrator, a poet-physician who returns to Portugal at the start of the Salazar dictatorship, with long dialogues that examine human nature as revealed in Portuguese history and culture. Saramago's practice of setting whimsical parables against realistic historical backgrounds in order to comment ironically on human foibles is exemplified in two novels: *A jangada de pedra* (1986; *The Stone Raft*; film 2002), which explores the situation that ensues when the Iberian Peninsula breaks off from Europe and becomes an island, and *O evangelho segundo Jesus Cristo* (1991; *The Gospel According to Jesus Christ*), which posits Christ as an innocent caught in the machinations of God and Satan. The outspoken atheist's ironic comments in *The Gospel According to Jesus Christ* were deemed too cutting by the Roman Catholic Church, which pressured the Portuguese government to block the book's entry for a literary prize in 1992. As a result of what he considered censorship, Saramago went into self-imposed exile on the Canary Islands for the remainder of his life.

Saramago also wrote poetry, plays, and several volumes of essays and short stories, as well as autobiographical works. His memoir *As pequenas memórias* (2006; *Small Memories*) focuses on his childhood. When he received the Nobel Prize in 1998, his novels were widely read in Europe but less well known in the United States; he subsequently gained popularity worldwide. He was the first Portuguese-language writer to win the Nobel Prize.

sensibility. Lyric poetry still flourishes. The tendency of fiction has been away from the romanticism of the 19th and early 20th centuries and toward realism. José Maria Eça de Queirós, whose works include *Os Maias* (1888; *The Maias*) and *A cidade e as serras* (1901; *The City and the Mountains*), was an outstanding realist novelist. In the first half of the 20th century, Aquilino Ribeiro was an exceptional regional novelist whose writings include *Jardim das tormentas* (1913; "Garden of Torments") and *O homem que matou o Diabo* (1930; "The Man Who Killed the Devil"), while José Maria Ferreira de Castro was a notable realist and author of *A selva* (1930; *The Jungle*) and *Os emigrantes* (1928; "The Emigrants"). The novelist, essayist, and poet Vitorino Nemésio received acclaim for his novel *Mau tempo no canal* (1944; "Bad Weather in the Channel"; Eng. trans. *Stormy Isles: An Azorean Tale*).

Censorship in the early to mid-20th century, during the regime of António de Oliveira Salazar, considerably stifled meaningful literary production. With the revolution and the end of the dictatorship in 1974, literature flourished; among the notable figures of the postrevolutionary period were Neorealist poet and writer Fernando Namora (1919–89), poet and diarist Miguel Torga (1907–95)—both country doctors—and novelist Vergílio Ferreira (1916–96). Eduardo Lourenço was a leading essayist, and younger writers, such as Margarida Rebelo Pinto, gained popularity. Admired novelists in the late 20th and early 21st centuries included Almeida Faria, José Cardoso Pires, António Lobo Antunes, and José Saramago, the last of whom won the Nobel Prize for Literature in 1998. Among Saramago's many works are *Memorial do convento* (1982; "Memoirs of the Convent"; Eng. trans. *Baltasar and Blimunda*); *O ano da morte de Ricardo Reis* (1984; *The Year of the Death of Ricardo Reis*), a tribute to Fernando Pessoa; and *O homem duplicado* (2002; *The Double*).

ARCHITECTURE

Portugal boasts several scores of medieval castles, as well as the ruins of several villas and forts from the period of Roman occupation; Romanesque and Gothic influences have given Portugal some of its greatest cathedrals. In the late 16th century a national style—Arte Manuelina—was synthesized by adapting several forms into a luxuriantly ornamented whole.

Outstanding examples of Portuguese architecture include the ornate Manueline-style Jerónimos Monastery in Lisbon; the Sé (cathedral) of Lisbon, in the facade of which the remains of Roman construction may still be seen; the Palace of Justice in Lisbon, a fine, soaring example of austere modern architecture; the castle and church of the Convent of Christ in Tomar; the late Portuguese Gothic abbey of Santa Maria da Vitória in Batalha; the granite Tower of the Clerics in Porto; and Braga's Romanesque cathedral. Lisbon's Baixa neighbourhood, in Pombaline style (named for Sebastião

Building at the edge of the Bairro Alto district of Lisbon. Maurits van der Hoofd

de Carvalho, marquês de Pombal, who rebuilt Lisbon after the 1755 earthquake), remains admirable today. As modern cities have expanded, there has been a revival of interest in traditional domestic and folk architecture, as is found in the hand-hewn stones of the Beiras, the low farms of the Alentejo, and the cottage chimneys in the Algarve.

Modern architecture has aroused considerable controversy. Some buildings with stark lines include the National Archives of Torre do Tombo, the Belém Cultural Centre, the grandiose Caixa Geral bank building, and the Expo '98 site in the Parque das Nações, which includes an oceanarium and a railroad station. Some contemporary architects have successfully blended classical Portuguese styles with modern functions; among these are Fernando Távora, Nuno Teotónio Pereira, and Álvaro Siza Vieira, who was

MANUELINE

Manueline was a particularly rich and lavish style of architectural ornamentation indigenous to Portugal in the early 16th century. Although the Manueline style actually continued for some time after the death of Manuel I (reigned 1495–1521), it is the prosperity of his reign that the style celebrates.

Portuguese wealth was dependent upon sea trade, and the vocabulary of Manueline decoration is decidedly nautical. When not made to resemble coral itself, moldings were encrusted with carved barnacles or covered with carved seaweed and algae. Stone ropes and cables form architectural string courses, and above the windows and doors heraldic shields, crosses, anchors, navigational instruments, and buoys are massed together in profusion. Contemporary ship accoutrements were turned into architectural motifs. Such vast building complexes as the church and convent of the Knights of Christ (original building, 12th century; rebuilt c. 1510–14) at Tomar or the Unfinished Chapels in the complex at Batalha are excellent examples of this unique style that existed for a few decades in the interval between the Gothic and the later High Renaissance and Mannerist domination of the arts in Portugal.

The profusion of dense ornament in Manueline architecture owes some debt to the contemporary Spanish, to the Flamboyant Gothic style of northern Europe, and to a revival of Moorish style.

responsible for the successful reshaping of Lisbon's Chiado area, a historic section of the city that suffered extensive fire damage in 1988.

VISUAL AND DECORATIVE ARTS

Sculpture found rich expression in the magnificent tombs of the 12th and 13th centuries, and late 18th-century Baroque wood sculptures, of which the crèches of Joachim Machado de Castro are the finest, also are outstanding. The Classical and Romantic traditions of Italy and France influenced Machado de Castro in the late 18th century and António Soares dos Reis a century later. A school of primitive painters headed by Nuno Gonçalves was prominent in the 15th century, and subsequently Flemish artists interpreted the native style, decorating palaces and convents and leaving a rich heritage of religious art. Notable among them is Josefa de Óbidos (Josefa de Ayala), known especially for her religious paintings in Óbidos and her still lifes. The 19th century saw another rebirth of national art with a late Romantic period. An era of naturalist realism that followed, dominated by António Silva Porto, José Malhoa, and Columbano Bordalo Pinheiro, gave way to the nonconformist imagery of the 20th century, such as that found in the work of José Almada Negreiros. Maria Elena Vieira da Silva, who did much of her work in France, was arguably the country's finest abstract painter. Carlos Botelho is notable for his street scenes of Lisbon.

Among the decorative arts, the Portuguese glazed tiles (*azulejos*) are outstanding. Many 16th- and 17th-century buildings are faced with tiles, and the rooms and halls of palaces and mansions exhibit blue-and-white tiled panels or motifs in other soft colours. Exceptionally fine examples are found in the Pátio da Carranca, the courtyard of the royal palace at Sintra; in the São Roque Church and the Fronteira Palace in Lisbon; and in the Quinta da Bacalhoa, a wine-making estate at Vila Fresca de Azeitão near Setúbal. A remarkable array of panels of decorative tiles from the 15th century onward are displayed in the National Tile Museum in Lisbon.

Pena Palace, Sintra, Portugal. George Holton/ Photo Researchers

MUSIC

Liturgical forms such as plainsong dominated early Portuguese music, but the secular tradition of troubadour singing became popular in the Middle Ages. Polyphonic music, employing multiple vocal parts in harmony, was developed in the 15th century. The Renaissance fostered a rich output of compositions for solo instruments and ensembles as well as for the voice. The modern revival of so-called academic music in Portugal was primarily the work of Luís de Freitas Branco, whose Neoclassic tradition has been perpetuated by Joly Braga Santos. The Calouste Gulbenkian Foundation (founded by and named for the oil magnate) continues to inspire much of the country's musical life. Composers acquiring prestige both at home and abroad include António Victorino d'Almeida, Jorge Peixinho, Miguel Azguime, Pedro Amaral, and João Pedro Oliveira. Orchestras of note include the Orquestra Sinfónica Portuguesa and the Gulbenkian Orchestra. Porto has had its own symphony orchestra since 1962, when the Chamber Orchestra was set up by the Gulbenkian Foundation. Lisbon also has a metropolitan orchestra, and the National Theatre of São Carlos in Lisbon, which was built in the late 18th century, has its own orchestra and ballet company. Among notable pianists, Maria João Pires has won worldwide acclaim.

Cultural centres such as the Belém Cultural Centre and the Culturgest, both

AMÁLIA DA PIEDADE REBORDÃO RODRIGUES

The Portuguese singer Amália da Piedade Rebordão Rodrigues (born July 23, 1920, Lisbon, Portugal—died October 6, 1999, Lisbon) won international fame with haunting and passionate renditions of fado. Amália, as she was known to her fans, debuted as a *fadista* while still a teenager. By the time she was 25, she had already launched her first international tour in Brazil and had recorded the first of an estimated 170 albums. In 1947 she starred in her first film, *Capas Negras* ("Black Capes"). As her fame increased, she began to stretch the traditional boundaries of fado. She incorporated Spanish and Mexican rhythms into her songs and used contemporary poets as a source for her lyrics.

Amália's impact on Portuguese culture and contemporary artists was incalculable, although her image was somewhat tarnished after the Revolution of the Carnations (1974), when accusations arose that she had collaborated with the recently toppled dictatorship. However, news that she had secretly funded the Portuguese Communist Party during the repressive rule of António de Oliveira Salazar (1932–68) helped to restore her status as the queen of fado. In 1990 she received the Grand Cross of the Order of Santiago, Portugal's highest honour.

in Lisbon, and commercial sponsorship have expanded opportunities for major concerts. Madredeus is among the most successful popular music groups. Singer Dulce Pontes is also widely admired, and Carlos Paredes is considered by many to have been Portugal's finest guitarist. Folk music and dancing and the traditional fado remain the country's fundamental forms of musical expression. When the renowned *fadista* (fado singer) Amália Rodrigues da Piedade Rebordão (known simply as Amália throughout the world) died in 1999, three days of national mourning were declared and campaigning in the country's general elections was temporarily suspended. Younger *fadistas* such as Mariza, Katia Guerreiro, and Cristina Branco gained an international audience in the early 21st century.

THEATRE AND MOTION PICTURES

Along with a small but lively theatre, the Portuguese film industry, aided by subsidies and coproductions, has made its mark. Major filmmakers include João Botelho and João César Monteiro. Manoel de Oliveira, who made his first film in 1931 and was considered one of the world's most innovative filmmakers, was still achieving critical successes and major awards into the early 21st century. His films include *Aniki-bóbó* (1942), *Francisca* (1981), *Os canibais* (1988; "The Cannibals"), *O convento* (1995; *The Convent*), and *Porto da minha infância* (2001; "Porto of My Childhood"). The actor Joaquim de Almeida gained an international following and appeared in many Hollywood films as well as in Maria de Medeiros's *Capitães de Abril* (2000; *Captains of April*), which chronicles the April 1974 revolution. There are performances of both serious plays and witty musicals at the National Theatre of Dona Maria II in Lisbon. State and Gulbenkian Foundation aid has given new life to the "little theatre" both in Lisbon and in the provinces. International opera, theatre, and ballet are prominent in regular seasons in the National Theatre of São Carlos, in Lisbon, and in other theatres.

CULTURAL INSTITUTIONS

Lisbon is home to the vast Calouste Gulbenkian Foundation and Museum—considered by many to be Portugal's best museum, with its collections of sculptures, ceramics, and paintings from around the world—and its modern art centre. Lisbon also has other notable museums covering a broad range of art, including the National Art Museum; the National Museum of Coaches, which has a fine collection of antique vehicles; the National Museum of Ancient Art, which has excellent displays of Portuguese painting; the National Museum of Medieval Art; the National Museum of Contemporary Art; the National Tile Museum; the Maritime Museum, which has displays of royal galleons; the Museum School of Decorative Arts, which trains craftsmen in furniture restoration, bookbinding, the repair of ancient tapestries, and other fine handicrafts; and the Casa Fernando Pessoa, an arts centre honouring the great poet. Outstanding museums are also found throughout the country. Porto, for example, contains the Soares dos Reis National Museum, the National Museum of Modern Art, which is housed in a pink Art Deco mansion, and the Museum of St. Francis, which displays thousands of skulls from catacombs. The Machado de Castro National Museum in Coimbra houses a vast collection of sculpture, and there is a regional museum in Aveiro. The National Library and the Ajuda Library in Lisbon have fine collections, while the National Archives of Torre do Tombo contain valuable national documents. Outside Lisbon, the library of the Mafra Convent and that of the University of Coimbra have historical importance.

SPORTS AND RECREATION

Bullfighting is a popular sport in Portugal and varies markedly from its Spanish counterpart. The Portuguese bullfighter, usually dressed in an 18th-century-style coat and tricornered hat, rides a horse and does not seek to kill the bull, the horns of which may be sheathed to protect the horse. The bullfighter is followed by young men called *forcados*, who confront the bull bare-handed.

Football (soccer), the most popular national sport, evokes intense emotion. The national team is among the world's finest, though it has often had disappointing results in the World Cup tournament. Portugal's most renowned player, Eusebio (originally from Mozambique), was one of the most prolific goal scorers in European

CRISTIANO RONALDO

Cristiano Ronaldo (born February 5, 1985, Funchal, Madeira, Portugal) was the 2008 Fédération Internationale de Football Association (FIFA) World Player of the Year and one of the greatest Portuguese football (soccer) players of all time. Ronaldo's father, José Dinis Aveiro, was the equipment manager for the local club Andorinha. (The name Ronaldo was added to Cristiano's name in honour of his father's favourite movie actor, Ronald Reagan, who was U.S. president at the time of Cristiano's birth.) At age 15 Ronaldo was diagnosed with a heart condition that necessitated surgery, but he was sidelined only briefly and made a full recovery. He first played for Clube Desportivo Nacional of Madeira and then transferred to Sporting Clube de Portugal (known as Sporting Lisbon), where he played for that club's various youth teams before making his debut on Sporting's first team in 2002.

A tall player at 6 feet 1 inch (1.85 metres), Ronaldo was a formidable athlete on the pitch. Originally a right-winger, he developed into a forward with a free-reined attacking style. He was able to mesmerize opponents with a sleight of foot that made sufficient space for openings in opposing defenses.

After a successful season with Sporting that brought the young player to the attention of Europe's biggest football clubs, Ronaldo signed with English powerhouse Manchester United in 2003. He was an instant sensation and soon came to be regarded as one of the best forwards in the game. His finest season with United came in 2007–08, when he scored 42 League and Cup goals and earned the Golden Shoe award as Europe's leading scorer, with 31 League goals. After helping United to a Champions League title in May 2008, Ronaldo captured FIFA World Player of the Year honours for his stellar 2007–08 season. He also led United to an appearance in the 2009 Champions League final, which they lost to FC Barcelona. Soon thereafter, Ronaldo was sold to Spain's Real Madrid—a club with which he had long been rumoured to want to play—for a record £80 million (about $131 million) transfer fee. His scoring prowess continued with his new team, and he netted the most goals (40) in La Liga history during the 2010–11 season (his record was broken the following season by his rival Lionel Messi of Barcelona). In 2011–12 Ronaldo helped Madrid capture a La Liga championship and scored a personal-best 46 goals during the League season.

On his home soil, after moving through the youth and under-21 ranks, Ronaldo had made his first appearance for Portugal's full national team against Kazakhstan in August 2003 (four days after his debut for United). He was a key player in Portugal's fourth-place finish at the 2006 World Cup and became the full-time captain of the national team in 2008. In 2012 his stellar play led Portugal to the semifinals of the European Championship, where the team was eliminated by rival Spain in a match that was decided by a penalty kick shoot-out.

football in the 1960s. In the 21st century his feats were rivalled by those of Cristiano Ronaldo, Portugal's biggest football star in a generation. As elsewhere in much of Europe, basketball has grown in popularity. In individual events Portugal's long-distance runners have proved exceptional, winning Olympic gold medals and world championships. Rosa Mota won the marathon at the 1988 Summer Games in Seoul, South Korea, a world championship title, and three European championships; and Carlos Lopes won the men's marathon at the Summer Games in Los Angeles (1984).

Portugal's long seacoast and mild climate make beachgoing a popular pastime, particularly in the Algarve. The country is also well known throughout the world for its many championship-level golf courses, especially in the south. In the 1990s Portuguese entrepreneurs began promoting Portugal as an ocean sports destination, drawing on a strong local tradition of sailing and surfboarding. As a result of this effort, the country has become a centre for scuba diving, with a number of attractive sites, including a dive over the wreckage of a British steamship that sank in 1847. Another favourite dive is Pelo Negro, a complex of shallow undersea canyons just beyond the beach at Leça da Palmeira. Skiing, particularly in the Estrela Mountains (which contain Portugal's highest peaks), is popular in winter. Visits to Portugal's many national parks are among the other popular recreational activities in the country.

MEDIA AND PUBLISHING

Before the revolution of 1974, all media in Portugal were censored. The 1976 constitution guaranteed freedom of the press. Readership of daily newspapers in Portugal is quite limited, particularly outside the urban centres. The nationalization of industry that began in 1974 encompassed the leading Lisbon newspapers, which had been owned by banks. Gradual reprivatization began in 1979. The daily *Diário de Notícias* (founded 1864) was long Portugal's most prestigious newspaper. With privatization, however, the position of *Diário* has been challenged. Leading dailies include *Público* (founded 1990) and *Correio da Manhã* (founded 1979), and one of the most widely read newspapers is the weekly *Expresso*. Despite Lisbon's prevalence in publishing, some regional daily newspapers, such as the *Jornal de Notícias* in Porto, enjoy wide circulation. The English-language *The Portugal News* is published weekly. Magazines of national and international news and review include the weekly *Visão*. In business and finance the magazine *Exame* and the newspaper *Semanário Económico* are leaders. Among the most widely read publications are *A Bola* (founded 1945), a daily sports paper, and *Maria*, a weekly magazine for women.

The broadcast media reach a much larger portion of the Portuguese population than do the print media. In 1975 all private radio broadcasting, except the church-owned Rádio Renascença, was nationalized. The reprivatization process has paralleled that of other industries. Radio broadcasting is dominated by two networks: Rádio Renascença, which offers both national and regional programming, and the state-run Radiodifusão Portuguesa (RDP), which has regional centres throughout the country and produces an international service (Radio Portugal). Ownership reform came much more slowly to television broadcasting, which since its inception had been limited to the state-owned Rádio e Televisão de Portugal (RTP). In 1991 two private companies—one (Sociedade Independente de Comunicação; SIC) financed by a publishing group and the other by the Roman Catholic Church—received television broadcasting licenses. Another private television company is Televisão Independente (TVI). A number of private satellite and cable companies offer access to premium channels and foreign broadcast networks for a monthly fee. The news agency Lusa provides extensive national and world coverage.

CHAPTER 5

PORTUGAL: ANCIENT TIMES TO 1640

In the 1st millennium BCE the Celtic Lusitani entered the Iberian Peninsula and settled the land, and many traces of their influence remain. According to national legend, though, Lisbon, the national capital, was founded not by Celts but by the ancient Greek warrior Odysseus. It is said that he arrived at a rocky headland near what is now Lisbon after leaving his homeland to wander the world and, liking what he saw, stayed there for a while. His departure was said to have broken the heart of the nymph Calypso, who, the legend goes, turned herself into a snake, her coils becoming the seven hills of Lisbon. Of course, had Odysseus actually come to Portugal, he would have found the land already well settled by the Lusitani.

Lusitani tribes battled the Romans for generations before acceding to empire, whereupon Rome established several important towns and ports. The Roman presence can be seen in the very name of the country, which derives from Portus Cale, a settlement near the mouth of the Douro River and the present-day city of Porto. Later, the descendants of the Romans and the Lusitani would live under Moorish rule for several centuries until an independent kingdom was established.

In constant battle and rivalry with Spain, its eastern neighbour, Portugal turned to the sea and, after Henry the Navigator's establishment of a school of navigation at Sagres, in time founded a vast overseas empire that would become Europe's largest and richest. Much of that empire was quickly lost, but even then Portugal retained sizable holdings along the African coast, in southern and eastern Asia, and in South America. Portugal remained a colonial power until the mid-1970s, when a peaceful revolution transformed the country from a dictatorship into a democratic republic. Long among the poorest countries of Europe, Portugal modernized in the last decades of the 20th century, expanding its economy from one based primarily on textile manufacture and livestock raising to include a range of manufactures and services.

PRE-ROMAN, ROMAN, GERMANIC, AND MUSLIM PERIODS

The earliest human remains found in Portugal are Neanderthal-type bones from Furninhas. A distinct culture first emerged in the Mesolithic (Middle Stone Age) middens of the lower Tagus valley, dated about 5500 BCE. Neolithic (New Stone Age) cultures entered from Andalusia, leaving behind varied types of beehive huts and passage graves. Agriculture, pottery, and the working of soft metals followed by the same route. In the 1st millennium BCE, Celtic peoples entered the peninsula via the Pyrenees, and many groups were projected westward by natural pressure. Phoenician and later Carthaginian influence reached southern Portugal in the same period. By 500 BCE, Iron Age cultures predominated in the north. Celtic hilltop settlements (*castros*)

retained their vitality after the Roman conquest.

After the Second Punic War (218–201 BCE), Rome dominated the eastern and southern seaboards of the Iberian Peninsula, and Celtic peoples who had partially absorbed the indigenous population occupied the west. A Celtic federation, the Lusitani, resisted Roman penetration under the brilliant leadership of Viriathus; however, after Viriathus was assassinated about 140 BCE, Decius Junius Brutus led a Roman force northward through central Portugal, crossed the Douro River, and subdued the Gallaeci. Julius Caesar governed the territory for a time. In 25 BCE Caesar Augustus founded Augusta Emerita (Mérida) as the capital of Lusitania, which incorporated present-day central Portugal. Gallaecia (Galicia), to the north of the Douro, became a separate province under the Antonines. In Roman times the present-day districts of Beja and Évora formed a wheat belt. The valley of the Tagus was famous for its horses and farms, and there were important mines in the Alentejo. Notable Roman remains include the Temple of Diana at Évora and the site of Conimbriga (Condeixa). Christianity reached Lusitania in the 3rd century and Galicia in the 4th.

After 406 CE, foreign invaders forced their way into Gaul and crossed the Pyrenees. A Germanic tribe, the Suebi, settled in southern Galicia, and their rulers resided at or near Bracara Augusta (Braga) and Portucale. The

ÉVORA

The city of Évora lies in a fertile valley surrounded by low hills 70 miles (110 km) east of Lisbon, in south-central Portugal. Originally known as Ebora, it was from 80 to 72 BCE the headquarters of the Roman commander Quintus Sertorius, and it long remained an important Roman military centre. Later it was called Liberalitas Julia because of certain municipal privileges bestowed upon it by Julius Caesar. About 712 Évora was conquered by the Moors, who named it Jabura, and it remained under Moorish rule until c. 1166. In the 15th–16th century the kings of Portugal began residing regularly in Évora. The city's bishopric, founded in the 5th century, was raised to an archbishopric in the 16th century. From 1663 to 1665 it was in Spanish hands. In 1832 Dom Miguel, pretender to the Portuguese throne, retreating before Pedro I (Dom Pedro), took refuge in Évora; in the hilltop citadel of neighbouring Évoramonte, the convention by which Miguel was banished was signed. Fought over for centuries, Évora has a coat of arms that features two severed human heads.

Évora's cathedral, originally a Romanesque building (1186–1204), was restored in Gothic style (c. 1400). São Francisco Church (1507–25) is a good example of the blended Moorish and Gothic architecture known as Manueline; it includes a 16th-century chapel created from the bones of some 5,000 monks. The city is the seat of the University of Évora, which was originally founded in 1559 to succeed the College of the Holy Spirit (Jesuit; founded in 1551) but was suppressed in 1759; it was reconstituted in 1973 as the University Institute of Évora, which gave way to the University of Évora in 1979. An inn, the Pousada dos Lóios, is situated on the grounds of the former convent of Lóios (15th century). Just outside the inn is the small Roman Temple of Diana (a name for which no valid authority exists), which dates from the 1st–3rd century CE. After 1640 the city became a centre for music study and performance in connection with the cathedral and university. The Museum of Évora includes archaeological and art exhibits. The historic centre of the city, with a defensive wall dating from the Roman, Moorish, and later periods and whitewashed houses adorned with azulejos (glazed tiles), was designated a UNESCO World Heritage site in 1986.

Suebi annexed Lusitania and for a time overran the rest of the peninsula, but the Visigoths subdued them and extinguished their monarchy in 469. There are no records until about 550, when the Suebic monarchy had been restored and was reconverted to Catholicism by St. Martin of Braga. When Muslim forces invaded in 711, the only serious Gothic resistance was made at Mérida; upon its fall the northwest submitted. Berber troops were placed in central Portugal and Galicia. When ʿAbd al-Raḥmān I set up the Umayyad monarchy at Córdoba in 756, there was some resistance in the west; indeed, Lisbon was independent for a few years in the early 9th century. The restoration of the Christian sees of Galicia, the discovery of the supposed tomb of St. James, and the erection of his shrine at Santiago de Compostela (Santiago) were followed by the organization of the frontier territory of Portucale in 868 by Vimara Peres; Coimbra was annexed by the Christians but later was lost again.

THE COUNTY AND KINGDOM OF PORTUGAL TO 1383

By the 10th century the county of Portugal (north of the Douro) was held by Mumadona Dias and her husband Hermenegildo Gonçalves and their descendants, one of whom was tutor and father-in-law to the Leonese ruler Alfonso V. However, when this dynasty was overthrown by the Navarrese-Castilian house of Sancho III Garcés (Sancho the Great), the western county lost its autonomy. Sancho's son Ferdinand I of Castile reconquered Coimbra in 1064 but entrusted it to a Mozarabic governor. When the African Almoravids annexed Muslim Spain, Alfonso VI, who ruled Castile and León (1072–1109), provided for the defense of the west by calling on Henry, brother of Duke Eudes (Odo) of Burgundy, whom he married to his illegitimate daughter Teresa and made count of Portugal. Thus, from 1095 Henry and Teresa (who used the title of queen) ruled Portugal and Coimbra. Upon Alfonso VI's death, his realms passed to his daughter Urraca, who was queen from 1109 to 1126, and her little son Alfonso (who became Alfonso VII upon Urraca's death). Henry of Portugal sought power but had achieved little when he died in 1112, leaving Teresa with an infant son, Afonso Henriques (later Afonso I). Teresa's intrigues with her Galician favourite, Fernando Peres of Trava, lost her the support of the Portuguese barons, and in 1128 followers of Afonso Henriques defeated her and drove her into exile.

Afonso Henriques became count of Portugal, and, although he was at first obliged to submit to Alfonso VII, his cousin, Afonso began to use the title of king, according to tradition following on his victory over the Muslims at Ourique on July 25, 1139 (though this may be more legend than history). In 1143 Alfonso VII accepted his cousin's autonomy, but the title of king was formally conceded only in 1179, when Afonso Henriques placed Portugal under the direct protection of the Holy See, promising an annual tribute. Afonso had captured Santarém (March 1147) and Lisbon (October 1147), the latter with the aid of English, French, German, and Flemish Crusaders bound for Palestine. An English priest, Gilbert of Hastings, became the first bishop of the restored see of Lisbon.

Although the new Moroccan dynasty of the Almohads struck back (1179–84), the Portuguese frontier was firmly established on the Tagus when Afonso I died (December 6, 1185). The new military order, the

Alfonso I, the first ruler of Portugal to be called king. Hulton Archive/Getty Images

Templars—including those of Calatrava (from *c.* 1156) and of Santiago (from *c.* 1170)—governed castles and territory on the frontier, and the Cistercians were responsible for the introduction of agriculture and architecture in central Portugal (Alcobaça).

THE KINGDOM AND THE RECONQUISTA

Although Afonso I granted charters to new settlements, it was his son Sancho I (reigned 1185–1211) who enfranchised many municipalities (*concelhos*), especially in eastern and central Portugal. The privileges of these communities were embodied in charters (*forais*), which attracted settlers from the more feudal north. Even Muslims were enfranchised, though many of them were enslaved. Assisted by transient Crusaders, Sancho captured Silves in the Algarve in 1189; however, the following year an Almohad army from Africa advanced to the Tagus, and, although Lisbon, Santarém, and Tomar stood firm, the Muslims recovered Silves in 1191, together with most of the land south of the Tagus. But peace was made before Sancho's death, and it was left to his son Afonso II (1211–23) to endeavour to strengthen the power of the throne at the expense of the church.

Although Afonso II was an unwarlike king, his followers were beside the Castilians at the great Christian victory in the Battle of Las Navas de Tolosa in 1212 and, again assisted by Crusaders, recovered Alcácer do Sal in 1217. Meanwhile, Afonso repudiated the bequests of large estates made by his father to his brothers and accepted those to his sisters only after a war with León and in a form, settled by the pope, that recognized Afonso's sovereignty. In the first year of his reign, Afonso called a meeting of the Cortes (parliament) at Coimbra, to which the nobility and prelates were summoned (representatives of the commoners were not to appear until 1254). Both estates obtained important concessions; in fact, the position of the church and the orders was now so strong that Afonso II and his successors were involved in recurrent conflicts with Rome. Afonso himself instituted (from 1220) *inquirições*, or royal commissions, to investigate the nature of holdings and to recover whatever had been illegally taken from the crown.

Little is known of the reign of his son Sancho II (1223–c. 1246), but the reconquest of the Alentejo was now completed, and much of the Algarve had also been retaken. When Sancho became king, he found the church in full ascendancy as a result of the agreement made before his father's death. At all events, his younger brother Afonso, who had become count of Boulogne through his marriage (1238) to Matilde, daughter of Raynald I, Comte (count) de Dammartin, was granted a papal commission (1245) to take over the government, and Sancho was ordered to be deposed by papal bull. When Afonso reached Lisbon (late 1245 or early 1246), he received the support of the church and of the inhabitants of Lisbon and other towns. After a civil war lasting two years, Sancho II retired to Toledo, dying there in January 1248.

On his arrival the count of Boulogne had already declared himself king as Afonso III, and the death of Sancho without issue gave his usurpation the mantle of legality. He brought together the divided kingdom, completed the reconquest of the Algarve, transferred the capital from Coimbra to Lisbon, and, fortified by the support of the towns, summoned the Cortes at Leiria, where in 1254 commoners representing the municipalities made their first appearance. Afonso III's conquest of the Algarve aroused the jealousy of Castile. Campaigns were fought in 1250 and 1252, and peace was made only by means of a marriage pact. Although still the husband of Matilde of Boulogne, Afonso married Beatriz, illegitimate daughter of Alfonso X of Castile, holding the disputed territory of the Algarve as a fief of Castile until the eldest son of the marriage should reach age seven, at which time the Algarve was to return to Portugal. This marriage led to a dispute with the Holy See, in which Afonso was placed under an interdict. Though beholden to Rome, Afonso refused to give way; in 1263 the bigamous marriage was legalized and his eldest son, Dinis, legitimized. Shortly afterward Afonso launched *inquirições* that deprived the church of much property. The prelates protested these actions of the royal commissions, and most of them subsequently left the country. Although

Afonso was excommunicated and threatened with deposition, he continued to defy the church until shortly before his death early in 1279.

The achievements of Afonso's reign—the completion of the Reconquista, the assertion of royal power before the church, and the incorporation of the commoners in the Cortes—indicate important institutional advances. Under his son Dinis (1279–1325), Portugal came into closer touch with western Europe. The chartering of fairs and the increased use of minted money bear witness to the growth of commerce, and the planting of pine forests to hold back the advancing sand dunes near Leiria illustrates Dinis's interest in furthering shipbuilding and agriculture. Having already adopted various measures to stimulate foreign trade, Dinis in 1317 engaged a Genoese admiral, Emmanuele Pessagno, to build up

SAINT ELIZABETH OF PORTUGAL

Saint Elizabeth of Portugal (born *c.* 1271—died July 4, 1336, Estremoz, Portugal) was the daughter of Peter III of Aragon and the wife of King Dinis (Denis) of Portugal. Her pious nature and her ability to defuse tensions between antagonistic parties earned her the bynames of the Holy Queen and the Peacemaker.

Elizabeth was named for her great-aunt St. Elizabeth of Hungary and received a strict religious education. In 1282 she was married to Dinis, a good ruler but an unfaithful husband. Despite the corrupt court life, Elizabeth maintained her devout habits, helped the sick and the poor, and founded charitable establishments. When her son Afonso rebelled against his father, Elizabeth rode between the two armies and reconciled father and son. She also helped settle disputes among other royal relatives. After Dinis died in 1325, she lived at Coimbra, Portugal, near a Poor Clare convent that she had founded, and devoted herself to people in need. She died on her way to the battlefield to make peace between her son, then King Afonso IV, and Alfonso XI of Castile. She was canonized in 1625. Her feast day is July 4.

his navy. He founded the University of Coimbra (at first in Lisbon) in 1290 and was both a poet and a patron of literature. Yet he was especially famed as the rei *lavrador* (farmer king) for his interest in the land.

Despite Dinis's attachment to the arts of peace, Portugal was involved in strife several times during his reign. In 1297 the Treaty of Alcañices with Castile confirmed Portugal's possession of the Algarve and provided for an alliance between Portugal and Castile. The mother of Dinis's son, the future Afonso IV (1325–57), was Isabel, daughter of Peter III of Aragon. This remarkable woman, later canonized as St. Elizabeth of Portugal and popularly known as the Rainha Santa (the Holy Queen), successfully exercised her influence in pursuit of peace on several occasions.

DISPUTES WITH CASTILE

Afonso IV (the Brave) was also involved in various disputes with Castile. Isabel, who had retired to the convent of Santa Clara at Coimbra, continued to intervene in favour of peace. However, upon Isabel's death in 1336 war broke out, and peace terms were not made until 1340, when Afonso, leading a Portuguese army, joined Alfonso XI of Castile in the great victory over the Muslims on the Salado River in Andalusia. Afonso's son Peter was married (1336) to Constança (died 1345), daughter of the Castilian infante Juan Manuel. Soon after the marriage,

however, Peter fell in love with her cousin Inês de Castro, with whom he had several children. Afonso was persuaded to allow the assassination of Inês in 1355, and one of the earliest acts of Peter I as king was to take vengeance on her murderers. During his short reign (1357–67), Peter devoted himself to the dispensation of justice; his judgments, which he executed himself, were severe and often violent, and his iron rule was tempered only by fits of reveling.

Ferdinand I (1367–83), Peter's son by Constança, inherited a wealthy throne almost free of external entanglements, but the dispute between Peter, king of Castile and León, and Henry of Trastámara (later Henry II) over the Castilian throne was raging. On the murder of Peter in 1369, several Castilian towns offered Ferdinand their allegiance, which he was unwise enough to accept. Henry II duly invaded Portugal, and, by the Peace of Alcoutim (1371), Ferdinand was forced to renounce his claim and to promise to marry Henry's daughter; however, he instead took a Portuguese wife, Leonor Teles, despite the fact that she was already married and against the wishes of the commoners of Lisbon. In 1372 Ferdinand made an alliance with the English through John of Gaunt, duke of Lancaster, who had married the elder daughter of Peter and claimed the Castilian throne. In 1372 Ferdinand provoked Henry II, who invaded Portugal and besieged Lisbon. Unable to resist, Ferdinand was forced to repudiate his alliance with John of Gaunt and to act as an ally of Castile, surrendering various castles and persons as hostages. It was only on the death of Henry in 1379 that Ferdinand dared to openly challenge Castile again. In 1380 the English connection was resumed, and in the following year John of Gaunt's brother Edmund of Langley, earl of Cambridge (afterward Edmund of Langley, 1st duke of York), took a force to Portugal for the invasion of Castile and betrothed his son Edward to Ferdinand's only legitimate child, Beatriz. In mid-campaign Ferdinand came to terms with the enemy (August 1382), agreeing to marry Beatriz to a Castilian prince. She did, in effect, become the wife of John I of Castile, and, when Ferdinand died prematurely decrepit, Leonor became regent and Castile claimed the Portuguese crown.

Leonor had long been the paramour of the Galician João Fernandes Andeiro, conde de Ourém, who had intrigued with both England and Castile and whose influence was much resented by Portuguese patriots. Opponents of Castile chose as their leader an illegitimate son of Peter I: John, master of Aviz, who killed Ourém (December 1383) and, being assured of the support of the populace of Lisbon, assumed the title of defender of the realm. Leonor fled first to Alenquer and then to Santarém, and the king of Castile came to her aid; soon, however, he relegated her to a Spanish convent. Lisbon was besieged for five months (1384), but an outbreak of plague forced the Castilians to retire.

THE HOUSE OF AVIZ, 1383–1580

The legitimate male line of Henry of Burgundy ended at Ferdinand's death, and, when the Cortes met at Coimbra in March–April 1385, John of Aviz was declared king (as John I) and became the founder of a new dynasty. This result was not unopposed, as many of the nobility and clergy still considered the queen of Castile the rightful heiress. However, popular feeling was strong, and John I had valuable and trusted allies in Nuno Álvares Pereira, "the Holy Constable," his military champion, and in João das Regras, his chancellor and jurist.

INDEPENDENCE ASSURED

A number of towns and castles still held out for Castile when in August 1385 John I of Castile and a considerable army made their appearance in central Portugal. Although much outnumbered, the Portuguese won the great Battle of Aljubarrota (August 14, 1385), in which the Castilian chivalry was dispersed and John of Castile himself barely escaped. The victory assured John I of his kingdom and made him a desirable ally. A small force of English archers had been present at Aljubarrota in support of the Portuguese. The Treaty of Windsor, concluded on May 9, 1386, raised the Anglo-Portuguese connection to the status of a firm, binding, and permanent alliance between the two crowns.

John of Gaunt duly went to the Iberian Peninsula in July 1386 and attempted an invasion of Castile in conjunction with John I. The invasion was not successful, but in 1387 the Portuguese king married John of Gaunt's daughter Philippa of Lancaster, who introduced various English practices into Portugal. The truce arranged with Castile in 1387 was prolonged at intervals until peace was finally concluded in 1411.

The victory of John I may be regarded as a triumph of the national spirit over the feudal attachment to established order. Because much of the older nobility sided with Castile, John rewarded his followers at their expense and the crown's. Meanwhile, commerce prospered, and the marriage of John's daughter Isabella to Philip III (the Good) of Burgundy was to be followed by the growth of close trading relations between Portugal and Philip's county of Flanders. With the conclusion of peace with Castile, John found an outlet for the activities of his frontiersmen and of his own sons in the conquest

Depiction of the Battle of Ajubarrota, from volume three of Chronique d'Angleterre (Chronicle of England) by Jean de Wavrin. British Library/Robana/Hulton Fine Art Collection/Getty Images

of Ceuta (1415), from which the great age of Portuguese expansion may be dated.

In 1437, during the short reign of John's eldest son, Edward (Duarte; 1433–38), an unsuccessful attempt to conquer Tangier was made by John's third son, Prince Henry the Navigator, and his younger brother Ferdinand (who was captured by the Moors and died, still unransomed, in 1443). Edward's son Afonso V (1438–81) was still a child when Edward died, and Edward's brother Pedro, duke of Coimbra (Dom Pedro), had himself made regent (1440) instead of the widow, Leonor of Aragon. However, Pedro's own regency was later challenged by the powerful Bragança family, descended from Afonso, illegitimate son of John of Aviz, and Beatriz, daughter of Nuno Álvares Pereira. This family continued to set the young king against his uncle, who was forced to resign the regency, driven to take up arms, and killed at Alfarrobeira (May 1449). Afonso proved unable to resist the demands of the Braganças, who now became the wealthiest family in Portugal. Having married Joan, daughter of Henry IV of Castile, Afonso laid claim to the Castilian throne and became involved in a lengthy struggle with Ferdinand and Isabella in the region of Zamora and Toro, where he was defeated in 1476. He then sailed to France in a failed attempt to enlist the support of Louis XI, and on his return he concluded with Castile the Treaty of Alcáçovas (1479), abandoning the claims

of his wife. Afonso never recovered from his reverse, and during his last years his son John administered the kingdom.

CONSOLIDATION OF THE MONARCHY

John II (1481–95) was as cautious, firm, and jealous of royal power as his father had been openhanded and negligent. At his reign's first Cortes, John exacted a detailed oath of homage that displeased his greatest vassals. A suspicion of conspiracy enabled him to arrest Fernando II, duke of Bragança, and many of his followers; the duke was sentenced to death and executed at Évora in 1484. As well as attacking the power of the nobility, John lessened the effects of the unfavourable treaty with Castile. Calculating and resolute, he later received the epithet "the Perfect Prince."

Predeceased by his legitimate son, John II was succeeded by his cousin the duke of Beja, as Manuel I (1495–1521), known as "the Fortunate." Manuel, who assumed the title of "Lord of the Conquest, Navigation, and Commerce of India, Ethiopia, Arabia, and Persia," inherited, because of the work of John II, a firmly established autocratic monarchy and a rapidly expanding overseas empire. Drawn toward Spain by the common need to defend their overseas interests as defined by the Treaty of Tordesillas (1494), Manuel nourished the hope that the whole peninsula could be united under the house of Aviz; to that end he married Isabella, eldest daughter of Ferdinand and Isabella. However, she died in 1498 while giving birth to a son, Miguel da Paz. This child, recognized as heir to Portugal, Castile, and Aragon, died in infancy. Manuel then married Isabella's sister Maria (died 1517) and eventually Eleanor, sister of the emperor Charles V.

As a condition of his marriage to Isabella, Manuel was required to "purify" Portugal of Jews. After Jews were expelled from Spain in 1492, John II had admitted many Jewish refugees; he had taxed the Jews heavily but was also to supply ships for them to leave Portugal. This was not done, however, and Manuel now ordered all Jews to leave within 10 months, by October 1497. On their assembly in Lisbon, every effort was made to secure their conversion by promises or by force. Some who resisted were allowed to go, but the rest were "converted" under promise that no inquiry would be made into their beliefs for 20 years. As "Christians," they could not be forced to emigrate, and, indeed, they were prohibited from leaving Portugal. In April 1506 a large number of these "new Christians," or Marranos, were massacred in Lisbon during a riot, but Manuel afterward protected the Marranos and allowed many to emigrate to Holland, where their experience with Portuguese trade was put at the service of the Dutch.

If Manuel failed to realize his dream of ruling Spain, his son John III (1521–57) lacked the power to resist Castilian influence. A pious, retiring man, he was ruled by his wife, Catherine, sister of Emperor Charles V, and encouraged the installation of the Inquisition (1536); the first *auto-da-fé* ("act of faith," a public condemnation or punishment of so-called heretics during the Inquisition) was held in 1540. The Society of Jesus (the Jesuits), established in 1540, soon controlled education in Portugal. In 1529 the settlement by the Treaty of Zaragoza (Saragossa) of a dispute over the possession of the Moluccas (an island group part of present-day Indonesia) removed an obstacle to Portuguese-Spanish understanding, and the line dividing Portuguese and Spanish interests in the New World (established by the Treaty of Tordesillas) was matched by a similar line in the Pacific. Meanwhile, this dual theoretical division of new lands between the Portuguese and Spanish and the Reformation had come between Portugal and its English ally.

John III was succeeded by his grandson Sebastian (1557–78), then only three years old. As a child Sebastian became obsessed with the idea of a Crusade against Morocco. Fanatically religious, he had no doubts of his own powers and listened only to flatterers. He visited Ceuta and Tangier in 1574 and began in 1576 to prepare a large expedition against Larache; his forces departed in June 1578 and on August 4 were utterly destroyed by the Moors in the Battle of the Three Kings near Alcazarquivir (Ksar el-Kebir). Sebastian and some 8,000 of his forces were killed, some 15,000 were captured, and only a handful escaped.

Sebastian was succeeded by his great-uncle, Cardinal Henry (1578–80), a brother of John III. His age and celibacy made it certain that the Portuguese throne would soon pass from the direct line of Aviz. Philip II of Spain, nephew of John III and husband (by his first marriage) of John's daughter Maria, had already made his preparations, and, when the cardinal-king died on January 31, 1580, Philip summoned the authorities to obey him. An army under the great duke of Alba entered Portugal in 1580; the resistance of António, prior of Crato (illegitimate son of John III's brother Luís), acclaimed António I at Santarém, collapsed; and Philip II of Spain became Philip I of Portugal (1580–98).

MEDIEVAL SOCIAL AND ECONOMIC DEVELOPMENT

Medieval Portugal comprised regions of considerable diversity. In the north the old aristocracy of Leonese descent owned large estates worked mainly by serfs. In the southern territory that had been reconquered from Muslim rule, there were many towns, often separated by districts almost barren and depopulated. Cistercian monks, who had reached Portugal by 1143, took the initiative in settling these areas; later kings such as Sancho I and Afonso III established *concelhos* (municipalities),

granting them chartered privileges designed to attract settlers. Tax concessions were often given, and freedom was promised to serfs or to Christian captives after a year's residence. In the south, however, the *concelhos* were burdened with defense duties. The *cavaleiros-vilãos* (villein knights) were obliged to horse and arm themselves; the *peões*, or less-substantial men, were required to serve as foot soldiers in defense of the country and perhaps also on a *fossado* (raid) into Muslim territory.

At court the king was advised by his *curia regis* (court or council), comprising the *majordomus curiae*, the head of the administration, the military chief or *signifer*, the *dapifer curiae* (steward of the household), the chancellor (an official whose origins in Portugal were Burgundian rather than Visigothic), and any members of the greater aristocracy, the *ricos-homens*, who might be at court. The *ricos-homens* also comprised the bishops and abbots and masters of the orders of knighthood; many held private civil or military authority. The lesser nobility were without such rights. Below them came various classes of free commoners, such as the *cavaleiros-vilãos* and the *malados*, men who had commended themselves to protectors. There were numerous serfs and slaves.

There had been several shifts in the social structure by the end of the medieval period. Many of the old aristocracy lost their position at the advent of the house of Aviz, and the new nobility, exemplified in the house of Bragança, was often of bureaucratic or ministerial origin. Representatives of the commoners, first attending the Cortes in 1254 on behalf of the *concelhos*, took an increasing part in politics. The Cortes were very frequently called during the reigns of John I, Edward, and Afonso V, but the avenues of power had become wider by the 16th century, and John III's proposal (1525) to call them only every 10 years aroused no opposition. Although the trade guilds were slow in developing, they took some part in determining local taxation in the 13th century. Trade increased, Portuguese merchants having had connections with the Low Countries from the time of Afonso Henriques and with England from the early 13th century. The political crisis of 1385 was followed by inflation and debasements; thereafter there was no national gold currency until 1435, when West African sources began to be tapped.

THE DISCOVERIES AND THE EMPIRE

The idea of expansion into Africa was a logical result of the completion of the Reconquista in the peninsula, and the conquest of Ceuta in North Africa (1415) probably provided the impulse toward further expansion. The simple idea of fighting the Muslims on their own soil was linked with more-complicated motives: the desire to explore in a scientific sense, the hope of finding a way to the rich spice trade of the Indies, and the impulse to spread the Christian faith. These purposes were gradually molded together into a national enterprise, though at first they represented the hopes and aspirations of one man, Prince Henry. The third son of John I and Philippa of Lancaster, known rather inaccurately as "the Navigator" (he himself never went farther afield than Tangier), Henry became (1420) master of the Order of Christ, which King Dinis had founded (1319). The resources of the order were used to draw together skilled geographers and navigators and to equip a series of expeditions that only gradually began to bear fruit.

The date of Prince Henry's earliest expedition was about 1418, visiting the island of Porto Santo; the first call at Madeira probably dates from 1419. An attempt was made to settle in the Canary Islands, and between 1427 and 1431 the Azores were visited by Portuguese seamen. Both the Azores and Madeira were then uninhabited, and their colonization proceeded fairly rapidly from about 1445. Sugar was exported to Europe and gave the islands great economic importance. Meanwhile, Prince Henry's ships were probing the African coast, passing Cape Bojador in 1434 and Rio de Oro in 1436. The unsuccessful expedition against Tangier (1437) was followed by a break in the explorations, but in 1439 Prince Henry was authorized to colonize the Azores; from 1440, further expeditions equipped with a new and lighter ship, the caravel, reached the Bay of Arguin (1443) and Cape Verde (1444) and by Henry's death (1460) had explored the coast as far south as Sierra Leone.

Under Afonso V, three military expeditions were sent against Morocco (1458, 1463, and 1471); by the last of them, Tangier and Arzila were captured. The African explorations were not entirely neglected, but it remained for John II, with his sharp sense of the national interest, to found a fortress and trading post in the Gulf of Guinea at Elmina (São Jorge da Mina, 1481–82). Diogo Cão explored the mouth of the Congo in 1482 and then advanced to Cape Cross, 200 leagues southward (1486). The Kongo kingdom converted to Christianity and allied itself with the Portuguese; its first Christian king, Afonso I (c. 1506–43), made M'banza Congo (renamed São Salvador do Congo in 1534) a centre of Portuguese influence, but the Kongo kingdom fell into internal strife, and Portuguese interests were transferred to the neighbouring kingdom of Angola.

TREATY OF TORDESILLAS

The Treaty of Tordesillas, signed on June 7, 1494, was an agreement between Spain and Portugal aimed at settling conflicts over lands newly discovered or explored by Christopher Columbus and other late 15th-century voyagers.

In 1493, after reports of Columbus's discoveries had reached them, the Spanish rulers Ferdinand and Isabella enlisted papal support for their claims to the New World in order to inhibit the Portuguese and other possible rival claimants. To accommodate them, the Spanish-born Pope Alexander VI issued bulls setting up a line of demarcation from pole to pole 100 leagues (about 320 miles) west of the Cape Verde Islands. Spain was given exclusive rights to all newly discovered and undiscovered lands in the region west of the line. Portuguese expeditions were to keep to the east of the line. Neither power was to occupy any territory already in the hands of a Christian ruler.

No other European powers facing the Atlantic Ocean ever accepted this papal disposition or the subsequent agreement deriving from it. King John II of Portugal was dissatisfied because Portugal's rights in the New World were insufficiently affirmed, and the Portuguese would not even have sufficient room at sea for their African voyages. Meeting at Tordesillas, in northwestern Spain, Spanish and Portuguese ambassadors reaffirmed the papal division, but the line itself was moved to 370 leagues (1,185 miles) west of the Cape Verde Islands, or about 46°30ʹW of Greenwich. Pope Julius II finally sanctioned the change in 1506. The new boundary enabled Portugal to claim the coast of Brazil after its discovery by Pedro Álvares Cabral in 1500. Brazilian exploration and settlement far to the west of the line of demarcation in subsequent centuries laid a firm basis for Brazil's claims to vast areas of the interior of South America.

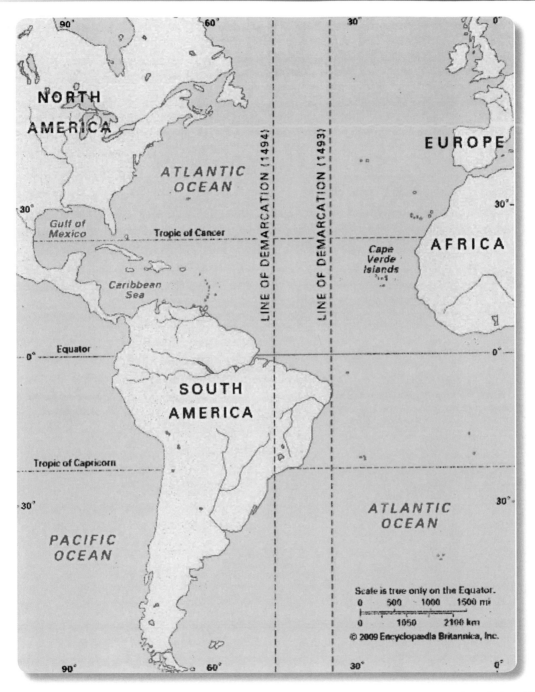

Map showing the line of demarcation between Spanish and Portuguese territory, as first defined by Pope Alexander VI (1493) and later revised by the Treaty of Tordesillas (1494). Spain won control of lands discovered west of the line, while Portugal gained rights to new lands to the east.

Paulo Dias de Novais founded Luanda, the first European-style city in western Africa south of the Equator, in 1576. In 1488 Bartolomeu Dias rounded the Cape of Good Hope and reached the East African coast, and the seaway to India lay open. Dias's return was followed in 1493 with the news that Christopher Columbus had, he thought, found the "Indies" by sailing across the Atlantic. Much as this news must have perturbed the Portuguese, Columbus brought no news of the spiceries or the cities of the East. John II ordered the preparation of an expedition to India by way of the Cape of Good Hope, though this sailed only after his death. John also contested the Spanish claim to all lands discovered west of the Atlantic, and, by the Treaty of Tordesillas, Spain's rights were limited to what lay more than 370 leagues west of the Cape Verde Islands. Thus the territory that was to become Brazil was reserved for Portugal.

The Treaty of Tordesillas had also confirmed Portugal's right to the exploration of Africa and the seaway to India. In July 1497 Vasco da Gama set sail with four ships on the first expedition to India. It reached Calicut (Kozhikode) on the southwestern coast of India the following spring, and the survivors made their way back to Lisbon in the autumn of 1499 with specimens of Oriental merchandise. A second fleet was prepared under Pedro Álvares Cabral, who touched the Brazilian coast (April 22, 1500) and claimed it for Portugal.

CONTROL OF THE SEA TRADE

In 1505 Francisco de Almeida arrived as viceroy of India and supported the ruler of Cochin against the *zamorin* (Hindu ruler) of Calicut. The control of sea trade, the chief source of Portuguese wealth in the East, was assured by the defeat of Muslim naval forces off Diu in 1509. Almeida's successor, Afonso de Albuquerque, conquered Goa (1510), which he made the seat of Portuguese power, and Malacca (1511); sent two expeditions to the Moluccas (1512 and 1514); and captured Hormuz in the Persian Gulf (1515). Soon after, Fernão Peres de Andrade reached Guangzhou (Canton) in China; in 1542 Portuguese merchants were permitted to settle at Liampo (Ningbo), and in 1557 they founded the colony of Macau (Macao).

Albuquerque was responsible for this conception of a system of strongpoints that secured Portuguese domination of trade with the Orient for nearly a century. Goa soon became the chief port of western India; Hormuz controlled the Persian Gulf, and Malacca became the gateway from the Indian Ocean to the South China Sea, while a string of fortified trading posts secured the coast of East Africa and the gulf and shores of India and Ceylon (Sri Lanka). Farther east, less-fortified settlements were established with the consent of the native rulers from Bengal to China, and the trade of the principal Spice Islands was in Portuguese hands. The preservation of the whole system was entrusted to a governor, who sometimes held the rank of viceroy, at Goa; although Portuguese arms had both triumphs and reverses, their control of the Oriental trade remained substantial, if never complete, until the 17th century, when the Dutch, at war with the joint crown of Portugal and Spain and deprived of their traditional trade with Lisbon, began to seek spices from their source and effectively demolished the Portuguese monopoly.

UNION OF SPAIN AND PORTUGAL, 1580–1640

After Philip II of Spain had occupied Portugal in 1580, the island of Terceira in the Azores held out for António of Crato, who himself sought alliances in England and France. In 1582 a French expedition to establish him in the Azores was defeated, and in 1589 an English attempt upon Lisbon, led by Sir Francis Drake and Sir John Norris, failed dismally. António died in Paris in 1595, but the true symbol of Portuguese independence was not him but King Sebastian himself. The Portuguese people refused to believe that he was dead and nourished a messianic faith in his reappearance, of which four pretenders sought to avail themselves, the last as late as 1600 and as far afield as Venice.

Meanwhile, Philip arrived in Portugal and was accepted as King Philip I (1580–98) by the Cortes held at Tomar in 1581. Philip sought to preserve Portuguese autonomy, to consider the union as a personal one like that of Aragon and Castile under Ferdinand and Isabella, to appoint only Portuguese to the administration, to summon the Cortes frequently, and to be accompanied by a Portuguese council in Madrid. However, these undertakings were neglected by his successor, Philip II (III of Spain; 1598–1621), and completely violated by Philip III (IV of Spain; 1621–40).

Portuguese resentment against Spanish rule was exacerbated by the failure of these kings to visit Portugal, the appointment of Spaniards to Portuguese offices, the loss of trade as a consequence of Spain's foreign wars, and the levying of taxation to sustain these wars. In 1624 the Dutch seized Bahia in Brazil, only to be expelled by a joint Spanish and Portuguese expedition the following year. But in 1630 the Dutch occupied Pernambuco in northeastern Brazil and the adjoining sugar estates, which they held for a generation. The final straw was the plan formulated in 1640 by Gaspar de Guzmán y Pimental, conde-duque de Olivares, to use Portuguese troops against the equally discontented Catalans. Two Portuguese insurrections, in 1634 and 1637, had failed to mount real threats, but in 1640 Spain's power was extended to the utmost by war with France and revolt in Catalonia. The French minister, Armand-Jean du Plessis, cardinal et duc de Richelieu, already had agents

JOHN IV

John IV (born March 18/19, 1604, Vila Viçosa, Portugal—died November 6, 1656, Lisbon) was made king of Portugal in 1640 as a result of the national revolution, or restoration, which ended 60 years of Spanish rule. He founded the dynasty of Bragança (Braganza), fought off Spanish attacks, and established a system of alliances.

John, duke of Bragança, the wealthiest nobleman in Portugal, married Luisa de Guzmán, daughter of the Spanish duke of Medina Sidonia. The Bragança duchy, founded in 1461, was a collateral of the extinct royal House of Aviz; and, when the restorers of independence overthrew the Spanish governor on December 1, 1640, they offered John the crown. On December 15 he was enthroned as John IV. Supported by the Cortes, the national assembly, he entrusted each province with its own defense and sent missions to seek recognition from France, England, and the Netherlands. His alliance with the English Stuarts (1642) was frustrated by the English Civil Wars, but in 1654 John made a new treaty with the English Commonwealth, which gained him military aid in return for trading privileges. The Dutch, already in possession of Pernambuco in northeastern Brazil, seized Angola but were expelled from both, while retaining their conquests in the East Indies. The Spanish were defeated at Montijo (May 26, 1644) and were blocked from further invasion.

John IV and his Queen Leonor governed through a royal council and a committee of the Cortes, the Board of Three Estates, and instituted the Overseas Council. He survived attempts at assassination and Spanish attempts to influence the Vatican to isolate the Portuguese church. John was a notable composer. At John's death his wife became regent for their son Afonso VI (ruled 1656–83). His daughter Catherine of Braganza married Charles II of England in 1662.

in Lisbon, and a leader was found in John, duke of Bragança, a grandson of the duchess Catherine (niece of John III) whose claims had been overridden in 1580 by Philip II of Spain. Taking advantage of the unpopularity of the governor, Margaret of Savoy, duchess of Mantua, and her secretary of state, Miguel de Vasconcelos, the leaders of the party of independence carried through a nationalist revolution on December 1, 1640. Vasconcelos was almost the only victim; the Spanish garrisons were driven out, and on December 15 the duke of Bragança was crowned as John IV (1640–56).

CHAPTER 6

INDEPENDENT PORTUGAL: FROM THE RISE OF THE BRAGANÇA DYNASTY TO THE 21ST CENTURY

In the centuries following its independence from Spain, Portugal's fortunes rose and fell, often as a result of external factors. Wealth from its overseas colonies—most notably Brazil—bolstered domestic prosperity, but a catastrophic earthquake in 1755 devastated Lisbon. The country became embroiled in the wars of the Napoleonic era, and the allegiances formed during that period served to bolster Portugal's territorial claims in Africa. The loss of Brazil, and the strife that led to that loss, marked the decline of the royal house of Bragança. The monarchy surrendered to republicanism in the late 19th century, and it, in turn, gave way to dictatorship in the 20th century. During this period Portugal lagged economically behind its European neighbours, and its once expansive colonial empire all but evaporated. The end of dictatorship was marked by a transitional period during which the military loomed large, but by the 1980s, full democracy was secure in Portugal, and the country greeted the 21st century as a founding member of the European Union.

THE HOUSE OF BRAGANÇA, 1640–1910

The success of the new regime was not finally assured until 1668, when Spain at last recognized Portuguese independence. Before that, faced with the threat of a Spanish invasion, John had sent missions to the courts of Europe in quest of alliances. France now refused a formal treaty. The Dutch, having seized northern Brazil, accepted a truce in Europe and proceeded to capture Angola from Portugal. In 1642

John negotiated a treaty with Charles I of England, but this was made void by Charles's execution in 1649. Meanwhile, the Portuguese defeated the Spaniards at Montijo (May 26, 1644) and warded off several invasions. In 1654 they made a treaty with the English Commonwealth, obtaining aid in return for commercial concessions. The Dutch were finally expelled from Pernambuco in northern Brazil. By a secret article of the Peace of the Pyrenees (November 7, 1659), France promised Spain that it would provide no further assistance to Portugal, but in 1661 Portugal signed a treaty of alliance with the restored English monarchy. In 1662 Charles II of England married John's daughter Catherine of Bragança and, in return for a large dowry including the cession of Bombay and Tangier, provided arms and men for the war with Spain. The Portuguese defense was organized by the German soldier Friedrich Hermann von Schönberg (later duke of Schomberg); in June 1663 Sancho Manuel, conde de Vila Flor, defeated Don Juan de Austria at Ameixial, and in June 1665 von Schönberg won the important victory of Montes Claros. Peace was finally made by the Treaty of Lisbon early in 1668.

When John IV died, his second son, Afonso VI (1656–83), was only age 13. Afonso's mother, Luísa de Gusmão, acted as regent until June 1662, when he began to rule. Afonso himself was feebleminded, but the country was capably governed by Luiz de Vasconcelos e Sousa, conde de Castelo Melhor, until 1667. At that point, the French princess, Maria Francesca of Savoy, who had married Afonso the previous year, entered into an intrigue with his more personable brother Peter, who later reigned as Peter II. They contrived to dismiss Castelo Melhor and to have Maria Francesca's marriage to Afonso annulled. She at once married Peter (1668), who was declared regent. Afonso, though still king, was kept a virtual prisoner in the Azores and at Sintra until his death.

During the reign of Peter II (1683–1706), Portugal recovered from the strain of the Spanish wars and began to benefit from the discovery of gold and precious stones in Brazil. The first gold strike in Minas Gerais took place in 1693, and, in the last years of the 17th century, considerable wealth was extracted; however, it was not until 1728, when diamonds were discovered, that the mineral wealth of Brazil formed a very substantial part of the revenue of the Portuguese crown.

THE 18TH CENTURY

In the War of the Spanish Succession (1701–14), Portugal's recent friends England and France fought on opposing sides. Although Peter initially sought to remain neutral, Portugal joined the Anglo-Austrian Grand Alliance in 1703 and provided a base for the archduke Charles (later Emperor Charles VI) to conduct his war for the Spanish throne. Then on December 27, 1703, the English envoy, John Methuen, concluded the treaty that bears his name, by which the exchange of port wine for English woolens became the basis for Anglo-Portuguese trade.

Sebastião José de Carvalho e Melo, the reform-minded minister of Portugal who virtually ruled the nation, with King Joseph I's knowledge and tacit permission, from 1750 to 1777. The Art Archive/ SuperStock

Although the treaty of 1654 had secured great privileges for English merchants in Lisbon, neither it nor the treaties of 1642 and 1661, by which the traditional alliance was restored, had created trade. This was now done, and, with the wealth that soon poured into Lisbon from Brazil, the English merchants gained a commanding position in the trade of Portugal. The political treaties of 1703 proved less fruitful. The Portuguese general António Luís de Sousa, marquês das Minas, entered Madrid in 1706, but French and Spanish forces were victorious at Almansa in 1707, and in 1711 the French admiral René Duguay-Trouin sacked Rio de Janeiro. At the conclusion of the war, Portugal negotiated a peace treaty with France (April 1713), but peace with Spain was not concluded until 1715.

Portugal under Peter's son John V (1706–50) attained a degree of prosperity unknown since the restoration of independence from Spain. The tax of a royal fifth levied on the precious metals and stones of Brazil gave the monarchy an independent source of wealth. The Cortes, which had met irregularly since 1640, was no longer summoned, and government was carried out by ministers appointed by the king. John V desired the absolute authority enjoyed by Louis XIV in France. John converted his wealth into papal and other dignities: the archbishop of Lisbon became a patriarch (1716); Pope Benedict XIV gave John the title "His Most Faithful Majesty" (1749); and royal academies, palaces, and libraries were inaugurated. But in his later years, his

ministers proved inadequate, and the kingdom sank into stagnation.

On John's death, his son Joseph (1750–77) appointed as minister Sebastião José de Carvalho e Melo (later conde de Oeiras and marquês de Pombal), who soon gained a complete ascendancy over the king and endeavoured to replace the stagnant absolutism with a more active type of despotism that, with some qualifications, deserves the epithet "enlightened." Pombal's full powers date from his efficient handling of the crisis caused by the disastrous Lisbon earthquake of November 1755, but even before this he had reformed the sugar and diamond trades, set up a national silk industry (1750), and formed one chartered company to control the sardine- and tunny-fishing industry of the Algarve and another to trade with northern Brazil. In 1756 he founded a board of trade with powers to limit the privileges enjoyed by the English merchants under the treaties of 1654 and 1661 and set up the General Company for Wines of Alto Douro to control the port wine trade. Industries for the manufacture of hats (1759), cutlery (1764), and other articles were established with varying success.

Pombal's methods were arbitrary and his enemies numerous. His reform of the wine industry provoked a riot in Porto (1757) that was savagely repressed. However, his principal victims were the Jesuits, who were expelled in 1759 from all the Portuguese dominions, and the nobility, in particular José Mascarenhas, duque de Aveiro, and the Távora family,

LISBON EARTHQUAKE OF 1755

A series of earthquakes occurred on the morning of November 1, 1755, causing serious damage to Lisbon and killing an estimated 60,000 people in that city alone. Violent shaking demolished large public buildings and about 12,000 dwellings. Because November 1 is All Saints' Day, a large part of the population was attending mass at the moment the earthquake struck; the churches, unable to withstand the seismic shock, collapsed, killing or injuring thousands of worshippers.

Modern research indicates that the main seismic source was faulting of the seafloor along the tectonic plate boundaries of the mid-Atlantic. The earthquake generated a tsunami that produced waves about 20 feet (6 metres) high at Lisbon and 65 feet (20 metres) high at Cádiz, Spain. The waves traveled westward to Martinique in the Caribbean Sea, a distance of 3,790 miles (6,100 km), in 10 hours and there reached a height of 13 feet (4 metres) above mean sea level. Damage was even reported in Algiers, 685 miles (1,100 km) to the east. The total number of persons killed included those who perished by drowning and in fires that burned throughout Lisbon for about six days following the shock. Depictions of the earthquakes in art and literature continued for centuries, making the "Great Lisbon Earthquake," as it came to be known, a seminal event in European history.

who were accused of an attack on the king (September 3, 1758), condemned, and executed (January 12, 1759). Having eliminated the Jesuits from the educational system, Pombal applied regalist principles in the reform of the University of Coimbra (1772) and the royal board of censorship (1768), which supervised the system of lower education from 1771.

While Pombal succeeded in modifying the ascendancy of the British merchants in Portugal, he invoked the English alliance in 1762 when Spain, prompted by the renewal of the Bourbon Family Compact with France, invaded Portugal. The Portuguese army was reformed by Wilhelm von Schaumburg-Lippe, and an English force was led by James O'Hara, 2nd Baron Tyrawley, and John Campbell, 4th earl of Loudoun. A peace treaty was signed in February 1763 at Fontainebleau. After Joseph's death on February 24, 1777, his daughter Maria I (1777–1816), who had married Joseph's brother and her uncle (Peter III), acceded to the throne; Pombal was dismissed (1777) and eventually found guilty on several charges. His successors made peace with Spain by the Treaty of San Ildefonso (1777).

THE FRENCH REVOLUTIONARY AND NAPOLEONIC WARS

After the death of Peter III in 1786 and her eldest son Joseph in 1788, Maria I suffered from melancholia. In 1792 her mental instability increased following news of the radical phases of the French Revolution, and she ceased to reign. Her surviving son ruled in her name, formally became prince regent in 1799, and on her death became John VI (1816–26). In 1793 Portugal joined England and Spain against France, sending a naval division to assist the English Mediterranean fleet and an army to the Catalan front. The Peace of Basel (July 1795), by which Spain abandoned its allies, left Portugal still at war. Although subjected to pressure from the French Directory and from the Spanish minister, Manuel de Godoy, Portugal remained unmolested until 1801, when Godoy sent an ultimatum and invaded the Alentejo. By the Peace of Badajoz (June 1801), Portugal lost the town of Olivenza and paid an indemnity.

From the Peace of Amiens (1802) until 1807, Portugal was once more immune from attack, though it was subjected to continuous pressure to break off the English connection. Napoleon sought to close all continental ports to British ships, but Portugal endeavoured to maintain neutrality. The secret Franco-Spanish Treaty of Fontainebleau (October 1807) provided for Portugal's eventual dismemberment by Napoleon I and Godoy. Already one of Napoleon's generals, Andoche Junot, was hastening across Spain with a French army, and on November 27 the prince regent and the royal family and court embarked on a fleet lying in the Tagus River and were escorted by British vessels to Brazil; the court remained at Rio de Janeiro for 14 years. Junot declared the Braganças deposed, but his occupation of Portugal was challenged in August 1808 by the arrival of Sir Arthur Wellesley (later duke

of Wellington) and 13,500 British troops in Mondego Bay. Winning the victories of Roliça (August 17) and Vimeiro (August 21), Wellington enabled his superiors to negotiate the Convention of Sintra (August 31), by which Junot was allowed to evacuate Portugal with his army.

A second French invasion (1808–09) led to Sir John Moore's death at La Coruña, Spain, in January 1809 and the reembarkation of the British forces. In February William Carr (later Viscount) Beresford was placed in command of the Portuguese army, and in March a French force under Marshal Nicolas-Jean de Dieu Soult advanced from Galicia and occupied Porto. Wellesley returned to Portugal in April, drove Soult from the north, and, after his victory of Talavera de la Reina in Spain (July), withdrew to Portugal.

The third French invasion followed in August 1810 when Marshal André Masséna with Marshal Michel Ney and Junot entered Beira province. Defeated by Wellington at Bussaco (September 27) near Coimbra, the French found themselves facing the entrenched lines of Torres Vedras, north of Lisbon, where they wintered amid great privations. By the spring of 1811 they could only retreat, and on March 5 they began the evacuation of Portugal, harassed all the way by English and Portuguese attacks and crossing the frontier after a defeat at Sabugal (April 3).

Portugal and France made peace on May 30, 1814. Portugal was represented at the Congress of Vienna, but it played little part in the settlement. The series of Anglo-Portuguese treaties concluded between the years 1809 and 1817, however, was important insofar as it extended many of the conditions of the Anglo-Portuguese alliance to Brazil and had an influence on the future of Africa. England's efforts to enlist Portuguese collaboration in suppressing the slave trade resulted in the treaty of January 22, 1815, and in the additional convention of 1817, by reason of which Portugal's claims to a considerable part of Africa were formally recognized.

CONSTITUTIONALISM

The Napoleonic campaigns caused great devastation in Portugal, and the absence of the royal family and the presence of a foreign commander (Beresford) combined with revolutionary agitation and the influence of Spanish liberalism to produce an atmosphere of discontent. On December 16, 1815, Brazil was raised to the rank of a kingdom united with Portugal, and John VI, who took the throne in March 1816, showed no desire to return to Portugal. In 1817 Beresford suppressed a conspiracy in Lisbon, and the Masonic leader General Gomes Freire de Andrade was executed. Unrest increased, and, when Beresford himself went to Brazil (March 1820) to press John to return, a constitutionalist revolution began in Porto (August 24, 1820); the revolution soon spread throughout the country and led to the formation of a junta in Lisbon (October 4). On October 10, when Beresford returned to Portugal,

he was not allowed to land, and British officers were expelled from the army. A constituent assembly was summoned that drew up a very liberal constitution, thus confronting John VI with an accomplished fact.

John's reluctance to return was at last overcome. Leaving his elder son Peter to govern Brazil, John landed at Lisbon on July 3, 1821. He swore to uphold the constitution, but his wife, Carlota Joaquina, and their second son, Michael, refused to take the oath and were sentenced to banishment, though this was not carried out. The Portuguese constitutionalists, not appreciating the determination of Brazil not to yield its status as a kingdom, sought to compel Pedro to return, but, rather than sacrifice the rule of the Braganças in Brazil, he declared Brazilian independence (September 7, 1822) and became emperor of Brazil as Pedro I. This enabled his brother Michael to appeal to absolutist forces in Portugal to overthrow the constitutionalists; an insurrection led by Michael almost succeeded (April 30, 1824), but, through the action of the foreign ministers, John VI was restored and Michael went into exile in Vienna (June 1824).

THE WAR OF THE TWO BROTHERS

John VI acknowledged the independence of Brazil in 1825, assuming pro forma the imperial title and then yielding it to Pedro. However, when John died (March 10, 1826), no provision had been made for the succession except that his daughter Maria Isabel was named regent. Pedro, as

Peter IV of Portugal, issued from Brazil a charter providing for a parliamentary regime by the authorization of the monarchy and not based on the sovereignty of the people. He then made a conditional abdication (May 1826) of the Portuguese throne in favour of his seven-year-old daughter Maria da Glória provided that she marry her uncle Michael and swear to accept the charter. This compromise could not be effective. The absolutists had hoped that Pedro would resign all rights to the Portuguese crown, and the council of regency hesitated to publish the charter until General João Carlos de Saldanha (later duque de Saldanha) forced their hand. In 1827 Michael took the oath and was appointed regent; he landed in Lisbon in February 1828, and his supporters at once began to persecute the liberals. A form of the Cortes met in Lisbon and in July 1828 repudiated Pedro's claims and declared Michael the rightful king.

Only Terceira Island in the Azores sustained the liberal cause. In June 1829, however, a regency on behalf of Maria da Glória was established in Terceira, and in 1831 Pedro, having abdicated the Brazilian throne, went to Europe and began to raise money and an army for the conquest of Portugal. In February 1832 the expedition sailed to Terceira, and in July the liberals, led by Pedro, disembarked at Mindelo near Porto, which they soon occupied. However, the rest of the country stood by Michael, who besieged the liberals in Porto for a year (July 1832–July 1833). By then enthusiasm for Michael had waned, and António José de Sousa Manuel, duque de Terceira, and Captain (later Sir) Charles Napier, who had taken command of the liberal navy, made a successful landing in the Algarve (June 1833). Terceira advanced on Lisbon, which fell in July 1833, and Michael capitulated at Evora-Monte in May 1834.

FURTHER POLITICAL STRIFE

The War of the Two Brothers ended with the exile of Michael (June) and the death of Pedro (September 24, 1834). Maria da Glória became queen as Maria II (1834–53) at age 15. While Maria necessarily came under the influence of the successful generals of the civil war, her principal aim was to defend her father's charter (which had been granted by the crown) from those who demanded a "democratic" constitution like that of 1822. In September 1836 the latter, thenceforth called Septembrists, seized power. The chartist leaders rebelled and were exiled, but by 1842 the Septembrist front was no longer united, and António Bernardo da Costa Cabral restored the charter.

In 1846 the movement of Maria da Fonte, a popular rising against higher taxation to improve roads and reforms in public health in which almost all parties joined, put an end to Costa Cabral's government but left Portugal divided between the Septembrists, who held Porto, and Saldanha, now in Queen Maria's confidence, in Lisbon. Saldanha negotiated for the intervention of other members of the Quadruple Alliance (formed in April 1834 by England, France, Spain, and Portugal), and a combined British and Spanish force received the surrender of the Porto junta in June 1847 and ended the war with the Convention of Gramido (June 29, 1847). Saldanha governed until 1849, when Costa Cabral resumed office only to be overthrown in April 1851. Saldanha then held office again for five years (1851–56), and the period of peace finally allowed the country to settle down. This "Regeneration" ended civil strife and established party government.

Maria II was succeeded by Peter V (1853–61), her eldest son by her second husband, Ferdinand of Saxe-Coburg. Peter, who married Stephanie of Hohenzollern-Sigmaringen in 1858, showed promise of being a capable monarch but died of typhoid fever on November 11, 1861. His brother Louis (1861–89) seemed to have inherited a country that had recovered from the Napoleonic invasions and from civil wars, political strife, and pronunciamentos (military coups). But, although the main parties were now defined as Historicals (i.e., radicals) and Regenerators (moderates), the alternation of governments gradually ceased to reflect public feeling, and, in the last years of Louis's reign, republicanism began to gain ground.

OVERSEAS EMPIRE

Brazil's independence in 1822 left Portugal's overseas empire a largely African one, with scattered small holdings in Asia (in western India mainly Goa, Damão [now Daman], and Diu; East Timor in Indonesia; and Macau in South China). Beginning in 1836, Portugal pursued a policy of African territorial expansion and economic enhancement, concentrating first on Angola and later on Mozambique and Portuguese Guinea (now Guinea-Bissau). Portugal's role in the European partition of Africa in the late 19th century was limited by its long-standing economic dependence on Great Britain. A colonial movement gained momentum in Lisbon, and a Portuguese scheme known as the "Rose-Coloured Map," which laid claim to a colony stretching across Africa from Angola to Mozambique, was recognized by France and Germany in 1886. However, Britain challenged Portugal's claim to territory in central Africa (in what are now Malawi and Zimbabwe) and issued an ultimatum, dated January 11, 1890, demanding the immediate withdrawal of Portuguese forces from the disputed regions. The ultimatum implicitly threatened, in the short run, the use of British naval force and, in the long run, an end to the venerable Anglo-Portuguese alliance, which dated from the late 14th century. The Lisbon government, obliged to comply, subsequently resigned. The ultimatum crisis rocked Portuguese public opinion, heightening imperial fever in the capital and principal towns, compromising the monarchy of King Charles I, and bolstering republicans.

Despite the failure of the central-corridor plan, Portugal retained a large African empire (about 8 percent of the continent). Two Anglo-Portuguese agreements—the 1891 boundary treaty and the so-called Windsor Treaty of October 14, 1899—safeguarded Portugal's sovereignty over its existing colonies and reaffirmed the ancient alliance.

THE RISE OF REPUBLICANISM

During the period from 1890 to 1910, the relatively stable politics of rotating governments under the constitutional monarchy disintegrated. Feuding monarchist parties and politicians agreed that Portugal faced severe economic, financial, and social problems, but they quarreled over solutions. The republicans increased their support in Lisbon and the larger towns as well as in the rural south. In 1906 João Franco, a prominent politician with reformist plans for saving the monarchy, was appointed premier. Unable to unite the factious monarchists, he began to govern by decree. Franco boldly undertook to reform finance and administration but was accused of illegal money transfers to Charles. These scandals were followed by rumours of further intrigue, and on February 1, 1908, Charles and his heir, Louis Philip, were assassinated in an open carriage in the streets of Lisbon. Whether the regicides were isolated fanatics or agents of a hidden organization such as the Carbonária, a republican secret society, the killings were applauded by the republicans, who immediately began their preparations for a final attack on the monarchy.

Only age 18 at his accession, Charles's younger son, King Manuel II (1908–10), was ill-equipped to solidify the crumbling monarchist factions. In the general elections of August 1910, both Lisbon and Porto voted in favour of a republic. On October 3 the murder by an insane patient of a leading republican figure, the distinguished psychiatrist Miguel Bombarda, offered the pretext for a rising that had already been organized. Armed civilians, soldiers, and the men aboard some ships in the Tagus, under the leadership of António Machado Santos, a key Carbonária figure, began the republican revolution on October 4; the next morning, Portugal's First Republic was declared from the balcony of the Lisbon City Hall. Manuel escaped via his yacht to Gibraltar and then to England, where he remained in exile until his death in 1932.

SOCIAL AND ECONOMIC CONDITIONS

The flow of wealth from Portugal's overseas territories and trading posts helped to sustain the court and capital but did little to improve the domestic economy, which remained largely rural. The favourable financial position of the late 15th century—derived from trade in slaves, gold, and spices—did not long survive into the 16th century, when the expenses of maintaining far-flung and unproductive foreign stations and the depredations of pirates quickly absorbed any surpluses. There were few native industries. Not only were manufactured goods such as cloth, tapestry, and metalware imported, but so were basic foodstuffs, salt meat, cured fish, and dairy produce. Agriculture was little regarded, and insufficient land was available for smallholdings. During the years of Spanish domination, the ports were closed to English merchants. By the time the ports were reopened, after 1640, the flow of trade had found new channels, and the Dutch and English had outstripped Portugal as colonial powers. The discovery of gold in Brazil at the end of the 17th century revived Portugal's economy, but gold production was in decline by 1750, while the diamond market was saturated. In the later 18th century a series of protectionist measures were introduced, many by Pombal. The Methuen Treaty (1703) with England had strengthened the port wine trade at the expense of Portuguese cloth; further attempts were later made to improve the export value of port wine. Support was also given for the production of woolen goods, linen, paper, porcelain, and cutlery and to the tunny and sardine fisheries. Pombal attempted to create an educated bourgeoisie, but the Portuguese textile industry could not withstand mechanized competition. After 1850 public works, railways, and ports were given priority, but it was not until the 20th century that any sustained attack upon Portugal's economic difficulties was undertaken.

THE FIRST REPUBLIC, 1910–26

The new regime formed a provisional government under the presidency of Teófilo Braga, a well-known writer. A new electoral law was issued giving the vote only to a restricted number of adult males. The provisional government presided over the election of a constituent assembly, which opened on June 19, 1911. The constitution was passed by the assembly on August 20, and the provisional government surrendered its authority a few days later (August 24) to the new president, Manuel José de Arriaga. Despite initial hopes that the republic would solve the massive problems inherited from the monarchy, Portugal soon became western Europe's most turbulent, unstable parliamentary regime.

Although a monarchist invasion led by Henrique de Paiva Couceiro in October 1911 was unsuccessful, the main danger to the new regime came from its internal divisions. For the moment, it was fairly united in support of abolishing the monarchy and disestablishing the Roman Catholic Church. The religious orders were expelled (October 8, 1910) and their property confiscated. New legislation banned the teaching of religion in schools and universities and annulled many religious holidays. Persecution of Catholics in the early years of the republic attracted international attention and brought the new political system into conflict with foreign diplomats, humanitarian organizations, and journalists. Indeed, though the government initiated advances in education, health, civic freedoms, and colonial development, positive results were overwhelmed by administrative instability, labour unrest, public violence, and military intervention in politics.

By 1912 the republicans were divided into Evolutionists (moderates), led by António José de Almeida; Unionists (centre party), led by Manuel de Brito Camacho; and Democrats (the leftist core of the original party), led by Afonso Costa. A number of prominent republicans had no specific party. The whirligig of republican political life offered little improvement on the monarchist regime, and in 1915 the army showed signs of restlessness. General Pimenta de Castro formed a military government and permitted the monarchists to reorganize, but a Democratic coup in May led to his arrest and consignment to the Azores, along with Machado Santos. Dominated by Costa's oratory, partisan press, and political machine, the Democrats' regime was in turn overthrown by another bloody military coup (December 1917), led by the former minister to Germany, Major Sidónio Pais.

The authoritarian, unstable "New Republic" of charismatic President Pais failed to pacify the feuding factions, and its collapse precipitated a brief civil war. Following Pais's assassination in Lisbon (December 14, 1918), republicans and monarchists fought a civil war (January 1919) in which the final armed effort to restore the monarchy failed, and political power was restored to the chastened Democrats. Four key tensions characterized the republic's troubled political system: (1) excessive factionalism, (2) the tendency of the factions to bear allegiance to personalities rather than to ideas, institutions, and the public interest, (3) disparity between the landholding patterns of the north (typified by *minifundias*—small subsistence farms) and the south (typified by *latifundias*—large estates worked by landless peasants), and (4) the concentration of economic development in Lisbon, at the expense of the provinces.

Though officially neutral, Portugal at the outbreak of World War I had proclaimed its adhesion to the English alliance (August 7, 1914) and on November 23 committed itself to military operations against Germany. On September 11 the first expedition left to reinforce the African colonies, and there was fighting in northern Mozambique, on the Tanganyika (now Tanzania) frontier, and in southern Angola, on the frontier of German South West Africa. In February 1916, in compliance with a request from Britain, Portugal seized German ships lying in Portuguese ports, and on March 9 Germany declared war on Portugal. A Portuguese expeditionary force under General Fernando Tamagnini de Abreu went to Flanders in 1917, and on April 9, 1918, the Germans mounted a major attack in the Battle of the Lys. Although the Allies won the war and Portugal's colonies were safeguarded, the 0.75 percent of the war indemnity paid by Germany to Portugal was scant compensation for the heavy costs incurred both in the field and at home, including the casualties of the African campaigns and the Western Front, the alienation of a portion of the army officer corps, crippling war debts to Britain, intense inflation, and a scarcity of food and fuel.

Former Evolutionist Almeida became the only president to complete his term during the First Republic, but the cycles of bankruptcy, corruption, public violence, and military insurrectionism continued. Finally, on May 28, 1926, the parliamentary republic was overthrown in a bloodless military coup that instituted what was to become western Europe's most long-lived authoritarian system.

THE DICTATORSHIP, 1926–74

The provisional military government was shortly taken over by General António Óscar de Fragoso Carmona, who favoured sweeping changes. In 1928, in the face of financial crisis, Carmona appointed António de Oliveira Salazar minister of finance with full powers over expenditure. A prominent professor of economics at the University of Coimbra, Salazar assembled a civilian elite of intellectuals and bureaucrats to steer the course of recovery. Budgetary surpluses became the hallmark of his regime, making possible large expenditures for social programs, rearmament, and infrastructure development. This progress, coupled with personal austerity and hard work, won Salazar the grudging collaboration of diverse parties and interest groups that included monarchists, conservative republicans, fascists, pseudofascists, nationalists, the church, business leaders, land barons, and the military establishment. As minister of colonies in 1930, he prepared the Colonial Act, assimilating the administration of the overseas territories to his system. In July 1932 Salazar became prime minister, a post he was to hold (along with other key ministries during crises) until 1968.

The new constitution of 1933 declared Portugal a "unitary, corporatist republic." Salazar's New State (Estado Novo) provided for a National Assembly, with deputies elected quadrennially as a bloc, and a Corporative Chamber comprising representatives of occupations. All seats in the assembly went to government supporters; the Corporative Chamber was not established until employers' and workers' syndicates were formed. The government regulated labour-management relations, banned strikes and lockouts, and monitored social welfare planning. Political parties were prohibited, and all eligible voters were encouraged to join the National Union, an approved loyalist movement. Ever mindful of the confusion that preceded it, the New State emphasized order over freedom and attempted to "neutralize" society through the use of censorship, propaganda, and political imprisonment. On the other hand, it partially restored the pre-1910 privileges of the church in law, society, and education.

During the Spanish Civil War (1936–39), Salazar backed the Nationalists led by General Francisco Franco, who triumphed and controlled all of Spain by the spring of 1939. In World War II, Portugal maintained official neutrality (while quietly favouring Britain) until Britain invoked the ancient Anglo-Portuguese alliance to obtain bases in the Azores. Portugal joined

António de Oliveira Salazar, in his capacity as prime minister, delivering a speech in 1938. AFP/ Getty Images

the North Atlantic Treaty Organization (NATO) as a founding member in 1949 but did not gain admission to the United Nations until 1955.

Portugal's foreign and colonial policies--Salazar's insistence on maintaining Portugal's colonies in Africa could only be sustained with difficulty at a time when the other European colonial empires in Africa were being dismantled--met with increasing difficulty both at home and abroad beginning in the 1950s. In the presidential election of 1958, General Humberto Delgado generated political heat after challenging the regime's candidate, Admiral Américo Tomás. Internationally, the tensions of the Cold War gave Portugal's largely undeveloped overseas empire a new significance. The determination of the Indian government to annex Portuguese India led to a severing of diplomatic relations (August 1955) and to mass invasions of the Portuguese possessions by Indian passive resisters. Portugal disputed but effectively lost the enclaves of Dadra and Nagar Haveli to India (despite a ruling by the International Court of Justice in April 1960 favouring Portugal), and on December 19, 1961, India took over Goa, Diu, and Daman.

Salazar had made it clear that he did not favour decolonization, and, when in early 1961 Angola was the scene of disturbances, he reinforced the troops in the African territories and took over the Ministry of Defense. Nevertheless, colonial wars erupted in Angola, Mozambique, and Portuguese Guinea between 1961 and 1964.

Despite its failure to rejuvenate agriculture and its reluctance to industrialize, perhaps the most important contribution of the New State was to the economy. Development plans, closely monitored by the demanding Salazar, were conservative but consistent. The government significantly reduced its debt, diminished its economic dependence on British investment, and tightly controlled foreign investment and did not openly encourage it until the mid-1960s, when expensive wars in Angola, Mozambique, and Portuguese Guinea prompted a revision of the investment code. The government also supported industry, though not massively, and emphasized infrastructure development over health, education, and welfare. From about 1960 until the inflation surge and energy crisis of 1973, Portugal experienced economic growth at an annual rate of 5 to 7 percent, which constituted a boom for western Europe's poorest country.

In September 1968 Salazar was incapacitated by a stroke. President Tomás invited Marcello Caetano, one of the architects of the New State, to form a government, but Salazar was never informed of this transition. On July 27, 1970, he died. Although Caetano was more worldly and less reserved than his predecessor, he proved unable to reverse the tide of Portugal's African wars, to alleviate the economic woes of 1973–74, or to avert revolution.

THE REVOLUTION OF THE CARNATIONS

Two developments galvanized the movement that was shortly to topple the dictatorship. The first occurred in mid-1973, when career army officers became alienated by a government measure commissioning militia officers for service in the colonial wars. The second incitement was the publication in February 1974 of the book *Portugal e o futuro* ("Portugal and the Future") by the colonial war hero General António de Spínola, who argued that the wars in Africa could not be settled by force of arms and advocated negotiated autonomy for the colonies and an alternative to Caetano's leadership. Some 200 to 300 officers calling themselves the Armed Forces Movement (Movimento das Forças Armadas; MFA), led by Francisco da Costa Gomes and other officers, planned and implemented the coup of April 25, 1974, which came to be known as the Revolution of the Carnations.

The revolution encountered little resistance from the dictatorship's remaining loyalists and won initial support from an urban middle class vexed by economic and political uncertainty. The transition to a functioning, consolidating, pluralist Portuguese democracy mirrored, though in a nonviolent way, the political course of the French Revolution: an early moderate-conservative phase (May 1974–March 1975) followed by a middle radical-leftist phase (March–late November 1975) and a final moderate reaction (late November 1975–June 1976).

After exiling Caetano and Tomás, a subgroup of the MFA calling itself the Junta of National Salvation filled the political vacuum, installing Spínola as president and commencing negotiation with the African nationalist movements. Independence was granted to Portuguese Guinea (as Guinea-Bissau) almost immediately after the revolution. The new regime abolished such instruments of repression as censorship, the paramilitary forces, and the secret police. Spínola, who opposed rapid independence for the colonies without free referendums, resigned in September 1974, launched a countercoup attempt that failed (March 1975), and fled into exile.

By this time, radical MFA elements and their leftist civilian allies in the Portuguese Communist Party and other Marxist-Leninist groups had won virtual control over the government in Lisbon, sections of the armed forces, and the media. The MFA itself was restructured and a Council of the Revolution installed with the support of six political parties. An election for a national assembly in April 1975 drew 92 percent of eligible voters, a record in western European history. The decolonization of the Cape Verde Islands and Mozambique was effected in July 1975. Portugal's remaining African territories achieved independence later the same year, thus ending a colonial involvement in Africa that had begun in 1415. However, in Angola full-scale, internationalized civil war followed Portugal's departure, and Indonesia forcibly annexed briefly independent East Timor, controlling the territory until 1999.

Political and social instability prevailed through most of 1975. More than half a million people fled to Portugal from the former African colonies, adding a refugee problem to the already volatile domestic situation; some 30 persons died in incidents of public violence, new political parties proliferated, and strikes were widespread. In 1975 the government also decided to nationalize banking, transport, heavy industries, and the media. In the Alentejo in southern Portugal, farmworkers expropriated latifundia and established communal farming. On November 25, 1975, moderate military elements crushed a radical leftist coup in the army and restored order.

THE 1976 CONSTITUTION AND SUBSEQUENT REFORMS

In April 1976 the Constituent Assembly approved a new constitution, which committed Portugal to socialism. Parliamentary elections held on April 25 produced no single majority party; the Socialists, the Popular Democrats (centre-right), the Social Democratic Centre Party (conservative), and the Communist Party (founded 1921) made the strongest showings, and the Socialist leader, Mário Soares, formed a minority government. In June,

General António Ramalho Eanes, who had been instrumental in preventing a radical leftist military coup in November 1975, won more than three-fifths of the valid votes cast in the presidential election.

Soares's minority government resigned in December 1977, primarily because it was unable to enact an effective austerity program. A number of volatile coalition governments followed, until in 1980, in the general election scheduled by the constitution, a centre-right coalition, the Democratic Alliance (Alianca Democrática), swept into power. The new government swiftly moved to revise the character of the 1976 constitution. The Assembly of the Republic approved a series of reforms that included reducing the powers of the president and abolishing the Council of the Revolution, which had been given the power to determine the constitutionality of laws and gave the military effective veto power over legislation. These constitutional reforms completed Portugal's transition to full civilian rule. Both government policy and public sentiment, as reflected in numerous elections and polls, favoured reprivatization of the largely nationalized economy, a de-emphasis on communal agriculture, and entry into the European Economic Community (EEC; later succeeded by the European Union [EU]) as soon as possible.

The alliance faltered in 1982, propelling the country into yet another crisis. President Eanes called an early general election for April 1983, and the Socialists, led by Soares, scored an inconclusive victory. Because Portugal urgently needed a stable, broadly based government to tackle its severe economic problems, Soares formed a coalition government with the Social Democrats (formerly the Popular Democrats). It successfully implemented an 18-month emergency program and a four-year modernization plan in its quest for admission to the EEC.

The coalition, though precarious, lasted until June 13, 1985. It survived several internal crises caused predominantly by a division within the Social Democrats between a left wing favouring the coalition and a right wing that opposed the coalition's economic policies. In May 1985 Aníbal Cavaco Silva, leader of the right wing, became head of the party. Almost immediately, Cavaco Silva questioned the viability of the coalition, voicing doubts especially on the subjects of labour and agrarian reform.

This crisis, which ended the coalition in June, had been intensified by nationwide strikes in the industrial and transport sectors led by communist unions and by demonstrations by parties on both the left and the right of the political spectrum calling for an end to the coalition government. Soares resigned, and in October 1985 the Social Democrats, campaigning on a platform advocating a free-market economy, became the largest single party in the Assembly of the Republic and were able to form a minority government with Cavaco Silva as prime minister. Portugal was admitted to the EEC on January 1, 1986, and on February 16 Soares became the country's first civilian president in 60 years. The parliamentary elections of 1987 marked another milestone as Cavaco

Silva's Social Democrats won the first clear majority in the Assembly since the 1974 revolution. A renewal of this mandate four years later provided the continuity necessary for carrying out reforms.

INTO THE 21ST CENTURY

By the end of the 20th century, Portugal's democracy had become solidified. With the military's withdrawal from politics and several revisions of the constitution, Portugal adopted what could be called a semipresidential system, which limited the president's powers by investing significant authority in the prime minister. Portugal developed a multiparty system in which two major parties (the Socialists and the Social Democrats) and several minor parties emerged. In 1995 Cavaco Silva left office, replaced by Socialist António Guterres; the following year, Soares was succeeded as president by Socialist Jorge Sampaio, the former mayor of Lisbon. In 1999 the government adopted the euro, the EU's single currency—which fully replaced the escudo as Portugal's sole currency in 2002—and also returned Macau, its last overseas territory, to Chinese rule. Sampaio was reelected in 2001, but in 2002 Guterres's government was ousted by the Social Democrats, whose leader, José Manuel Durão Barroso, formed a centre-right coalition government and promised to reduce taxes and spending and privatize some public services. Economic problems beset the new government, which in 2005 lost power to the Socialists, whose

JOSÉ MANUEL BARROSO

José Manuel Barroso (born March 23, 1956, Lisbon, Portugal) served as prime minister of Portugal from 2002 to 2004 and became president of the European Commission in 2004. He was born to parents who hailed from the region of Valpaços, one of the poorer areas of Portugal. The difficulties of growing up under the dictatorship of António de Oliveira Salazar influenced the development of Barroso's political ideas, and he joined a Maoist student group while attending the University of Lisbon; he would later distance himself from that decision. After receiving a law degree there (1978), Barroso continued his studies at the University of Geneva, where he earned a European studies degree and a master's degree (1981) in political science. He then began an academic career, serving as a teaching assistant at both of his alma maters. He also taught at Georgetown University in Washington, D.C., where he did research for a Ph.D. In 1979 he founded the University Association for European Studies.

Barroso joined Portugal's centre-right Social Democratic Party (Partido Social Democrata; PSD) in 1980. When the party's Aníbal Cavaco Silva was elected prime minister in 1985, he appointed Barroso undersecretary of state for the home affairs ministry. Two years later Barroso moved to secretary of state for the ministry of foreign affairs, before his promotion to minister of foreign affairs. He lost that post after the PSD's 1995 defeat by Portugal's Socialist Party, but he rose to party president in 1999. He was continually reelected—while simultaneously serving as vice president of the European People's Party—until the 2002 parliamentary elections, which returned the PSD to power and made Barroso prime minister of Portugal.

In 2004 Barroso resigned from the Portuguese government to accept the post of president of the European Commission, the main executive body of the European Union. In 2009 the European Parliament approved a second five-year term for Barroso.

leader, José Sócrates, became prime minister. In 2006 Cavaco Silva returned to politics with a successful run for the presidency, scoring a victory on the first ballot against a split Socialist ticket.

Perhaps a reflection of the tremendous progress made by Portugal in establishing a successful democracy and in fully integrating itself into Europe, a Portuguese, Durão Barroso, was named president of the European Commission in 2004. Nevertheless, Portugal continued to experience several troubling problems. Despite economic growth during the 1990s, high unemployment persisted. Also of concern to political leaders were continued poverty in rural and urban areas, a growing gap between rich and poor, and administrative and labour inefficiency. Moreover, too large a share of Portugal's population over age 40 had little formal education, and Portugal remained among western Europe's poorest countries.

The protection of Portugal's historic heritage became a serious issue; Portugal's economy was partly dependent on tourism, but its fragile environment was endangered by the impact of tourism, urban sprawl, and a failure to limit and control air, water, and soil pollution brought on by growth and development. The increasing depopulation of interior rural areas, the result in part of urbanization and rural-urban migration, was an issue of major concern. Rural and provincial areas of Portugal experienced the steady loss of population to urban areas such as Greater Porto, Coimbra, and Lisbon. This movement further hampered agriculture, which faced stiff competition from other EU countries, and limited the availability of educational, health, and social services in rural areas. As Portugal increasingly evolved into an urban society, political leaders attempted to achieve a balance between growth and development (modernization) and the need to protect consumers, the public interest, and the rare but vulnerable environment.

By the beginning of the 21st century, Portugal had benefited from substantial improvements in health, communications, transportation, welfare, and education. The new pluralist democracy provided citizens with historically unprecedented civil liberties. Nevertheless, the country's empire had vanished, and Portugal was highly dependent on imports of energy, capital, and food. During the 1990s, as a partner in further European integration, Portugal was under great pressure to conform to rigorous EU standards, procedures, and rules. New layers of administration were established, and trade, travel, employment, and other barriers started to fall in 1993, when Portugal began preparing for full economic and monetary union with other EU members.

From 1988 through 2000, Portugal celebrated many historical feats. Notably, the government sponsored commemorations of Portuguese exploration, including the 500th anniversaries of Bartolomeu Dias's 1488 voyage that rounded the Cape of Good Hope and the founding of Brazil by Pedro Álvares Cabral in 1500. In 1998 Lisbon hosted the World's Fair (Expo '98), which also marked the 500th anniversary of the arrival of Vasco da Gama in Asia following his discovery of an all-water route from Europe. As the celebrations ended and the 21st century began, many wondered how the new Portugal would conceive of its national tradition and what effect European integration would have on the country's self-image and national identity.

Support for Sócrates and the Socialists eroded as Portugal weathered the global economic crisis throughout 2007–08, and in the 2009 parliamentary elections the ruling party held onto power but fell short of an absolute majority. Sócrates struggled to preserve his minority government as the Portuguese economy continued to spiral downward throughout 2010. As unemployment topped 10 percent, government efforts to stimulate the economy caused the budget deficit to skyrocket, and Portugal's sovereign debt rating was downgraded by investment agencies. In response the Socialists passed a series of austerity measures in November 2010 that cut public-sector wages and increased the sales and value-added tax rates. Cavaco Silva was reelected president by a comfortable margin in January 2011, an event that was widely interpreted as an endorsement of stability and continuity, though fewer than half of eligible voters participated in the polling. Portugal's economic problems persisted into 2011.

In March 2011 Sócrates's proposal for a new round of spending cuts and tax increases (the fourth such austerity package in a year) was soundly rejected by the parliamentary opposition, prompting the prime minister's resignation and setting the stage for a snap election. In early May Sócrates's caretaker government and the EU and the International Monetary Fund came to an agreement in principle for a bailout of some 78 billion euros (about $116 billion). The agreement was contingent, however, on acceptance by the entire EU, which was less than certain, largely because of the opposition to bailouts expressed by the True Finn party, which had gained prominence in recent elections in Finland. In the June 2011 legislative election, the Socialists were defeated by the Social Democrats, who promptly secured a parliamentary majority by forming a coalition with the centre-right Social Democratic Centre–Popular Party (Centro Democrático Social–Partido Popular; CDS-PP). The new prime minister, Social Democrat leader Pedro Passos Coelho, vowed to implement economic policies that would not only meet the austerity guidelines imposed by the EU and the IMF but exceed them. Portugal saw its credit rating downgraded to junk status in January 2012, and the government responded with increasingly harsh cuts. The announcement of an additional round of tax hikes and public-sector layoffs triggered a wave of protests in October 2012 as demonstrators, facing an unemployment rate that topped 15 percent, expressed their weariness of austerity.

CHAPTER 7

SPAIN: THE LAND AND ITS PEOPLE

Located in extreme southwestern Europe, Spain occupies about 85 percent of the Iberian Peninsula, which it shares with its smaller neighbour Portugal. Spain is a storied country of stone castles, snowcapped mountains, vast monuments, and sophisticated cities, all of which have made it a favoured travel destination.

The country is bordered to the west by Portugal, and to the northeast it borders France, from which it is separated by the tiny principality of Andorra and by the great wall of the Pyrenees Mountains. Spain's only other land border is in the far south with Gibraltar, an enclave that belonged to Spain until 1713, when it was ceded to Great Britain in the Treaty of Utrecht at the end of the War of the Spanish Succession. Elsewhere the country is bounded by water: by the Mediterranean Sea to the east and southeast, by the Atlantic Ocean to the northwest and southwest, and by the Bay of Biscay (an inlet of the Atlantic Ocean) to the north. The Canary (Canarias) Islands, in the Atlantic Ocean off the northwestern African mainland, and the Balearic (Baleares) Islands, in the Mediterranean, also are parts of Spain, as are Ceuta and Melilla, two small enclaves in North Africa (northern Morocco) that Spain has ruled for centuries.

The Spanish flag and crest.
Encyclopædia Britannica, Inc

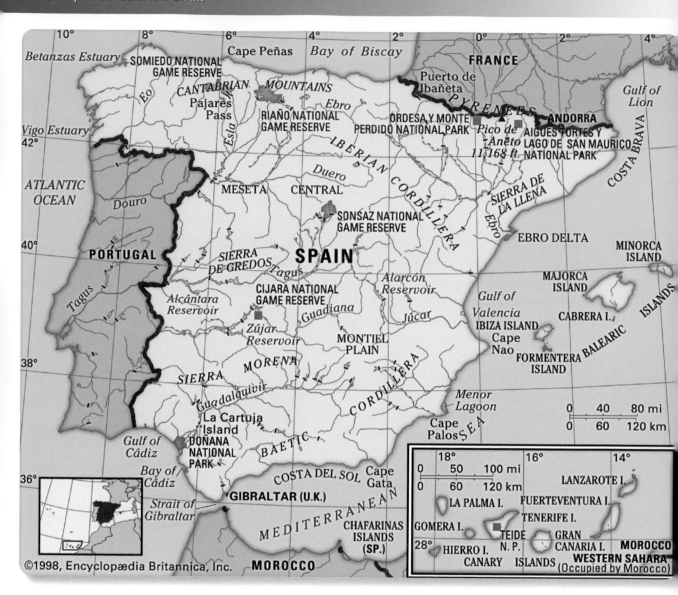

Physical map of Spain.

The country is geographically and culturally diverse. Its heartland is the Meseta, a broad central plateau half a mile above sea level. Much of the region is traditionally given over to cattle ranching and grain production; it was in this rural setting that Miguel de Cervantes imagined Don Quixote tilting at the tall windmills that still dot the landscape in several places. In the country's northeast are the broad valley of the Ebro River, the mountainous region of Catalonia, and the hilly coastal plain of Valencia. To the northwest is the Cantabrian Mountains, a rugged range in which heavily forested, rain-swept valleys are interspersed with tall peaks. To the south is the citrus-orchard-rich and irrigated lands of the valley of the Guadalquivir River, celebrated in the renowned lyrics of Spanish poets Federico García Lorca and Antonio Machado; over this valley rises the snowcapped Sierra Nevada. The southern portion of the country is desert, an extension of the Sahara made familiar to Americans through the "spaghetti western" films of the 1960s and early '70s. Lined with palm trees, rosemary bushes, and other tropical vegetation, the southeastern Mediterranean coast and the Balearic Islands enjoy a gentle climate, drawing millions of visitors and retirees, especially from northern Europe.

MADRID

Madrid is the capital of Spain and of Madrid *provincia* (province). The city and province form a *comunidad autónoma* (autonomous community) in central Spain. The city is Spain's arts and financial centre.

(continued on next page)

The Puerta de Alcalá, built in 1778, remains a key landmark in Madrid. © Digital Vision/Getty Images

(continued from previous page)

Madrid's status as the national capital reflects the centralizing policy of the 16th-century Spanish king Philip II and his successors. The choice of Madrid, however, was also the result of the city's previous obscurity and neutrality; it was chosen because it lacked ties with an established, nonroyal power, rather than because of any strategic, geographic, or economic considerations. Indeed, Madrid is deficient in other characteristics that might qualify it for a leading role. It does not lie on a major river, as so many European cities do. (The 16th–17th century dramatist Lope de Vega, referring to a magnificent bridge over the distinctly unimposing waters of the Manzanares, suggested either selling the bridge or buying another river.) Madrid does not possess mineral deposits or other natural wealth, nor was it ever a destination of pilgrimages, although its patron saint, San Isidro, enjoys the all-but-unique distinction of having been married to another saint. Even the city's origins seem inappropriate for a national capital: its earliest historical role was as the site of a small Moorish fortress on a rocky outcrop—part of the northern defenses of what was then the far more important city of Toledo, located about 43 miles (70 km) south-southwest.

Madrid was officially made the national capital by Philip III, an entire generation after Philip II took the court to Madrid in 1561. Under the patronage of Philip II and his successors, Madrid developed into a city of curious contrasts, preserving its old, overcrowded centre, around which developed palaces, convents, churches, and public buildings.

Spain's countryside is quaint, speckled with castles, aqueducts, and ancient ruins, but its cities are resoundingly modern. The Andalusian capital of Sevilla (Seville) is famed for its musical culture and traditional folkways; the Catalonian capital of Barcelona for its secular architecture and maritime industry; and the national capital of Madrid for its winding streets, its museums and bookstores, and its around-the-clock lifestyle. Madrid is Spain's largest city and is also its financial and cultural centre, as it has been for hundreds of years.

RELIEF

Spain accounts for five-sixths of the Iberian Peninsula, the roughly quadrilateral southwestern tip of Europe that separates the Mediterranean Sea from the Atlantic Ocean. Most of Spain comprises a large plateau (the Meseta Central) divided by a mountain range, the Central Sierra (Sistema Central), which trends west-southwest to east-northeast. Several mountains border the plateau: the Cantabrian Mountains (Cordillera Cantábrica) to the north, the Iberian Cordillera (Sistema Ibérico) to the northeast and east, the Sierra Morena to the south, and the lower mountains of the Portuguese frontier and Spanish Galicia to the northwest. The Pyrenees run across the neck of the peninsula and form Spain's border with France.

There are two major depressions, that of the Ebro River in the northeast and that of the Guadalquivir River in the southwest. In the southeast the

Isolated farmstead in the region of La Mancha in the southern Meseta Central, south-central Spain. Robert Frerck/Tony Stone Images

Baetic Cordillera (Sistema Penibético) runs broadly parallel to the coast to merge with the mountains of the Iberian Cordillera. Along the Mediterranean seaboard there are coastal plains, some with lagoons (e.g., Albufera, south of Valencia). Offshore in the Mediterranean, the Balearic Islands are an unsubmerged portion of the Baetic Cordillera. The Canary Islands in the Atlantic are of volcanic origin and contain the highest peak on Spanish territory, Teide Peak, which rises to 12,198 feet (3,718 metres) on the island of Tenerife.

Spain has some of the oldest as well as some of the youngest rocks of Europe. The entire western half of Iberia, with the exception of the extreme south, is composed of ancient (Hercynian) rocks; geologists refer to this Hercynian block as the Meseta Central. It constitutes a relatively stable platform around which younger sediments accumulated, especially on the Mediterranean side. In due course these sediments were pushed by major earth movements into mountain ranges. The term *meseta* is also used by geographers and local toponymy to designate the dominating relief unit of

Ibiza city and port, of the Balaeric Islands, Spain. Josef Muench

central Iberia. As a result, the Meseta Central defined by relief is subdivided by geology into a crystalline west (granites and gneisses) and a sedimentary east (mainly clays and limestones). The northern Meseta Central, which has an average elevation of 2,300 feet (700 metres), corresponds to the tablelands, or plateau, of Castile and León, although it is in fact a basin surrounded by mountains and drained by the Douro (Duero) River. The southern Meseta Central (the Meseta of Castile–La Mancha) is some 330 feet (100 metres) lower. Its relief is more diverse, however, owing to heavy faulting and warping caused by volcanic activity around the Calatrava Plain and to two complex river systems (the Guadiana and the Tagus) separated by mountains. Its southern plains rise gradually to the Sierra Morena. The southeastern side of this range drops almost vertically by more than 3,300 feet (1,000 metres) to the Guadalquivir depression. Dividing the northern and southern Mesetas are the Central Sierras, one of the outstanding features of the Iberian massif. Their highest points—Peñalara Peak at 7,972 feet (2,430 metres) and Almanzor Peak at 8,497 feet (2,590 metres)—rise well above the plains of the central plateau. In contrast, the granitic Galician mountains, at the northwestern end of the Hercynian block, have an average elevation of only 1,640 feet (500 metres), decreasing toward the deeply indented (ria) coast of the Atlantic seaboard.

Part of Alpine Europe, the Pyrenees form a massive mountain range that stretches from the Mediterranean Sea to the Bay of Biscay, a distance of some 270 miles (430 km). The range comprises a series of parallel zones: the central axis, a line of intermediate depressions, and the pre-Pyrenees. The highest peaks, formed from a core of ancient crystalline rocks, are found in the central Pyrenees—notably Aneto Peak at 11,168 feet (3,404 metres)—but those of the west, including Anie Peak at 8,213 feet (2,503 metres), are not much lower. The mountains fall steeply on the northern side but descend in terraces to the Ebro River trough in the south. The outer zones of the Pyrenees are composed of sedimentary rocks. Relief on the nearly horizontal sedimentary strata of the Ebro depression is mostly plain or plateau, except at the eastern end where the Ebro River penetrates the mountains to reach the Mediterranean Sea.

A series of sierras trending northwest-southeast forms the Iberian Cordillera, which separates the Ebro depression from the Meseta and reaches its highest elevation with Moncayo Peak

Cows grazing high in the central Pyrenees, Huesca province, Spain. age fotostock

at 7,588 feet (2,313 metres). In the southeast the Iberian Cordillera links with the Baetic Cordillera, also a result of Alpine earth movements. Although more extensive—more than 500 miles (800 km) long and up to 150 miles (240 km) wide—and with peninsular Spain's highest summit, Mulhacén Peak, at 11,421 feet (3,481 metres), the Baetic ranges are more fragmented and less of a barrier than the Pyrenees. On their northern and northwestern sides they flank the low-lying and fairly flat Guadalquivir basin, the average elevation of which is only 426 feet (130 metres) on mainly clay strata. Unlike the Ebro basin, the Guadalquivir depression is wide open to the sea on the southwest, and its delta has extensive marshland (Las Marismas).

DRAINAGE

Although some maintain that "aridity rivals civil war as the chief curse of [historic] Spain," the Iberian Peninsula has a dense network of streams, three of which

EBRO RIVER

The Ebro, Spain's longest river, rises in springs at Fontibre near Reinosa in the Cantabrian Mountains, in the Cantabria province in the northern part of the country. It flows for 565 miles (910 km) in a southeasterly course to its delta on the Mediterranean coast in Tarragona province, midway between Barcelona and Valencia. The Ebro has the greatest discharge of any Spanish river, and its drainage basin, at 33,000 square miles (85,500 square km), is the largest in Spain; the river drains about one-sixth of the country. Because it plunges through the coastal mountain ranges by a series of deep gorges and defiles, the Ebro is navigable upstream for only 15 miles (25 km), from its delta to the city of Tortosa.

The Ebro's interior basin is arid, poor, and sparsely populated. Irrigation has been intensified there since the mid-20th century—though it is still limited to the main floodplains in the middle reaches of the river between Tudela, Navarra, and Zaragoza (site of the Imperial Canal system, begun in the 16th century) and to the interfluves on the north-central plain around Caspe—and is augmented by the Lodosa and Tauste canals. The modern networks of irrigation canals between the Bárdenas project and the Monegros and Cinca valleys are impressive. The upper part of the Ebro River basin, the Rioja Alta, around Logroño, gives its name to the Rioja wine produced there.

The Ebro receives water from more than 200 tributaries. Those on the left bank (including the Segre-Cinca, Gállego, and Aragón rivers), which originate in the rainy Pyrenees, contribute the overwhelming majority of the Ebro's volume; the right-bank tributaries are smaller and originate in the Iberian Cordillera. The largest tributaries have been utilized for hydroelectric power and irrigation. A system of major dams produces a significant portion of Spain's hydroelectric power, chiefly in the upper La Noguera valleys. Extensive lignite deposits in the southeastern, or lower, part of the basin are used to produce thermoelectric power.

rank among Europe's longest: the Tagus at 626 miles (1,007 km), the Ebro at 565 miles (909 km), and the Douro at 556 miles (895 km). The Guadiana and the Guadalquivir are 508 miles (818 km) and 408 miles (657 km) long, respectively. The Tagus, like the Douro and the Guadiana, reaches the Atlantic Ocean in Portugal. In fact, all the major rivers of Spain except the Ebro drain into the Atlantic Ocean.

The hydrographic network on the Mediterranean side of the watershed is poorly developed in comparison with the Atlantic systems, partly because it falls into the climatically driest parts of Spain. However, nearly all Iberian rivers have low annual volume, irregular regimes, and deep valleys and even canyons. Flooding is always a potential hazard. The short, swift streams of Galicia and Cantabria, draining to the northwestern and northern coasts, respectively, have only a slight or, at most, modest summer minimum. The predominant fluvial regime in Spain is thus characterized by

The Júcar River flowing past a 14th-century castle at Cofrentes, Valencia, Spain. Robert Frerck/Odyssey Productions

a long or very long summer period of low water. This is the regime of all the major arteries that drain the Meseta as well as those of the Mediterranean seaboard, such as the Júcar and the Segura: for example, from August to September the Guadiana River usually has less than one-tenth of its average annual flow.

Only the Ebro River has a relatively constant and substantial flow—19,081 cubic feet (540 cubic metres) per second at Tortosa—coming from snowmelt as well as rainfall in the high Pyrenees. In comparison, the flow of the Douro is only 5,050 cubic feet (143 cubic metres) per second. The flow of many Iberian streams has been reduced artificially by water extraction for purposes such as irrigation. Subterranean flow is well-developed in limestone districts.

SOILS

There are five major soil types in Spain. Two are widely distributed but of limited extent: alluvial soils, found in the major valleys and coastal plains, and poorly developed, or truncated, mountain soils. Brown forest soils are restricted to humid Galicia and Cantabria. Acidic southern brown earths (leading to restricted crop choice) are prevalent on the crystalline rocks of the western Meseta, and gray, brown, or chestnut soils have developed on the calcareous and alkaline strata of the eastern Meseta and of eastern Spain in general. Saline soils are found in the Ebro basin and coastal lowlands. Calcretes (subsoil zonal crusts [toscas], usually of hardened calcium carbonate) are particularly well-developed in the arid regions of the east: La Mancha, Almería, Murcia, Alicante (Alacant), and Valencia, as well as the Ebro and Lleida (Lérida) basins.

Soil erosion resulting from the vegetation degradation suffered by Spain for at least the past 3,000 years has created extensive badlands, reduced soil cover, downstream alluviation, and, more recently, silting of dams and irrigation works. Particularly affected are the high areas of the central plateau and southern and eastern parts of Spain. Although the origins of some of the spectacular badlands of southeastern Spain, such as Guadix, may lie in climatic conditions from earlier in Quaternary time (beginning 2.6 million years ago), one of the major problems of modern Spain is the threat of desertification—i.e., the impoverishment of arid, semiarid, and even some humid ecosystems caused by the joint impact of human activities and drought. Nearly half of Spain is moderately or severely affected, especially in the arid east (Almería, Murcia), as well as in much of subarid Spain (the Ebro basin). The government has adopted policies of afforestation, but some authorities believe that natural vegetation regrowth would yield more speedy and more permanent benefits.

CLIMATE

Spain is characterized by the overlap of one fundamental climatic division (between humid and semiarid and arid zones) by another (the threefold division of the peninsula into maritime, continental, and mountain climates). This complexity results from the peninsula's size, which is large enough to generate a continental thermal regime; its location close to the Atlantic Ocean and North Africa, exposing it to both maritime and Saharan influences; and its mountainous relief, which not only produces its own climatic zones but also exaggerates local aridity through the creation of rain shadows on the mountains' leeward sides.

The Pyrenees and the Cantabrian ranges play an important role in the Spanish climate, holding the warm, dry subtropical airstream over Spain during the summer months. In general, westerly winds from the North Atlantic are dominant most of the year, while the warm, dry Saharan airstream blows less frequently. Some local or seasonal winds are notable: the easterly *levante* (levanter) can bring as many as 15 consecutive days of dry, clear weather to the coastal strip in the region of the Strait of Gibraltar; the *leveche* brings a hot, dry, dust-laden wind that blights vegetation in spring from the southern sector to the Spanish Levantine lowlands (the provinces of Castellón, Valencia, and Alicante); and in spring and summer a wind from the same sector, the *solano*, carries unbearably hot, dry, suffocating weather over the Andalusian plain. Northern Spain, from Galicia to northern Catalonia (Catalunya, or Cataluña), is characterized by a temperate humid or maritime type of climate, having high rainfall and an average temperature in January of 43 °F (6 °C) near the coast but less than that inland and in the mountains. A Coruña (La Coruña) has a moderate annual temperature, ranging from 48 °F (9 °C) in winter to 64 °F (18 °C) in summer, and the annual rainfall is about 38 inches (965 mm). The rest of the peninsula has a Mediterranean type of climate with continental tendencies—i.e., hot toward the coast, relatively cold in the interior, humid only in the mountains, and dry elsewhere. Thus Albacete, in the southeastern part of the southern Meseta, varies between 40 °F (4 °C) in the winter and 75 °F (24 °C) in the summer, while the annual rainfall is less than 15 inches (380 mm). The valleys of the Ebro and the Guadalquivir also have a continental climate, the Ebro drier and colder and the Guadalquivir warmer and more humid. Catalonia, Valencia, and the Balearic Islands enjoy more temperate weather, with higher rainfall in Catalonia, while the Canary Islands have a subtropical Atlantic climate.

PLANT AND ANIMAL LIFE

Nearly half of Spain is covered by spontaneous vegetation of some sort, but only a small proportion (largely confined to the mountains) is classified as dense woodland. Northern Spain has heath and deciduous woodland (oak, beech). The mountains of the northern Meseta and the Iberian and Baetic cordilleras carry deciduous Portuguese oak; those of the central Pyrenees, the Iberian ranges, and the Central Sierras have diverse pine species. The rest, more than half of Spain, has a Mediterranean vegetation characterized by evergreen oak (*Quercus ilex*) and other drought-resistant plants commonly reduced to scrub status (*matorral*). An esparto grass (*Lygeum spartum*) is found in the steppes of La Mancha and the southeast; the esparto products of Spain (paper, rope, basketry), however, come from an associated alfa grass (*Stipa tenacissima*). Poplar and eucalyptus have become widespread since the 19th century.

The proximity of Africa has given Spain more African species of wildlife than are found in the other Mediterranean peninsulas, while the Pyrenean barrier and the general extent of the country explain the number of indigenous species. The European wolf and the brown bear survive in the scarce wild areas of the northeast. The Barbary ape is possibly indigenous but is more likely an import from North Africa. It survives only under protection, at Gibraltar. The wild boar, ibex (wild goat), and red and fallow deer are more common. More than half of the bird species of Europe are found in Coto Doñana National Park, at the mouth of the Guadalquivir; the Spanish imperial eagle and other large species such as the eagle owl, the buzzard, and several varieties of pheasant are native to the high Pyrenees. Desert locusts have been known to invade southern Spain from North Africa.

The country's waters contain a diversity of fish and shellfish, especially in the southeast where Atlantic and Mediterranean waters mix (the Alborán Sea). Species include red mullet, mackerel, tuna, octopus, swordfish, pilchard

(*Sardinia pilchardus*), and anchovy (*Engraulis encrasicholus*). Demersal (bottom-dwelling) species include hake and whiting. Striped dolphin and the long-finned whale inhabit the waters off southeastern Spain, and the bottle-nose dolphin is found off the Ebro delta. Overfishing has tended to alter the balance of species.

ETHNIC GROUPS

Spain has been invaded and inhabited by many different peoples. The peninsula was originally settled by groups from North Africa and western Europe, including the Iberians, Celts, and Basques. Throughout antiquity it was a constant point of attraction for the civilizations of the eastern Mediterranean. From c. 1100 BCE the Phoenicians, the Greeks, and the Carthaginians began to establish settlements and trading posts, especially on the eastern and southern coasts. These outsiders found a mosaic of peoples, collectively known as the Iberians, who did not have a single culture or even share a single language. A kingdom called Tartessus, which flourished between 800 and 550 BCE, ruled much of the valley of the Guadalquivir. Elsewhere political organization was less sophisticated, consisting of a number of city-states in the coastal regions and of clans in the interior and the northwest.

IBERIAN PEOPLE

The Iberians were a prehistoric people of southern and eastern Spain who later gave their name to the whole peninsula. The waves of migrating Celtic peoples from the 8th to 6th century BCE onward settled heavily in northern and central Spain, penetrated Portugal and Galicia, but left the indigenous Bronze Age Iberian people of the south and east intact. Greek geographers give the name Iberian, probably connected with that of the Ebro (Iberus) River, to tribes settled on the southeastern coast, but, by the time of the Greek historian Herodotus (mid-5th century BCE), it applied to all the peoples between the Ebro and Huelva rivers, who were probably linguistically connected and whose material culture was distinct from that of the north and west. There were, however, areas of overlap between the Iberian and Celtic peoples, as in the Celtiberian tribes of the northeastern Meseta Central and in Catalonia and Aragon.

Of the Iberian tribes mentioned by classical authors, the Bastetani were territorially the most important and occupied the Almería region and mountainous Granada region. The tribes to the west of the Bastetani are usually grouped together as "Tartessian," after the name Tartessos given to the region by the Greeks. The Turdetani of the Guadalquivir River valley were the most powerful of this group. Culturally the tribes of the northeast and of the Valencian coast were greatly influenced by the Greek settlements at Emporion (modern Ampurias) and in the Alicante region, those of the southeast by influences from the Phoenician trading colonies at Malaca (Málaga), Sexi (Almuñéca), and Abdera (Adra), which later passed to the Carthaginians.

(continued on next page)

(continued from previous page)

On the east coast the Iberian tribes appear to have been grouped around independent city-states. In the south there were monarchies, and the treasure of El Carambolo, near Sevilla (Seville), has been thought to be that of a ruler of Tartessos. Religious sanctuaries have yielded bronzes and terra-cotta figures, especially in mountainous areas. There is a wide range of ceramics in the distinctive Iberian styles. Exported pottery has been found in southern France, Sardinia, Sicily, and Africa; and Greek imports were frequent. The splendid *La dama de Elche* ("The Lady of Elche"), a bust with characteristic headdress and ornaments, also shows classical influence. The Iberian economy had a rich agriculture and mining and metallurgy.

The Iberian language, a non-Indo-European tongue, continued to be spoken into early Roman times. Along the east coast it was written in Iberian script, a system of 28 syllabic and alphabetic characters, some derived from Greek and Phoenician systems but most of unknown origin. Many inscriptions in the script survive. Few words, however, except place-names on the coinage struck by many cities in the 3rd century BCE, can be understood. The Iberians retained their writing system until the Roman conquest, when the Latin alphabet came into use. Although the modern Basque language was formerly thought to be the descendant of Iberian, many scholars now believe the two languages to be separate.

THE ROMANS

The Phoenician and Greek presence was limited to small coastal regions. The Carthaginians were the first to move inland; late in the 3rd century BCE they set out to conquer as much of the peninsula as they could. Yet their success led to intervention in Iberia from the Romans, who quickly drove out the Carthaginians and conquered much of the peninsula. The Romans, however, had to deal with a number of revolts, and it was only in 19 BCE, after almost 200 years of warfare, that they secured their rule over all of Iberia. The Romans brought Iberia under a single political authority for the first time but did not try to impose a single culture on the inhabitants. Nevertheless, much of the indigenous elite adopted Roman culture and became Roman citizens, particularly in the south and east, where the Roman presence was strongest.

THE VISIGOTHS

Roman power in Spain collapsed during the 5th century CE when a number of Germanic peoples—the Suebi, the Alani, the Vandals, and finally the Visigoths—invaded the peninsula. At the end of the 6th century, King Leovigild brought all of Spain under Visigothic rule, and his son Reccared imposed a single religion, Catholic Christianity, on the country.

THE MUSLIMS

Visigothic rule did not last long. In 711 Muslim Arabs invaded Spain from North Africa and defeated the Visigothic ruler, King Roderick. They quickly conquered almost the entire peninsula and established Muslim states in Spain that were to last until 1492.

RECENT ARRIVALS

The Muslims were the last new peoples to arrive in Spain in large numbers for many centuries. Indeed, from the 16th century on and especially during the 100 years after 1860, Spain was a country of emigration rather than immigration. This began to change in the 1980s when Spain's new position as a highly industrialized and relatively prosperous country made it attractive to people from the developing world. For the first time since the Middle Ages, Spain received large numbers of immigrants. By the early 21st century there were several million legal foreign residents and illegal immigrants in Spain, the latter concentrated mainly in Andalusia (Andalucía), in metropolitan Madrid and Barcelona, and in the Balearic and Canary islands. Most foreign residents came from other countries of the European Union (EU) and from Latin America. Many also arrived from Morocco, often crossing the Strait of Gibraltar in small boats, and from sub-Saharan Africa, arriving often at the Canary Islands; there also are significant numbers of Asians and Europeans from non-EU countries. Since 1985 Spanish governments have passed several laws on foreigners, which have made it more difficult for people to enter Spain and easier for the authorities to deport them.

Promulgated in 2000 (and subsequently modified), the Law on the Rights and Freedoms of Foreigners in Spain and Their Social Integration sought to end the restrictive policies of the previous 15 years, terminating the practice of repatriating illegal immigrants and giving legal status to any employed illegal immigrant who resided in Spain for at least two years. In 2005 legislation legalized the status of many immigrant workers. The law also gave immigrants most of the same rights as Spanish citizens (except the right to vote).

THE GITANO MINORITY

The one ethnic minority of long standing in Spain is the Roma (Gypsies), who are known in Spain as Gitanos. Their traditional language is Caló. Many of them have assimilated into the mainstream of Spanish society, but others continue to lead their traditional nomadic way of life. The Gitanos were at one time most numerous in southern Spain, and, while there continue to be large populations in Andalusian cities such as Almería, Granada, and Murcia, large communities now exist in Madrid and Barcelona as well. Flamenco, an expressive song-dance form, has long been associated with the Gitanos.

Considerable prejudice and discrimination have existed against the Gitanos in Spain and are still prevalent today. But Gitanos have begun to create their own political organizations, such as the

Union of the Gitano People (Unión del Pueblo Gitano; also known as the Unión Romaní), and some have been elected to parliament. There also are government programs that promote Gitano culture.

LANGUAGES

The official language of Spain is Castilian. It is the country's most widely spoken language, and outside Spain it is generally known as Spanish. The constitution of Spain allows for its autonomous communities to recognize their dominant regional languages and dialects as having official status along with Castilian. The statutes of 6 of the 17 autonomous communities stipulate the following "co-official" languages: Catalan in Catalonia and in the Balearic Islands, Valencian in Valencia, Galician (Gallego) in Galicia, and Euskera (Basque) in the Basque Country and in some Euskera-speaking territories of Navarra. Although not named a co-official language of Asturias, Bable (Asturian) is protected and promoted under the community's statutes, as are local Aragonese dialects in Aragon. In addition, Aranese, spoken in the Aran Valley, is safeguarded in a provision by the region's government, the autonomy of Catalonia. All of these languages except Euskera are Romance languages (i.e., they evolved from Latin). With no relation to any other language of the world, Euskera is what is known as a language isolate. Within their respective regions of dominance, many of the languages of Spain are taught regularly in school and are used in newspapers and radio and television broadcasts.

SPANISH LANGUAGE

Spanish is a Romance language (Indo-European family) spoken by more than 358 million people in Spain, the Americas, Australia, and Africa. In the early 21st century, Mexico had the greatest number of speakers (more than 85 million), followed by Colombia (more than 40 million), Argentina (more than 35 million), the United States (more than 31 million), and Spain (more than 30 million). Spanish was the official language of all these countries except the United States. The earliest written materials in Spanish, in the form of glosses on Latin texts, date from the 10th century, and works of literature in Spanish first appeared about 1150.

Spanish is also known (particularly in Latin America, but increasingly in Spain itself) as Castilian, after the dialect from which modern standard Spanish developed. That dialect arose in the 9th century around the town of Burgos in north-central Spain (Old Castile) and, as Spain was reconquered from the Moors, spread southward to central Spain (New Castile) around Madrid and Toledo by the 11th century. In the late 15th century the kingdoms of Castile and Leon merged with that of Aragon, and Castilian became the official language of all of Spain. The regional dialects of Aragon, Navarra, Leon, Asturias, and Santander were crowded out gradually and today survive only in secluded rural areas. Galician (a language with many similarities to Portuguese), spoken in northwestern Spain, and Catalan, spoken in eastern and northeastern Spain, were also much reduced but began a resurgence in the late 20th century.

The dialect of Spanish used in Arab-occupied Spain prior to the 12th century was called Mozarabic. A remarkably archaic form of Spanish with many borrowings from Arabic, it is known primarily from Mozarabic refrains (called *kharjahs*) added to Arabic and Hebrew poems.

Outside the Iberian Peninsula, Spanish is spoken in virtually all of Central and South America except Brazil (where Portuguese is spoken), as well as in the Canary Islands, parts of Morocco, and the Philippines. Latin American Spanish has a number of regional dialects; all are derived from Castilian but differ in several points of phonology from European Spanish. Typical of Latin American Spanish is the use of the /s/ sound where Castilian has the lisplike /th/ sound (for words spelled with a *z* or *c* before *e* or *i*) and replacement of the Castilian /ly/ sound (spelled *ll*) with a /y/ sound or even with the /zh/ sound of the *z* in English *azure* or the *j* in French *jour*.

In Spanish the case system of Latin has been completely lost except for subject and object forms for pronouns. Nouns are marked for masculine or feminine gender, and plurals are marked by the addition of *-s* or *-es*; adjectives change endings to agree with nouns. The verb system is complex but, by and large, regular: it uses indicative, imperative, and subjunctive moods; preterite, imperfect, present, future, conditional, and a variety of perfect and progressive tenses; and passive and reflexive constructions.

CASTILIAN

Castilian, which contains many words of Arabic origin, began as a dialect spoken in northern Spain. It became the language of the court of the kingdoms of Castile and León in the 12th century, and the dominance of Castile within Spain allowed it to become the official language of the state.

There are differences in accent and, to a lesser extent, in vocabulary in Castilian as it is spoken in various regions of the country. The most significant difference is in the pronunciation of *c* before *i* or *e*. In northern Castile, where the language is said to be spoken in its purest form, this is pronounced as an English *th*; in southern and western Spain it is pronounced as an English *s*. The prominence of people from these latter regions in the colonization of Latin America led to their pronunciation becoming the standard in American Spanish. The Cervantes Institute promotes the Spanish language and Spanish culture in many countries.

CATALAN

Catalan is closely related to Occitan (Provençal), a language spoken in southern France. It is spoken by more than four-fifths of the population in Catalonia, Valencia, and the Balearic Islands. But there are differences in the way Catalan is spoken in these three regions, and in the 1980s there were politically motivated disputes as to whether Valencian was a Catalan dialect or a distinct language. Catalan literature, which has a long and distinguished history, flourished especially during the Middle Ages. However, it declined after the 15th century before reviving again in the period known as the Renaixença ("Renaissance"), which began in the mid-19th century.

GALICIAN

Spoken in Galicia, in the northwestern corner of Spain, the Galician language (Gallego) is closely related to Portuguese, although it has been influenced by Castilian Spanish throughout the modern period. It was the language of courtly literature until the 14th century, when it was displaced by Castilian. From then until the late 19th century, when a literary revival began, its use was limited to everyday speech, and it was more common in the countryside than in the cities due to a tradition of spoken Galician at home. Most of the population of Galicia is bilingual in Galician and Castilian.

EUSKERA

Euskera is the most distinctive language spoken in Spain. Neither a Romance nor an Indo-European language, it predates the arrival of the Romans in Spain. Until the end of the 19th century, Euskera was spoken mostly in the countryside, and, unlike the other peninsular languages, it had no significant literary tradition. In the 20th century, especially after it became the official language of the Basque Country (Euskera: Euskadi; Spanish: País Vasco) in 1978, Euskera grew in popularity and was increasingly used in literature, journalism, and the electronic media. Moreover, it has been the regional government's policy to extend its use in education and public administration. About one-third of the region's population speaks Euskera, and another one-sixth comprehends it. The largest proportion of Euskera speakers live in the province of Guipúzcoa.

RELIGION

Roman Catholicism became the official religion of Spain in 589 and has been closely identified with the country ever since. The advent of political liberalism at the beginning of the 19th century led to a series of conflicts between church and state, especially over land ownership and the control of education. Even so, Catholicism remained the official religion of the state until the Second Republic (1931–36). After the Spanish Civil War, General Francisco Franco restored it as the state religion, and it retained that status until the proclamation of the constitution of 1978. Since then Spain has had no official religion, but the Roman Catholic Church continues to receive financial support from the state. The legalization of divorce and abortion along with educational reforms in the 1980s brought the church into conflict with the government once again but with less intensity than previously.

The vast majority of the population is Roman Catholic, yet for many—and especially for those born after 1950—this has little meaning beyond being baptized, married, and buried within the church. There are several hundred thousand non-Catholic Christians in Spain. American-based denominations such as the Jehovah's Witnesses and the Seventh-day Adventists as well as the Church of Jesus Christ of Latter-day Saints (Mormons) have been active in the country since the 1970s. In addition, there are hundreds of thousands of adherents of Islam, whose numbers have grown rapidly because of immigration. Some 100,000 Jews fled Spain during the Spanish Inquisition in the late 15th century, when the inquisitor general Tomás de Torquemada persuaded the country's rulers to expel any Jew who refused to be baptized. To remain in the country, many Jews converted to Christianity (becoming known as *conversos*); those known as Marranos converted to Christianity but continued surreptitiously to practice Judaism. Restrictions on Judaism were eased only in the 20th century, and by the early 21st century there were some 15,000 Jews in Spain.

SETTLEMENT PATTERNS

The impact on the Spanish landscape of some 35,000 years of human occupation has been both diverse and profound. Human activity in prehistoric times undoubtedly led to changes in vegetation, soils, microrelief, and microclimate. However, influences from northern Europe (Celtic), the eastern Mediterranean (Phoenician, Ligurian, and eventually Roman), and North Africa (Iberian) contributed more obviously to what was to become the "traditional landscape" of Spain. Thus, most of Spain's major towns have ancient origins: they began as Celtiberian settlements (Soria); as Phoenician colonies (Cádiz) and Phoenician or Greek trading emporiums (Tarragona, Ampurias, and Málaga); and as Roman commercial centres along the Mediterranean coast or military and administrative centres in the north and west, at nodal points in the road system (Mérida, León, and Zaragoza [Saragossa]). Such towns were surrounded by zones of intensive, irrigated agriculture (the *barros* of Évora, Portugal, the *vegas* of Mérida and Zaragoza, the *huertas* of the east coast).

The Roman legacy of a gridiron town plan is preserved in many northern centres (e.g., in Barcelona and Zaragoza) but has been largely obliterated in the cities of the south and east by Muslim urban elements. In towns such as Valencia, Córdoba (Cordova), Toledo, Almería, Granada, and Sevilla (Seville), the marketplace, mosque, and high-walled domestic compounds, often with watered gardens, dominate an intricate alley network. Like their Roman antecedents, these early medieval Muslim centres were surrounded by rich agricultural *huertas*; in both towns and *huertas* water usage was rigorously controlled by institutions such as the Tribunal de las Aguas de la Vega de Valencia.

Alley in Toledo, Spain.© Digital Vision/Getty Images

After the Reconquista (Reconquest), the establishment of isolated single farms (*alquerías*) within the *huertas* increased. In Castile and León, medieval urban settlement developed from Christian military foundations in an open landscape of extensive dry farming. Centres such as Pamplona, Burgos, Soria, Valladolid, and Salamanca comprised a series of walled nuclei until new squares and broad streets were laid out in the 17th century. Rural settlement in León and in the mountains of northern Andalusia focused on the ecclesiastical granges of the Reconquista, developing into small villages. In Castile and León, castles similarly gave rise to clusters of hamlets. Much of this rural settlement was the result of spontaneous peasant colonization based on a now largely lost communal farming (open-field) system. In contrast, in Castile–La Mancha (Castilla–La Mancha), lower Aragon, Andalusia, Extremadura, and parts of the Alentejo, Portugal, the rural settlement pattern testifies to the more-organized resettlement schemes of the Reconquista in the southern Meseta. Here the four great Christian military orders (the Hospitallers, the Templars, the Order of Santiago, and the Order of Calatrava) acquired vast territories, which they defended with fortresses and huge, widely spaced villages, the latter sometimes now so large as to take on an urban aspect (agrotowns). Among these, in parts of Andalusia and Alentejo, are the courtyard farms (*cortijos, montes*) of the latifundios (very large estates).

MIGRATION

Spaniards participated fully in the massive 19th- and early 20th-century European immigration to the Americas. Between 1846 and 1932 nearly five million Spaniards went to the Americas, mostly to South America in general and to Argentina and Brazil in particular. Only Britain, Italy, Austria-Hungary, and Germany had more emigrants. Significant numbers of Spaniards also immigrated to Algeria and France.

The pattern of Spanish emigration changed after World War II. Continental Europe, especially France, West Germany, and Switzerland, displaced Latin America as the favoured destination for Spanish emigrants. Between 1962 and 1976 almost two million Spaniards, mainly from Andalusia and Galicia, went to other European countries. Since the 1980s, however, as the Spanish economy improved, there has been very little permanent emigration from Spain. Indeed, there was a reverse in migration flows, as more than 20,000 Spanish citizens, many of them retired, returned from other European countries each year. This tide turned again in the early 21st century as Spain's economy soured, and by 2012 the unemployment rate had topped 25 percent. More than half of Spaniards under age 25 were unable to find work, and recent university graduates increasingly looked abroad for opportunities.

Traditionally the number of emigrants has been dwarfed by the number of people moving within Spain itself. Almost 10 million Spaniards moved from one province to another between the early 1970s and mid-1990s, significantly affecting the distribution of population within the country. Until the mid-1970s, most internal migrants left rural areas seeking industrial jobs in the larger cities, especially Madrid and Barcelona, and in the Basque Country and Valencia. During the 1980s the decline of Spain's traditional industries prompted a return migration to the less-industrialized provinces. In the 1990s the focal points for migration were medium-sized cities (with 10,000 to 50,000 inhabitants), regions with strong service sectors, and the fringes of large and medium metropolitan areas.

URBANIZATION

During the first half of the 20th century, most Spaniards lived in villages or in towns of fewer than 10,000 people, but by the end of the century about three-fourths of the population lived in urban areas. The most intense growth took place in a handful of the largest cities: Madrid, Barcelona, Valencia, Sevilla, Zaragoza, Málaga, and Murcia. Spanish cities recorded some of the highest population densities in the Western world. This explosive urban growth occurred with very little planning, and many migrants to the cities could find housing only in cheaply constructed apartment blocks in outlying districts that lacked adequate municipal services.

Since 1978 democratically elected municipal governments in many cities have tried to alleviate some of the worst effects of the uncontrolled urban boom of the 1960s. They acquired more parkland and began to provide a variety of public cultural facilities. Meanwhile, growth in the larger metropolitan areas has shifted from the central cities to the suburbs. Even smaller cities, such as Valladolid, León, and Granada, have begun to suburbanize.

DEMOGRAPHIC TRENDS

Spain experienced the traditional preindustrial pattern of high birth and death rates throughout the 19th and early 20th centuries, but both began to decline shortly after 1900. The slow but continuous fall of birth rates stalled during the 20 years after the Spanish Civil War, when the Franco regime (1939–75) followed policies that encouraged large families. In the late 1960s the decline resumed. The low birth rate, which was especially marked among young women, contributed to a rate of natural increase that was near zero at the end of the 20th century, though in the beginning of the 21st century there was an upturn fuelled by the birth rate among the immigrant population.

Death rates declined steadily after 1940, although they rose slightly during the 1990s as the population aged. However, life expectancy in Spain increased dramatically, and by the end of

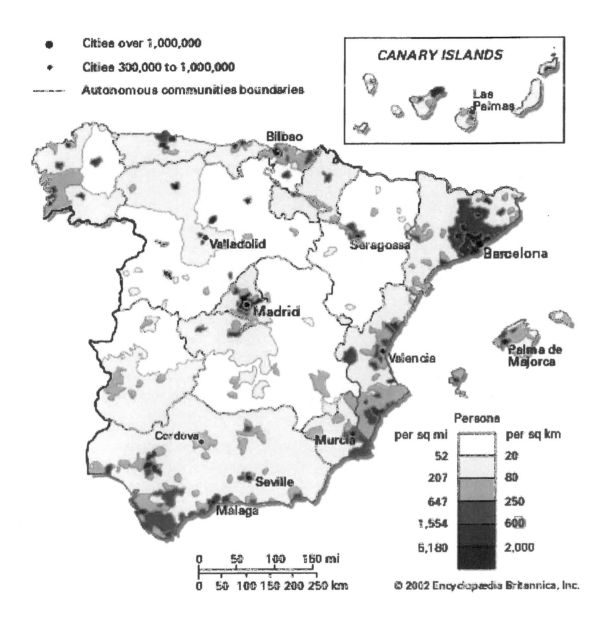

- ● Cities over 1,000,000
- ✦ Cities 300,000 to 1,000,000
- ----- Autonomous communities boundaries

CANARY ISLANDS

Las Palmas

Bilbao

Valladolid

Saragossa

Barcelona

Madrid

Valencia

Palma de Majorca

Cordova

Murcia

Seville

Malaga

Persons per sq mi	per sq km
52	20
207	80
647	250
1,554	600
6,180	2,000

0	50	100	150 mi
0	50 100 150 200 250 km		

© 2002 Encyclopædia Britannica, Inc.

Population density of Spain.

the 20th century it was among the highest in the world. The greatest improvement was in the area of infant mortality. The striking overall change was a result of the higher standard of living made possible by the economic "miracle" of the 1960s and by the general availability of high-quality medical care through the government-sponsored system.

By the 1990s Spain's major demographic indicators were similar to those of other industrialized countries of western Europe. As birth rates and death rates declined and life expectancy increased, the Spanish population aged significantly during the final decades of the 20th century, posing a growing challenge to the Spanish economy and society.

The Spanish population grew rapidly in the 30 years after the Civil War, in part because the death rate fell more quickly than the birth rate but also because of changes in marriage patterns. In the years immediately after the war, economic hardship discouraged people from marrying, and the average age at first marriage rose. By the mid-1940s, however, the percentage of those who married grew significantly (especially among women), reaching its highest level between 1955 and 1960 and remaining high until the mid-1970s, when it began to decline markedly. Likewise the average age at first marriage decreased until the 1990s, when it began climbing again. By the end of the 20th century the average age of first marriage for women had risen again (to between 25 to 29), and the average age at which women had their first child was about 30.

Beginning in the 1970s, Spaniards also began to have fewer children, and at the turn of the 21st century the total fertility rate was one of the lowest in Europe and well below the rate of replacement. The size of the average household also declined during this period, and the number of Spaniards living in traditional households, composed of a married couple and their children, also dropped.

CHAPTER 8

THE SPANISH ECONOMY

The Spanish economy began to industrialize in the late 18th century, and industrialization and economic growth continued throughout the 19th century. However, it was limited to a few relatively small areas of the country, especially to Catalonia (where textile manufacture took hold) and the Basque Country (where iron and steel were made). The overall pace of economic growth was slower than that of the major western European countries, so that by the early 20th century Spain appeared poor and underdeveloped compared with countries such as Great Britain, Germany, France, and even Italy.

The Spanish Civil War and its aftermath left Spain even farther behind, and the economic policies of the Franco regime failed to revitalize the economy. For nearly two decades after the war, the government followed a policy of autarky, or national economic self-sufficiency, similar to the policies of the pre-World War II fascist regimes in Germany and Italy. This approach entailed high levels of government intervention through highly protective tariffs, currency regulation, marketing boards for agriculture, and import controls. There was also a high degree of government ownership, realized through the National Industrial Institute (INI), which was created in 1941 to develop defense-related industries and other industries ignored by the private sector. The self-imposed economic isolation was reinforced by the Western democracies, which shunned Spain after 1945 because of its "fascist" government. Spain did not receive Marshall Plan aid from the United States and was excluded from a number of international organizations.

Spain's autarkic policies were a failure, and by the late 1950s the country was on the verge of economic collapse. This crisis led to a major change in economic policy, and in 1959 a team of technocrats announced the Economic Stabilization Plan. This plan allowed a less-restrained market economy and the fuller integration of Spain into the international capitalist economy. The Stabilization Plan set the stage for the period of rapid economic growth known as the Spanish economic miracle. From 1960 until 1974 Spain's economy grew an average of 6.6 percent per year, more quickly than that of any country in the world except Japan, and agriculture fell from being the most important sector of the economy in terms of employment to the least.

Spain's economic miracle occurred during a period of high prosperity in the West, and it was largely dependent on these favourable external circumstances. Three factors were especially important. The first was foreign investment in Spain. Limited under the policy of autarky, it increased rapidly once the economy had been liberalized. The United States was the most important source, followed by West Germany. The second significant factor was tourism. General prosperity made foreign travel possible for many Europeans and North Americans. With its many beaches, warm climate, and bargain prices, Spain became an attractive destination, and tourism quickly became the country's largest industry. The third factor was emigrant remittances. From 1959 to 1974 more than

one million Spaniards left the country. The vast majority went to Switzerland, West Germany, and France, countries whose growing economies were creating a massive demand for unskilled labour. There they joined Portuguese, Italians, Yugoslavs, and Turks as "guest workers." These emigrants sent large sums of money back to Spain—more than $1 billion in 1973 alone.

The great dependence on external conditions, however, made Spain's economic growth vulnerable to economic changes elsewhere as the Franco era ended. The oil crisis of 1973, which initiated an extended period of inflation and economic uncertainty in the Western world, brought Spain's economic growth to a halt. Political instability following Franco's death in 1975 compounded these problems. The clearest sign of change was the dramatic increase in unemployment. The unemployment rate rose from 4 percent in 1975 to 11 percent by 1980, before peaking at more than 20 percent in 1985.

Economic growth returned, however, during the late 1980s, spurred by industrial restructuring and integration into the European Economic Community (EEC). Although growth rates were well below those of the 1960s, they were still among the highest in western Europe. Unlike the earlier boom, this one was accompanied by high inflation and continuing high unemployment, which, though lower than in previous years, were nonetheless significantly higher than the EEC averages. Although unemployment began to drop, at 16 percent in 1990 it was almost double the average for the EEC. Young people trying to join the workforce for the first time were hit particularly hard.

During the 1990s, Spain's economy stabilized, unemployment declined (largely because of the rapid expansion of the services sector), and inflation eased. This economic recovery resulted partly from continuing integration into the single European market and from the government's stability plan, which reduced budget deficits and inflation and stabilized the currency. The government pursued this policy of economic stabilization to enable Spain to qualify for the European economic and monetary union outlined in the 1991 Maastricht Treaty (formally the Treaty on European Union). The government also began privatizing state-owned enterprises. Moreover, Spain succeeded in qualifying for the euro, the EU's common currency; in 1999 the euro was introduced as a unit of exchange, although the Spanish peseta (the value of which was locked to that of the euro) remained in circulation until 2002. In the early 21st century, Spain had one of the strongest economies in the EU. Foreign direct investment in the country tripled from 1990 to 2000. Moreover, since 2000, a large number of South Americans, eastern Europeans, and North Africans have immigrated to Spain to work in the construction industry, which contributes about one-tenth of the gross domestic product (GDP).

The global financial downturn that began in 2008–09 took root in the euro zone, and Spain was one of the hardest-hit countries. Spanish banks, undercapitalized and suffering the effects of a burst housing bubble, dragged down an already ailing economy. The government's initial attempts to stimulate the economy proved insufficient, and Spanish bond yields—the benchmark of the country's ability to borrow—rose to dangerous levels. Unemployment skyrocketed as a succession of governments introduced austerity measures in an effort to restore confidence in the Spanish economy. In 2012 Spain accepted a €100 billion (about $125 billion) bailout package from the EU, the European Central Bank, and the International Monetary Fund to recapitalize its banks.

AGRICULTURE

Because of the relative decline of agriculture since the 1960s, Spain's rural population decreased and many farms disappeared. Spanish agriculture has remained relatively backward by western European standards: capital investment per hectare is about one-fifth the average for the Organisation for Economic Co-operation and Development (OECD), and the vast majority of farms are small. Since Spain joined the EEC in 1986, the Spanish agricultural sector has had to respect Europe-wide policies. As a result, many small-scale operations, especially in grape growing and dairying, had to cease. Since the mid-1990s, however, the amount of agriculturally productive land (especially land dedicated to organic farming) in Spain has increased through irrigation and the conversion of fallow lands.

Vegetables, fruits, and cereals are the principal crops, accounting for about three-fourths of Spain's agricultural production (in terms of value), with cereals the principal crops. Barley and wheat, the major crops in Spain, predominate on the plains of Castile-León, Castile–La Mancha, and Andalusia, while rice is grown in coastal Valencia and southern Catalonia. Corn (maize), grown in the north, is a major fodder product. Other crops include cotton; tobacco (grown in Extremadura); sugar beets (grown mainly in the Duero and Guadalquivir valleys); olives (produced in the south), a large portion of which are used for oil; and legumes (beans, lentils, and chickpeas). Fruit growing is also significant, with citrus fruits, especially oranges (grown in the regions of Valencia and Murcia), being of greatest importance. Other fruit crops include apples, apricots, bananas, pears, peaches, and plums. Spain also produces vegetables (especially tomatoes, onions, and potatoes) and nuts (almonds).

Because Spain is one of the world's largest producers of wine, grape growing is of considerable importance. The main wine-producing areas are La Rioja, the Penedès in Catalonia, Valdepeñas in Castile–La Mancha, the Duero valley in Valladolid, and Málaga and Jerez de la Frontera in Andalusia, which is also the centre of sherry production. The raising of livestock accounts for just under half the value of Spain's total agricultural output. Pigs are raised mainly in Castile-León, Aragon, and Catalonia, and pork leads meat production in Spain, followed by poultry, beef, and lamb. In the Atlantic coastal regions and the dry southern interior, sheep and dairy cows are raised.

FORESTRY

Forests cover more than one-third of the total land area of Spain, with much of this woodland in the Cantabrian Mountains. Forestry contributes only a tiny fraction to Spain's agricultural production. Important forestry products are cork, eucalyptus, oak, pine, and poplar. Because centuries of erosion, harvesting of firewood, and the creation of pastureland had resulted in the disappearance of many of the country's forests, the government initiated reforestation efforts in the 1940s that are still in progress.

FISHING

With about 5,000 miles (8,000 km) of coastline, Spain has long had an important fishing industry, which relies on fishing grounds off its coast and as far away as the Pacific and Indian oceans. The main fishing ports are in the northwest, especially Vigo and A Coruña. The activities of the commercial fishing fleet led to conflicts between Spain and a number of other countries, especially Morocco and Canada. On a number of occasions Spanish fishermen have been arrested for fishing illegally in these countries' waters. Spain's total catch declined during the 1980s and '90s, but the fishing sector still accounted for about 1 percent of GDP, and fish remain an important component of the Spanish diet. Moreover, as the catch from sea fishing has declined, Spanish producers have increasingly developed coastal fish farming as an alternative.

RESOURCES AND POWER

Spain has one of Europe's most important and varied mining industries. Coal—produced mainly in the Cantabrian Mountains, the eastern Iberian Cordillera, and the Sierra Morena—accounts for a significant proportion of the country's total mineral production. Other major products include metals such as iron, copper, lead, zinc, tungsten, uranium, mercury, and gold. In order to compete with other EU countries, however, the Spanish mining industry has been forced to restructure. This need has been most urgent in Asturias, where it has led to strong protests by coal miners against government policies.

Spanish miners sing in solidarity during a protest march in Madrid in 2012. The miners were protesting subsidy cuts within Spain's coal mining industry. Denis Doyle/Getty Images

Despite the long-standing prominence of the mining industry, in general, Spain's mineral resources are limited, and the country's once-plentiful coal reserves are no longer sufficient for its energy needs. Moreover, Spain has virtually no petroleum of its own, and the commercial potential of its natural gas fields is limited. As a result, Spain, once a mineral-exporting country, now imports minerals on a large scale, including both coal and petroleum.

Thermal power plants, located near coal fields or ports that receive imported oil, supply about half of Spain's electricity needs. The country also relies heavily on hydroelectric power, mainly provided by its northern rivers, which create about one-sixth of its electricity. To address its energy shortage, the Spanish government adopted an ambitious nuclear energy program in the 1960s. The first nuclear power plant began operating in 1968, and several additional plants went online in the 1980s. In 2006 the 1968 plant was closed, and the government sought to move toward renewable energy. In fact, in the early 21st century, Spain became one of the EU's leading exponents of renewable energy, including solar and wind power. In 2007 solar thermoelectric power plants opened near Sevilla, and there are wind parks throughout the country.

MANUFACTURING

Spain's early industrialization took place behind high tariff walls, and most industries remained small in scale, partly because of a lack of adequate raw materials and investment capital and partly because of weak domestic demand. Historically, industrial production has been concentrated on the northern coast and in the Basque Country, Catalonia, and the Madrid area while other parts of Spain underwent little industrial development. The liberalization of the economy in the 1960s and the influx of foreign investment, however, added a number of large firms. It also helped Spanish industry to diversify. The most striking example of this change was the automobile industry. Before 1960 Spain built few motor vehicles, but by the end of the 1980s it was producing 1.5 million vehicles in factories owned by Ford, Renault, General Motors, and the Spanish firm SEAT (largely owned by Volkswagen). During the 1990s, further liberalization of Spanish industry took place as the government privatized state-owned industrial enterprises, and telecommunications deregulation spurred an expansion of infrastructure. Meanwhile, Spanish firms, encouraged by government policy, began to address their traditional reliance on imported technologies by increasing their budgets for research and development.

Iron, steel, and shipbuilding have long been the dominant heavy industries in Asturias and the Basque Country, but in the 1970s and '80s they began to decline because of outdated technology and rising energy costs. Much of this heavy industry was replaced by firms specializing in science and technology, a reflection of the government's large-scale investment in the development of biotechnology, renewable energy sources, electronics, and telecommunications. The production of cotton and woolen textiles, paper, clothing, and footwear remains significant in Catalonia and neighbouring Valencia. Other leading industries include the manufacture of chemicals, toys, and electrical appliances (televisions, refrigerators, and washing machines). Consumer-oriented industries, such as food processing, construction, and furniture making, are located either close to their consumer markets in the larger cities or in rural areas where agricultural products and timber are close at hand. At the beginning of the 21st century, Madrid, Catalonia, and the Basque Country continued to dominate metallurgy, capital goods, and chemical production, but industrial production in a variety of sectors had expanded to new regions, such as Navarra, La Rioja, Aragon, and Valencia.

FINANCE

During the Franco regime, Spanish banks played a primary role in industrial growth and came to control much of the country's industry. The banking sector was so highly regulated that even the number of branches a bank could maintain was controlled. It was only at the very end of the regime, in 1974, that banking experienced the same kind of liberalization that had been applied to the economy as a whole

in the 1960s. In 1978 foreign banks were permitted to operate in Spain, and by the 1990s dozens of foreign banks had established branches. By the late 1990s, however, the foreign share of the banking market had declined as some foreign banks left the country and others were acquired by Spanish banks. Capital flight became a major concern in the 21st century, as both domestic and international account holders, fearing for the solvency of Spanish banks in the wake of the eurozone crisis, shifted their funds abroad.

The central bank is the Banco de España (Bank of Spain). Having complied with the criteria for convergence, Spain joined the economic and monetary union of the EU in 1998, and the Banco de España became part of the European System of Central Banks. In addition to being the government's bank, the Banco de España supervises the country's private banks. It is responsible to the Ministry of the Economy. In 1999 Spain adopted the euro as its official monetary unit, and in 2002 the euro replaced the peseta as the national currency.

Although Spain has a large number of private banks, the banking industry has long been dominated by a handful of large institutions. During the 1990s, in preparation for incorporation into the European monetary union, the government encouraged bank mergers to create more-competitive financial institutions, a trend that continued with renewed intensity in the 21st century. This process produced three large banking groups: Banco Santander, the Banco Bilbao

Vizcaya Argentaria, and CaixaBank. Even the strongest Spanish banks, however, are of only moderate size by global standards, and at the beginning of the 21st century only Banco Santander ranked among the world's leading financial institutions. Spain's banks grew dramatically in the first decade of the 21st century, but much of that growth was fueled by a housing and construction bubble that burst in 2009. The collapse in real estate prices, combined with a freeze in global credit markets, left Spain's banks exposed and overleveraged. Government intervention in the banking sector reached its peak in May 2012 with the nationalization of Bankia, Spain's fourth-largest bank and its largest mortgage lender.

Spain has traditionally had a second distinct set of banks known as *cajas de ahorros* (savings banks). These not-for-profit institutions originally were provincially or regionally based and were required to invest a certain amount in their home provinces, but they were later opened to all parts of the country. Surpluses were put into reserves or were used for local welfare, environmental activities, and cultural and educational projects. The largest of the savings banks is the Barcelona-based La Caja de Ahorros y de Pensiones (the Bank for Pensions and Savings), popularly known as "La Caixa." La Caixa is the largest shareholder in the CaixaBank financial group, proof that the boundary between savings banks and commercial banks had become somewhat blurrier in the 21st century. This distinction was almost completely erased in the wake of the 2009 financial crisis, as reforms within the savings banking sector led to widespread consolidation and commercialization. Indeed, the troubled Bankia group was created in 2010 by the merger of seven regional savings banks, and further restructuring within

BANCO SANTANDER, SA

Banco Santander, SA—formerly (1999–2007) BSCH, SA (Banco Santander Central Hispano, SA),—is the leading financial group in Spain and one of the largest in Europe. It offers services in traditional commercial banking, private banking, investment banking, treasury, and asset management. Headquarters are in Madrid.

BSCH was formed as a result of the 1999 merger of Banco Santander (founded 1857) and Banco Central Hispano. Prior to this merger, Banco Santander had acquired Banco Banesto in 1994, and Banco Central had merged with Banco Hispano Americano in 1991. The company has a strong presence in Spain, Portugal, Germany, Italy, Belgium, and Latin America. It also has operations in New York, London, and Paris.

In the early 21st century the company engaged in a series of sales and acquisitions, maintaining a strong international presence. As part of an effort to achieve a more uniform image, BSCH was legally renamed Banco Santander, SA in 2007.

the sector was seen as a necessary step to strengthening it against future shocks.

Spain has stock exchanges in Madrid, Bilbao, Barcelona, and Valencia. Yet even the largest, the Madrid exchange, is quite small by international standards. The stock exchanges were deregulated in 1989, and during the 1990s their importance increased.

TRADE

Spain's foreign trade grew rapidly during the late 20th century. The long-established pattern of imports outweighing exports continued, though earnings from tourism and other services balanced the country's trade deficit in tangible goods. The largest share of Spain's foreign trade is conducted within the EU; its two largest trading partners are France and Germany, and there is significant trade with Portugal, the United Kingdom, and Italy. Outside of Europe the largest and most important trading partners are the United States and China. Spain also engages in significant trade with Japan.

During the mid-20th century, Spain was mainly an exporter of agricultural products and minerals and an importer of industrial goods. By the early 21st century, this pattern had changed, reflecting the increasing sophistication of the country's economy. The main imported goods continued to be largely industrial in nature, including machinery and electrical equipment, motor vehicles, chemical and petroleum products, base metals, seafood, and paper products. But the principal exports included not only agricultural products but also motor vehicles, machinery and electrical equipment, processed iron products, chemical products, and clothing and footwear.

SERVICES

Compared with many western European countries, Spain's service sector is less developed, but it is still a major sector of the Spanish economy. Tourism is among Spain's leading industries, and the country is one of the world's top tourist destinations. Spain receives more than 55 million visitors annually—more than 10 million more people than the country's entire population. Most visitors are European, with British, French, and German tourists making up the majority. At the beginning of the 21st century, the tourism sector accounted for about one-tenth of Spain's GDP and employment. Spain's central government is responsible for tourism policies and for promoting tourism overseas, while regional authorities promote tourism in their own provinces.

LABOUR AND TAXATION

Spain's 1978 constitution recognized the right of unions to exist and the right of all citizens, except those in the military, to join them. Both collective bargaining and the right to strike are guaranteed. The constitutional provisions regarding unions were fleshed out in the Workers' Statute of 1980 and the Organic Law of Trade Union Freedom, which went into effect in 1985. The Workers' Statute eliminated government involvement in labour relations, leaving negotiations to unions and management. Within firms, elected delegates or workers' committees deal with management on issues of daily working conditions, job security, and, in some cases, wages. Worker representatives are elected for four-year terms.

There are a number of trade union federations, but the union movement as a whole is dominated by two: the General Union of Workers (Unión General de Trabajadores; UGT), which is affiliated with the Spanish Socialist Workers' Party (Partido Socialista Obrero Español; PSOE) and is organized by sections (economic branches) and territorial unions; and the Workers' Commissions (Confederación Sindical de Comisiones Obreras; CC.OO.), which is affiliated with the Communist Party and is also structured by sectional and territorial divisions. Other unions include the Workers' Syndical Union (Unión Sindical Obrera; USO), which has a strong Roman Catholic orientation; the Independent Syndicate of Civil Servants (Confederación Sindical Independiente de Funcionarios); the Basque Workers' Solidarity (Euzko Langilleen Alkartasuna–Solidaridad de Trabajadores Vascos; ELA-STV),

which is independent but has ties to the Basque Nationalist Party; and the General Confederation of Labour (Confederación General del Trabajo; CGT), the tiny remnant of the once-powerful anarcho-syndicalist union organization. Overall, with about one-sixth of its workforce belonging to unions, Spain has one of the lowest levels of unionization in Europe.

The outstanding feature of union activity after the demise of the Franco regime was the willingness of the major union organizations to sign agreements with the government and the employers' organizations regarding employment, wage restraint, and social policy. Many such pacts were agreed upon between the late 1970s and the late 1990s.

The unions became less accommodating under the Socialist governments of Felipe González. The thrust of González's economic policies was to make the Spanish economy more competitive in preparation for the full economic integration of the EU in the 1990s. This program included the reconversion through reprivatization or closing of money-losing state corporations, especially in the country's "rust belt" of Asturias and the Basque Country, and the reduction of public spending in order to control the deficit.

The major unions refused to agree to further pacts with employers and the government. The UGT became much more critical of the PSOE, with which it had always been affiliated, and began to cooperate more closely with the CC.OO.

In 1983 the government's reconversion program prompted a series of strikes, mass demonstrations, and riots, especially in the north. In December 1988 the UGT and CC.OO. jointly called a widely supported national one-day general strike to protest the government's policies. Plans for the downsizing of the coal, iron, and steel industries in Asturias also led to a one-day general strike in the region in October 1991. At the beginning of the 21st century, Spanish unions were working for increased job opportunities and greater job security for all workers. They also supported the idea of a more equitable distribution of wealth among regions and social groups, though unionization in Spain is still quite low.

There are three levels of taxation in Spain. Taxes may be imposed by the national government, the regional governments, and local authorities. Tax rates are progressive, ranging from about three-tenths of income to more than half. Spain has a corporate tax and a value-added tax.

TRANSPORTATION AND TELECOMMUNICATIONS

Well into the 19th century, movement within much of Spain was difficult. The rivers were inadequate for transportation, and the many mountain ranges formed major barriers to overland travel. The situation improved with the construction of railroads. The first line, between Barcelona and Mataró, was built in 1848 and the second, between Madrid and Aranjuez, was built three years later. Most of the railroads were constructed by foreign investors, although the Spanish government provided major subsidies and other inducements. At the end of the 19th century, two groups of French investors controlled four-fifths of the railways in Spain.

In 1941 the rail system was nationalized, and virtually all the lines were incorporated into the National Network of Spanish Railroads (Red Nacional de los Ferrocarriles Españoles; RENFE). There are also regionally operated lines in the Basque Country, Valencia, and Catalonia. Lines generally start in Madrid and radiate outward in all directions. Transverse lines serve the Mediterranean and Ebro valley corridors. New equipment—including the Talgo, a light train designed by a Spaniard—was introduced in the 1960s and '70s, and much of the track was electrified. However, the system constantly ran up huge losses, and in the 1980s a number of lines were eliminated. In 1990 the government announced a massive, long-term investment program for RENFE, the main goal of which was the introduction of superspeed trains, Alta Velocidad Española (AVE). These high-speed trains, first used on the Madrid-Sevilla line for the Expo '92 world's fair, make the journey from Sevilla to Madrid in less than three hours. An AVE train route between Madrid and Barcelona opened in 2008.

The construction of a modern road network came after the building of the railways and was mostly achieved in the second half of the 20th century. The first motorway was begun in 1967. Like the railways, the road system is radial in design, with Madrid as its hub. Traffic on Spanish roads increased dramatically in the late 20th century, and both highways and city streets became heavily congested as the number of vehicles increased dramatically. In response, during the 1990s and the beginning of the 21st century, the central governments advanced plans to cover the country with an almost complete network of roads, some of which would be financed through private investment, and a toll system was proposed to fund highway maintenance.

The busiest of Spain's many commercial airports, and one of the busiest in Europe, is Madrid's Barajas Airport. Barcelona too has a major airport, and areas of tourism also serve international flights. The largest Spanish airline, the formerly government-owned Iberia, flies both domestic and international routes. Several other domestic and foreign airlines operate both regularly scheduled and charter flights, the latter accounting for a significant proportion of traffic to tourist destinations. By the end of the 20th century, increases in air travel made air traffic congestion a concern.

Largely surrounded by water, Spain has extensive coastlines and is heavily dependent on maritime transport, especially for international trade: more than four-fifths of imports and more than two-thirds of exports pass through the ports. Spain has one of the largest merchant marines in the world as well as one of the world's most important fishing fleets. General traffic is very heavily concentrated in relatively few of Spain's many ports, most notably in Algeciras (province of Cádiz), Barcelona, Bilbao, Las Palmas, Santa Cruz de Tenerife, Tarragona, and Valencia. Other important ports include Huelva, Cartagena, A Coruña, and Ceuta. A fishing fleet is concentrated mainly in Galicia and the Basque Country.

During the 1980s and '90s the telecommunications and information technology sectors developed quickly, mainly in or near Madrid and Barcelona. Two major companies, Telefónica (reorganized in 2000 into several companies)

TELEFÓNICA SA

The Spanish company Telefónica SA is one of the world's leaders in the telecommunications industry. Its headquarters are in Madrid. Telefónica is the main service provider in Spanish- and Portuguese-speaking markets. The company offers a wide range of services, including fixed and mobile telephony, Internet and broadband, content management, directories, applications, and customer-relations management. It was created in 1924 under the name of Compañía Telefónica Nacional de España (CTNE), whose shareholder was New York's International Telephone and Telegraph Corporation (later renamed ITT Corporation). The company was nationalized in 1945 and, under the control of the Spanish government, was the country's sole telephone operator until 1997. It became entirely privately owned in 1999. Telefónica adopted its current name in 1988. At the turn of the 21st century, it had a significant presence in some 15 countries and was operating companies in approximately 40 countries; the bulk of the company's growth was occurring in Latin America.

In 1994 Telefónica launched the mobile-telephone provider Movistar, under which it thereafter began integrating its brands in an effort to achieve a more uniform image. Owing to shrinking demand and profitability in the telecommunications sector following the collapse of the dot-com boom in the late 1990s, Telefónica engaged in a series of sales, acquisitions, and joint ventures in the early 21st century.

and Grupo Corporativo ONO, dominate the country's telephone and cable television markets. Although initially much of the telecommunications sector was government-controlled, from 1998 the sector was liberalized and fully deregulated. Consumer use of various telecommunications products generally lagged behind that of the rest of western Europe, but the growth in the sector during the 1990s raised use to the European average. Internet use also grew rapidly during the late 1990s and into the early 21st century.

CHAPTER 9

SPANISH GOVERNMENT AND SOCIETY

From 1833 until 1939 Spain almost continually had a parliamentary system with a written constitution. Except during the First Republic (1873–74), the Second Republic (1931–36), and the Spanish Civil War (1936–39), Spain also always had a monarchy.

From the end of the Spanish Civil War in April 1939 until November 1975, Spain was ruled by Gen. Francisco Franco. The principles on which his regime was based were embodied in a series of Fundamental Laws (passed between 1942 and 1967) that declared Spain a monarchy and established a legislature known as the Cortes. Yet Franco's system of government differed radically from Spain's modern constitutional traditions.

Under Franco the members of the Cortes, the *procuradores*, were not elected on the democratic principle of one person, one vote but on the basis of what was called "organic democracy." Rather than representing individual citizens, the *procuradores* represented what were considered the basic institutions of Spanish society: families, the municipalities, the universities, and professional organizations. Moreover, the government—appointed and dismissed by the head of state alone—was not responsible to the Cortes, which also lacked control of government spending.

In 1969 Franco selected Juan Carlos de Borbón, the grandson of King Alfonso XIII, to succeed him as head of state. When Franco died in 1975, Juan Carlos came to the throne as King Juan Carlos I. Almost immediately the king initiated

CORTES

The Cortes developed in the Middle Ages when elected representatives of the free municipalities acquired the right to take part in the deliberations of the Curia Regis (Latin: "King's Court") on certain matters. They were admitted because of the crown's need for financial aid beyond that provided by its customary levies and because of the crown's lack of legal right to impose extra taxation without the consent of the municipalities.

In both Leon and Castile the Cortes were in existence by the early 13th century. Their functions and procedures were similar, and, after the union of the two crowns in 1230, they often held joint meetings—a normal procedure after 1301. Parliaments also functioned in Catalonia from 1218, Valencia (1283), Aragon (1274), and Navarre (1300). The Cortes of Leon and Castile were composed of three estates: nobles, clergy, and the *procuradores* (attorneys or town clerks) of the *concejos* (fortified municipalities), who bore *poderes* (written instructions) from their electors. The king convened the Cortes' meetings when and where he pleased. During the 14th century the *procuradores* dominated the Cortes because only they could authorize the special taxation needed by the crown. The meetings consisted of negotiations, not true debates.

In Castile, after the failed revolt of the townsmen known as *comuneros* (1520–21), the *hidalgos* (lower nobility) were the only surviving force in the Cortes, and even they ceased to exercise much real power. In Portugal the Cortes ratified the succession of the House of Avis (1385) and of Philip II (1580) and was active after the restoration of independence (1640). But in Spain the Cortes of Catalonia did not meet after the revolt of 1640; nor did that of Valencia after 1645 or that of Castile after 1685. In 1709 the Cortes of Aragon and Valencia were merged with that of Castile, as was that of Catalonia in 1724, though the meetings were held solely to recognize the heir to the crown. In the 18th century Portugal's Cortes did not meet at all.

In 1812 the Spanish Cortes met at Cádiz and adopted the first liberal constitution. Although it was overthrown in 1814, the Cortes was restored in 1820 and was adopted by Portugal in the same year. In both countries the word was henceforth applied to the national parliament.

During the reign of Francisco Franco, the name Cortes Españolas ("Spanish Courts") was used from 1942 for the rubber-stamp, nondemocratic legislature. Following the transition to democracy in the 1970s, the official name of the legislature was changed to Cortes Generales ("General Courts").

a process of transition to democracy that within three years replaced the Francoist system with a democratic constitution.

The product of long and intense negotiations among the leading political groups, the Spanish constitution was nearly unanimously approved by both houses of the legislature (it passed 551–11 with 22 abstentions) in October 1978. In a December referendum, the draft constitution was then approved by nearly 90 percent of voters. The constitution declares that Spain is a constitutional monarchy and advocates the essential values of freedom, justice, equality, and political pluralism. It also provides for the separation of powers into executive, legislative, and judicial branches. Although the monarch is the head of state and the country's highest representative in international affairs, the crown's role is defined as strictly neutral and apolitical. The monarch is also commander in chief of the armed forces—though without actual authority over them—and the symbol of national unity. For example, when the new democratic constitution was threatened by a military coup in 1981, Juan Carlos in military uniform addressed the country on national television, defusing the uprising and saving the constitution. The monarch's most important functions include the duty to summon and dissolve the legislature, appoint and accept the resignation of the prime minister and cabinet ministers, ratify laws, declare wars, and sign treaties decided upon by the government.

The legislature, known as the Cortes Generales, is composed of two chambers (*cámaras*): a lower chamber, the Congress of Deputies (Congreso de los Diputados), and an upper chamber, the Senate (Senado). As with most legislatures in parliamentary systems, more power is vested in the lower chamber. The Congress of Deputies has 350 members, who are elected to four-year terms by universal suffrage. The Senate is described in the constitution as the "chamber of territorial representation," but only about one-fifth of the senators are actually chosen as representatives of the autonomous communities. The rest are elected from the 47 mainland provinces (with each province having four senators), the islands (the three largest having four and the smaller ones having one each), and Ceuta and Melilla (having two each).

The executive consists of the prime minister, the deputy prime minister, and the members of the cabinet. After consultation with the Cortes, the monarch formally appoints the prime minister; the cabinet ministers, chosen in turn by the prime minister, are also formally appointed by the monarch. The executive handles domestic and foreign policy, including defense and economic policies. Since the executive is responsible to the legislature and must be approved by a majority vote, the prime minister is usually the leader of the party that has the most deputies. The Congress of Deputies can dismiss a prime minister through a vote of no confidence.

REGIONAL GOVERNMENT

For most of the period after 1800, Spain was a highly centralized state that did not recognize the country's regional diversity. Decades of civil unrest followed Isabella II's accession to the throne in 1833, as factions warred over the role of the Roman Catholic Church, the monarchy, and the direction of Spain's economy. The constitution of the short-lived First Republic called for self-governing provinces that would be voluntarily responsible to the federal government; however, decentralization led to chaos, and by 1875 the constitutional monarchy was restored. For the rest of the 19th century, Spain remained relatively stable, with industrial centres such as the Basque region and Catalonia experiencing significant economic growth while most of the rest of Spain remained poor. Following Spain's defeat in the Spanish-American War (1898), many Spaniards viewed their country's political and economic systems as unworkable and antiquated. Groups in Catalonia, the Basque region, and Galicia who wanted to free their regions from the "Castilian corpse" began movements for regional autonomy, and a number of influential regional political parties consolidated their strength. One of the stated goals of the Second Republic was to grant autonomy to the regions, as it did to Catalonia and the Basque provinces; however, self-government for these regions was not reinstated after the Civil War.

During the Franco years the democratic opposition came to include regional autonomy as one of its basic demands. While the 1978 constitution reflected this stance, it also was the product of compromise with the political right, which preferred that Spain remain a highly centralized state. The result was a unique system of regional autonomy, known as the "state of the autonomies."

Article 2 of the constitution both recognizes the right of the "regions and nationalities" to autonomy and declares "the indissoluble unity of the Spanish nation." Title VIII states that "Adjoining provinces with common historic, cultural and economic characteristics, the islands and the provinces with a historical regional identity" are permitted to form autonomous communities.

The constitution classifies the possible autonomous communities into two groups, each of which has a different route to recognition and a different level of power and responsibility. The three regions that had voted for a statute of autonomy in the past—Catalonia, the Basque provinces, and Galicia—were designated "historic nationalities" and permitted to attain autonomy through a rapid and simplified process. Catalonia and the Basque Country had their statutes approved in December 1979 and Galicia in April 1981. The other regions were required to take a slower route, although Andalusia was designated as an exception to this general rule. It was not a "historic nationality," but there was much evidence, including mass demonstrations, of significant popular support for autonomy. As a result, a special, quicker process was created for it.

By May 1983 the entire country had been divided into 17 *comunidades autónomas* (autonomous communities): the Basque Country, Catalonia, Galicia, Andalusia, Asturias, Aragon, Balearic Islands, Canary Islands, Cantabria, Castile and León, Castile-La Mancha, Extremadura, Navarra, La Rioja, and the regions of Madrid, Murcia, and Valencia. In 1995 two autonomous cities, Ceuta and Melilla, were added.

The basic political institutions of each community are similar to those of the country as a whole. Each has a unicameral legislature elected by universal adult suffrage and an executive consisting of a president and a Council of Government responsible to that legislature.

The powers (*competencias*) to be exercised by the regional governments are also stated in the constitution and in the regional statute of autonomy. However, there were differences between the "historic nationalities" and the other communities in the extent of the powers that were initially granted to them. For the first five years of their existence, those communities that had attained autonomy by the slow route could assume only limited responsibilities. Nevertheless, they had control over the organization of institutions, urban planning, public works, housing, environmental protection, cultural affairs, sports and leisure, tourism, health and social welfare, and the cultivation of the regional language (where there was one). After five years these regions could accede to full autonomy, but the meaning of "full autonomy" was not clearly defined. The transfer of powers to the autonomous governments has been determined in an ongoing process of negotiation between the individual communities and the central government that has given rise to repeated disputes. The communities, especially Catalonia and Andalusia, have argued that the central government has dragged its feet in ceding powers and in clarifying financial arrangements. In 2005 the Cortes granted greater autonomy to Catalonia, declaring the region a nation in 2006.

By the beginning of the 21st century, the Spanish state had yet to achieve a form of regional government that was wholly acceptable to all its communities, but, whenever that happens, it will almost inevitably be an asymmetrical form in which the range of powers held by the regional governments will vary widely from one community to another.

LOCAL GOVERNMENT

There are two further levels of government below the national and regional—*provincias* and *municipios* (provinces and municipalities). Their powers and responsibilities are set out in the Basic Law on Local Government (1985).

The provinces, in existence since 1833, originally served as transmission belts for the policies of the central government. Although they still perform this function, the provinces now also bring together and are dependent on the governments of the municipalities.

There are more than 8,000 municipal governments (*ayuntamientos*). Each has a council, a commission (a kind of cabinet), and a mayor (*alcalde*). Municipal councillors are elected by universal adult suffrage through a system of proportional representation. As in elections to the national parliament, votes are cast for party lists, not for individual candidates.

Political map of Spain.

Municipal governments may pass specific local regulations so long as they conform to legislation of the national or regional parliament. While municipal governments receive funds from the central government and the regions, they can also levy their own taxes; in contrast, provincial governments cannot.

A provincial council (Diputación Provincial) is responsible for ensuring that municipalities cooperate with one another at the provincial level. The main function of these councils is to provide a range of services not available to the smaller municipalities and to develop a provincewide plan for municipal works and services. There are no provincial councils in the autonomous regions that comprise one province (Asturias, Navarra, La Rioja, Cantabria, Madrid, and Murcia). In the Basque Country, provincial councils are elected directly by universal adult suffrage. The islands, too, choose their corporate body by direct election; each of the seven main Canary Islands and the main Balearic Islands elect island councils (Cabildo Insular and Consell Insular, respectively).

JUSTICE

The judicial system, known as the *poder judicial,* is independent of the legislative and executive branches of government. It is governed by the General Council, which comprises lawyers and judges.

There are a number of different levels and types of courts. At the apex of the system is the Supreme Court, the country's highest tribunal, which comprises five chambers. The National Court (Audiencia Nacional) has jurisdiction throughout Spain and is composed of three chambers (criminal, administrative, and labour). Each autonomous community has its own high court of justice (Tribunal Superior de Justica), and all the provinces have high courts called the *audiencias* that try criminal cases. Below these are courts of first instance, courts of judicial proceedings (which do not pass sentences), penal courts, and municipal courts. Created by law in 1981 and reporting to the Cortes, the ombudsman (*defensor del pueblo*) defends citizens'

rights and monitors the activities of all branches of government.

The Constitutional Court (Tribunal Constitucional), which is not part of the judiciary, is responsible for interpreting the constitution and the constitutionality of laws and for settling disputes between central and regional powers regarding constitutional affairs. The Constitutional Court is composed of 12 members who are formally appointed by the monarch after being elected by three-fifths of both the Congress of Deputies and the Senate (four members each) and by the executive and the General Council (two members each).

POLITICAL PROCESS

Voting is open to all citizens age 18 years or older. For elections to the Congress of Deputies, held every four years, each of the 50 provinces serves as an electoral district, with the number of deputies representing it determined by its population. Under a proportional representation electoral system governed by the d'Hondt formula, ballots are cast for a province-wide party list rather than for candidates representing individual constituencies. This formula favours large parties and less-populated areas.

About four-fifths of the members of the Senate are directly elected via a plurality system at the provincial level. Each province is entitled to four representatives; voters cast ballots for three candidates, and those with the most votes are elected. Because representation is not based upon population, in the Senate smaller and more-rural provinces generally are overrepresented in relation to their overall population. The remainder of the senators are appointed by the regional legislatures. For elections to the European Parliament, held every five years, and local elections, residents who are citizens of other EU countries are eligible to participate. Spain is among the countries with the highest proportion of women members of parliament, with women generally constituting about three-tenths of the Chamber of Deputies and about one-fourth of the Senate.

Electoral participation declined markedly after the initial enthusiasm of the transition to democracy, and by the early 1980s political commentators spoke of a *desencanto* ("disenchantment") with the political system. Indeed, although support for democracy remained solid, the voting abstention rate increased throughout the 1980s, especially in local and regional elections. The trend was reversed in the 1990s, when about four-fifths of the electorate voted in national elections; however, in 2000 nearly one-third of the electorate abstained. Voter participation increased again in 2004, when about three-fourths of the electorate voted, only slightly greater than the heavy turnout for the 2008 election.

The constitution recognizes political parties as "the major instruments of political participation." The Law of Political Parties (1978) provided them with public funding based on the number of seats they held in parliament and the number of votes received.

NATIONAL PARTIES

The Spanish political scene is at once simple and complex. The simplicity rests in the fact that, since the beginning of democratic elections in 1977, national politics have been dominated by a small number of parties. From 1977 until 1982 Spain was governed by the Union of the Democratic Centre (Unión de Centro Democrático; UCD), and the major opposition party was the Spanish Socialist Workers' Party (Partido Socialista Obrero Español; PSOE). The only other national parties of importance were the right-wing Popular Alliance (Alianza Popular; AP) and the Spanish Communist Party (Partido Comunista de España; PCE).

In 1982 the PSOE came to power and governed until 1996. The UCD subsequently split into a number of smaller parties and was replaced as the leading opposition force by the Popular Party (Partido Popular; PP), which in 1989 became the successor to the AP. After faring badly in the national elections of 1982, the PCE became one of the founding members of the United Left (Izquierda Unida; IU) coalition in 1986.

The PP won a plurality in the elections of 1996 and formed a government with the support of Basque and Catalan nationalist parties. The PSOE assumed leadership of the opposition. By 2000 the PP controlled the majority of provincial and autonomous governments, and in that year it solidified its position by winning an absolute majority in the Cortes. In March 2004, however, following a series of terrorist bombings in Madrid—originally attributed by the government to the Basque separatist group ETA but subsequently linked to Islamic militants—the PSOE ousted the PP from national government. In 2008 the PSOE government won a second term, but the economic crisis that came to a boil in 2009 proved the party's undoing. Amid widespread voter dissatisfaction, PSOE Prime Minister José Zapatero advanced the date of the scheduled 2012 general election to November 2011, and in that event the PP won a convincing victory.

REGIONAL PARTIES

There also are parties that exist at the regional level only, with at least one in each of the 17 autonomous communities. Of these, the two most important are Convergence and Union (Convergència i Unió; CiU), a coalition of liberal and Christian democratic parties in Catalonia, and the Basque Nationalist Party (Basque: Euzko Alderdi Jeltzalea [EAJ]; Spanish: Partido Nacionalist Vasco [PNV]), commonly referred to as the EAJ-PNV, which espouses a traditionally rooted moderate Christian nationalist ideology. The CiU has governed Catalonia for most of the period since 1979. The EAJ-PNV has led the regional government of the

Basque Country since it was established in 1980 (ruling on its own or in coalition), and it has won a number of the region's seats in the Congress of Deputies and the Senate. Other regional parties include the Canary Islands Coalition (Coalición Canaria; CC), with a centre-right ideology; the Galician Nationalist Bloc (Bloque Nacionalista Galego; BNG), a left-wing group; Basque Solidarity (Eusko Alkartasuna; EA), a left-wing party composed of former EAJ members; the Republican Left of Catalonia (Esquerra Republicana de Catalunya; ERC), which advocates independence for Catalonia; and the Valencian Union (Unió Valenciana; UV), a centre-right nationalist party.

MINOR PARTIES

The complexity of Spanish political life since the transition to democracy lies in the existence of a very large number of minor political parties. In the early 21st century there were several minor parties operating at the national level: the Spanish Green Party (Partido Verde Español; PVE), the Liberal Party (Partido Liberal; PL), and the Spanish Workers' Party–Communist Unity (Partido de los Trabajadores de España–Unidad Comunista; PTE-UC).

One interesting feature of Spanish politics is that the authoritarian or non-democratic right has remained almost totally insignificant. During the last quarter of the 20th century, no political group claiming to be the heir to Francoism ever won more than 1 percent of the vote in a national election.

SECURITY

Traditionally, Spain had compulsory nine-month military service for all adult males. However, beginning in 2002, conscription was ended and the military became professionalized. Spain's national defense is supplemented by its membership in the North Atlantic Treaty Organization, and the United States maintains a naval base at Rota and an air base at Morón de la Frontera.

Domestic order is maintained by the National Police Corps (Cuerpo Nacional de Policía), which is primarily responsible for national investigations and security in urban areas, and the Civil Guard, established in 1844, which maintains security in rural areas and on the highways and controls the borders. These bodies were unified under the Ministry of the Interior to provide more efficiency in responding to security issues.

The state of the autonomies, a product of negotiation and compromise at the time of the transition to democracy, has come to be widely accepted by the Spanish people and by their political organizations, with one significant exception—the militant Basque nationalist movement, which has sought total independence and used terrorism as its principal method. As a result, domestic terrorism is a major concern of the Spanish police.

The nationalist movement in the Basque provinces before the Spanish Civil War was nonviolent. The inflexible centralism of the Franco regime and its repression of any expression of regional difference, however, were instrumental in stimulating the development of a more radical nationalism among Basque youth in the 1950s. Euzkadi Ta Azkatasuna (Basque Homeland and Liberty), best known by its Basque acronym, ETA, was created in 1959 and, influenced by anti-imperialist struggles in the developing world, quickly took up armed opposition. In December 1973 ETA assassinated Admiral Luis Carrero Blanco, Franco's handpicked successor as head of the government.

So long as ETA was seen to be fighting against the Franco dictatorship, it received considerable sympathy both inside and outside the Basque provinces. Its continued use of violence during and after the transition to democracy cost it whatever support it had enjoyed in the rest of Spain. In the Basque Country itself the continuing use of terror led to much public revulsion and to demonstrations demanding the end to violence. Nevertheless, Batasuna, the political party generally considered to be the political wing of ETA, won between 15 and 20 percent of the votes cast in the Basque Country in regional and national elections until the Supreme Court voted to ban the party in 2003. As of the early 21st century, Basque terrorism had claimed more than 800 lives, and numerous cease-fire agreements had failed to result in a lasting peace. In 2011, however, ETA declared that it would permanently and unilaterally renounce violence as a means of achieving its political ends. In addition to combatting ETA's violence, the Spanish government in the early 21st century dedicated considerable resources to investigating and thwarting the activities of groups in Spain linked to al-Qaeda's international terrorist network.

Other autonomous communities have had similar but much smaller and less significant illegal organizations whose terrorist activities have ceased, including the Terra Lliure (Free Country) in Catalonia and Exército Guerrilheiro do Pobo Galego Ceibe (Free Galician Guerrilla People's Army) in Galicia.

HEALTH AND WELFARE

Since the 1960s Spain's increasing prosperity and the generalized availability of government-sponsored health care have combined to cause dramatic improvements in levels of health and well-being. By the beginning of the 21st century, life expectancy in Spain was among the highest in the world. Spain also had more doctors per capita than most other countries of the EU.

The health system is administered by the national Ministry of Health through a department known as the National Institute of Health (Insalud). However, as the system of regional autonomy developed, much of the responsibility for health care devolved to the regional governments, first to Andalusia, Galicia, the Basque Country, Catalonia, Valencia, the Canary Islands, and Navarra and later to other regions. The system provides a full range of services in clinics and in general and specialized hospitals. By the 1970s most villages had a doctor who received a salary from the Ministry of Health. During the 1980s a reform allowed people to attend any public clinic they wished; previously they had to go to the one that served their neighbourhood.

Health care is not a government monopoly, though all but a very small percentage of the population seeks treatment at state-run clinics. Many doctors have their own offices and clinics outside the government-funded system, and many private insurance plans are available. In addition, as part of planned health-care reform measures, some public hospitals and clinics are to be transferred from state to private administration.

The government, through its ad hoc social security office, provides a number of other social services, including unemployment insurance, old-age pensions, maternity and sickness benefits, and disability payments. These services are financed through deductions from workers' pay, employer contributions, and general tax revenues from the state. Additional services by local authorities attempt to meet urgent health care needs of underserved groups.

HOUSING

During the Franco era, housing shortages and standards were a major problem. In

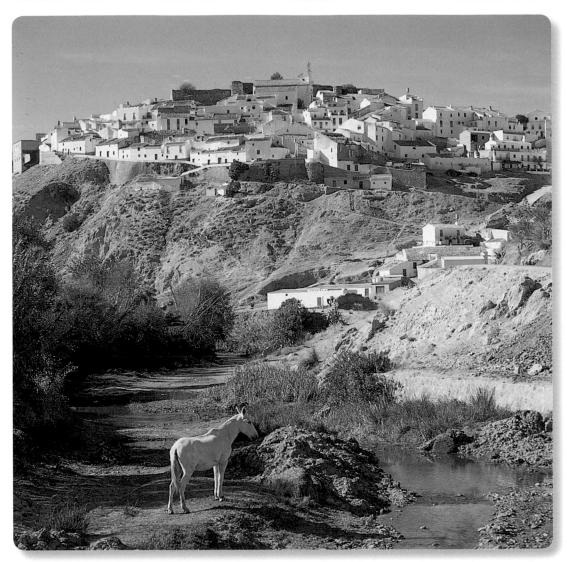

A village in Andalusia, Spain, showing housing typical of the region. © David Warren/SuperStock

1961 the government passed a National Housing Plan, which resulted in the construction of millions of homes over the next two decades. However, many of these homes were geared to affluent middle-class families; thus, by the 1980s, housing shortages were severe and conditions were still considered poor. After the election of the socialist government in 1982, significant resources were directed at housing. However, population growth continued to outstrip housing construction, and at the beginning of the 21st century many considered housing to be the country's most pressing social problem. That perception, coupled with low interest rates and an infusion of foreign investment capital, fueled a construction boom that added millions of jobs to the Spanish economy. When the real estate and construction bubble popped in 2009, thousands of developers went under, and Spain's banks were saddled with more than €180 billion (about $225 billion) in toxic assets. In 2012 financial analysts estimated that excess inventory in the housing sector, combined with high levels of household debt, would erase many of the gains made by the real estate market in the previous decade.

More than three-fourths of housing stock is owner-occupied. House types vary from region to region, but by and large multistory dwellings are characteristic of mountain and pastoral districts, while single-story or low houses with courtyards arranged in different ways according to the local economy are typical of the lowlands. Land reform, industrialization, and depopulation have significantly changed the character of many rural districts. In rural areas in particular, the housing stock is relatively old, with more than half of all units built prior to 1960. Increasingly, population concentration in urban areas created difficult housing conditions and resulted in the rapid increase in housing prices, exacerbating problems for individuals with low incomes. These prices peaked in 2007–08, and the subsequent housing bust saw home values drop by as much as 75 percent. Because this adjustment had catastrophic effects on the rest of the economy, few were able to take advantage of the lowered prices, and much of the excess housing stock sat empty.

EDUCATION

Spain's first comprehensive public education plan was contained in the Moyano Law of 1857. It remained basically unchanged until 1970, when the General Law on Education was passed. Since then many other education reforms have taken place.

The school system has a number of levels: preschool (to age 6), primary school for ages 6 or 7 to 11, secondary school for ages 12 to 16 (which includes technical and vocational schools), baccalaureate school for ages 17 and 18, and university. Education is free and compulsory for children between the ages of 6 and 16. Literacy exceeds 95 percent of the population.

Historically, the state and the Roman Catholic Church have clashed over education. Spain still has a large private education sector, almost all of which is Catholic, but since the 1960s the predominance of the state has been clearly established, especially in secondary education. In the 1980s the Catholic schools, most of which received substantial subsidies from the state, were subjected to closer government control, and religious education was removed as an obligatory subject. With regional autonomy, control over education in some parts of the country was transferred from the central to regional governments. As a result, the study of Catalan, Galician, and Euskera became obligatory in their respective regions, whereas in the past these languages had not been taught at all.

After 1960 there was a dramatic increase in the availability of schooling at all levels. The change was greatest with regard to universities. Until 1960 there were only 12 universities in the country, and higher education was the privilege of a very small elite. By the end of the 20th century, there were more than 60 public and private universities, some of which were operated by the Catholic church. Access to a university education became more democratic as well: in the 1980s almost half of Spain's university students had parents who had received no more than an elementary school education. By the early 21st century more than two-thirds of Spain's college-age population was attending a university. Among the largest and most-prestigious universities in Spain are the Complutense University of Madrid (founded 1508), the University of Barcelona (1450), the University of Granada (1526), the University of Sevilla (1502), the University of Salamanca (1218), the University of Valencia (1499), and the University of the Basque Country (1968).

UNIVERSITY OF SALAMANCA

The University of Salamanca was founded in 1218 under Alfonso IX, but its real beginnings date from 1254, when, under Alfonso X, grandson of the founder, three chairs in canon law and one each in grammar, arts, and physics were established. From that time until the end of the 16th century, Salamanca was one of the leading centres of learning in Europe, ranking with Paris, Bologna, and Oxford. Francisco de Vitoria, in his lectures there (1526–46), set forth some of the fundamental principles of international law, and the scholar and poet Luis de León lectured in the university from 1561 until his death in 1591, except for the years 1572–76, when he was a prisoner of the Inquisition on a charge of unorthodoxy; a room in the university is still known as his *aula* (lecture hall).

The university was at its peak in 1584, with nearly 7,000 students. A decline began at the end of the 16th century, and by 1875 enrollment was down to 391. In the early 19th century, a quarter of Salamanca containing many university buildings was destroyed by the French when the defeat of Napoleon ended their occupation of Spain (for its present buildings, *see* Salamanca). The university continued ecclesiastical until 1835, after which it was forcibly secularized. The contemporary university has faculties of philosophy and letters, law, science, medicine, and pharmacy.

CHAPTER 10

SPANISH CULTURAL LIFE

As in much of western Europe, the culture of Spain was marked decisively by the period of Roman rule. In language, religion, and even architectural traditions, the Romans left a lasting legacy. However, the subsequent course of Spanish history added elements to the country's cultural development that were missing or much weaker in other European countries. The most important differences stem from the Arabic-speaking Muslims from the Middle East and North Africa who invaded Spain in 711 CE and dominated much of the country for almost 800 years. The Muslim cultural influence was very strong, especially in the area of language; indeed, the Spanish language has taken more words from Arabic than from any other source except Latin. Through contact with Muslims, Christian Europe was able to recover much of the cultural and intellectual heritage of Classical antiquity. It also gained access to many scientific advances made by Muslims. Spain's cultural mix was further enriched by the presence of a large and influential Jewish population, and medieval Spain witnessed one of the periods of greatest cultural achievement in Jewish history.

During the early modern and modern periods, Spain's culture was fairly homogeneous. The one significant exception was the presence and persistence of early languages other than Castilian in some parts of the country. Two of these, Catalan and Galician (Gallego), developed significant literary traditions during the Middle Ages. From the 16th century on, however, they lost ground to Castilian and increasingly became limited to everyday use, especially among the peasantry. This had always been the case with the third language, Euskera (Basque), which never had a significant literary tradition.

Beginning in the 19th century, all three languages enjoyed a revival. In the 20th century the Franco regime prohibited the public use of languages other than Castilian, but this did not lead to their disappearance. Instead, the use of these languages, both in daily life and in high culture, increased greatly when they became the official languages in the autonomous regions established under the constitution of 1978. They are now taught in the schools and are used in the press and on television and radio.

For much of its history, and especially after the Reconquista was completed in 1492, Spain has been strongly identified with the Roman Catholic Church. To a large extent this identification and the virtual religious monopoly that the church has enjoyed since the 16th century have been artificially imposed. Members of the two large religious minorities were forced to convert or leave the country: the Jews in 1492 and the Muslims in 1502. From 1478 until 1834 religious uniformity was enforced by the church court, the Inquisition.

In the 19th and 20th centuries the Roman Catholic Church sought to have, and for much of that time succeeded in having, the government declare Roman Catholicism as the state religion, even though a large part of the population was nonpracticing or even anticlerical. The church also encouraged the government to limit or even prohibit the practice of other faiths. State support for the Catholic church was strongest during the Franco regime, but since 1978 Spain has had no official religion. Today Spaniards enjoy complete freedom of religion, although Roman Catholicism remains an important cultural influence. Thus, at the beginning of the 21st century, the expression of cultural diversity is easier than it was for at least 500 years. Ironically, this came at the same time that Spain became increasingly drawn into a homogeneous global culture.

DAILY LIFE AND SOCIAL CUSTOMS

Daily life in early 21st-century Spain looks little different from that in other industrialized countries of the West. There remain, however, some important practices that are peculiar to Spain. The most obvious, especially for foreign visitors, is the organization of the day and the scheduling of meals. Lunch, which is the main meal of the day, is eaten between 2:00 and 3:00 *pm*. Traditionally it was followed by a nap—the famous siesta—but, because most people now commute between home and work, this custom is in decline. Supper, a lighter meal, is also taken late, between 9:00 and 10:00 *pm*, or even later during the hot summer months.

Business, shopping, and school hours reflect this pattern. There is a long break—generally two to five hours long—in the middle of the day, during which most businesses are closed and the streets are not very busy. (The few exceptions are bars, restaurants, and the large department stores, which do not close at midday.) The main daily television news is broadcast at this time, as are some of the most popular programs. The workday resumes in the late afternoon, between 4:30 and 5:00 PM, and continues until about 8:00 PM.

FOOD AND DRINK

Bars, which are open all day, generally serve food as well as drink, and it is a widespread custom to go for a snack before meals, especially on non-working days. The most well-known bar food, known as tapas, usually consists of prepared dishes, many of which are quite elaborate and are often smaller-sized versions of main-course dishes. There are hundreds of different tapas, but a few typical ones are mushrooms in garlic sauce, marinated seafood, Spanish omelette, lamb brochettes, and octopus in paprika sauce.

Spanish cooking varies greatly from region to region, linked to local products and traditions. Galicia, for example, is famed for its seafood, including dishes of baby eels and Vizcayan-style codfish; Catalonia is renowned for meat and vegetable casseroles; and Valencia is the homeland of paella, a rice dish made with seafood, meats, and vegetables. From Andalusia comes gazpacho, a delicious cold soup made of tomatoes, garlic, and cucumber, while the cattle-producing region of Castile boasts succulent roasts and air-dried hams. Spanish food is frequently thought to be very spicy, but, apart from a few dishes that contain small amounts of a mild chili pepper, the most piquant ingredient in general use is paprika; otherwise, dishes are likely to be flavoured with such spices as tarragon and saffron. The most widely eaten meats are pork, chicken, and beef, but in much of the country lamb is eaten on special occasions. Very fond of both fish and shellfish, Spaniards are among the world's largest consumers of seafood. Legumes, especially lentils and chickpeas, also form an important part of the Spanish diet.

PAELLA

Paella is a dish of saffron-flavoured rice cooked with meats, seafood, and vegetables. Originating in the rice-growing areas on Spain's Mediterranean coast, the dish is especially associated with the region of Valencia. Paella takes its name from the *paellera*, the utensil in which it is cooked, a flat round pan with two handles; paella is traditionally eaten from the pan.

To prepare paella, pieces of meats such as chicken, pork, or rabbit and seafood such as clams, shrimps, mussels, crayfish, and squid are sauteed in olive oil with onions, garlic, and herbs and removed from the pan. Rice, tomatoes, saffron, and stock are simmered together, the meats and seafood mixed in, and the dish is garnished with peas, pimientos, and other vegetables. Traditional paellas are made out of doors over a wood fire.

Spaniards frequently drink wine and beer with their meals. They also commonly drink bottled mineral water, even though in most parts of the country the tap water is perfectly safe. At breakfast and after meals, strong coffee is the almost universal drink. Few people drink tea, but herbal infusions such as chamomile are popular. Soft drinks, both domestic and imported, are widely available.

INTERNATIONALIZATION OF CULTURE

The Franco regime sought to preserve what it understood as Spain's long-standing traditions and to impose a strict Roman Catholic morality on the country. However, the economic policies of the 1960s that opened Spain up to foreign investment and tourism and encouraged Spaniards to work in other European countries also invited foreign influences, which undermined the government's desire to protect or isolate Spanish culture. Since the 1960s Spanish culture, particularly the youth culture, has increasingly become part of a homogeneous, heavily American-influenced international culture.

For young people the most significant aspects of international culture are rock and contemporary dance music, both of which make up a considerable portion of the music played on Spain's radio stations. Beginning with the Beatles in the 1960s, many leading foreign rock groups have given concerts in Spain's major cities. In the 1990s dance clubs on the island of Ibiza frequented by young British vacationers became a hotbed for techno music, first called Balearic Beat by some. There are also a large number of Spanish rock musicians, but few of these have achieved much recognition outside the country. The most successful of Spain's popular singers is undoubtedly Julio Iglesias, whose music appealed to an older audience.

The internationalization of culture also can be seen in a variety of other ways. American fast-food chains have franchises in all the major cities, and much of the television programming and many of the popular films are foreign, the bulk of the programs and films being from the United States.

FESTIVALS AND HOLIDAYS

Traditionally, most holidays in Spain have been religious in origin. At the national level the most important of these are Holy (or Maundy) Thursday, Good Friday, Easter Monday, Corpus Christi, the Feast of Saint James (July 25), and All Saints' Day (November 1). The most important day of the Christmas period, and the day on which children receive presents, is the Day of the Three Kings, or Epiphany (January 6).

By contrast, nonreligious, civic holidays have been relatively insignificant. The Franco regime declared July 18, the day on which the Spanish Civil War began, a national holiday, but that was abandoned after the demise of the regime. Since 1978 the official national holiday has been Constitution Day (December 6). Catalonia and the Basque Country have their own official "national" holidays, and each of the autonomous communities celebrates itself with a regional holiday.

One important holiday is both religious and civic. October 12 is the Day of the Virgin of El Pilar and also the day on which the "discovery" of America is celebrated (a counterpart to the celebration of Columbus Day in the United States); it has been called at different times the Day of the Race (Día de la Raza) and Hispanic Day (Día de la Hispanidad).

Every village and town has its own annual holiday fiesta, and these are probably the most important holidays in the daily lives of the Spanish people. These holidays are religious in origin, honouring the local patron saint or the Virgin Mary, but the religious component is often much less important than the dancing and bullfights that take place. Some of these celebrations, such as the Fiesta de San Fermín in Pamplona (with its famous

The running (encierro) *of the bulls during the Fiesta de San Fermín, Pamplona, Spain.* © Blaine Harrington

running of the bulls), the Sevilla fair, and the Fallas of Valencia, have become internationally famous and have turned into major tourist attractions. A thoroughly secular, unique festival is held in the little town of Buñol, near Valencia, where each August thousands of residents and visitors gather to hurl tomatoes at one another. The festival, called La Tomatina, began as a symbolic repudiation of harsh rule during the Franco era. It now celebrates the summer tomato harvest, but it is also a fine excuse to drink red wine, eat paella, and enjoy one another's company.

THE ARTS

Spain has a long, varied, and distinguished artistic heritage, which includes some of the most important figures in the Western cultural tradition. A partial list would include novelists Miguel de Cervantes (the most important figure of Spanish literature) and Benito Pérez Galdós, dramatists Pedro Calderón de la Barca and Lope de Vega, painters Diego Velázquez, Francisco de Goya, and Pablo Picasso, and filmmaker Luis Buñuel.

The period from about 1500 to 1681, known as the Golden Age, is considered the most brilliant era of Spain's artistic history, with enduring contributions made in the fields of literature, theatre, architecture, and painting. Still, at no time has Spain ceased to be a culturally vital country, and the 20th century in particular proved a highly productive and creative one; indeed, its first few decades came to be called the Silver Age.

The Spanish Civil War marked a break in the development of the arts. Many leading artists and intellectuals went into exile at the end of the war. Within Spain the Franco regime practiced a sweeping censorship that limited artistic expression. Nevertheless, many Spanish artists made major contributions throughout the 20th century. Some sought inspiration in the country's history and folk traditions; others joined the most modern currents in their fields.

MUSIC

Spain's contributions to world culture are many, but none has been so universally well-accepted as its musical heritage, especially that of music performed on stringed instruments. Noteworthy Spanish composers include Fernando Sor (1778–1839), Isaac Albéniz, Enrique Granados, Manuel de Falla, and Joaquín Rodrigo, all of whom drew heavily on popular and regional music for their inspiration. In the hands of Spanish composers, the guitar moved from Rom (Gypsy) folk instrument to a staple of symphonies; from Spain have come such masters as Manitas de Plata, Andrés Segovia, Paco de Lucia, and countless flamenco and classical artists of great distinction. The flamenco tradition, derived from a marriage of Arabic and Spanish folk songs, carried over into southern Spain's unique "Rock Andaluz" movement of the 1970s and '80s, centred in Sevilla. In the 1990s Ibiza, a popular holiday destination in the Balearic Islands, emerged as a global capital of electronic music. Electronic artists and disc jockeys from around the world converge on the island each summer to perform at nightclubs and private parties, and music-related tourism has become a vital part of Ibiza's economy.

Spain is also well represented in classical opera, with Plácido Domingo, José Carreras, Alfredo Kraus, and Montserrat Caballé among the most renowned singers. The leading classical instrumentalists of the century were cellist Pablo Casals, pianist Alicia de Larrocha, and guitarist Narciso Yepes.

PABLO CASALS

The Spanish-born cellist and conductor Pablo Casals (born December 29, 1876, Vendrell, Spain—died October 22, 1973, Río Piedras, Puerto Rico) was known for his virtuosic technique, skilled interpretation, and consummate musicianship. Casals made his debut in Barcelona in 1891 after early training in composition, cello, and piano. After further study in Madrid and Brussels he returned to Barcelona in 1896 as principal cellist at the Gran Teatro del Liceo. By this time he had established his innovative technique; by making his left-hand positions more flexible and using a freer bowing technique, he created an individual style marked by seeming effortlessness and a singing tone. Casals toured internationally between 1898 and 1917 and formed a celebrated trio with Alfred Cortot (piano) and Jacques Thibaud (violin). Having won an international reputation as a cellist, Casals helped found in 1919 the École Normale de Musique in Paris and also established and conducted the Orquestra Pau Casals in Barcelona.

An outspoken opponent of Fascism, he was forced to move in 1936 to Prades in Catalan France. He refused to return to Spain after the Spanish Civil War (1936–39) and announced his retirement from public performance in 1946 to protest worldwide recognition of the Franco regime in Spain; in 1950, however, he returned to recording and conducting, choosing spoken over silent protest. In 1956 he moved to Puerto Rico, from which place he continued his personal musical crusade for peace until his death. Casals was a romantic who eschewed the drier, literal interpretations of modernism. His love for the works of J.S. Bach formed the core of his sensibilities. He revitalized appreciation of Bach's cello music, especially with his masterful rendition of the six unaccompanied suites for cello.

LITERATURE

Spain's loss of its empire in Latin America following the Spanish-American War (1898) provided the impetus for many Spanish writers, poets, and scholars to restore a sense of national pride. In their work, writers such as José Ortega y Gasset, Pío Baroja, Vicente Blasco Ibáñez, and Antonio Machado y Ruiz examined Spain's heritage and its role in the modern world. They and others who took up similar concerns came to be known as the Generation of '98. These writers helped revitalize Spanish letters and opened the doors for Spanish cultural development in the 20th century.

GENERATION OF 1898

The Generation of 1898 were the novelists, poets, essayists, and thinkers active at the time of the Spanish-American War (1898) who reinvigorated Spanish letters and restored Spain to a position of intellectual and literary prominence that it had not held for centuries. The shock of Spain's defeat in the war, which left it stripped of the last vestiges of its empire and its international prestige, provided an impetus for many writers and thinkers to embark on a period of self-searching and an analysis of Spain's problems and its destiny.

The term Generation of 1898 was used loosely at the turn of the century but was elaborated by the literary critic Azorín in critical essays that appeared in various periodicals and were collected in his *Clásicos y modernos* (1913). It was soon generally applied to the writers who concerned themselves with Spain's heritage and its position in the modern world. Never an organized movement or school, the Generation of 1898 worked in diverse fields and styles and rarely agreed on approaches or solutions to Spain's problems, but all had in common a desire to shake the Spanish people out of what they saw as apathy and to restore a sense of national pride.

Joaquín Costa, Ángel Ganivet, and Miguel de Unamuno are generally considered precursors of the Generation of 1898, but many literary historians consider Ganivet and, usually, Unamuno as members of the group proper. Other outstanding figures are Azorín himself, the philosopher and critic José Ortega y Gasset, the novelists Pío Baroja, Vicente Blasco Ibáñez, and Ramón María del Valle-Inclán, and the poets Antonio Machado y Ruiz and Manuel Machado y Ruiz. In their revitalization of Spanish letters, they brought a new seriousness of purpose to the Spanish novel and elevated the essay—critical, psychological, philosophical—to a position of literary importance. At the same time, they brought to Spain an awareness of foreign trends in literature and thought that enabled the Spanish people to reassess their own values in the context of the modern world, thus awakening a national consciousness that paved the way for Spanish cultural development in the 20th century.

Many of Spain's 20th-century authors have achieved international recognition, including five who won the Nobel Prize for Literature: dramatists José Echegaray (1904) and Jacinto Benavente (1922), poets Juan Ramón Jiménez (1956) and Vicente Aleixandre (1977), and novelist Camilo José Cela (1989).

The most famous writer of the century, however, was poet and playwright Federico García Lorca. Executed by the Nationalists in the early days of the Spanish Civil War, he became a symbol of art perishing at the hands of fascism. García Lorca's poetry is often couched in illusive symbolism and, like his plays, draws heavily on the folklore of his native Andalusia and especially on that of the Roma (Gypsies), or Gitanos. The suppression of instinct by social convention and the repression of women are the major themes of his plays (perhaps influenced by his own homosexuality), some of which continue to be produced and which inspired two films by Spanish director Carlos Saura in the 1980s.

Among the leading poets of the last half of the 20th century were Leopoldo Panero, Luis Rosales, Blas de Otero, Gabriel Celaya, Juan Luis Panero, Andrés Trapiello, Claudio Rodríguez, José Hierro, and Pedro Gimferrer, who wrote in Catalan as well as in Castilian. Prominent female poets in the late 20th and early 21st centuries included María Victoria Atencia, who was known for poetry inspired by domestic situations, for her cultivation of the themes of art, music, and painting, and for her later existentialist contemplations; Pureza Canelo, who was known especially for her ecological poetry and feminist volumes; Juana Castro; Clara Janés; and Ana Rossetti, who was noteworthy for her erotic verse. Contemporary Spanish poetry often uses colloquial language and explores intimate and social themes.

During the early 20th century many novelists experimented with form and technique and put less emphasis on plot and character. In the post-Civil War period a new generation of novelists, including Rosa Chacel, Miguel Delibes, and Carmen Laforet, avoided such experimentation and returned to a more traditional approach. Several noted writers, including Camilo José Cela, Luis Martín-Santos, and Rafael Sanchez

Ferlosio, focused on postwar social problems.

The late 20th-century novel showed a variety of trends. One was the use of everyday language to tell realistic stories, often based on historical events. At the other extreme were highly intellectual novels by writers such as Juan Benet Goitia and his small group of followers. In addition, some novelists, such as Terenci Moix and, later in his career, Juan Goytisolo, were strongly drawn to non-Western cultures. Among the ranks of leading novelists were Eduardo Mendoza, Carmen Martín Gaite, José Luis Sampedro, Javier Marías, Juan José Millàs, Antonio Muñoz Molina, and Antonio Gala. The detective novel became a popular genre after the 1970s, largely through the influence of Manuel Vázquez Montalbán; the work of his younger contemporary Arturo Pérez-Reverte, who writes both intellectual thrillers and historical novels, has been widely translated. During the 1980s and 1990s, new fictional paradigms emerged as exiles returned; new subgenres included the feminine neo-Gothic novel, science fiction, adventure novels, and the thriller. Despite this proliferation of modes, many novelists continued producing what might be considered "traditional" narrative. José Jiménez Lozano investigated Inquisitorial repression, recondite religious issues, and esoteric historical themes drawn from a variety of cultures in such novels as *Historia de un otoño* (1971; "History of Autumn") and *El sambenito* (1972;

"The Saffron Tunic"). He received the Cervantes Prize in 2002, as had Delibes (1993) and Cela (1995) before him. Francisco Umbral—a prolific journalist, novelist, and essayist often compared to 17th-century satirist Francisco Gómez de Quevedo y Villegas for his style and to 19th-century journalist Mariano José de Larra for his biting critiques of contemporary society—won the Cervantes Prize in 2000.

THEATRE

Spain has been an important centre of world theatre since the Roman era, when playwrights such as Lucius Annaeus Seneca, a native of Córdoba, produced popular and enduring works that would exert great influence in the 16th and 17th centuries—the so-called Golden Age. Whereas medieval drama tended to be closely tied to the Roman Catholic Church, focusing on miracle and Passion plays and on religious themes, the pioneering 16th-century dramatist Juan del Encina helped revive classical theatrical forms. During this profoundly inventive period, a national theatre emerged, fuelled by the energies of artists such as Lope de Vega, Guillén de Castro, Tirso de Molina, Pedro Calderón de la Barca, and Miguel de Cervantes.

A time of relative quiet and cultural conservatism followed, as Spanish theatre became a shadow of the French—an irony, given that Pierre Corneille, Jean Racine, and Molière borrowed many themes and characters from Spanish

Golden Age originals. To further the irony, it was a French dramatist and stage director, Juan de Grimaldi, who helped revive the Spanish theatre in the 1820s by both translating French plays into Spanish and commissioning new works by Spanish writers. In the 19th and early 20th centuries, playwrights José Echegaray, Gregorio Martínez Sierra, and Jacinto Benavente helped elaborate this identifiably Spanish theatre, which would arguably reach its zenith in the work of Federico García Lorca. Although, as with other aspects of art and culture, the long Franco era discouraged theatrical experimentation, García Lorca's work informed that of playwrights such as Antonio Buero Vallejo, Antonio Gala, Adolfo Marsillach, Josep María Flotats, and Fernando Fernán Gómez. These and other writers have produced a significant body of theatrical work in Spanish as well as in other national and regional languages, such as Catalan and Basque. Most modern playwrights are active as well in other literary genres and media, such as poetry and filmmaking.

VISUAL ARTS

Spain's most important 20th-century painters and sculptors were all part of the international avant-garde. The most famous, Pablo Picasso, is considered by many to be the most influential European artist of the 20th century. Other leading figures were Juan Gris, Joan Miró, and Salvador Dalí. Among sculptors, the best-known figure internationally was Eduardo Chillida. Among the leading artists of the late 20th and early 21st centuries were the painters Antoni Tàpies, Miguel Barceló, Rafael Canogar, Manuel Millares, and Antonio Saura, along with the sculptors Pablo Serrano, Julio González, Pablo Gargallo, and Alberto Sánchez.

PABLO PICASSO

The Spanish painter, sculptor, printmaker, ceramicist, and stage designer Pablo Picasso (born Pablo Ruiz y Picasso, October 25, 1881, Málaga, Spain—died April 8, 1973, Mougins, France) was one of the greatest artists of the 20th century. Trained by his father, a professor of drawing, he exhibited his first works at age 13. After moving permanently to Paris in 1904, he replaced the predominantly blue tones of his so-called Blue Period (1901–04) with the hues of pottery and flesh in his Rose Period (1904–06). His first masterpiece, *Les Demoiselles d'Avignon* (1907), was controversial for its violent treatment of the female body and the masklike faces derived from his study of African art.

From 1909 to 1912 Picasso worked closely with Georges Braque—the only time Picasso ever worked with another painter in this way—and they developed what came to be known as Cubism. The artists presented a new kind of reality that broke away from Renaissance tradition, especially from the use of perspective and illusion. Neither Braque nor Picasso desired to move into the realm of total abstraction in their Cubist works, although they implicitly accepted inconsistencies such as different points of view, different axes, and different light sources in the same picture. By 1912 they had taken Cubism further by gluing paper and other materials onto their canvases. Between 1917 and 1924 Picasso designed stage sets for five ballets for Sergey Diaghilev's Ballets Russes.

In the 1920s and '30s, the Surrealists spurred him to explore new subject matter, particularly the image of the Minotaur. The Spanish Civil War inspired perhaps his greatest work, the enormous *Guernica* (1937), whose violent imagery condemned the useless destruction of life. After World War II he joined the Communist Party and devoted his time to sculpture, ceramics, and lithography, as well as to painting. In his late years he created variations on the works of earlier artists, the most famous being a series of 58 pictures based on *Las Meninas* of Diego Velázquez. For nearly 80 of his 91 years, Picasso devoted himself to an artistic production that contributed significantly to and paralleled the whole development of modern art in the 20th century.

ARCHITECTURE

Antoni Gaudí was the most famous Spanish architect as well as one of the most unusual architects of the early 20th century. Through an eclectic approach, he created a unique style reminiscent of the Mudéjar, an architectural style blending Muslim and Christian design. Despite Gaudí's posthumous prominence, during his life he had no influence outside of Spain and little influence within it. Most of Gaudí's work was done in Barcelona. His most famous building is the unfinished Expiatory Temple of the Holy Family. Spain's leading architects of the late 20th and early 21st centuries—some of whom attained international renown—included Josep Lluís Sert, Eduardo Torroja, Sanz de Oiza, Ricardo Bofill, José Rafael Moneo, and Santiago Calatrava.

CINEMA

Spain's film industry has always been small and economically fragile. A large number of the films shown in Spanish cinemas in the 21st century were imported, from other European countries and, above all, from the United States.

The Spanish film director Luis Buñuel is considered one of the greatest filmmakers of all time. Because he was in exile during the Franco regime, most of his films were made outside of Spain, first in Mexico and then in France.

The cinema suffered greatly from the censorship of the Franco regime, and it began to recover only at the end of the 1950s with the work of Juan Antonio Bardem and Luis García Berlanga. After 1970 a number of Spanish directors, such as Carlos Saura, Pilar Miró, Victor Erice, and Pedro Almodóvar, achieved critical success both in Spain and abroad. José Luis Garcí's *Begin the Beguine* (1982) won the Academy Award for best foreign-language film, as did Fernando Trueba's *Belle Epoque* (1992). However, Spanish films were not generally economically successful abroad, the one major exception being Almodóvar's comedies, especially *Women*

PEDRO ALMODÓVAR

Pedro Almodóvar (born September 25, 1949, Calzada de Calatrava, Spain) is known for colourful melodramatic films that often feature sexual themes. As a young man, Almodóvar moved to Madrid with the hopes of attending the Spanish national film school, but it had recently been closed under dictator Francisco Franco's rule. With this avenue blocked, Almodóvar purchased a Super-8 camera and began making his own short films.

His first feature-length film, *Pepi, Luci, Bom y otras chicas del montón* (1980; *Pepi, Luci, Bom, and Other Girls like Mom*), which Almodóvar also wrote, explores the punk rock scene in Madrid in the years after Franco's death. Ostensibly a comedy, the film also traffics in themes of rape, corruption, and revenge. After several other early efforts, Almodóvar wrote and directed a series of films starring Antonio Banderas. The first two films, *Matador* (1986) and *La ley del deseo* (1987; *Law of Desire*), deal with the intersection between violence and sexual desire. A dizzying farce called *Mujeres al borde de un ataque de nervios* (1988; *Women on the Verge of a Nervous Breakdown*) won international acclaim, including an Academy Award nomination for best foreign-language film. Almodóvar followed it with *¡Átame!* (1990; *Tie Me Up! Tie Me Down!*), which attracted criticism from women's advocacy groups for a plot in which a mentally ill man (played by Banderas) successfully persuades a woman he has kidnapped to fall in love with him.

Almodóvar's reputation soared with *Todo sobre mi madre* (1999; *All About My Mother*), which he also wrote. The film—the bittersweet story of a woman's search for her recently deceased son's father—won an Academy Award for best foreign-language film, and Almodóvar was honoured as best director at the Cannes film festival. He received similar praise for the emotionally charged *Hable con ella* (2002; *Talk to Her*), for which he garnered an Oscar for best original screenplay, in addition to a nomination for best director. Almodóvar subsequently directed *La mala educación* (2004; *Bad Education*), which takes on sexual abuse within the Roman Catholic Church; the family drama *Volver* (2006; "To Return"); and *Los abrazos rotos* (2009; *Broken Embraces*), a stylish exercise in film noir. The latter two films starred Penélope Cruz.

After more than 20 years, Almodóvar reteamed with Banderas for *La piel que habito* (2011; *The Skin I Live In*), a psychological thriller about a plastic surgeon who performs experiments on a woman whom he holds captive.

on the Verge of a Nervous Breakdown (1988), *Tie Me Up! Tie Me Down!* (1990), and *All About My Mother* (1999), the last of which won an Academy Award for best foreign-language film.

By the late 1990s a new generation of directors, benefiting from government tax incentives and increased exposure on the international film festival circuit, had begun to attract attention outside Spain. In the first years of the 21st century, intellectually ambitious ghost stories such as Alejandro Amenábar's *The Others* (2001) emerged as a genre that easily found audiences outside the country. Amenábar's *The Sea Inside* (2004) won the Academy Award for best foreign-language film, and his *Biutiful* (2010) earned nominations for best foreign-language film as well as for best actor (for the film's lead, Javier Bardem).

MUSEUMS

Foremost among Spain's many art museums is the Prado Museum in Madrid, which began construction at the end of the 18th century and was completed in the early 19th century. Many of its paintings came from royal collections of the 16th and 17th centuries. The Prado also has an annex housing 19th- and early 20th-century art.

PRADO MUSEUM

Located in Madrid, the Prado Museum houses the world's richest and most comprehensive collection of Spanish painting, as well as masterpieces of other schools of European painting, especially Italian and Flemish art. The Prado's building had its start in 1785 when Charles III commissioned the architect Juan de Villanueva to design a natural-science museum. The construction of the Neoclassical-style building was interrupted during the Napoleonic Wars, but it was completed under Ferdinand VII in 1819 and was opened to the public as the Royal Museum of Painting. In 1868 it became the National Museum of the Prado after the exile of Isabella II, who had enlarged the collection with paintings from the royal palaces and the Escorial.

The Prado's holdings originally consisted of the art collected by the Habsburg and Bourbon monarchs of Spain. The collection of Charles V (reigned 1516–56) was enlarged by Philip II (1556–98); both of these kings were important patrons of Titian. The royal holdings were further enlarged by Philip IV (1621–65), who commissioned his court painter, Diego Velázquez, to purchase paintings in Italy for him. Philip V (1700–46) added many French Baroque works to the collection, and Ferdinand VII assembled together all the paintings from the various royal collections (except those in the Escorial) in the new building of the Prado. In 1872 the museum acquired many notable paintings that were formerly owned by Spanish convents and monasteries. Further additions to the collections, as well as to the building, were made in the 20th century. In 1971 the Prado annexed the nearby Casón del Buen Retiro, which was built in 1637 as a ballroom for the Buen Retiro Palace. Work on a new wing began in 2002 and was completed in 2007. Designed by architect Rafael Moneo, it expanded the museum by more than 235,000 square feet (22,000 square metres).

The Prado contains the most complete collections in the world of the works of El Greco, Velázquez, and Francisco de Goya, as well as of such Spanish masters as José de Ribera and Francisco de Zurbarán. The museum also has important works by Hiëronymus Bosch, Pieter Bruegel the Elder, Raphael, Tintoretto, Paolo Veronese, Peter Paul Rubens, Rembrandt, Anthony Van Dyck, Nicolas Poussin, Claude Lorrain, and Antoine Watteau. It also has a fine collection of Greco-Roman statuary. In 1981 Pablo Picasso's *Guernica* (1937), named for the Basque town bombed in 1937 by the fascists, was added to the Prado's collection. However, in a controversial move, the mural painting was permanently transferred to the Queen Sofía Museum in 1992. This reflected the desire of the Prado's curators to focus on works dating from the 19th century and earlier.

Other outstanding museums in Madrid include the Spanish Museum of Contemporary Art, the Joaquín Sorolla Museum, and the Thyssen Bornemisza Museum. The Queen Sofía Museum (Museo Nacional Centro de Arte Reina Sofía), which opened in the early 1980s, is dedicated to modern and contemporary art. Important museums outside the capital include the Picasso Museum and the Museum of Art of Catalonia in Barcelona, the National Museum of Sculpture in Valladolid, the El Greco Museum in Toledo, the Guggenheim Museum in Bilbao, and the Museum of Spanish Abstract Art in Cuenca.

There are a large number of special-interest museums. Some of them are national institutions, such as the National Archaeological Museum in Madrid and the Sephardic Museum in Toledo, but many more are provincial or local institutions. There are also numerous museums attached to cathedrals and other religious institutions.

LIBRARIES AND ARCHIVES

Spain has some 6,500 public and private libraries. Some important ones, such as the libraries of the palatial royal monastery of El Escorial near Madrid and of the

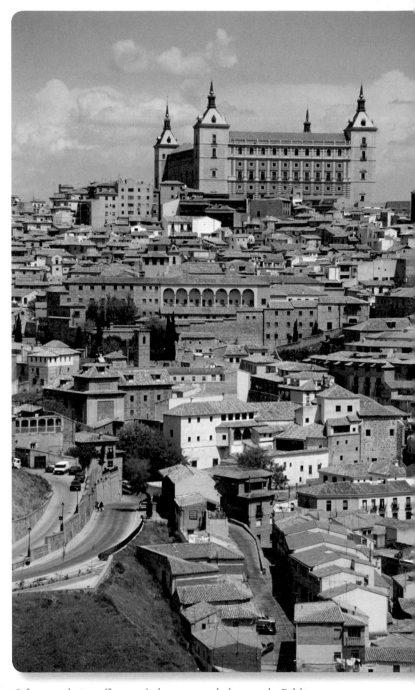

A former alcázar *(fortress) that currently houses la Biblioteca de Castilla-La Mancha (a regional library) and military museum in Toledo, Spain.* © Getty Images

University of Salamanca, date back more than four centuries. Others are more recent, notably the National Library in Madrid, which was created in the 19th century.

Spain has a vast number of public and private archives of various sorts: local, provincial, regional, and national. The most important are the National Historical Archive in Madrid, the General Archive of the Administration in Alcalá de Henares, the Archive of the Civil War in Salamanca, the General Archives of Simancas (established in 1540), and the Royal Archives of Aragon in Barcelona. Perhaps the most important for people outside Spain is Sevilla's Archives of the Indies, which hold an immense quantity of documentation about Spain's former empire in the Americas.

ACADEMIES AND INSTITUTES

Spain's oldest and most famous academy is the Royal Spanish Academy. Founded in 1713 under Philip V, the first Bourbon king, it was modeled on the French Academy in Paris. Its most important task is to "cultivate and set standards for the purity and elegance of the Castilian language"; since 1951 it has done this in cooperation with similar scholarly institutions in Latin American countries to promote the lexicographical corpus of Spanish in the world. As part of this work, it publishes a massive dictionary intended to be the definitive work of its kind for the language.

There are a number of other cultural and intellectual academies and institutes, most of which date from the 18th and the 19th centuries. These include the San Fernando Royal Academy of Fine Arts, the Royal Academy of History, and the Royal National Academy of Medicine. The most prestigious institution for research is the Council for Scientific Research (Consejo Superior de Investigaciones Científicas; CSIC), an autonomous public research organization based in Madrid and affiliated with the government Ministry of Education and Science. It was created in 1940 by the Franco regime to promote and manage research. Today there are branches of the CSIC throughout Spain, with the largest number of research centres being located in Madrid.

In its attempt to put itself at the centre of the international Spanish-language cultural world, Spain awards the Cervantes Prize, comparable to the Nobel Prize for Literature for all authors writing in Spanish. Among the recipients have been many of the leading Latin American writers. An agency for international cooperation maintains economic and cultural ties with the countries of Latin America and other countries with cultural links to Spain.

One of the most interesting cultural initiatives was the creation in 1991 of the Cervantes Institute. This government agency, modeled on the British Council and the German Goethe Institute, is responsible for promoting the study of Spanish language and culture abroad. In the early 21st century, the Cervantes Institute operated in more than 60 cities in some 30 countries throughout the world.

SPORTS AND RECREATION

Sports play an important part in the daily life of the Spanish people, and each region has its favourite forms of play. In mountainous Catalonia, skiing and other winter sports are popular; along the Valencia coast, windsurfing, scuba diving, and surfing have countless enthusiasts; in the Basque provinces, jai alai (a kind of racquetball) is a favourite pastime; and in Asturias and Andalusia, equestrian events draw large numbers of spectators and participants alike.

Despite the international controversy over bullfighting, the *corrida de toros* ("running of bulls") is still fairly popular in Spain. A staple of Spanish culture dating back to antiquity, bullfighting is considered the national spectacle, a rich pageant more akin to a beautifully choreographed ballet than a sporting event. It is seen as a heroic, albeit bloody, test of wills involving courage, intelligence, grace, and elegance. Spain's foremost matadors have been national heroes of mythic stature, as Manolete was in the 1940s. The season runs from March to October, with bullfights typically occurring on Sunday afternoons in major cities and in almost every town during local festivals. The mecca of bullfighting in Spain is in Madrid, at the Las Ventas bullring.

Spain's National Olympic Committee was founded and recognized in 1924. The 1992 Summer Olympic Games were held in Barcelona, where Spanish athletes earned 13 gold medals, including for football (soccer), swimming, running, and walking.

Spaniard Juan Antónío Samaranch served as president of the International Olympic Committee from 1980 to 2001.

Football was introduced into Spain by the British at the end of the 19th century (British miners established the first Spanish football club, Recreativo, in Huelva in 1889), and a professional league was set up in the 1920s. By the 1950s football had surpassed bullfighting in popularity. Spain's leading clubs have a distinguished record in European competitions; indeed, Real Madrid and FC Barcelona are two of football's most famous organizations. The Spanish men's national team won the Union of European Football Associations (UEFA) European championship in 1964 but then was long saddled with a reputation for failing to win "big" international matches. Spectacularly reversing its fortunes, Spain won the 2008 UEFA championship, the 2010 World Cup, and another UEFA championship in 2012 with a team that some characterized as the greatest national team in the sport's history.

At the end of the 1980s, football was challenged by basketball, whose popularity soared after Spain won the silver medal in the sport at the 1984 Olympics. In the early 21st century, a pair of Spanish brothers, Pau and Marc Gasol, became stars in the National Basketball Association. Other popular spectator sports include hockey on roller skates, motorcycle racing, and tennis. Cycling also has a large following, and Spanish cyclist Miguel Indurain was a multiple winner of the Tour de France.

REAL MADRID

Playing in all-white uniforms, which are responsible for the club's nickname, "Los Blancos," Real Madrid is one of the world's best-known professional football (soccer) teams, with fans in many countries. Real Madrid grew out of Football Club Sky, a team formed in Madrid in 1897. The club was officially founded in 1902 and joined the Royal Spanish Football Federation in 1909. Real Madrid played at a variety of venues until ambitious club president Santiago Bernabéu spearheaded the construction of the stadium that bears his name. Opened in 1947, the Bernabéu holds more than 80,000 spectators and was the venue for the 1982 Fédération Internationale de Football Association (FIFA) World Cup final.

The European Cup was first held during the 1955–56 season, with a prestigious field consisting of clubs that had won their own country's league championship. Real Madrid was the tournament's first winner, defeating French club Stade de Reims in the final. It continued on a run of European dominance that no team has matched since. Gifted players such as Ferenc Puskás, Alfredo Di Stefano, Paco Gento, Hector Rial, and Miguel Muñoz helped the club win the first five European Cups in a row. The club's play in the 1960 European Cup final against the West German team Eintracht Frankfurt—a 7–3 Real victory—is widely considered one of the finest club performances of all time. Real has won a total of nine European Cup/Champions League titles, more than any other team.

Real Madrid has won more Spanish top-division (La Liga) championships than any other Spanish side. The club has also won the Copa del Rey, the main Spanish cup competition, many times, as well as multiple Spanish Super Cups and two Union of European Football Associations (UEFA) Cups (1985 and 1986).

Real's local competition is Atlético Madrid, but the club's biggest rivalry is with FC Barcelona. The tension between the football clubs from Spain's two biggest cities was amplified by a struggle between the teams in the 1950s to sign the talented Argentinian striker Alfredo Di Stefano, who reneged on a proposed deal with Barcelona to sign with Madrid, helping Real become a football power in the 1950s and '60s. Matches between Barcelona and Real Madrid are known as El Clásico ("The Classic") and are watched throughout Spain, in large part because the two sides symbolize for many the ongoing political and cultural difficulties between Castilian (Real) and Catalonian (Barcelona) Spain.

From the late 1990s Real Madrid spent enormous sums on luring some of the world's most famous foreign players to the club, where they are known as *galácticos* ("superstars"). Those players were often the most expensive (by transfer fee) footballers in the world and included such stars as David Beckham, Luis Figo, Ronaldo, Zinedine Zidane, Kaká, and Cristiano Ronaldo.

Historically, the country has had a fairly poor record in protecting its natural resources, including Spain's rare wetlands Doñana National Park, from industrial development; despite this, Spaniards are avid users of their country's many parks and picturesque countryside.

MEDIA AND PUBLISHING

At the beginning of the 21st century, Spain had nearly 200 daily newspapers. By far the most widely read, and the most influential, is the liberal , published in Madrid and in other important cities and regions. *ABC* and *El Mundo* are also leading dailies. Published continuously in Barcelona since 1881, the conservative *La Vanguardia* has the widest Castilian-language readership in Catalonia. The leading regional daily newspapers are *El Periódico* in Catalonia, *La Voz de Galicia* in Galicia, and *El Correo Español-El Pueblo Vasco* in the Basque Country, all published in Castilian. There are other newspapers serving regional and local interests that are published in local languages. There are also several newspapers that specialize in areas such as sports and business. *Marca*, a sport daily, is the most widely disseminated daily newspaper in Spain. By the late 1990s most leading newspapers also published digital versions on the Internet. Yet, despite this large number of newspapers, overall readership in Spain is low by European standards, and most Spaniards get their news from nonprint sources.

There also are many weekly and monthly magazines published in Spain. The most popular and successful are those, such as *¡Hola!*, that deal largely in gossip about the lives of celebrities, both national and international. On the other hand, there are also a number of serious political magazines. In general, the boom in publishing that occurred in the aftermath of Franco's death had receded by the early 21st century.

Television was introduced into Spain in 1956. During the Franco regime and the first few years of the constitutional monarchy, there were only two television stations, both part of the government-owned and -controlled Radio-Televisión Española (RTVE). They still broadcast today, solely in Castilian, and have been split into separate organizations: Radio Nacional de España (RNE) and Televisión Española (TVE). Radio Exterior de España (REE) provides overseas services, broadcasting in 10 languages.

In 1983 the Catalan and Basque autonomous governments established television stations that broadcast in the regional languages; a Galician-language station began operation two years later. At the end of the 1980s, the number of television stations available to Spaniards increased rapidly. Moreover, in 1989 the government introduced legislation permitting the establishment of privately owned television stations. Three of these began to broadcast in 1990, and in subsequent years several others began operations. There are now several hundred television stations serving national, regional, and local audiences. At the same time, the availability of satellite dishes, which many Spaniards acquired, gave them access to channels broadcasting in a variety of languages, especially English, French, German, and Italian.

The most popular types of programs include game shows, soap operas, sports, movies, and dramatic series. Much of the programming comes from the United States, but a number of soap operas (*telenovelas*) from South America are very popular.

Radio broadcasting began on a small scale in the 1920s. A government station, Radio Nacional de España (RNE), was set up by the Nationalists during the Spanish Civil War, but the government never established the same kind of monopoly over radio that it held over television. The number of privately owned radio stations increased markedly during the 1980s and '90s, such that there were more private than public stations in the early 21st century.

CHAPTER 11

SPAIN: PREHISTORY THROUGH THE VISIGOTHS

The many and varied cultures that have gone into the making of Spain—those of the Castilians, Catalonians, Lusitanians, Galicians, Basques, Romans, Arabs, Jews, and Roma (Gypsies), among other peoples—are renowned for their prolific contributions to the world's artistic heritage. The country's Roman conquerors left their language, roads, and monuments, and many of the Roman Empire's greatest rulers were Spanish, among them Trajan, Hadrian, and Marcus Aurelius. The Moors, who ruled over Spain for nearly 800 years, left a legacy of fine architecture, lyric poetry, and science; the Roma contributed the haunting music called the *cante jondo* (a form of flamenco), which, wrote García Lorca, "comes from remote races and crosses the graveyard of the years and the fronds of parched winds. It comes from the first sob and the first kiss." Even the Vandals, Huns, and Visigoths who swept across Spain following the fall of Rome are remembered in words and monuments, which prompted García Lorca to remark, "In Spain, the dead are more alive than the dead of any other country in the world."

In 1492, the year in which the last of the Moorish rulers were expelled from Spain, ships under the command of Christopher Columbus reached America. For 300 years afterward, Spanish explorers and conquerors traveled the world, claiming huge territories for the Spanish crown—a succession of Castilian, Aragonese, Habsburg, and Bourbon rulers. For generations Spain was arguably the richest country in the world, and certainly the most far-flung. With the loss of its overseas empire throughout the 18th and 19th centuries, however, Spain was all but forgotten in world affairs, save for the three years during which the ideologically charged Spanish Civil War (1936–39) put the country at the centre of the world's stage, only for it to become ever more insular and withdrawn during the four decades of rule by dictator Francisco Franco which ensued. Following Franco's death in 1975, a Bourbon king, Juan Carlos, returned to the throne and established a constitutional monarchy. The country has been ruled since then by a succession of elected governments, some socialist, some conservative, but all devoted to democracy.

ALTAMIRA

Altamira is a cave in northern Spain that is famous for its magnificent prehistoric paintings and engravings. It is situated 19 miles (30 km) west of the port city of Santander, in Cantabria *provincia*. Altamira was designated a UNESCO World Heritage site in 1985. The cave, discovered by a hunter in 1868, was visited in 1876 by Marcelino Sanz de Sautuola, a local nobleman. He returned

Altamira, Spain, designated a World Heritage site in 1985.

in 1879 to excavate the floor of the cave's entrance chamber, unearthing animal bones and stone tools. On one visit in the late summer, he was accompanied by his eight-year-old daughter, Maria, who first noticed the paintings of bison on the ceiling of a side chamber. Convinced of the antiquity of the paintings and the objects, Sanz de Sautuola published descriptions of his finds in 1880. Most prehistorians of the time, however, dismissed the paintings as modern forgeries, and it was not until the end of the 19th century that they were accepted as genuine.

The Altamira cave is 971 feet (296 metres) long. In the vestibule numerous archaeological remains from two main Paleolithic occupations—the Solutrean (about 21,000 to 17,000 years ago) and the Magdalenian (about 17,000 to 11,000 years ago)—were found. Included among these remains were some engraved animal shoulder blades, one of which has been directly dated by radiocarbon to 14,480 years ago. The lateral chamber, which contains most of the paintings, measures about 60 by 30 feet (18 by 9 metres), the height of the vault varying from 3.8 to 8.7 feet (1.2 to 2.7 metres); the artists working there were thus usually crouched and working above their heads, never seeing the whole ceiling at once. The roof of the chamber is covered with paintings and engravings, often in combination—for example, the bison figures that dominate were first engraved and then painted. These images were executed in a vivid bichrome of red and black, and some also have violet tones. Other featured animals include horses and a doe (8.2 feet [2.5 metres] long, the biggest figure on the ceiling), as well as other creatures rendered in a simpler style. Numerous additional engravings in this chamber include eight anthropomorphic figures, some handprints, and hand stencils. The other galleries of the cave contain a variety of black-painted and engraved figures. In many cases the creator of the images exploited the natural contours of the rock surface to add a three-dimensional quality to the work.

The black paint used in the drawings was determined to be composed largely of charcoal, which can be radiocarbon dated. By the turn of the 21st century, this method had been applied to several images on the Altamira ceiling. Scientists now believe the ceiling paintings date from c. 14,820 to 13,130 years ago. In July 2001 an exact facsimile of the cave's decorated chamber, entrance chamber, and long-collapsed mouth was opened to the public at the site.

PREHISTORY

Human fossils in Spain belong to modern humans (*Homo sapiens*), the Neanderthals (*H. neanderthalensis*), and even earlier members of the human lineage, possibly *H. erectus* or *H. heidelbergensis*. A large number of bones have been recovered from caves at Atapuerca, Burgos, which come from sediments that are at least 300,000 years old. Other important sites are at Torralba and Ambrona (Soria), where elephants (*Palaeoloxodon antiquus*) were trapped accidentally in marshy ground and their remains scavenged. From these sites were excavated shouldered points fashioned from young elephant tusks, as well as hundreds of stone implements (hand axes, cleavers, and scrapers on flakes, made from chalcedony, quartzite, quartz, and even limestone) and wooden objects. Pieces of charcoal show that fire was known and used. But *H. erectus* or *H. heidelbergensis* humans were already living in Spain as early as 1.2 million years ago, as indicated by finds at Atapuerca and by stone tools recovered from beaches in the Algarve (Mirouço), Huelva (Punta Umbria), and Cadiz (Algeciras) and the terraces of the lower Guadalquivir, Tagus, Manzanares, and Ter rivers. Choppers, angular balls, and flakes from the terraces of the Jabalón River (Ciudad Real) are older than 700,000 years and perhaps more than 1,000,000 years.

Fossils of Neanderthals were found at Bañolas (Girona) and Cova Negra (Valencia). Fully developed Neanderthals, some represented by well-preserved skulls, come from more than 10 different localities throughout Spain, including Los Casares, Carigüela, Gabasa, and Zafarraya, with a cluster in Gibraltar (Forbes' Quarry, Gorham's Cave, and La Genista).

The appearance of modern humans (*H. sapiens*) in Spain after 35,000 BCE opened a new era, when material culture acquired an innovating velocity it never lost. Flint tools became more varied and smaller, and bone and antler were used for harpoons, spears, and ornaments. Needles from El Pendo Cave (Cantabria) hint at sewn clothing of furs and skins. Most remarkable were the intellectual achievements, culminating in the Paleolithic (Old Stone Age) caves found in the Cantabrian Mountains of northern Spain. These caves were painted, engraved, and sculpted and visited intermittently between 25,000 and 10,000 BCE. On the walls and ceilings are images of cold-weather animals—such as bison,

mammoths, Przewalski's horse, aurochs (wild oxen), and woolly rhinoceroses. Predators such as bears, wolverines, and lions are rarely represented, and depictions of humans are extremely scarce. Many caves (such as the group of caves at El Castillo, Cantabria) show rows of coloured dots, arrowlike marks, negative impressions of human hands, and signs interpreted as vulvas. Animals may be drawn skillfully in black outlines, like the horses at Ekain (Guipúzcoa), or painted in polychrome, as at Altamira (Cantabria), and in bichrome, as at Tito Bustillo (Asturias). These are scenes and standard compositions, but figures are also drawn singly (Puente Viesgo, Cantabria), engraved repeatedly, or drawn on top of other representations. Although the main animals hunted for food were red deer, ibex (mountain goat), and reindeer, the most common depictions are of aurochs, bison, and horses. Salmon, a seasonal food, was rarely drawn, and plants never appear. Similar themes occur on portable objects made of bone and antlers and on stone plaques. At the habitation site of the cave of Parpalló (Valencia), thousands of engraved stone plaques accumulated; although their interpretation is difficult, it should be stressed that Paleolithic art follows conventions. Figures are placed formally within selected caves (probably sanctuaries), with meanings hidden from modern eyes. Paleolithic visitors left stone lamps and pine firebrands as well as footprints and hand marks on muddy surfaces in the French caves of Fontanet, Isturitz (Haristoi), and Lascaux.

The complexity of the Paleolithic mental universe is demonstrated by the mortuary practice in two graves in the Cueva Morín (Cantabria), where four mutilated burials survived as casts formed by a compact, greasy sediment that had replaced the bodies. The dead were accompanied by meat offerings and ochre and buried below low mounds, on top of which ritual fires burned.

After 10,000 BCE the climatic changes accompanying the end of the last glaciation led to the disappearance of cold-tolerant game and the flooding of their grazing lands near the coasts. Hunters responded by widening their range of food and collecting quantities of marine shellfish. Such adaptations can be seen in caves as far apart as Santimamiñe (Guipúzcoa), Costalena (Zaragoza [Saragossa]), and Dos Aguas (Valencia). More than 7,500 figures painted by these hunters and gatherers are known from all over the eastern and southern Iberian Peninsula, dating from 7000 to 3500 BCE and giving tantalizing glimpses of their society. Located in the open air, usually beneath rock overhangs or in protecting hollows, are animated representations of people dancing (two women in voluminous skirts at Dos Aguas; three women in skirts and two nude ithyphallic men at the Barranco del Pajarejo, Albarracín), fighting, robbing honey, stalking red deer, and hunting wild goats. Some scenes are constructed around a narrative. The Remigia Cave and the series of 10 cavities with outstanding paintings at the Cingle de La Gasulla (Castellón) next to it show

scenes of remarkable activities; in cavity IX two matched groups of archers, led by a man sporting a headdress, are engaged in hand-to-hand combat, while nearby in the rock shelter of Les Dogues another combat pits two bands of archers rhythmically against each other at close range. Bees are depicted more than 200 times, often near hives, and in cavity IV of the Cingle de la Ermita del Barranc Fondo (La Valltorta, Castellón) a scene shows a long fibre ladder with men climbing it to reach a hive defended by oversized bees. Other well-preserved groups of paintings are found at Minateda and Alpera (Albacete) and around Bicorp (Valencia).

The craft of pottery making and the cultivation of domestic cereals and livestock that characterize the Neolithic (New Stone Age) economy in Europe reached Spain from the central Mediterranean, and perhaps from northwestern Africa, after 6000 BCE. Although agriculture and husbandry were known early in eastern and southern Spain, they were assimilated extremely slowly and irregularly. Caves and sites conveniently located for hunting, like those around Montserrat (Barcelona) and at La Sarsa (Valencia) and Carigüela (Granada), were still preferred, and people lived in extended families or small bands. A different pattern prevailed in southwestern Spain and Portugal, where the advent of the Neolithic Period came later, between 4500 and 3800 BCE. By 4000 BCE the first big collective tombs were built from boulders, and by 3500 BCE funerary monuments were prominent in the landscapes of Alentejo (Portugal), Extremadura, and the Atlantic littoral. Veritable megalithic cemeteries arose around Pavia and Reguengos de Monsaraz (Alentejo).

Significant changes in technology and social organization occurred after 3200 BCE. Skills in copper working were accompanied by a tendency to live in larger village communities. Differences in natural resources and population density meant that regions developed unequally, and centres of innovation are known all around the southern and southwestern coasts of Spain and Portugal. Particularly impressive is the settlement at Los Millares (Almería), which extends over five acres (two hectares) and is protected by triple walls of stone reinforced with towers at regular intervals. A formidable barbican with arrow slits and guard chambers projected from the gateway. These defenses stretch over 330 yards (300 metres) and cut off a triangle of land high above the Andarax River, with a cemetery of more than 70 collective tombs lying just outside the walls. On the nearby hills, 10 or 15 smaller citadels watched over the natural approaches to the village. Modest dwellings lay inside, and an especially large building was used as a workshop to melt copper and to cast objects in simple molds; the metal wastes and crucibles show that pure copper and copper mixed with a small amount of arsenic as a hardening agent were regularly selected. Mines and copper smelting slags of this date are known from the Alhamilla highlands, less than 12 miles (20 km) to the east. Smaller,

undefended villages are known from El Barranquete and Almizaraque (Almería). The agricultural economy was based on growing wheat and barley, raising common domestic animals such as cattle, pigs, sheep, and goats, and probably tilling small areas of river bottomland, the only land plentifully watered in this arid region. Varied grave goods such as copper implements, personal ornaments, and decorated vessels for drinking and feasting (called bell beakers from their distinctive shape) indicate a stratified tribal society at Los Millares with marked inequality of riches and access to the good things in life. The defenses and multiple forts suggest social instability and the raiding and fighting that went with it. Similar villages and their megalithic tombs are known in the western outskirts of Sevilla (Seville), eastward at the Cabezo del Plomo (Murcia), and at Vila Nova de São Pedro and Zambujal north of Lisbon (Portugal).

Many Copper Age villages were abandoned by 2000 BCE, and Bronze Age settlement shifted to new sites, sometimes only a few hundred yards away. Steep hilltops were favoured for their inaccessibility, and in southeastern Spain the custom of burying people below the floors of their houses replaced the collective practices of the Copper Age societies. Social stratification is very marked at settlement sites like El Argar and El Oficio (Almería), where the richest women were adorned with silver diadems while their male consorts were equipped with bronze swords, axes, and polished pottery. At

Fuente-Álamo (Almería) the elite lived apart from the village, in square stone houses with round granaries and a water cistern nearby. Such customs were practiced with less intensity on the southern Meseta, where fortified hamlets known as *motillas* dominated a flat landscape. In eastern and northern Spain people did not live in villages at all but in hamlets such as Moncín (Zaragoza) or on isolated family farms such as El Castillo (Frías de Albarracín, Teruel). In the wetter regions of Spain and Portugal, along the Atlantic coast and Bay of Biscay, so-called *castros*—small settlements fortified with a deep ditch and inner bank—arose, with a flourishing bronze industry linked to southern Britain and France and a custom of burying hoards of metal tools and weapons. Mining for copper ores was practiced at El Milagro and Aramo (Asturias), where the last miners abandoned their antler picks and levers deep in the underground galleries. Such differences in settlement patterns and customs indicate that Bronze Age Spain was not homogeneous but a social mosaic that included centralized tribal societies as well as looser associations based on smaller units. Such Bronze Age societies were prospering when Phoenician sailors reached Spain about 800 BCE.

PHOENICIANS

Venerable historical traditions recount the Phoenician voyages to found new cities. Utica, on the Tunisian coast of North Africa, was reputedly founded in 1178 BCE, and by 1100 BCE the Phoenician city of Tyre supposedly had a Spanish colony at Gadir (Cadiz). Although intriguing, these historical traditions are unsupported by evidence. Excavations confirm that the Phoenicians settled in southern Spain after 800 BCE, shortly after the traditional founding of the greatest Phoenician colony, Carthage (now in Tunisia). Their search for new commodities led them ever farther westward and was the reason for their interest in southern Spain's mineral wealth. The untapped lodes of silver and alluvial deposits of tin and gold provided essential raw materials with which to meet the increasing Assyrian demands for tribute. By 700 BCE silver exported from the Río Tinto mines was so abundant that it depressed the value of silver bullion in the Assyrian world. This is the background for Phoenician interest in the far west.

Phoenician commerce was conducted by family firms of shipowners and manufacturers who had their base in Tyre or Byblos and placed their representatives abroad. This accounts for the rich tombs of Phoenician pattern found at Almuñécar, Trayamar, and Villaricos, equipped with metropolitan goods such as alabaster wine jars, imported Greek pottery, and delicate gold jewelry. Maritime bases from the Balearic Islands to Cadiz on the Atlantic were set up to sustain commerce in salted fish, dyes, and textiles. Early Phoenician settlements are known from Morro de Mezquitilla, Toscanos, and Guadalhorce and shrines from Gorham's Cave in Gibraltar and the Temple of Melqart on the island of Sancti Petri near Cadiz. After the fall of Tyre to the Babylonians in 573 BCE and the subjugation of Phoenicia, the early prosperity faded until the 4th century. Many colonies survived, however, and Abdera (Adra), Baria (Villaricos), Carmona (Carmo), Gadir (Cadiz), Malaca (Málaga), and Sexi (Almuñécar) thrived under the trading system established by Carthage for the central and western Mediterranean. Eivissa (Ibiza) became a major Carthaginian colony, and the island produced dye, salt, fish sauce, and wool. A shrine with offerings to the goddess Tanit was established in the cave at Es Cuyram, and the Balearic Islands entered Eivissa's commercial orbit after 400 BCE. In 237 BCE, shortly after its defeat in the First Punic War, Carthage launched its conquest of southern Spain under Hamilcar Barca, Hannibal's father, and founded a new capital at Cartago Nova (Cartagena) in 228 BCE. After the death of Hamilcar, Hannibal continued Carthaginian expansion in Spain, reaching the Ebro River—the limit imposed by Rome in the settlement of the First Punic War. A diplomatic dispute over Seguntum, a Roman ally in Carthaginian Spain, led to the outbreak of the Second Punic War in 218 BCE. Despite Hannibal's invasion of Italy and near victory there, Carthage suffered a crushing defeat in Spain in 206 at the hands of Publius Cornelius Scipio (Scipio Africanus the Elder) and ultimately lost the war.

GREEKS

Greeks from Phocaea reached Spain's shores, but by 575 BCE they had established only two small colonies as offshoots of Massilia (Marseille) in the extreme northeast, at Emporion (Ampurias) and Rhode (Rosas). There was, however, an older Archaic Greek commerce in olive oil, perfumes, fine pottery, bronze jugs, armour, and figurines carried past the Strait of Gibraltar by the Phoenicians. It developed between 800 and 550 BCE, peaking sharply from 600 to 550, and was directed along the southern coast in precisely the areas of most intense Phoenician influence and settlement.

Connected with this early commerce in the late 7th century are the stories collected by Herodotus about the kingdom of Tartessos (Tartessus) and its ruler, King Arganthonios, who befriended the Greek captain Kolaios after his vessel was blown off course. Tartessos was portrayed as a mineral emporium where Kolaios exchanged his merchandise for a fortune in silver bullion. The Greeks remembered this kingdom as a legendary world beyond their reach. Tartessos, in fact, was the late Bronze Age society in southwestern Spain that included the mines of the Tinto River in its territory; it flourished between 800 and 550 BCE.

After 450 BCE there was renewed Greek interest in Spain, although directed to the eastern peninsula rather than to the west and south. Greek objects were widely traded by Carthaginian middlemen, as the shipwreck at El Sec (Palma de Mallorca) suggests. The vessel sank with a mixed cargo including millstones, ingots, and decorated Greek pottery, some scratched with personal Punic names such as "Slave of Melqart" (MLQRT'BD) or "Baal is Merciful" (B'HLM).

IBERIANS

The indigenous Bronze Age societies reacted vigorously to the culture of the Phoenicians and then the Greeks, adopting eastern Mediterranean values and technologies. At first the process of assimilation was exclusive, affecting few people; then it gathered pace and volume, drawing entire societies into the transformation. Everywhere the process of change was rapid and intense, lasting a few generations between 700 and 550 BCE. As old patterns of patronage were overturned with the arrival of new prestige goods outside the control of the former rulers, new adventurers came onto the scene. Their traces can be seen in rich tombs around Carmona at cemeteries such as El Acebuchal, Setefilla, and in Huelva at the cemetery of La Joya. Princely wealth from La Joya included a chariot of walnut wood, an ivory casket with silver hinges, bronze mirrors, tiered incense burners, and ornate libation jugs. Gold jewelry is known from many spectacular treasures in southern Spain, of which the regalia from El Carambolo (Sevilla) and the mixture of jewels, engraved scarabs, and tableware of silver and glass from Aliseda (Cáceres) are good examples. Glass and ivory were imported, but the impressive goldwork of filigree and granulation was probably western Phoenician craftsmanship.

By 550 BCE a distinctive Iberian culture can be recognized throughout the entire south and east of the peninsula. The name Iberian was the one used by Classical writers, although it referred to a culture having an ethnic and linguistic diversity that remained politically distinctive until its incorporation into the Roman Empire. Iberian civilization had an urban base, and indigenous cities arose after 600 BCE, imitating aspects of the Phoenician and Greek colonies. They were especially large and numerous in western Andalusia (Andalucía), at Ategua, Cástulo, Ibros, Osuna, Tejada la Vieja, and Torreparedones, and, somewhat later, also at the other end of the Iberian world, in northeastern Spain at Calaceite (Teruel), Olérdola, Tivissa (Tarragona), and Ullastret (Girona). Cities were political centres with territories; while some joined into confederacies, others were independent city-states. The urban heartland in western Andalusia prospered uninterruptedly from 550 BCE, but many towns in southern and eastern Spain were destroyed in the middle of the 4th century amid political turbulence attributed to Carthaginian influence.

The economy continued to be based on agriculture, though supplemented with cultivated grapes and olives of eastern origin. Ironworking was introduced by the Phoenicians, and iron was available everywhere for basic agricultural tools by 400 BCE; forging inlaid and damascened weapons brought the blacksmiths' art to a peak. The fast potter's wheel allowed mass production of crockery and storage vessels. There were many regional centres of production, and the artistic repertoire grew from geometric designs in the early stages to complex figurative compositions after 300 BCE. Important centres arose at Archena, Elx (Elche), Liria, and Azaila, whose artisans depicted scenes from Iberian myth and legend. Mining for silver continued at the Tinto River, expanding up the Guadalquivir valley to the area around Cástulo and to the coast around Cartagena. The scale of extraction at the Tinto River was enormous, and the Phoenician and Iberian workings built up more than six million tons of silver slag. Silver was abundant in Iberian society and was widely used for tableware among the upper class. An outstanding treasure from Tivissa has dishes engraved with religious themes.

Figurative stone sculpture shows Greek influence in the sophisticated modeling of human forms—especially in the friezes from Porcuna—and of animals. Sculptures of deer, griffins, horses, and lions were used as emblems to decorate tombs and were either placed on top of freestanding columns, as at Monforte de Cid, or displayed on tiered monuments. There are sphinxes from Agost and Salobral and a tower tomb from Pozo Moro (Albacete), built by 500 BCE, which is decorated with bas reliefs of the Lord of the Underworld in a style reminiscent of 8th-century sculpture from northern Syria. Temples at the Cerro de los Santos (Albacete) and Cigarralejo (Murcia) yielded hundreds of stone human and horse figurines, respectively, while bronze was favoured for statuettes at the sanctuary of Despeñaperros (Jaén). Striking funerary sculptures of enthroned ladies, bejeweled and robed, from Elx and Baza represent the Carthaginian goddess Astarte; the throne had a side cavity to receive cremations.

Three native writing systems developed in Iberia. An alphabet derived from Phoenician signs was used in the southwest by 650 BCE, and alphabets based on Greek models arose in the southeast and in Catalonia after 425 BCE. Many inscriptions exist, including letters inscribed on rolled-up lead sheets found in houses at Mogente (Valencia) and Ullastret, but they cannot be read. Only the names of places and some personal names can be recognized. The Iberian writing systems remained in use until the Roman conquest.

CELTS

Inland Spain followed a different course. To the west and north developed a world that has been described as Celtic. Iron was known from 700 BCE, and agricultural and herding economies were practiced by people who lived in small villages or, in the northwest, in fortified compounds called *castros*. The people spoke Indo-European languages (Celtic, Lusitanian) but were divided culturally and politically into dozens of independent tribes and territories; they left behind hundreds of place-names. Celts, living on the central mesetas in direct contact with the Iberians, adopted many Iberian cultural fashions, including wheel-made pottery, rough stone sculptures of pigs and bulls, and the eastern Iberian alphabet (inscriptions on coins and on the bronze plaque from Botorrita [Zaragoza]), but they did not organize themselves into urban settlements until the 2nd century BCE. Metalworking flourished, and distinctive neck rings (torques) of silver or gold, along with brooches and bangles, attest to their technical skills. The Mediterranean way of life reached the interior only after the Romans conquered Numantia in 133 BCE and Asturias in 19 BCE.

SPAIN AND THE ROMAN CONQUEST

The Romans became interested in Spain after the conquest of much of the region by Carthage, which had lost control of Sicily and Sardinia after the First Punic War. A dispute over Saguntum, which Hannibal had seized, led to a second war between Rome and Carthage.

Although the Romans had originally intended to take the war to Spain on their own initiative, they were forced to do so defensively to prevent Carthaginian reinforcements from reaching Hannibal after his rapid invasion of Italy. Roman generals, however, had great success, conquering large sections of Spain before a disastrous defeat in 211 BCE forced them back to the Ebro River. In 210 Scipio Africanus resumed Rome's effort to remove the Carthaginians from Spain, which was achieved following the defeat of the Carthaginian armies at Baecula

(Bailén) in 208 and Ilipa (Alcalá del Río, near Sevilla) in 207. Scipio returned to Rome, where he held the consulship in 205, and went on to defeat Hannibal at Zama in northern Africa in 202.

After the expulsion of the Carthaginians from Spain, the Romans controlled only that part of the peninsula which had been affected by the war: the eastern seaboard and the valley of the river Baetis (Guadalquivir). Although over the next 30 years the Romans fought almost continuously, chiefly against Iberian tribes of the northeast, against the Celtiberians in the northeastern Meseta, and against the Lusitanians in the west, there is little sign that this opposition to Roman rule was coordinated, and, although the area under Roman control increased in size, it did so only slowly. The region was divided into the two military areas (*provinciae*) of Nearer and Further Spain (Hispania Citerior and Hispania Ulterior) in 197, after which elected magistrates (praetors) were sent out, usually for two-year periods, to command the armies; the Romans, however, were more interested in winning victories over Spanish tribes (and so gaining the accolade of a triumph—a ceremonial victory march through the city of Rome) than in establishing any organized administration. After the campaigns of Tiberius Sempronius Gracchus (father of the famous tribune of the same name) and Lucius Postumius Albinus in 180–178, treaties were arranged with the Celtiberians and probably with other tribes, as a result of which Roman taxation seems to have become more regular.

In the middle of the 2nd century, during a period when Rome was not otherwise occupied by fighting in the eastern Mediterranean or Africa, large-scale wars broke out in Celtiberia in the northern part of the Meseta and in Lusitania, which resulted in a series of consuls (senior magistrates) being sent to Spain. These struggles continued sporadically for the next two decades, during which Roman armies were defeated on several occasions, notably in 137 when an entire army commanded by the consul Gaius Hostilius Mancinus was forced to surrender to the Celtiberians. The war against the Lusitanians was ended only by the assassination of their leader, Viriathus, in 139, and the Celtiberians were finally subdued in 133 by the capture of their main town, Numantia (near modern Soria), after a prolonged siege conducted by Publius Scipio Aemilianus (Scipio Africanus the Younger), the grandson by adoption of Hannibal's opponent.

In the 1st century BCE Spain was involved in the civil wars afflicting the Roman world. In 82 BCE, after Lucius Cornelius Sulla captured Rome from the supporters of Gaius Marius (who had died four years earlier), the Marian governor of Nearer Spain, Quintus Sertorius, relying partly on his good relations with local Spanish communities, successfully frustrated the attempts of two Roman commanders, Quintus Metellus Pius and the young Pompey, to regain control of the peninsula, until Sertorius's assassination in 72 resulted in the collapse of his cause. During the wars between Julius Caesar and Pompey, Caesar rapidly secured Spain by a victory over the Pompeians at Ilerda (Lleida); but after Pompey's murder in Egypt in 48 his sons, Gnaeus and Sextus Pompey, raised the south of the peninsula and posed a serious threat until Caesar himself defeated Gnaeus at the Battle of Munda (in present-day Sevilla province) in 45. Not until the reign of Augustus, who, after the defeat of Mark Antony at the Battle of Actium in 31, became master of the entire Roman Empire, was the military conquest of the peninsula complete. The last area, the Cantabrian Mountains in the north, took from 26 to 19 BCE to subdue and required the attention of Augustus himself in 26 and 25 and of his best general, Marcus Vipsanius Agrippa, in 19. It was probably after this that the peninsula was divided into three provinces: Baetica, with its provincial capital at Corduba (Córdoba); Lusitania, with its capital at Emerita Augusta (Mérida); and Tarraconensis (still called Hispania Citerior in inscriptions), based on Tarraco (Tarragona).

ROMANIZATION

It does not seem that the Romans pursued a policy of deliberate "Romanization" of their Spanish provinces, at least for the first two centuries of their presence there. Scipio left some of his wounded veterans at Italica (Santiponce, near Sevilla) in 206, and the Roman Senate allowed a settlement of 4,000 offspring of Roman soldiers and native women to be established at Carteia (near Algeciras) in 171. Further veteran settlements were probably placed at Corduba and Valentia (Valencia) during the 2nd century BCE. There had certainly been migration from Italy to the silver-mining areas in the south during this period, and in Catalonia Roman villas, whose owners were producing wine for export, appeared at Baetulo (Badalona) before the end of the 2nd century. It was not until the period of Julius Caesar and Caesar Augustus, however, that full-scale Roman-style foundations (*coloniae*) were established for the benefit of Roman legionary veterans, some on already-existing native towns (as at Tarraco), some on sites where there was relatively small-scale habitation previously, as at Emerita Augusta. By the early 1st century CE there were nine such foundations in Baetica, eight in Tarraconensis, and five in Lusitania. An inscription from one of these colonies, the *colonia* Genetiva Iulia at Urso (Osuna), which contains material from the time of its foundation under Julius Caesar, shows a community of Roman citizens with their own magistrates and religious officials, a town council, and common land assigned to the town.

During the reign of Augustus and through the period up to the overthrow of the emperor Nero in 68 CE, native communities also began to model themselves on the Roman pattern, setting up public buildings (including a forum, buildings for local government, temples, and bath-houses); some acquired the status of *municipium*, by which the inhabitants gained the so-called Latin right, which afforded privileges under Roman law and allowed the magistrates of the town to become Roman citizens. This process was advanced rapidly during the reign of the Flavian emperors—Vespasian (69–79 CE), Titus (79–81 CE), and Domitian (81–96 CE). Vespasian is said to have granted the Latin right to all the communities of Spain, and, although this is almost certainly an exaggeration, epigraphic evidence from towns in Baetica (especially a long inscription on six bronze tablets from Irni [near Algámitas, Sevilla] unearthed in 1981) reveals the existence of a general charter for these Latin *municipia* issued in the reign of Domitian, requiring them to adopt the forms of Roman law and to organize themselves on lines not unlike those used by the *coloniae* of Roman citizens. It is likely that this particular interest in Spain resulted from the support given by Spanish communities to Servius Sulpicius Galba, who, while governor of Tarraconensis in 68 CE, had participated in the uprising against Nero and had been emperor for a few months in 68–69.

The extent to which the upper classes in the towns and cities of Spain, of both immigrant and native stock, were part of the elite of the Roman Empire as a whole in the 1st century CE can be seen by the appearance of men of Spanish origin in the life of Rome itself. These include the philosopher and writer Lucius Annaeus Seneca (*c.* 4 BCE–65 CE) from Corduba, who was the tutor and subsequent adviser to Nero, and the poet Martial (*c.* 38–*c.* 103 CE), born at Bilbilis (near Calatayud)—a *municipium* since the time of Augustus—who was active in Rome under the Flavian emperors. A growing number of Roman senators were natives of Spain, including Trajan and Hadrian, who later became emperors (98–117 CE and 117–138 CE, respectively); both came from Italica.

The same period saw a progressive reduction in the number of Roman troops stationed in the peninsula. During the Cantabrian War under Augustus the number of legions had risen to seven or eight, but these were reduced to three by the reign of his successor, Tiberius, and to one by the time of Galba's accession. From Vespasian's time to the end of the empire the legionary force in Spain was limited to the VII Gemina Felix legion, stationed at Legio (León) in the north. Both this legion and the other auxiliary units in Spain seem to have been recruited increasingly from the peninsula itself, and recruits from Spain served throughout the Roman world, from Britain to Syria. From the time of Vespasian onward, military activity in Spain itself was restricted in scope and occasional, such as the repulsion of an attack by the Mauri (probably Imazighen

Statue of the Roman emperor Trajan, who was a native Italica, Spain. Stevan Kordic /Shutterstock.com

[Berbers]) from Africa in the 170s and raids by barbarians during the chaotic period of the later 3rd century, which, according to some late sources, involved the sack of Tarraco. It seems probable that the legion VII Gemina was split in the late 3rd or 4th century, with one part being transferred to the *comitatenses*, the mobile army that accompanied the emperor. Certainly the remaining forces in Spain, further reduced by the removal of soldiers to fight in the civil war that followed the attempt by the usurper Constantine to seize power from the emperor Honorius in 406, were unable to provide much resistance to the Vandals, Suebi, and Alani, who swept across the Pyrenees in 409.

ADMINISTRATION

From the time of Augustus, the work of the provincial governors, who under the Roman Republic had been commanders in military areas, became more focused on the administration of their provinces. Baetica, the most thoroughly pacified of the three Augustan provinces, was governed by a proconsul chosen by the Senate in Rome, while Tarraconensis and Lusitania had governors appointed directly by the emperor (*legati Augusti*). These provincial divisions continued to be used down to the time of the emperor Diocletian (284–305 CE), who subdivided Tarraconensis into three sections—Gallaecia, Tarraconensis, and Carthaginiensis. In Baetica, financial matters were handled by another magistrate (*quaestor*), as had been the case under the republic, while in Augustus's provinces this work was done by imperial agents (*procuratores Augusti*). The administration of law, which had always been the responsibility of the provincial commanders, was undertaken at a number of centres, each of which had a district (*conventus*) attached to it: in Baetica these were Corduba, which was the provincial capital, Astigi (Ecija), Gades (Cadiz), and Hispalis (Sevilla); in Tarraconensis, Tarraco itself, Caesaraugusta (Zaragoza), Nova Carthago (Cartagena), Clunia (Peñalba de Castro), Asturica (Astorga), Lucus Augusti (Lugo), and Bracara Augusta (Braga); and, in Lusitania, Scallabis (Santarém), Pax Iulia (Beja), and the provincial capital, Emerita Augusta. The larger number in Tarraconensis, the result of the larger geographic size of that province, led to the appointment of an additional official (the *legatus iuridicus*) to help with the work, at least from the time of the emperor Tiberius (14–37 CE) onward. The extent to which the governor was regarded as the source of law in the province can be seen from the requirement set forth in the charters issued to *municipia* that local magistrates should post, at the place where they dispensed justice, a copy of the governor's edict specifying which categories of legal suits he was prepared to hear.

ECONOMY

The economy of Roman Spain, as throughout the ancient world, was primarily agricultural. In addition to the food grown for local consumption, there was a considerable export trade in agricultural products, which has been demonstrated by the investigation of shipwrecks and amphorae found in Spain and elsewhere in the Roman world. Particularly important are the amphorae from Monte Testaccio, a hill in Rome, still some 160 feet (50 m) high, that is composed mostly of the remains of amphorae in which olive oil had been carried from Baetica to Rome in the first three centuries CE. Wine from Baetica and Tarraconensis, even though not highly regarded in Rome, was shipped in quantity from the 1st century BCE to the mid-2nd century CE. Spain also was famous for the production of piquant fish sauces, made especially from tuna and mackerel, of which the most reknowned was *garum*. Glass, fine pottery, and esparto grass (for making ropes and baskets) were also exported from Spain. Mining was another highly important economic activity; Spain was one of the most important mining centres in the Roman world.

RELIGION

Religion in Spain was shaped by the spread of Roman control. Along the eastern coast and in the Baetis valley the anthropomorphic deities of the Romans absorbed or replaced earlier nonanthropomorphic gods, particularly in the Romanized towns and cities. In areas of Greek and Phoenician colonization, local gods were readily identified with Roman ones, the most striking example being the cult of Hercules/Melqart at Gades. In the north and west, native deities survived longer. In the imperial period the worship of the emperor was widespread, especially in the provincial capitals, where it provided a focus for expressions of loyalty to the emperor, and priesthoods in the imperial cult were an important part of the careers of local dignitaries. Mystery religions from the eastern Mediterranean appeared in the 1st and 2nd centuries CE, particularly that of the Egyptian goddess Isis. Christianity became established in the 2nd century, and the extent of its organization is attested not only by accounts of martyrdoms during the 3rd century but also by the records of one of the earliest councils at Elvira, about 306. It is noteworthy that Hosius (Ossius; *c.* 257–357), bishop of Corduba, acted as religious adviser to the emperor Constantine after his conversion in 312.

ROMAN REMAINS

Monumental remains of the Roman occupation can be seen throughout Spain, of which some of the most remarkable are the city walls of Tarragona and Lugo, the aqueducts at Segovia, Mérida, and Tarragona, the reservoir, theatre, and public buildings at Mérida, the bridges at Alcántara and Córdoba, and the towns of Italica and Ampurias (Emporion). Particularly fine collections of Roman art and remains can be seen in the National Archaeological Museums in Madrid and Tarragona and the provincial archaeological museums in Mérida, Sevilla, Zaragoza, and Barcelona, as well as in Conimbriga (in Portugal).

VISIGOTHIC SPAIN TO *C.* 500 CE

Roman rule in Spain, and elsewhere in the Western Empire, was undermined during the 5th century by the migrations of Germanic tribes that had settled along the Roman frontier and that came under pressure from expansion by the Huns. One such group, subsequently known as the Visigoths, a people that lived along the Danube River and converted to Arian Christianity, was authorized by the emperor Valens to settle in the empire in 376. Mistreatment by local officials and the failure of the empire to uphold its end of the bargain caused the Goths to revolt. In the subsequent Battle of Adrianople in 378, Valens was killed and his armies were destroyed by the Goths. Despite the extent of their victory, the Goths came to terms with the emperor Theodosius I and settled in the empire as *foederati* ("federated allies"). Theodosius's heirs, however, were less successful at containing the various Germanic peoples that had moved into the empire. In 406 the Ostrogoths attempted to invade Italy, and the efforts to stop them allowed the Vandals, Alans, and Suebi (Suevi) to enter Gaul and then Spain. After ravaging the country for two years, the Suebi and the Asding Vandals settled in the northwestern province of Galicia (Gallaecia). The Siling Vandals occupied Baetica in the south, and the Alans, an Iranian people, settled in the central provinces of Lusitania and Carthaginiensis. For the time being, only Tarraconensis remained entirely under Roman control.

The Visigoths also posed difficulties for Theosodius's heirs. The new king, Alaric, rose in rebellion soon after the death of the emperor in 395 but was kept in check by the general Stilicho. Rome's failure to make concessions to Alaric and the massacre of barbarian soldiers in the imperial army following Stilicho's execution in 408 led to Alaric's invasion of Italy and sack of Rome in 410, which sent shock waves throughout the empire. Alaric died soon after, however, and was succeeded by Athaulf, who moved into southern Gaul. Failing to win recognition for his people as *foederati*, or allies, of the empire, he was forced into Tarraconensis, where he was assassinated in 415. Under his successor, Wallia (415–418), the Romans acknowledged the Visigoths as allies and encouraged them to campaign against the other barbarian tribes in the peninsula. Those Alans and Siling Vandals who survived Visigothic attacks sought refuge with the Asdings and the Suebi in Galicia. In 418 the Roman emperor Honorius authorized the Visigoths to settle in Gaul in the provinces of Aquitania Secunda and Narbonensis.

The Suebi and the Asding Vandals meanwhile continued to lay waste to Spain. Led by King Gaiseric (Genseric), the Vandals crossed the Strait of Gibraltar into North Africa in 429. They subjugated that province and governed it and the Balearic Islands until the Byzantine reconquest in 534. In Spain the Suebi, initially pagans, accepted Arianism, but in the middle of the 6th century they were converted to Roman Catholic Christianity by St. Martin of Dumio, bishop of Braga. Their independent kingdom in Galicia survived until the Visigoths subdued it in 585.

The Visigoths, as allies of Rome, aided in the defense of Gaul against Attila and the Huns. However, the unchecked deterioration of the Western Empire resulted in the rupture of the fragile alliance between Rome and the Visigoths. Under the rulership of Euric (466–484), the Visigoths founded an independent kingdom in southern Gaul, centred at Toulouse. In Spain the Visigoths drove the Suebi back into Galicia and occupied Tarraconensis and part of Lusitania. For the moment the provinces of Baetica and Carthaginiensis were left to take care of themselves.

Despite the collapse of imperial rule in Spain, Roman influence remained strong. The majority of the population, probably about six million, were Hispano-Romans, as compared with 200,000 barbarians. Hispano-Romans held many administrative positions and continued to be governed by Roman law embodied in the Theodosian Code. The Codex Euricianus ("Code of Euric"), which was completed in 475 or 483 or under Euric's son a generation later, was written in Latin and designed as the personal law of the Visigoths. It also addressed relations between Euric's Roman and Visigothic subjects. In 506 Euric's son Alaric II (484–507) published a legal code, known as the Breviarium Alariciarum ("Breviary of Alaric") or the Lex Romana Visigothorum ("Roman Law of the Visigoths"), which was based on the Theodosian Code and meant to serve the needs of the Roman population.

Visigothic dominance over southern Gaul came to an end when Clovis I and the Franks defeated Alaric II at Vouillé in 507. As a consequence of Frankish expansion, the Visigoths were compelled to penetrate more deeply into Spain, where their kings eventually established themselves at Toledo (Toletum). Meanwhile, as part of his effort to reconquer the Western Empire, the Byzantine emperor Justinian took advantage of struggles among the barbarians to regain control of the southern and eastern coasts of Spain. For about 70 years the Byzantines maintained a foothold in that part of the peninsula.

Although the Visigoths had been in contact with the Roman world for more than a century before their effective settlement in Spain and had acquired a veneer of Romanization, significant legal, cultural, social, and religious differences kept them apart from the Hispano-Roman population. Aside from different languages and disparities in education, these diverse peoples were subject to distinct bodies of law. Although the Visigoths were Christian, they held to the Arian heresy against the Roman Catholic Christianity of the Hispano-Romans. The Visigothic king was theoretically ruler of only his own people, whereas the Hispano-Romans continued to profess allegiance to a rapidly vanishing imperial authority. A Roman law that prohibited

A page from the Code of Euric, a set of laws enforced in Spain during Visigothic rule. Universal Images Group/Getty Images

intermarriage between the two peoples was, however, abolished in the late 6th century. Still, the task of bringing the two peoples together and of achieving some sort of political and cultural unity was a formidable one.

THE VISIGOTHIC KINGDOM

The Hispano-Roman population did not easily absorb the Visigoths. Because the Suebi maintained an independent kingdom in Galicia and the Basques steadfastly opposed all attempts at subjugation, the Visigoths did not control the entire peninsula. To the great satisfaction of the Hispano-Romans, Byzantine authority was restored in the southeast early in the 6th century. However, in the second half of the century Leovigild (568–586), the most effective of the Visigothic monarchs, advanced the unification of the peninsula by conquering the Suebi and subduing the Basques. Ruling from Toledo in the centre of the peninsula, he transformed Visigothic kingship by adopting the throne and other Roman symbols of monarchy. A committed Arian Christian, Leovigild sought to unify the kingdom by encouraging conversion of the Catholic Hispano-Roman population to his faith. Despite his efforts to bring the Arian faith more in line with Catholic teaching and his emphasis on conversion rather than compulsion, Leovigild's attempt was ultimately unsuccessful and may have contributed to the failed revolt of his son Hermenegild (later St. Hermenegild), who had accepted Roman

Catholicism and hoped, perhaps, to become king. Hermenegild's rebellion, however, may have been incidental to his conversion, and Leovigild's policy of uniting this people through religion would be vindicated by his other son, Reccared.

Recognizing that the majority of the people adhered to the Catholic faith, Reccared (586–601) repudiated his father's religion and announced his conversion to Catholicism. As the Gothic nobles and bishops followed his lead, a principal obstacle to the assimilation of Visigoths and Hispano-Romans was lifted. Thereafter, the Hispano-Romans, no longer expecting deliverance by Byzantium, developed a firm allegiance to the Visigothic monarchy. As a consequence, Swinthila (621–631) was able to conquer the remaining Byzantine fortresses in the peninsula and to extend Visigothic authority throughout Spain.

Not only was the conversion of the Visigoths a sign of the predominance of Hispano-Roman civilization, but it also brought the bishops into a close relationship with the monarchy. Indeed, both Hermenegild and Reccared had close ties with St. Leander of Sevilla, who was involved with their conversions and was the brother of the encyclopaedist Isidore. Kings, imitating Byzantine practice, exercised the right to appoint bishops, the natural leaders of the Hispano-Roman majority, and to summon them to the Councils of Toledo. Although the Councils of Toledo were essentially ecclesiastical assemblies, they had an exceptional impact on the government of the realm. The bishops, once they had heard a royal statement concerning current issues, enacted canons relating to church affairs, but they also touched on secular problems, such as royal elections or cases of treason. Through their councils the bishops provided essential support for the monarchy, but, in striving to achieve a peaceful and harmonious public order, the bishops sometimes compromised their independence.

The hostility of the nobility to hereditary succession and an absence of natural heirs tended to preserve the elective character of the monarchy. Because the Visigoths had a reputation for assassinating their kings, the bishops tried to safeguard the ruler by means of an anointment ceremony. The holy oil manifested to all that the king was under God's protection and now had a sacred character. The bishops, hoping to eliminate the violence associated with a royal election, also devised the procedures to be followed. The royal household (*officium palatinum*), which imitated the Roman imperial model, assisted the king in governing, but when necessary the king also consulted assemblies of magnates and notables (*aula regia*). Dukes, counts, or judges were responsible for the administration of provinces and other territorial districts surviving from Roman times. Self-government had long since disappeared in the towns. Agriculture and animal husbandry were the mainstays of the economy. Evidence suggests that commercial and industrial activity were minimal.

The predominance of the law of the Hispano-Roman majority over that of the Visigoths was another manifestation of the ascendancy of Roman civilization. The form and content of the Liber Judiciorum,

LIBER JUDICIORUM

The Liber Judiciorum, the Visigothic law code that formed the basis of medieval Spanish law, was promulgated in 654 by King Recceswinth and was revised in 681 and 693. Although called Visigothic, the code was written in Latin and owed much to Roman tradition.

The primary innovation of the code was the designation of territorial laws. Of the 500 laws in the code, many were revisions of those dating from the time of King Leovigild (d. 586). They dealt with 12 areas: laws and legal administrators; courts; matrimony; families and inheritances; contracts; crimes and the use of torture; robbery; crime against property; the right of asylum (especially with reference to deserters from military service); the draft and division of landed estates; laws governing doctors and merchants; and laws for the punishment of heretics, public officials, and Jews.

The main contemporary value of the code is its detailed picture of the constitutional organization of the Visigothic kingdom and the information it provides about the "vulgar law"—i.e., Roman law adapted to fit the economic and social conditions of the late Roman Empire. The code continued to be used by the Christian judges of Muslim Spain, and it benefited from the renewed prestige of the Visigothic tradition that emerged during the Christian Reconquista.

a code of law promulgated about 654 by the Visigothic king Recceswinth (649–672), was fundamentally Roman. Although Germanic elements (such as the test of innocence by the ordeal of cold water) were included, the code consistently accepted the principles of Roman law, and, unlike Germanic customary law, it was meant to have territorial rather than personal application. The Liber Judiciorum was a principal part of the Visigothic legacy received by medieval Spain.

The extraordinary cultural achievements of the 7th century also testify to the continuing impact of the Roman heritage. The most prolific author was St. Isidore, bishop of Sevilla (Hispalis) from about 600 to 636, a friend and counselor of kings. In addition to his history of the Visigoths and theological treatises, his chief contribution to medieval civilization was the *Etymologiae* (*Etymologies*), an encyclopaedic work that attempted to summarize the wisdom of the ancient world.

Toward the end of the 7th century, a critical time in Visigothic history began. The deposition, through deception, of King Wamba (672–680), a capable ruler who tried to reform the military organization, was a portent of future problems. As agitation continued, Wamba's successors made scapegoats of the Jews, compelling them to accept the Christian religion and threatening them with slavery. After the death of Witiza (700–710), the persistent turbulence of the nobility thwarted the succession of his son and allowed Roderick, duke of Baetica (710–711), to claim the throne. Determined to oust Roderick, Witiza's family apparently summoned the Muslims in North Africa to their aid. Subsequently, Ṭāriq ibn Ziyād, the Muslim governor of Tangier, landed at Calpe (Gibraltar) in 711 and routed King Roderick and the Visigoths near the Guadalete River on July 19. The triumphant Muslims rapidly overran Spain, meeting only feeble resistance from the leaderless Visigoths. Although the kingdom of the Visigoths vanished, its memory inspired the kings of Asturias-León-Castile to begin the reconquest of Spain.

CHAPTER 12

CHRISTIAN SPAIN: FROM THE MUSLIM INVASION TO ABOUT 1479

Despite ongoing warfare among its various Christian kingdoms, a recurring theme in Christian Spain from the Islamic invasion of the 8th century to the coming of the Catholic Monarchs, Ferdinand and Isabella, in the late 15th century was the unification of the Iberian Peninsula under Christian rule. The Islamic conquest disrupted whatever measure of unity the Visigoths had achieved and raised new religious, cultural, legal, linguistic, and ethnic barriers to assimilation with the native population. A number of tiny Christian states eventually rose from obscurity in the northern mountains and, prompted by self-preservation and religio-cultural hostility toward Islam, initiated the Reconquista (Reconquest). Christian success was in direct proportion to the strength of Islamic Spain at any given time. When Islamic power waned, the Christians usually advanced their frontiers. The kings of Asturias-León-Castile, declaring themselves the heirs of the Visigoths, claimed hegemony over the entire peninsula. However, the rulers of Portugal, Navarre (Navarra), and Aragon-Catalonia (Spanish: Cataluña; Catalan: Catalunya), whose frontiers began to be delineated in the 11th and 12th centuries, repudiated and often undermined the aspirations of their larger neighbour. The Reconquista was nearly completed by the middle of the 13th century, by which time the Muslims retained only the small kingdom of Granada (Arabic: Gharnāṭah) in vassalage to Castile until 1492.

The Trastámara dynasty, which came to power in Castile in the late 14th century, gave a new impetus to the search for peninsular unity by using marriage, diplomacy, and war to acquire dominion over the neighbouring Christian kingdoms. At the same time, the Trastámaras struggled to extend royal power against the resistance of the nobles. Ferdinand and Isabella linked Aragon and Castile by marriage and also brought the Reconquista to a conclusion by conquering Granada. However, as they were unable to incorporate Portugal into a family union by marriage, the unification of the peninsula was incomplete. The political union of Castile and Aragon could not by itself, of course, overcome the two realms' centuries-old diversity of languages, laws, and traditions.

THE CHRISTIAN STATES, 711–1035

Soon after the Islamic invasion, fleeing Visigothic nobles and the mountaineers of Asturias united under the leadership of Pelayo (718–737), a Gothic lord, in opposition to the Muslim forces. Later generations acclaimed Pelayo's victory over the Muslims at Covadonga, about 718, as the beginning of the Reconquista and the "salvation of Spain." Alfonso I (739–757) expanded the Asturian kingdom by occupying Galicia after the withdrawal of rebellious Imazighen garrisoned there. He also created an uninhabited no-man's-land between Christian and Islamic Spain by devastating the Duero River valley to the south. The Basques apparently recovered their independence in the western Pyrenees, while the Franks drove the Muslims from Septimania (southwestern France) and moved into northeastern Spain. Although Charlemagne failed to take Zaragoza (Saraquṣṭah) in 778, his troops captured Barcelona in 801 and occupied Catalonia. This region, later known as the Spanish March, consisted of several counties under Frankish rule and long maintained strong political and cultural connections first to the Carolingian empire and then to the kingdom of France. Thus, for several centuries Catalans looked to the north.

By contrast, the Asturians turned to the south. After advancing his chief seat to Oviedo, Alfonso II (791–842) attempted to recreate Visigothic institutions. In the late 9th century Alfonso III (866–910) took advantage of internal dissension in Islamic Spain to plunder enemy territory and to seize notable strongholds such as Porto. He also initiated the repopulation of the lands reaching southward to the Duero that had been deserted for about a century. His construction of numerous castles to defend his eastern frontier against Muslim assaults gave that area its distinctive character and thus its name, Castile. During this time the earliest known Christian chronicles of the Reconquista were written, and they deliberately tried to demonstrate the historical connection between the Visigothic and Asturian monarchies. Portraying themselves as the legitimate heirs of Visigothic authority and tradition, the Asturians self-consciously declared their responsibility for the Reconquista of Islamic Spain.

However, Asturian leadership did not go unchallenged: King Sancho I Garcés (905–926) began to forge a strong Basque kingdom with its centre at Pamplona in Navarre, and Count Wilfred of Barcelona (873–898)—whose descendants were to govern Catalonia until the 15th century—asserted his independence from the Franks by extending his rule over several small Catalan counties.

The apparent weakness of Islamic Spain and the growth of the Asturian kingdom encouraged García I (910–914) to transfer the seat of his power from Oviedo southward to the city of León. Nevertheless, any expectation that Islamic rule was set to end was premature. During the 10th century the caliphs of Cordóba (Qurṭabah) not only restored order and unity in Islamic Spain but also renewed their raids on the Christian north. Although the Christians suffered great destruction, they occasionally won some victories. The triumph of Ramiro II (931–951) over the great caliph ʿAbd al-Raḥmān III at Simancas in 939 was extraordinary, but within his own dominions Ramiro encountered increasing hostility from the Castilians. As a frontier people hardened by exposure to the dangers of daily Islamic raids, they were disinclined to bow to Leonese tradition and law. Fernán González (c. 930–970), the count of Castile, defied Ramiro and established the foundations for the later independence of Castile.

With Islamic power steadily increasing in the later 10th century, the Christians suffered a corresponding decline. When ambassadors representing Ramiro III of León (966–984), Sancho II Garcés of Navarre (970–994), Count Borrell II of Barcelona (c. 940–992), and García Fernández, count of Castile (970–995), pledged homage and paid tribute to the caliph at Cordóba, the abject status of the Christian rulers was manifest for all to see. Yet, despite their acknowledgement of Islamic hegemony, the Leonese kings, adhering to Asturian custom, continued to assert their rights as heirs to the Visigothic tradition. Their claim to domination over the entire peninsula was now expressed in the idea of a Hispanic empire centred at León. As the century drew to a close, the imperial idea surely offered some comfort when Abū ʿĀmir al-Manṣūr (Almanzor), who exercised dictatorial authority in the caliph's name, regularly ravaged all the Christian states. His semiannual plundering expeditions in the north not only brought many slaves to Cordóba but also helped to divert the Muslims from his usurpation of power. After defeating Count Borrell in 985, he burned Barcelona and three years later plundered León; in 997 he sacked the great Christian shrine of Santiago de Compostela. However, with the death of al-Manṣūr, the caliphate of Cordóba disintegrated.

The demise of Islamic rule allowed the Christian states to breathe easily again. The ensuing civil wars among the Muslims enabled Ramon Borrell, count of Barcelona (992–1018), to avenge past affronts by sacking Cordóba in 1010. Alfonso V of León (999–1028) exploited

King Ramiro II, who defeated Islamic forces in 939 but faced opposition from his subjects in Castile.
DEA/G. Dagli Orti/De Agostini/Getty Images

the situation to restore his kingdom and to enact the first general laws for his realm in a council held at León in 1017. Once the threat of Islam seemed to be removed, the Christian rulers resumed old quarrels. Sancho III Garcés (the Great), king of Navarre (1000–35), was able to establish an undisputed ascendancy in Christian Spain for some years. As communication with the lands of northern Christendom increased, French influence grew ever stronger. French pilgrims trod the newly developing route to Compostela; monastic life was reformed according to the Cluniac observance; and various northern social ideas and customs altered the life of the nobility. Already in control of the counties of Aragon, Sobrarbe, and Ribagorza, and including Count Berenguer Ramon I of Barcelona (1018–35) among his vassals, Sancho III continued his aggrandizement by overrunning the county of Castile and challenging Bermudo III of León (1028–37). Sancho completed his triumph by seizing the city of León and taking the title of emperor in 1034, but his death the next year brought an end to the unity he had achieved.

THE MEDIEVAL EMPIRE, 1035–1157

By extending his rule over all the Christian states except Catalonia, Sancho III made an apparent advance toward the unification of Christian Spain. By choosing to treat his dominions as a private patrimony to be divided among his sons, however,

he turned away from the Leonese tradition of a united, indivisible kingdom. He assigned the kingdom of Navarre to García III (1035–54); Castile to Ferdinand I (1035–65); and Aragon to Ramiro I (1035–63), who annexed Sobrarbe and Ribagorza in 1045 after the murder of a fourth brother, Gonzalo. As each of the brothers assumed the title king, Castile and Aragon thenceforward were regarded as kingdoms. Bermudo III recovered León after Sancho III's death, but Ferdinand I defeated and killed him in 1037. Taking possession of the kingdom of León, he also assumed the imperial title. During the ensuing 30 years Ferdinand sought hegemony over all of Spain, triumphing over his brothers on the battlefield, capturing Coimbra, and reducing the Muslim rulers (*reyes de taifas*) of Toledo (Ṭulayṭulah), Sevilla (Ishbīliya), and Badajoz (Baṭalyaws) to tributary status.

Meanwhile, Count Ramon Berenguer I of Barcelona (1035–76) was actively fostering Catalan interests and relationships among the lords of Languedoc in southern France. He also published the earliest legal texts included in the compilation of Catalan law later known as the Usatges de Barcelona ("Usages of Barcelona").

Adhering to his father's practice, just before his death Ferdinand I divided his realms between his sons: Sancho II (1065–72) received Castile, and Alfonso VI (1065–1109) obtained León. However, the two brothers quarreled, and, following Sancho's murder in 1072, Alfonso VI assumed the kingship of both Castile and León. Before acknowledging him as their monarch, the Castilian nobility forced Alfonso to swear that he had not caused his brother's death. Among Alfonso's new Castilian vassals was Rodrigo Díaz de Vivar, known to history as El Cid Campeador (from the Arabic *sīdī*, meaning "lord"). Driven into exile by jealousies at court, he entered the service of the Muslim king of Zaragoza and later provided protection for the king of Valencia.

At first Alfonso VI took advantage of the disunity among the kingdoms of Islamic Spain to demand tribute from them, but he eventually determined to subjugate them. The surrender of Toledo in 1085 not only extended his frontiers to the Tagus River but also had great symbolic value. Possession of Toledo, the ancient seat of the Visigothic monarchy, enhanced Alfonso's claims to peninsular supremacy, which he expressed when he styled himself "Emperor of Toledo" as well as "Emperor of Spain." According to Muslim sources, he described himself as "Emperor of the Two Religions," thus underscoring his dominion over both Christians and Muslims. Thousands of Muslims and Jews, who in earlier times usually had retreated southward rather than submit to Christian rule, elected to remain within his kingdom. Also living in Toledo and the vicinity were many Mozarabs, or Arabic-speaking Christians. In succeeding generations the interaction among these differing religious and cultural traditions became especially tense.

Frightened by the fall of Toledo, the other Muslim kings of Spain appealed for help to the Almoravids of Morocco, an ascetic Islamic sect of Amazigh (Berber) zealots. After routing Alfonso's army at Zalacca (Al-Zallāqah) in 1086, the Almoravids also overran Islamic Spain's petty kingdoms. By restoring Islamic Spain's unity, the Almoravids halted any further progress in the Reconquista and forced Alfonso to remain on the defensive thereafter. Although El Cid

EL CID

Rodrigo Díaz de Vivar (born c. 1043, Vivar, near Burgos, Castile—died July 10, 1099, Valencia) was a Castilian military leader and national hero. His popular name, El Cid (from the Spanish Arabic *al-sid*, "lord"), dates from his lifetime. Brought up at the court of Ferdinand I, the Cid served the king's eldest son, Sancho II, in his campaign to gain control of León. On Sancho's death he shifted to the service of Alfonso VI, whom he had formerly opposed. His unauthorized raid on the Moorish kingdom of Toledo (1081) prompted Alfonso to send him into exile. He then entered the service of the Muslim rulers of Zaragoza, becoming known as a general who was never defeated in battle. Alfonso tried unsuccessfully to win him back during the Almoravid invasion of Spain. The Cid maneuvered to gain control of the Moorish kingdom of Valencia, finally succeeding in 1094. He was speedily elevated to the status of national hero, and his exploits were celebrated in a heroic biography and a famous 12th-century epic poem.

successfully repulsed the Almoravid attack on Valencia, his followers had to abandon the city after his death in 1099. Subsequently all of eastern Spain as far north as Zaragoza came under Almoravid domination.

As Christians and Muslims contended for control of the peninsula, steadily increasing northern European influences emphasized the links of Christian Spain with the wider world of Christendom. The leading proponent of the general reform of the church, Pope Gregory VII (1073–85), demanded liturgical uniformity by requiring the acceptance of the Roman liturgy in place of the native Mozarabic rite that dated to earliest times. He also claimed papal sovereignty over Spain, but, when the Spanish rulers ignored him, he did not pursue the issue. While French monks and clerics found opportunities for ecclesiastical advancement in Spain, numerous French knights came to take part in the wars of the Reconquista. The most fortunate among them, the cousins Raymond and Henry of Burgundy, married Alfonso VI's daughters, Urraca and Teresa, and thereby became the ancestors of the dynasties that governed León and Portugal until the late 14th century.

After succeeding her father, Urraca (1109–26), then widowed, married Alfonso I (the Battler), who served as the king of Aragon and Navarre from 1104–34. The tension and conflict that plagued their marriage from the beginning finally caused Alfonso I to withdraw to Aragon. Alfonso VII (1126–57), Urraca's son by Raymond of Burgundy, restored the prestige of the Leonese monarchy. His coronation as emperor—the first and last imperial coronation in Spain—in the cathedral of León in 1135 was intended to assert Leonese claims to ascendancy throughout Spain; however, the newly formed federation of Aragon and Catalonia and the newly independent kingdom of Portugal soon offered a daunting challenge to Leonese predominance.

After dissolving his marriage to Urraca, Alfonso I extended his frontiers to the Ebro River by seizing Zaragoza in 1118. Then, marching directly into the heart of Islamic Spain, he liberated the Mozarabs of Granada (Gharnāṭah) and settled them in Aragon. Thereafter, the Mozarabic population left in Islamic Spain appears to have been minimal. Before he died, Alfonso willed his realms to the military orders of the Hospitallers (Knights of Malta) and Templars and to the Church of the Holy Sepulchre in Jerusalem, but his people rejected this arrangement. The Navarrese, who had been ruled by the kings of Aragon since 1076, chose their own monarch, García IV Ramírez (1134–50), and the Aragonese asked Ramiro II (1134–37), the deceased king's brother, to leave the monastic life and accept the kingship. After marrying and fathering a child, Petronila, who could inherit the kingdom, Ramiro returned to his monastery. Petronila was betrothed in 1137 to Count Ramon Berenguer IV of Barcelona (1131–62), who assumed responsibility for the governance of the kingdom. Alfonso II (1162–96), the child of this marriage, united under his rule the kingdom of

Aragon and the county of Barcelona. Usually referred to as the Crown of Aragon, the federation of the kingdom and the county endured until the Middle Ages despite countless vicissitudes and disparate linguistic and cultural traditions. Catalonia soon emerged as a maritime power in the Mediterranean, while Aragon, an inland kingdom with an agricultural and pastoral economy, was controlled by a landed aristocracy. Both regions retained their characteristic customs and laws and vigorously opposed all efforts at assimilation.

The county of Portugal—originally part of the kingdom of León—which Alfonso VI had assigned to Teresa and Henry of Burgundy, also began to move from autonomy to independence. Teresa and Henry's son, Afonso I Henriques (1128–85), repudiated Leonese suzerainty and took the royal title about 1139. By becoming a papal vassal and promising to pay a yearly tribute, he hoped to safeguard himself against Leonese reprisals. Only in 1179 did the pope formally address him as king.

Meanwhile, internal dissension and the rise of the Almohads, a new Islamic Amazigh confederation based in Morocco, led to the disintegration of the Almoravid empire. The Christian rulers, seizing the opportunity offered by civil war among the Muslims, raided at will throughout Islamic Spain and conquered some important places. Afonso I, aided by a fleet of Crusaders from northern Europe, captured Lisbon in 1147, while Alfonso VII and Ramón Berenguer IV, supported by a fleet from Pisa (Italy), seized the great seaport of Almería (Al-Marīyah) on the southeastern coast. The fall of Tortosa (Ṭurṭūshah) and Lérida (Lāridah) to the count of Barcelona in the next year advanced the county's frontier to the mouth of the Ebro and concluded the expansion of Catalonia. Nevertheless, the Almohads, after crushing the Almoravids, invaded the peninsula and recovered Almería in 1157. By subjugating all of Islamic Spain, the Almohads were effectively able to halt any further Christian advance.

THE RISE OF CASTILE AND ARAGON

Alfonso VII subverted the idea of a Leonese empire, and its implied aspiration to dominion over a unified peninsula, by the division of his kingdom between his sons: Sancho III (1157–58) received Castile and Ferdinand II (1157–88) received León. Although the Christians remained on the defensive in the face of Almohad power, Alfonso VIII of Castile (1158–1214) and Alfonso II of Aragon concluded a treaty in 1179 apportioning their expected conquest of Islamic Spain between them. Castile retained the right of reconquest to Andalusia and Murcia (Mursīyah), while Aragon claimed Valencia. Nevertheless, Alfonso VIII's efforts to dominate the other Christian rulers provoked contention and warfare and thwarted any concerted effort against the Almohads.

Thus, in 1195 the king of Castile suffered a disastrous defeat by the Almohads at Alarcos (Al-Arak), south of Toledo. The other Christian monarchs, acknowledging that the Almohads threatened them all, came to terms with Castile. With the collaboration of Sancho VII of Navarre (1194–1234) and Peter II of Aragon (1196–1213) and Portuguese and Leonese troops, in 1212 Alfonso VIII triumphed over the Almohads at Las Navas de Tolosa (Al-ʿIqāb). The victory by the Christian forces was significant, marking the beginning of the end of the Almohad empire and opening Andalusia to the Christians.

While the kings of Aragon took an active role in the Reconquista, as counts of Barcelona they also had important relationships in southern France, where several lords were their vassals. When Pope Innocent III proclaimed a Crusade to check the spread of the Albigensian heresy throughout that area, Peter II, though no friend of the heretics, realized that his feudal rights and interests there were endangered by the arrival of northern French knights. In 1213 Peter was defeated and killed by the Crusading army at Muret after he went to the aid of his brother-in-law, the count of Toulouse. In the generation after his death, Catalan ambition and power were steadily curtailed in southern France.

As the Almohad empire fell apart in the second quarter of the 13th century, the Christian rulers reconquered nearly all of Spain. James I of Aragon (1213–76) utilized Catalan naval power in 1229 to conquer the kingdom of Majorca (Mayūrqah), the first significant step in Catalan expansion in the Mediterranean. The subjugation of the kingdom of Valencia was more difficult, especially as James was diverted temporarily by the expectation of acquiring Navarre. When Sancho VII died without children, the people of Navarre accepted his nephew, Count Theobald of Champagne (1234–53), as their king. Thereafter, French interest in Navarre steadily increased. Forced to give up his aspirations there, James I resumed the war against the Muslims and captured Valencia in 1238, bringing thousands of Muslims under his rule.

Meanwhile, Alfonso IX of León (1188–1230) drove southward to the Guadiana River (Wadi Ānā) and captured Mérida (Māridah) and Badajoz in 1230, clearing the way to Sevilla. When he died, his son Ferdinand III, already king of Castile (1217–52) by reason of inheritance from his mother, Berenguela, a daughter of Alfonso VIII, succeeded him as king of León. Henceforth Castile and León were permanently united. Using the combined resources of the two kingdoms, Ferdinand conquered Córdoba in 1236, Murcia in 1243, Jaén (Jayyān) in 1246, and Sevilla in 1248. The Muslims retained only the kingdom of Granada, whose rulers were obliged to pay an annual tribute to Castile. As a vassal kingdom, Granada by itself was not a threat, but, when supported by the Muslims of Morocco, this last outpost of Islamic power in Spain caused great difficulty for the Christians.

SOCIETY, ECONOMY, AND CULTURE

The development of Christian society and culture in the first 300 years after the Islamic conquest was slow, but major changes occurred more quickly in the 12th and 13th centuries. The size of the population grew, communication with northern Europe intensified, commerce and urban life gained in importance, and the Reconquista was executed with greater success than ever.

By the middle of the 13th century, the kingdoms of Castile-León, Aragon-Catalonia, Navarre, and Portugal reached the frontiers that they would keep, with minimal alteration, until the end of the Middle Ages. As a confederation of the kingdoms of Aragon, Valencia, and Majorca and the principality of Catalonia, the Crown of Aragon had a distinctive character among the Christian states.

The idea of hereditary succession gained early acceptance, but the vestiges of election could still be detected in the acclamation of a new king. Following Visigothic custom, the king occasionally was anointed and crowned. Peter II of Aragon, who received his crown in Rome from the pope, became a papal vassal and held his kingdom as a papal fief. The principal officials of the royal household were the chancellor, usually an ecclesiastic, who was responsible for the issuance of royal letters and the preservation of records; the *mayordomo*, a magnate, who supervised the household and the royal domain; and the *alférez* (Catalan: *senyaler*), also a magnate, who organized and directed the army under the king's command. The *merinos* or, later, *adelantados*, who functioned as provincial governors in Castile, were also drawn from the nobility. The Catalan counties initially were part of the Carolingian empire, but the various counts gradually achieved independence. The counts of Barcelona had gained an effective sovereignty over all of Catalonia by the 11th century. Under the count's direction, vicars (*vegueres*) and bailiffs (*batlles*), responsible respectively for justice and taxes, administered the Catalan territorial subdivisions. The privilege of immunity granted to bishops, magnates, monasteries, and military orders prohibited royal officials from dispensing justice or levying taxes in immune lands, except in cases of negligence. The immunities of the archbishop of Compostela in Galicia and those of the military orders south of Toledo were among the most important.

Feudal ideas emphasizing private and personal relationships exerted great influence on the governmental and military organization of the Christian kingdoms—most fully in Catalonia, where French influence was strong. As vassals holding fiefs of the count of Barcelona, the Catalan nobles owed him military and court service, and they often had vassals of their own. In the western states, royal vassals usually held land in full ownership rather than in fief. As vassals of the king or count, the magnates, called *ricos hombres* (i.e., rich or powerful men) in the west and *barones* in Catalonia, functioned as his chief counselors and provided the bulk of the royal military forces. Nobles of the second rank, known variously as *infanzones*, *caballeros*, or *cavallers*, generally were vassals of the magnates.

Agriculture and pasturage were the principal sources of wealth in the Christian states, as the king, landlords, and nobles gained their income primarily through the exploitation of landed property. Peasants dwelling on noble estates cultivated the soil and owed various rents and services to their lords. The serfs (*solariegos* in Castile, *payeses de remensa* in Catalonia), who were effectively bound to the land, bore the heaviest burden. The rights (the so-called "evil usages") of Catalan lords were such that they could abuse their serfs at will. Castilian peasants living on lands known as *behetrías* were free to choose their lord and to change their allegiance whenever they wished, but their right to do so was challenged in the 13th century. Life on the frontier attracted many peasants because, while it exposed them to risk and adventure, it also promised freedom. Like pioneers in all ages, they developed a strong sense of personal worth and independence.

The progress of the Reconquista made possible the colonization of the Duero valley, where fortified urban centres (*concejos*), each surrounded by a broad dependent rural area, were established. Royal charters (*fueros*) set down the rights and obligations of the settlers and allowed them to choose their own magistrates (*alcaldes*) and to govern themselves. The basis of the municipal economy was sheep and cattle raising and the booty won by the urban militia in the wars of the Reconquista. Industry and commerce were of secondary importance. The towns of Aragon and Catalonia had little autonomy, but some Catalan towns began to develop as important mercantile centres. The urban population increased significantly, and trade and industry began to develop substantially following the conquest of the Islamic cities of Toledo, Zaragoza, Lisbon, Cordova, Valencia, and Sevilla. Increasing numbers of craftsmen tried to protect their interests by organizing guilds. Merchants who made their living by large-scale commercial activity based on the use of money as a medium of exchange and credit instruments also became more numerous. A native overseas carrying trade began to develop as a result of the growth of shipbuilding at Santander, Barcelona, and other seaports.

Many thousands of Muslims and Jews came under Christian rule as a result of the Reconquista. The Mudéjares, as subject Muslims were called, were located mainly in country areas, but important Muslim quarters were also found in the towns. Jews, who were chiefly urban dwellers, engaged in trade and money-lending and often contracted to collect royal taxes. Both Muslims and Jews were required to pay a regular tribute, but otherwise they were allowed to worship freely and to administer their own affairs according to Islamic or Judaic law. On occasion, however, Christians assaulted their Jewish neighbours.

The increasing administrative, military, and economic importance of the towns eventually led the crown to summon municipal representatives to attend the royal council along with prelates and magnates. Alfonso IX convened the first such council (*curia plena*) at León in 1188, but similar assemblies appeared in the other states early in the 13th century. Later known as the Cortes, these assemblies performed a variety of functions, one of the most important of which was to give consent to the levy of extraordinary taxes necessitated by the king's ever-increasing financial obligations as royal activities and responsibilities steadily expanded. The growth of parliamentary institutions was a common European phenomenon, though it is noteworthy

MUDÉJAR

The term *Mudéjar* (from the Arabic *mudajjan*, "permitted to remain") describes any of the Muslims who remained in Spain after the Reconquista, or Christian reconquest, of the Iberian Peninsula (11th–15th century). In return for the payment of a poll tax, the Mudéjars—most of whom converted to Islam after the Arab invasion of Spain in the 8th century—were a protected minority, allowed to retain their own religion, language, and customs. With leaders assigned by the local Christian princes, they formed separate communities and quarters in larger towns, where they were subject to their own Muslim laws.

The Mudéjars were highly skilled craftsmen who created an extremely successful mixture of Arabic and Spanish artistic elements. The Mudéjar style is marked by the frequent use of the horseshoe arch and the vault, and it distinguishes the church and palace architecture of Toledo, Córdoba, Sevilla (Seville), and Valencia. The Mudéjar hand is also evident in the ornamentation of wood and ivory, metalwork, ceramics, and textiles; and their lustre pottery is second only to that of the Chinese.

By the 13th century, the Mudéjars, especially those in the kingdom of Castile, had abandoned Arabic for the Castilian spoken by their Christian neighbours. They continued to write in Arabic, however, giving rise to their characteristic *aljamiado* literature.

Although valued for their artistic and economic contributions, the Mudéjars faced increasing difficulties as Christian princes strengthened their grip on Spain, imposing an intolerable tax burden on the Mudéjars and demanding forced labour and military service from them. The Mudéjars also were expected to wear distinctive clothing and by the 14th century were forbidden to pray in public. When Granada, the last Muslim stronghold in Spain, fell in 1492, the situation of the Mudéjars deteriorated even more rapidly. They were now forced to leave the country or convert to Christianity. Those who stayed and accepted baptism, the Moriscos (Spanish: "Little Moors"), often did not truly convert and practiced their Islamic faith secretly. Christian authorities continued to persecute them, and by 1614 the last of an estimated three million Spanish Muslims had been expelled from the peninsula.

that it occurred at such an early date in the peninsular kingdoms.

Another consequence of the Reconquista was the restoration of former bishoprics or the expansion of existing ones. The five metropolitan sees of Toledo (which claimed the primacy), Tarragona, Braga, Compostela, and Sevilla formed the principal ecclesiastical divisions in Spain. From the 12th century the papacy intervened more frequently in peninsular affairs. The reforms of the French monasteries of Cluny and Citeaux had a profound effect on monastic life in the 11th and 12th centuries. The mendicant orders of Franciscans and Dominicans (the latter founded by the Spaniard Domingo de Guzmán) established themselves in the peninsula in the early 13th century. The military orders of the Templars and the Hospitallers, both founded in the Holy Land, came to Spain in the 12th century, but in the second half of that century several native orders were organized—Calatrava, Alcántara, Santiago, and Avis. The knights followed a modified form of the monastic life, but they also played an increasingly important role in the military struggle against Islam.

Ancient cultural traditions were preserved by the clergy, who also authored the few books that have survived from the early centuries of the Reconquista. In the 8th century Bishops Elipandus of Toledo and Felix of Urgel advocated the teachings of Adoptionism, a Christian heresy that maintained that Christ in his humanity was the adopted son of God. The dispute over this teaching gave rise to several polemical works and brought condemnations from Charlemagne and his court and Popes Adrian I and Leo III. In the 9th century Eulogius and Alvarus of Córdoba produced many books defending their fellow Mozarabic Christians who had blasphemed Muhammad publicly in Córdoba and were then martyred by the Muslims of the city. Christians in Spain, however, not only involved themselves in writing polemics against Islam but participated in the important work of translating the Qur'ān and other Islamic religious texts in the 12th century for Peter the Venerable, the abbot of Cluny. Early in the 13th century Alfonso VIII of Castile and Alfonso IX of León founded the Universities of Palencia and Salamanca, respectively, for the study of theology, philosophy, and Roman and canon law. Although Palencia ceased instruction by the middle of the century, Salamanca eventually attained international renown. The appearance in the mid-12th century of the first great epic in the Castilian tongue, *Poema del Cid* (*The Poem of the Cid*), signaled the beginning of the development of a significant vernacular literature. Although the literary production of Spanish authors was still limited, through his historical works Rodrigo Jiménez de Rada, archbishop of Toledo (died 1247), fixed the standard for Spanish historiography for centuries to come.

CASTILE AND LEÓN, 1252–1479

As the kings of Castile endeavoured to strengthen monarchical power in the late medieval centuries, they encountered a stiff challenge from the nobility, who tried to use the institutions of government for their own interests. The struggle for power commenced during the reign of Alfonso X (the Learned, 1252–84), who is perhaps best known for the literary and scientific achievements under his direction by scholars whom he summoned to his court. His aim to gain control of the Moroccan ports giving access to the Iberian Peninsula provoked a revolt in 1264–66 by the Mudéjares of Andalusia and Murcia, abetted by the king of Granada. Elected Holy Roman emperor in 1257, Alfonso spent the next 17 years engaged in a vain effort to counter a rival claimant and to secure papal acceptance. His expenditure of great sums of money on this enterprise and his innovations in taxation and legislation eventually brought about a grave challenge to his rule.

Alfonso concluded that a uniform royal law was necessary to overcome the multiplicity and diversity of local and regional laws, such as the municipal *fueros* and the Liber Judiciorum used in León (which Ferdinand III had translated into Castilian as the Fuero Juzgo). The Espéculo, a code of law intended for use in the royal court, and the Fuero Real, a code of municipal law meant for the towns of Castile and Extremadura, were drawn up and likely promulgated in 1254. Between 1256 and 1265 royal jurists, drawing heavily on Roman law, revised and amplified the Espéculo, which in its new form came to be known as the Siete Partidas (Seven Divisions). The nobles and the towns objected to these changes in the law and

in 1272 compelled the king to confirm their traditional laws and customs. To underscore their opposition to royal policy, the magnates went into exile in Granada for two years. Following this setback, the pope in 1274 refused to recognize Alfonso's imperial claims, and the king's eldest son and heir, Fernando de la Cerda, died in 1275 while hastening to repel a Moroccan invasion. A dispute over the succession then ensued between the adherents of Fernando de la Cerda's son, Alfonso, and the king's second son, Sancho. Although the king recognized Sancho, their relationship deteriorated, in part because Alfonso X's ill health rendered him less able to carry out his duties and caused him to act arbitrarily. In 1282 an assembly of nobles, prelates, and townsmen transferred the responsibilities of government from the king to Sancho. While the Muslims continued to threaten the kingdom externally, Castile was torn apart by civil war until the king's death.

During the reign of Sancho IV (1284–95), domestic and foreign supporters of his nephew maintained a steady opposition. At the same time, Sancho had to defend the realm against another Muslim invasion from Morocco. Thus began a long struggle to control the Strait of Gibraltar and to close that invasion route. During the minority of Ferdinand IV (1295–1312), new efforts were made in favour of Alfonso de la Cerda, but in 1304 he renounced all claims to any portion of the Crown of Castile. Although the king seized Gibraltar in 1309, the Muslims regained possession a quarter century

Depiction of King Alfonso XI (center, on horseback) fighting in the Battle of Salado River. The victory effectively quashed Moroccan attempts to gain a stronghold in Spain. Universal Images Group/Getty Images

later. The minority of Alfonso XI (1312–50) witnessed new disorders, but when Alfonso reached adulthood he brutally crushed his enemies among the nobility. Aided by his Christian neighbours, he gained a great triumph over the allied Islamic forces from Granada and Morocco at the Salado River in 1340 and thus ended for good all Moroccan attempts to establish a base in Spain. He captured Algeciras (Al-Jazīrah al-Khaḍrāˇ) four years later, but he was unable to take the nearby fortress of Gibraltar because he fell victim to the Black Death.

During the reign of Peter the Cruel (1350–69), the monarchy and the nobility again came into violent conflict. Challenging the king's right to rule, his half brother, Henry of Trastámara, an illegitimate son of Alfonso XI, appealed to France for support. Backed by a mercenary army commanded by the Frenchman Bertrand du Guesclin, Henry was able to eject Peter from the kingdom in 1366. In order to recover his throne, the king enlisted the help of Edward, prince of Wales, and a combined Anglo-Castilian army defeated Henry of Trastámara at Nájera in 1367. After Edward's withdrawal, however, Henry and du Guesclin defeated and killed Peter at Montiel in 1369.

As the first of the Trastámara dynasty, Henry II (1369–79) had to maintain his rights to the throne against his peninsular neighbours and domestic enemies. He eventually overcame his opponents and was even able to assist his French allies by providing a fleet to attack English shipping. As an ally of France, Henry's son John I (1379–90) acknowledged the Avignonese pope during the Great Schism. The Trastámara family's aspirations to acquire the other peninsular kingdoms were first manifested when John claimed Portugal by right of marriage. His invasion in 1385 roused the Portuguese national spirit, and he suffered a grievous defeat at Aljubarrota. Then John of Gaunt, duke of Lancaster, claiming the Castilian throne as the husband of Peter I's daughter, landed in Galicia in 1386. Although John was aided by the Portuguese, he was unsuccessful and came to terms in 1388. The marriage of his daughter Catherine to Henry III, John I's oldest son, ended the hostility between the two branches of the Castilian royal family.

The nobility took advantage of the minority of Henry III (1390–1406) to pursue their own gain at royal expense, but, once the king reached adult age, he strongly asserted his power. However, royal prestige and authority suffered terribly during the long reign of his son, John II (1406–54). The king's uncle, Fernando de Antequera, who acted as regent, maintained stability until he was elected king of Aragon in 1412. John II, a weak and disinterested monarch, allowed Álvaro de Luna, the royal favourite, to dominate him and to direct royal policy. Fernando's sons, Henry and John of Navarre, tried to gain control of the king and the organs of government, but Luna successfully thwarted their schemes. Luna retained effective authority during most of the reign, but in 1453 he incurred the king's wrath and was summarily executed.

The nobles continued to engage in an intense struggle for influence and power in the reign of Henry IV (1454–74). Although Juan Pacheco, marqués de Villena, initially gained ascendancy over the king, others vied for royal favour. The nobles, alleging Henry's impotence, refused to accept the legitimacy of the infanta Joan, who they declared was the child of the queen and of the king's most recent favourite, Beltrán de la Cueva. Because of that account, the young girl was derided as "La Beltraneja." Henry IV repudiated her and recognized his sister Isabella as heir to the throne in the Pact of Los Toros de Guisando in 1468. Although Villena and his supporters hoped to control Isabella, they soon learned that they could not. Without first seeking her brother's consent as she had promised, in 1469 Isabella married Ferdinand, son and heir of John II of Aragon. An angry Henry IV denounced her and tried to exclude her from the succession, but when he died she was proclaimed Queen Isabella I (1474–1504). Afonso V of Portugal, who was betrothed to Joan, invaded Castile on her behalf, but in 1479 Joan abandoned her rights to the throne. Ferdinand's accession to the Aragonese throne in the same year brought about a personal union of Aragon and Castile.

CASTILIAN INSTITUTIONS, SOCIETY, AND CULTURE

In the 13th century the recovery of the idea of the state, as reflected in Roman law and Aristotle's *Politics*, profoundly influenced the development of the Castilian monarchy. As the one primarily responsible for maintaining the well-being of the state, the king (God's vicar on earth, according to the Siete Partidas and numerous other medieval texts) tended to concentrate power in his own hands. The royal bureaucracy, now largely directed by jurists, attempted to strengthen royal authority in every way. Although contemporaries were wary of Roman law, its influence continually expanded. The place of Roman law and legal procedure in the courts was secured when Alfonso XI promulgated the Ordenamiento de Alcalá in 1348. Henry II reorganized the royal tribunal (*audiencia*), but its development was not completed until the end of the Middle Ages. In the pursuit of greater centralization of power, the crown took advantage of the persistent factionalism in the towns to intervene frequently in municipal administration. The lower classes were denied any civic role, as the urban knights, a non-noble aristocracy, controlled town affairs. The knights also struggled to win noble status for themselves, with its accompanying exemption from taxation. The crown dispatched *corregidores* (governors) to the towns to restrain violence and to supplant local governmental officials. Although this was initially a temporary expedient, by the 15th century it had become a permanent institution.

Both the nobility and the representative assembly of the municipalities, the Cortes, challenged the royal inclination toward absolutism. In 1386 John

I, responding to the demands of the Cortes, included representatives of the three estates (consisting of the nobility, the church, and the towns) in the royal council (*consejo real*) where they could regularly monitor royal policy. That plan did not succeed, because in the 15th century the nobility came to dominate the council and used it to further their own interests. Throughout the realm the power and influence of the magnates continued to grow, as they were entrusted with various territorial administrative responsibilities, including the posts of *adelantado mayor* (governor) in Castile, Murcia, and Andalusia. In order to retain their favour, the Trastámara kings granted them vast territorial lordships as well as lordships over some of the principal municipalities. This was a serious loss for the monarchy, as the cities and towns had long been the chief supporters of royal authority. As a mentality favourable to the aristocracy came to the fore in the 15th century, the magnates became ever more brazen in arrogating royal rights to themselves.

The role of the Cortes in the political life of the kingdom was especially important from about 1250 to 1350 and again during the reigns of Henry I and John I, who hoped to use it to strengthen their hold on the throne. The Cortes was convened frequently to consent to taxation (*servicio*) for fixed terms and for specific purposes. Both Ferdinand IV and Alfonso XI explicitly stated that they would not levy an extraordinary tax without the consent of the Cortes, and John I agreed to let the Cortes audit his accounts. The monarch often enacted ordinances in the Cortes, and if he accepted petitions presented by that body, they became the law of the land. John II and Henry IV curtailed the role of the Cortes and abused the rights that it had gained in the 14th century. At times the crown appointed municipal procurators and summoned fewer and fewer towns, so that eventually only 18 were called to represent the entire realm. Indeed, many towns held in lordship by the magnates, who claimed to speak for them, lost their right to attend the Cortes.

The predominance of agriculture and pasturage in the Castilian economy continued. As the Reconquista opened vast pasturelands in Extremadura and Andalusia, sheep and cattle grazing acquired new importance. The Mesta, a kingdomwide organization of sheep owners chartered originally by Alfonso X, had great economic and political power. Although the manufacture of woolen cloth became important in the towns, the urban middle class was not especially strong, and an effective guild organization never really matured. Forged during the Reconquista, the urban aristocracy's military mentality impeded its participation in trade and crafts. While the ports of the Bay of Biscay maintained a substantial trade with England, Flanders, France, and Portugal, the Genoese, who were solidly established at Sevilla, the chief southern port, had a great share in the overseas trade originating there.

Following the outbreak of the Black

Death in the middle of the 14th century, the population declined sharply, and there was serious social and economic unrest. In 1351 Peter I (the Cruel) tried to guarantee stability by enacting the Ordenamiento de Menestrales, which required workers to accept the same wages as before the plague. Owing to popular agitation, a great pogrom against the Jews erupted in 1391 and rapidly spread throughout the peninsula. Forced to choose Christianity or death, many Jews converted. A number of these *conversos*, freed of earlier legal restraints, now attained prominence in public life, but they were always suspected of continuing privately to observe Jewish practices. The demand that they demonstrate *limpieza de sangre*—i.e., that their ancestry was unsullied by Jewish or Muslim blood—was intended to exclude them from any important place in government or the church.

The cultural integration of Castile into western Europe was now complete. The development of Castilian as a literary language owed much to Alfonso X, whose stimulus to learning has been described as having prompted an intellectual renaissance. Under his patronage both the *General estoria* ("General History") and the *Estoria de Espanna* ("History of Spain") were written; astronomical tables were arranged, and translations of Arabic scientific works were undertaken; and the Siete Partidas was compiled. The *Cantigas de Santa María* ("Songs to the Virgin") is a collection of more than 400 poems written in Galician, a language considered appropriate for lyric poetry; the poems are generally assumed to be the work of Alfonso himself, and many of them constitute a royal autobiography. Alfonso's nephew, Don Juan Manuel (died 1348), authored many works, including *El Conde Lucanor; o, el libro de Patronio* (1328-35; "Count Lucanor; or, The Book of Patronius", a collection of fables and folk tales with a didactic intent) and the *Libro de los estados* (a treatise on social classes). Juan Ruiz, the archpriest of Hita (died *c.* 1350) and one of the great medieval poets, took a satirical look at love; his *Libro de buen amor* (1330; expanded 1343; *Book of Good Love*) intersperses ribald and comic poems of love with beautiful hymns in praise of the Virgin Mary. The history of this period was recorded in a succession of royal chronicles. Pedro López de Ayala (died 1407), a brilliant writer who searched for motives and realized the importance of social and institutional developments, wrote excellent chronicles of Peter I, Henry II, John I, and Henry III. During the reign of John II, who was a patron of poets and scholars, the Italian Renaissance influenced Castilian writers and thinkers, including the marqués de Santillana (died 1458), whose lyric poems have great beauty; Jorge Manrique (died 1479), who reflected on the vanities of the world in the *Coplas por la muerte de su padre* (*Verses on the Death of His Father*); and Fernán Pérez de Guzmán (died *c.* 1460), who sketched the characters and personalities in the court of Henry III in the *Generaciones y semblanzas* (*Generations and Sketches*).

ARAGON, CATALONIA, AND VALENCIA, 1276–1479

In the late Middle Ages the Crown of Aragon experienced a confrontation between the monarchy and the nobility similar to that which occurred in neighbouring Castile. As Roman law and its practitioners gained in influence, there were protests in both Aragon and Catalonia, and James I confirmed the customary law of Aragon in an assembly at Ejea in 1265. He also agreed that the *justicia*, a judge appointed by the king from the ranks of the knights rather than from among the professional jurists, should adjudicate litigation involving the nobles. A critical stage in relations between the crown and the nobles was reached during the reign of Peter III (the Great; 1276–85), the heir to Aragon, Catalonia, and Valencia (the kingdom of Majorca fell to the share of his younger brother James).

Peter III's conquest of Sicily, where he reigned as Peter I, was the second major step in the Mediterranean expansion of Catalonia, marking the beginning of a long international struggle with serious domestic complications. Although the papacy had awarded Naples and Sicily to Charles of Anjou, Peter's wife represented Hohenstaufen claims to them. Taking advantage of the Sicilian Vespers, a rebellion by Sicilians against Charles's rule, Peter occupied Sicily in 1282. Pope Martin IV not only excommunicated and deposed Peter but also offered Aragon to a French prince. Seizing the opportunity created by these difficulties, the Aragonese nobles organized a union to uphold their liberties and in 1283 compelled the king to grant their demands, which were set down in the document known as the General Privilege. Peter agreed to convene the Cortes each year and confirmed the right of the *justicia* to hear the lawsuits of the nobility. He made similar promises in Valencia and Catalonia, where the allegiance of his subjects was more secure. After the pope proclaimed a Crusade, King Philip III of France led the Crusading army against Peter but failed to achieve success. Thereafter the disposition of Sicily remained the chief concern of Peter's three sons.

Alfonso III (1285–91), who inherited the mainland dominions, and his younger brother James, who received Sicily, valiantly tried to overcome the formidable opposition of the pope, the king of France, and the house of Plantagenet (Anjou). Alfonso seized Majorca because his uncle James had aided the French during their Crusade against Aragon. Once again the Aragonese nobles challenged the king, forcing him in 1287 to confirm his father's General Privilege and to permit the nobles to control the appointment of certain royal councillors. After succeeding his brother as king of Aragon, James II (1291–1327) tried to secure an unchallenged title to that kingdom by yielding his rights to Sicily in 1295 and returning Majorca to his uncle James. Pope Boniface VIII awarded Sardinia to James II as compensation.

In 1302 the pope reluctantly agreed to accept the third brother, Frederick, who had been proclaimed as king of Sicily. The Catalan Company, a mercenary troop idled by the end of the Sicilian wars, transferred its activities to the Byzantine Empire and in 1311 gained dominion over the duchy of Athens. Although neither Sicily nor Athens came under the direct rule of the king of Aragon, they remained bastions of Catalan influence and power in the Mediterranean.

After securing a favourable alteration of his frontier with Murcia, James II occupied Sardinia in 1325. As Genoa disputed Aragonese rights there, his successors, Alfonso IV (1327–36) and Peter IV (the Ceremonious; 1336–87), were forced to wage a series of wars. Accusing his cousin, the king of Majorca, of disloyalty, Peter IV annexed Majorca permanently to the Crown of Aragon in 1343. In 1347 Peter provoked a constitutional crisis by naming his daughter as heir to the throne rather than his brother, the count of Urgel, who argued that women were excluded from the succession. The Aragonese union, which had been relatively inactive in the previous reign, again confronted the king and compelled him to confirm the privileges granted by his predecessors. The Valencian nobility also organized a union and exacted similar concessions. The devastation caused by the Black Death and the royalist victory over the Aragonese union at Epila in 1348 enabled Peter to dissolve the union and to annul its privileges. The union never again threatened the crown.

After mid-century, Peter I of Castile invaded the Crown of Aragon, prompting Peter IV to back Henry of Trastámara's claims to the Castilian throne, but Henry subsequently refused to reward him with any territorial concessions. That disappointment was offset to some extent by the reincorporation of Sicily into the dominions of the Crown of Aragon in 1377. Peter IV remained neutral during the Great Schism, but his son John I (1387–95) acknowledged the pope of Avignon. Both John and his younger brother and successor, Martin (1395–1410), had to attend constantly to agitation and unrest in Sardinia and Sicily. When Martin died without immediate heirs, the Crown of Aragon faced an acute crisis. Claimants were not lacking, but none enjoyed wide popularity. The estates of Aragon, Valencia, and Catalonia appointed nine commissioners to meet at Caspe to resolve the issue. The Compromise of Caspe, announced in 1412, determined that Fernando de Antequera, brother of King Henry III of Castile, had the best claim to the throne by right of inheritance. The accession of Ferdinand I (1412–16), the first of the Trastámara dynasty to rule in Aragon, prepared the way for the eventual union of Aragon and Castile. By withdrawing obedience from the Avignonese pope Benedict XIII, Ferdinand helped to terminate the schism.

Alfonso V (the Magnanimous; 1416–58) opted to pursue ambitions in Italy and generally neglected his peninsular domains. After occupying the Kingdom of Naples in 1442, he hoped to lord it over the rest of Italy and to extend his influence and power into the eastern Mediterranean. A spirit of discontent fostered by his long absence from Aragon provoked a crisis during the reign of his brother, John II (1458–79). John inherited the mainland kingdoms as well as Sicily, while Ferrante, Alfonso V's illegitimate son, obtained Naples. John had already added another kingdom to the Trastámara holdings when he married the queen of Navarre in 1420. By quarreling with his son, Prince Charles of Viana, he antagonized many and provoked the open hostility of the Catalans. Charles's sudden death in 1461 led many to believe that he had been poisoned by John. Already restive because of economic and social uncertainties, the Catalans revolted and offered the principality to other potential rulers. Louis XI of France seized the opportunity to occupy Roussillon and Cerdagne, thereby laying the foundation for future enmity between France and Spain. By 1472 John II had suppressed the Catalan revolt; subsequently he aided his daughter-in-law Isabella in acquiring the Castilian crown. His son Ferdinand succeeded him as king of Aragon and Sardinia, and his daughter Eleanor inherited Navarre.

ARAGONESE INSTITUTIONS AND SOCIETY

Aragon, Catalonia, and Valencia constituted the nucleus of the Crown of Aragon during the late Middle Ages. James II declared in 1319 that these three states formed an indissoluble union. At various times Majorca, Sicily, Sardinia, and Naples were added to, separated from, and finally reunited with the Crown of Aragon. Peter IV and the people of Valencia opposed a plan to dismember the kingdom of Valencia for the benefit of the king's younger brother. When the Catalans revolted against John II and unsuccessfully tried to secede, the Aragonese federation faced the threat of dissolution, but it was able to hold together. Ever since Peter II had offered his dominions in fief to the papacy in 1204 several popes had intervened directly in Aragonese affairs and had even tried to dispose of the throne.

Dominated by jurists favouring royal absolutism, the bureaucracy of the Crown of Aragon became highly complex. Peter IV carefully structured the administration around four principal officials—the chancellor, the chamberlain, the *mayordomo*, and the *mestre racional* (chief financial officer). The employment of nonnatives in administrative positions was vigorously opposed in each of the federated states. Although Peter IV abolished the Aragonese union, the *justicia*, who were appointed and removed by the king at will, continued to adjudicate lawsuits concerning the nobility.

As his father's lieutenant, the king's oldest son usually was appointed procurator general for all the realms. A procurator or governor-general permanently represented the crown in Valencia and Majorca, which the king visited only occasionally. A vicar or *justicia* also acted in the name of the crown in the towns, which enjoyed a greater degree of self-government than before. Executive authority in Barcelona was entrusted to a council of five who were responsible to a larger *consell de cent*, or council of 100.

The fundamental law for Catalonia and Majorca continued to be the Usages of Barcelona, and in 1251 James I pledged that Roman law would not supplant them. He provided the newly conquered kingdom of Valencia with the Fori Regni Valentiae (1240), a code of law largely Roman in substance. In 1247 he promulgated the Code of Huesca, a compilation of the customary law of Aragon; the code, which originally defined Aragon's territory, came to embody the criminal and civil legal code in Aragon. As new laws were added, the Aragonese legal code was reorganized as the Fueros de Aragón, which included the Code of Huesca and the General Privilege, in the 15th century.

A vigorous parliamentary structure emerged in the Crown of Aragon. Each of the peninsular states (Aragon, Catalonia, and Valencia) had a parliament, and the king occasionally assembled a general parliament of all three. The development of Catalan constitutionalism received a strong impetus from two significant pledges made by Peter III in the Corts (parliament) of Barcelona in 1283. He declared that he would convene an annual Corts "to treat of the good estate and reformation of the land" and that he would not make any general statute for Catalonia without its consent. The Corts did not meet annually thereafter, but the constitutions and *capitols de Corts*

enacted during these meetings testify to its legislative role. The parliaments in Aragon, Catalonia, and Valencia also voted on taxes. Not trusting the monarchy, the Catalans established a commission to control the collection and disbursement of taxes authorized by the Corts. In the late 14th century this commission, known as the Diputació del General de Catalunya or simply the Generalitat, became permanent. When the Corts was not in session, the Generalitat represented the Catalan community and defended Catalan liberties against royal encroachments. Early in the 15th century similar agencies were established in Aragon and Valencia.

The Aragonese economy was dominated by agriculture and pasturage. A numerous class of Mudéjares, Muslims living under Christian rule and retaining many of their own institutions, farmed the land in lower Aragon and Valencia. The main industry in the Catalan towns, where a strong guild organization developed, was the manufacture of woollen cloth. Barcelona and Valencia—trading with Tunis, Alexandria, Sicily, Sardinia, the Holy Land, and the Black Sea area—ranked among the major Mediterranean seaports. To represent their interests, Catalan merchants and consuls resided in many of the principal African ports. Catalan maritime law, compiled about 1370 in the *Llibre del consolat de mar* (*Book of the Consulate of the Sea*), enjoyed wide European recognition and usage.

Following the havoc caused by the Black Death, recurrent social and economic crises disturbed the peace and provoked the massacre of the Jews in Valencia and other cities in 1391, as well as other violent acts. Financial uncertainty, the failure of many private banks, and the decline of trade in the later 14th century compounded problems. In Barcelona the agitation of the popular party (the Busca) against the ascendancy of the wealthy urban aristocracy (the Biga) helped to foment the Catalan revolt against John II. Hoping to win their liberty, the serfs, or *payeses de remensa*, joined the rebellion.

ARAGONESE CULTURE

Culture flourished in the Crown of Aragon in the late Middle Ages. After James II founded the University of Lledia (Lérida) in 1300—the first in Aragon—other universities were established at Huesca, Barcelona, and Zaragoza. Two Dominicans—St. Raymond of Penyafort (died 1275), a great canonist, and St. Vincent Ferrer (died 1419), a preacher of exceptional eloquence—were outstanding representatives of the university tradition. Several works of history, generally regarded as gems of Catalan literature, helped to shape the vernacular as a literary language: *The Chronicle of James I*, purportedly written by the king himself; Bernat Desclot's *Chronicle of the Reign of King Peter III*; Ramon Muntaner's *Chronicle*, reporting the adventures of the Catalan Company; and the *Chronicle of Peter IV*, of which the king claimed to be the author. Ramon Llull (died 1315), who was equally facile in Latin, Catalan, and Arabic, was the most prolific writer of the times. Primarily an active propagandist concerned with the recovery of the Holy Land and the conversion of the Muslims, Llull also was a philosopher, theologian, and mystic. Among his principal writings were the romantic *Book of the Lover and the Beloved, Blanquerna*, and *Book of the Order of Chivalry*. *Lo Crestià*, an encyclopaedic work dealing with moral and political theory, was the best-known work of Francesc Eiximenis (died 1409). The poet Ausiàs March (died 1459) explored the psychological dimensions of love.

CHAPTER 13

MUSLIM SPAIN

In the second half of the 7th century CE, Byzantine strongholds in North Africa gave way before the Arab advance. Carthage fell in 698. In 705 al-Walīd I, the sixth caliph of the Umayyad dynasty, the first great Muslim dynasty centred in Damascus, appointed Mūsā ibn Nuṣayr governor in the west; Mūsā annexed all of North Africa as far as Tangier (Ṭanjah) and made progress in the difficult task of propagating Islam among the Imazighen. The Christian ruler of Ceuta (Sabtah), Count Julian (variously identified by the Arab chroniclers as a Byzantine, a native Amazigh, or a Visigoth), eventually reached an agreement with Mūsā to launch a joint invasion of the Iberian Peninsula.

The invasion of Spain was the result both of a Muslim readiness to invade and of a call for assistance by one of the Visigothic factions, the "Witizans." Having become dispossessed after the death of King Witiza in 710, they appealed to Mūsā for support against the usurper Roderick. In April or May of 711 Mūsā sent an Amazigh army headed by Ṭāriq ibn Ziyād across the passage whose modern name, the Strait of Gibraltar, derives from Jabal al-Ṭāriq; in July they were able to defeat Roderick in a decisive battle.

Instead of returning to Africa, Ṭāriq marched north and conquered Toledo (Ṭulayṭulah), the Visigothic capital, where he spent the winter of 711. In the following year Mūsā himself led an Arab army to the peninsula and conquered Mérida (Māridah) after a long siege. He reached Ṭāriq in Toledo in the summer of 713. From there he advanced northeast, taking Zaragoza (Saraqusṭah) and invading the country up to the northern mountains; he then moved from west to east, forcing the population to submit or flee. Both Mūsā and Ṭāriq were recalled to Syria by the caliph, and they departed in 714 at the end of the summer; by then most of the Iberian Peninsula was under Muslim control.

The rapid success of the Islamic forces can be explained by the fact that Hispano-Visigoth society had not yet succeeded in achieving a compact and homogeneous integration. The Jews, harassed by the legal ordinances of Toledo, were particularly hostile toward the Christian government. Moreover, the Muslim conquest brought advantages to many elements of society: the burden of taxes was generally less onerous than it had been in the last years of the Visigoth epoch; serfs who converted to Islam (*mawālī*; singular: *mawlā*) advanced into the category of freedmen and enrolled among the dependents of some conquering noble; and Jews, who were no longer persecuted, were placed on an equal footing with the Hispano-Romans and Goths who still remained within the Christian fold. Thus, in the first half of the 8th century, a new society developed in Muslim Spain. The Arabs were the ruling element; a distinction was made between *baladiyyūn* (i.e., Arabs who had entered Spain in 712 under Mūsā) and Syrians (who arrived in 740 under Balj ibn Bishr). Below them in status were the Imazighen, who made up the majority of the invading troops, whose numbers and influence continued to grow over the course of centuries because of their steady influx from Africa. Then came the native population who had converted to Islam, the *musālimah*, and their descendants, the *muwallads*; many of them were also *mawālī* (i.e., connected by patronage with an Arab) or even themselves of Amazigh lineage. This group formed the majority of the population because during the first three centuries social and economic motives induced a considerable number of natives to convert to Islam. Christians and Jews who kept their religion came next in the social hierarchy, but their numbers decreased in the course of time. Finally, there was a small group of slaves (Ṣaqālibah)—captives from the northern peninsula and other European countries—and black captives or mercenaries.

The period between 711 and 756 is called the dependent emirate because Muslim Spain, or Al-Andalus, was dependent on the Umayyad caliph in Damascus. These years were marked by continuous hostilities between the different Arab factions and between the various social groups. Nonetheless, Muslim expansion beyond the Pyrenees continued until 732, when the Franks, under Charles Martel, defeated the Muslims, led by the emir 'Abd al-Raḥmān al-Ghāfiqī, near Tours. This battle marked the beginning of the gradual Muslim retreat. A major Amazigh uprising against the Arabs in North Africa had powerful repercussions in Muslim Spain; it caused the depopulation of the northwestern peninsula, occupied at that time mainly by Imazighen, and brought the Syrian army of Balj to Al-Andalus, which introduced a new motive for discord. This situation changed with the establishment of an independent emirate in 756 by ʿAbd al-Raḥmān I al-Dākhil, an Umayyad prince who, having succeeded in escaping from the slaughter of his family by the ʿAbbāsids and in gaining power in Al-Andalus, became independent of them politically (not religiously; he did not adopt the title of caliph).

THE INDEPENDENT EMIRATE

The dynasty of the Andalusian Umayyads (756–1031) marked the growth and perfection of the Arabic civilization in Spain. Its history may be divided into two major periods—that of the independent emirate (756–929) and that of the caliphate (929–1031)—and may be interpreted as

MOSQUE-CATHEDRAL OF CÓRDOBA

The original structure of the Mosque-Cathedral of Córdoba was built by the Umayyad ruler ʿAbd ar-Raḥman I in 784–786 with extensions in the 9th and 10th centuries that doubled its size, ultimately making it one of the largest sacred buildings in the Islamic world. The ground plan of the completed building forms a vast rectangle measuring 590 by 425 feet (180 by 130 metres), or little less than St. Peter's Basilica in Rome. About one-third of this area is occupied by the Patio de los Naranjos ("Court of the Oranges") and the cloisters that surround it on the north, east, and west.

Passing through the courtyard, one enters on the south a deep sanctuary whose roof is supported by a forest of pillars made of porphyry, jasper, and many-coloured marbles. Some 850 pillars divide this interior into 19 north-to-south and 29 east-to-west aisles, with each row of pillars supporting a tier of open horseshoe arches upon which a third and similar tier is superimposed. The most exquisite decoration in the whole complex is found in the third mihrab, or prayer niche, a small octagonal recess roofed with a single block of white marble that is carved

in the form of a shell and has walls inlaid with Byzantine-style mosaics and gold.

Since 1236 the former mosque has served as a Christian cathedral, and its Moorish character was altered in the 16th century with the erection in the interior of a central high altar and cruciform choir, numerous chapels along the sides of the vast quadrangle, and a belfry 300 feet (90 metres) high in place of the old minaret.

Interior, Great Mosque of Córdoba, Spain, begun 785. Alfonso Gutierrez Escera/Ostman Agency

revolving around three persons of like name—'Abd al-Raḥmān I (756–788), 'Abd al-Raḥmān II (822–852), 'Abd al-Raḥmān III (912–961)—and the all-powerful *ḥājib* (chief minister) Abū 'Āmir al-Manṣūr (976–1002).

'Abd al-Raḥmān I organized the new Arab state. Vigorously checking all dissident elements, he endeavoured to base his power on the Eastern aristocracy affiliated with his house and heaped upon it property and riches, though he nonetheless treated it ruthlessly when it showed signs of rebellion. He protected the religious authorities who represented orthodoxy, and, through a series of punitive campaigns, he held in check the Christians of Asturias. In the eastern part of the country he was troubled by intrigues of the 'Abbāsids, and in the north he had to cope with the ambitions of Charlemagne, who menaced the valley of the Ebro (Ibruh). As discussed above, Charlemagne failed; he was forced to raise the siege of Zaragoza, and in the course of his retreat the Basques attacked and destroyed his rear guard at Roncesvalles (778), an event which is celebrated in the great medieval epic *The Song of Roland*. The Franks had to be content with occupying the upper valleys of the Pyrenees. The Frankish advance ended with the Muslim seizure of Girona (Jerunda) in 785, Barcelona (Barjelūnah) in 801, and Old Catalonia, which were later taken back by the Franks and formed part of the Spanish March.

'Abd al-Raḥmān I's successors, Hishām I (788–796) and al-Ḥakam I (796–822), encountered severe internal dissidence among the Arab nobility. A rebellion in Toledo was put down savagely, and the internal warfare caused the emir to increase the numbers of Slav and Amazigh mercenaries and to impose new taxes to pay for them.

'Abd al-Raḥmān II inaugurated an era of political, administrative, and cultural regeneration for Muslim Spain, beginning a sharp "Orientalization" or, more precisely, an "Iraqization." 'Abd al-Raḥmān's most severe problems sprang from his restless vassals in the Ebro valley, especially the convert Banū Qāsī family and the Mozarabs. Incited by the extremist chiefs Alvarus and Eulogius (the latter being canonized after his death), the Mozarabs sought to strengthen their Christian faith through the aura of martyrdom and began to publicly revile the Prophet Muhammad, an action punishable by death from 850 onward, according to Mozarabic sources. The emir sought to persuade the blasphemous to retract, but, failing in his attempts, he imposed the death penalty. The "vogue" of seeking martyrdom was a reaction of the conservative Mozarabic party against the growing "Arabization" of their coreligionists. The conflict ended in 859–860, and, despite official tact, this provocation by the Christians led to the execution of 53 people and was finally disavowed by the ecclesiastical authorities.

In foreign policy, 'Abd al-Raḥmān II conducted intensive diplomatic activity, exchanging ambassadors with the Byzantine Empire and with the Frankish king Charles II (the Bald) and maintaining friendly relations with the sovereigns of Tāhart, who lent military support to Muslim Spain. He confronted the constantly growing incursions of the Vikings (Norsemen), whom he defeated in the vicinity of Sevilla. Furthermore, he established permanent defenses against the Viking invaders by creating two naval bases, one facing the Atlantic at Sevilla and another on the Mediterranean shore at Pechina near Almería.

His successors Muḥammad I (852–886), al-Mundhir (886–888), and ʿAbd Allāh (888–912) were confronted with a new problem, which threatened to do away with the power of the Umayyads—the *muwallads*. Having become more and more conscious of their power, they rose in revolt in the north of the peninsula, led by the powerful Banū Qāsī clan, and in the south (879), led by ʿUmar ibn Ḥafṣūn. The struggle against them was long and tragic; Ibn Ḥafṣūn, well protected in Bobastro and in the Málaga mountains, was the leader of *muwallad* and even Mozarabic discontent in the south of Al-Andalus, but his defeat in 891 at Poley, near Córdoba, forced him to retreat and hide in the mountains. ʿAbd Allāh, however, was unable to subdue the numerous rebels and thus left a weak state for his grandson, the great ʿAbd al-Raḥmān III, who from 912 was able to restore order. He subdued all of Al-Andalus, from Jaén (Jayyān) to Zaragoza (Saraqusṭah), from Mérida (Māridah) to Sevilla (Ishbīliyah), and the Levant. He even challenged Ibn Ḥafṣūn successfully—especially after the latter's political error of reverting to the Christianity of his Spanish ancestors, a move that caused the desertion of numerous *muwallads* who regarded themselves as good Muslims. When Ibn Ḥafṣūn died in 917, his sons were forced to capitulate, and in 928 ʿAbd al-Raḥmān III captured the theretofore impregnable fortress of Bobastro.

THE CALIPHATE OF CÓRDOBA

One of the first international political problems that ʿAbd al-Raḥmān III faced was that of his juridical status vis-à-vis the ʿAbbāsid caliphate at Baghdad. As long as religious unity existed in the Islamic dominions, the Umayyads in Spain were resigned to acknowledge the religious leadership of Baghdad. However, when the heterodox caliphate of the Fāṭimids developed in Tunis after 910, ʿAbd al-Raḥmān III proclaimed himself caliph and adopted the caliphal title of al-Nāṣir in 929. This new caliphate, the caliphate of Córdoba (Qurṭubah), was to rule Al-Andalus for more than a century.

Al-Nāṣir's internal situation was already almost assured; the last bulwarks of resistance were not long in capitulating (Toledo, 933), and thereafter he was able to devote all his efforts to foreign affairs. As to Christian Spain, his successes were meagre, and, what was more serious, he suffered a severe defeat in 939 at Simancas (Shānt Mānkas). Afterwards, however, the internal debilitation of the kingdom of León enabled him to restore his predominance on the peninsula by political means. He consolidated his position through a series of embassies to Otto I, the emperor in Germany and the most powerful figure in Christian Europe, to the Christian sovereigns of the peninsula, to the pope, and to Constantinople. His sovereignty was also acclaimed by the corsair enclave in Fraxinetum (Frakhshinīṭ; modern-day La-Garde-Freinet), in southern France.

In Tunis the Fāṭimids fought the establishment of an empire that would reach as far as the Atlantic and encompass Al-Andalus. In order to forestall Fāṭimid hegemony in the Maghrib, the Islamic area of northwestern Africa, al-Nāṣir occupied the North African ports of Melilla (Malīlah) and Ceuta (931). Intense naval warfare between the two western caliphates coincided with clashes on land in the Maghrib and attempts at subversive wars in the enemy states in northwest Africa. In the latter area, al-Nāṣir nearly overthrew the Fāṭimid caliphate by supporting the rebel Abū Yazīd al-Nukkārī; the conflict between the Umayyads and the Fāṭimids dragged on and ended in 969, when the latter conquered Egypt and lost interest in the Maghrib, thus leaving a power vacuum that was rapidly filled by the Umayyads.

Al-Nāṣir was succeeded by his son al-Ḥakam II (961–976), who adopted the caliphal title of al-Mustanṣir. His peaceful reign succeeded in resolving the problem of the Maghrib, thanks to the strategic ability of General Ghālib and the policy of the intendant, Abū ʿĀmir al-Maʿāfirī, who soon became the all-powerful al-Manṣūr (Spanish: Almanzor), the Victorious One.

On al-Mustanṣir's death, his throne was occupied by his son Hishām II al-Muˇayyad, a minor. Hishām grew up under the tutelage of his mother, Aurora, and of the prime minister, Jaʿfar al-Muṣḥafī, who before long was liquidated by al-Manṣūr. The latter succeeded in eliminating all temporal power of the caliph, whom he dominated, and acquired complete power for himself.

Al-Manṣūr won control over a great part of the Maghrib, which he transformed into the viceroyalty of Córdoba, and he halted the expansion of the Christian kings from the north through a series of raids—usually every six months—in which he sacked nearly every Christian capital on the peninsula. With the support of a professional army consisting predominantly of Imazighen, many of them recent arrivals from Africa who obeyed him blindly, he managed to dispense with the Arab aristocracy, which for the most part was pro-Umayyad, and to hold in check the influence of the slaves, whose numbers had been increasing since al-Nāṣir had placed them in posts of high responsibility. But this balancing of forces—Arab aristocracy, Imazighen, and slaves—could be sustained only by the strong hand of a ruler such as himself.

Al-Manṣūr played the role of a grand lord. A protector of poets and scholars, he concealed his rationalism under a cloak of piety and was the darling of the *faqīhs* (scholars versed in the traditions of Islam); he contrived to attract to himself the outstanding poets of the era. By the time of his death, he had won more than 50 raids and succeeded in leaving a robust and well-organized state for his son ʿAbd al-Malik al-Muẓaffar.

Al-Muẓaffar (1002–08) continued his father's policies, hemming in Hishām II and fighting against the Christians. After Al-Muẓaffar's premature death, his brother ʿAbd al-Raḥmān Sanchuelo took the reins of power, but he lacked the fortitude to maintain the structure built by his father. An uprising that sought to vindicate the political rights of Hishām II resulted in Sanchuelo's death and brought about the beginning of the end of the Umayyad dynasty in Spain.

THE ṬĀʾIFAS

The death of ʿAbd al-Raḥmān Sanchuelo in 1009 ushered in 21 years of unrest, during which the social and political unity—among "Andalusians" (Arabs, Imazighen who had settled in Al-Andalus a long time earlier, and the population that had converted to Islam), Imazighen who had arrived fairly recently, and the slaves—fell apart. The consequence of those years of anarchy was the formation of numerous independent kingdoms, or *ṭāʾifas*, which may be classified into the following: (1) "Andalusian" factions in the three capitals of the frontier area (Zaragoza, Toledo, and Badajoz), in the valleys of the Guadalquivir (Wadi Al-Kabīr), and in the transition zone from the Ebro to the Tagus (Tajo) valley, (2) "new" Imazighen in Granada, Málaga, and four small southern *ṭāʾifas*, and (3) groups of slaves in the east.

The political history of the period comprises an uninterrupted series of internecine wars. Preeminent is the confrontation between the Arab factions, under the leadership of Sevilla (Ishbīliyah) and governed by the dynasty of the Banū ʿAbbād, and the Imazighen, presided over by Granada. Little by little, Sevilla united southern Al-Andalus under its aegis, exclusive of Granada and Málaga. This state was ruled by al-Muʿtaḍid, a sovereign devoid of scruples, who pretended at first to have found the vanished Hishām II al-Muʿayyad (at most, the pretender was a mat maker from Calatrava who bore some resemblance to the old caliph), and then by al-Muʿtaḍid's son, the poet-prince al-Muʿtamid. In the east, except for a brief period when the petty state of Denia (Dāniyah) built a powerful fleet that enabled it to stage incursions throughout the western Mediterranean as far as Sardinia, the various *ṭāʾifas* preserved a certain static and dynastic equilibrium; farther to the north, the various *ṭāʾifas* also spent their time embroiled in interminable internal quarrels.

This fragmentation facilitated the expansion of the Christian states of the north, which, lacking the demographic potential to repopulate the lands they had succeeded in occupying, wisely annexed only those that they were capable of repopulating and garrisoning. The Christian states also imposed a heavy economic burden of tribute on the *ṭā'ifas*. Christian armies forced the Andalusian petty kings to buy peace by paying annual tribute, the famous *parias*. The tribute revitalized the economy of the Christian states, but it created sharp friction between the Muslim authorities and their subjects. The *ṭā'ifas* constantly had to increase the yield from their imposts, and they constantly laid new and heavier tax burdens on their subjects; when cash was lacking, they devalued the currency, minting low-standard coins that were not accepted by the Christians. This in turn gave rise to new tax increases and to popular discontent, which was considerably aggravated by the legalistic party of the *faqīhs*. Furthermore, the extravagant luxury and lavish public outlays of the local petty courts rendered Al-Andalus ripe for the foreign intervention that came when the Castilians occupied Toledo (1085), the key to the Meseta Central and to the entire peninsula. The factional chiefs, alarmed by the Christian advance, called in the help of the Almoravids, the powerful Amazigh confederation then exercising hegemony over northwestern Africa.

THE ALMORAVIDS

The Almoravid ruler Yūsuf ibn Tāshufīn entered the Iberian Peninsula from North Africa and slowly advanced to the fields of Al-Zallāqah, north of Badajoz (Baṭalyaws), where in 1086 he defeated a Castilian army under Alfonso VI. However, unable to further exploit his victory, he returned to the Maghrib. For two years Almoravid policy in Spain remained indecisive, but it appears that the siege of Aledo (1088) convinced Yūsuf ibn Tāshufīn of the urgent necessity of putting an end to the *ṭā'ifas* if he was going to rescue Spanish Islam. From 1090 he deposed their rulers, beginning with those of Granada and Málaga; the next year he dethroned the rulers of Almería and Sevilla, followed by the leader of Badajoz in 1093. Only Rodrigo Díaz de Vivar (the Cid), exiled from his native Castile by King Alfonso VI, was able to resist the Africans, and he established an independent kingdom in Valencia—a new *ṭā'ifa*. The figure of the Cid—the Lord (Spanish Arabic: *al-sīd*), a title that the Arabs conferred upon him—is quite curious. He first served as a mercenary in the *ṭā'ifa* of Zaragoza, after which he became an independent prince in the east, ruling over states that were mainly inhabited by Muslims. He had the good fortune, however, of finding efficient administrators from among the Mozarabs residing in his states; further, his superb grasp of Almoravid tactics enabled him to overcome his numerical inferiority. Upon his death, Valencia remained under the control of his forces until 1102, when they were forced to evacuate it and seek refuge in Castile. Following the fall of Valencia, the Almoravids were unopposed, and in 1110, under the leadership of 'Alī ibn Yūsuf (1106–43), they were able to occupy Zaragoza.

However, the conquest of Zaragoza marked the beginning of the Almoravid decline. The Aragonese king, Alfonso I (the Battler), and his stepson, Alfonso VII of Castile, launched renewed Christian assaults against the entire frontier of Islam in Spain. In 1118 Zaragoza fell into the hands of Alfonso I, who reconquered a large part of the valleys of the Jalón and of the Jiloca. After 1121 the Almoravids experienced serious difficulties in Africa as a result of the preachings of an Amazigh reformer, Muḥammad ibn Tūmart, and could not successfully withstand the Christian onslaught; indeed, they had to hire Christian mercenaries to help them. A resounding Almoravid victory over the Aragonese at Fraga (Ifragah) in 1134 bore no fruit, because the Almoravids lacked the resources to exploit it.

THE ALMOHADS

In Africa the Almohad dynasty finally triumphed, and ʿAbd al-Muˇmin (1130–63), successor to Ibn Tūmart, turned his attention to Spain and to the integration of all the Muslim states—the second ṭāʾifas—formed under the shield of the latest internecine wars caused by the Almoravid decline. Of these states, those under Ibn Mardanīsh (1147–72)—who was successful with Christian help in becoming the master of Valencia, Murcia, and Jaén and in securing Granada and Córdoba—especially stood out.

The Almohads assumed the title of caliph, introduced a series of severe religious measures, and sought to strengthen their states through religious

unification—i.e., by compelling the Jews and Christians to either convert to Islam or emigrate. Two great sovereigns, Abū Yaʿqūb Yūsuf (1163–84) and Abū Yūsuf Yaʿqūb al-Manṣūr (1184–99), raised western Islam to the zenith of its power. Benefiting from the quarrels that divided the Christians, al-Manṣūr defeated the king of Castile, Alfonso VIII, in 1195 at the Battle of Alarcos (Al-Arak); despite this victory, however, he proved unable to exploit his triumph—repeating the fate that had befallen the Almoravids after al-Zallāqah. Years later, during the reign of his successor Muḥammad al-Naṣīr (1199–1214), the Christians avenged this defeat in the Battle of Las Navas de Tolosa (Al-ʿIqāb). This battle created a power vacuum into which stepped some of the ṭāʾifas, prominent among which were those of Banū Hūd of Murcia (Mursīyah) and of the Naṣrids of Arjona (Arjūnah). The policies of the two emirs were quite divergent: Muḥammad ibn Hūd (1228–38) emphasized resistance on the part of the Muslims against the Christians who, led by Ferdinand III, were occupying the Guadalquivir valley; by contrast, Muḥammad I ibn al-Aḥmar (ruled in Granada 1238–73) acknowledged himself to be a vassal of the king of Castile and even helped him against his own Muslim coreligionists. This realistic policy enabled him to preserve in his possession the territory of what are the modern provinces of Málaga, Granada, and Almería, together with portions of neighbouring provinces. Thus, after the middle of the 13th century and the reconquest of Jaén (Jayyān), Córdoba, Sevilla, and Murcia by the Castilians and of Valencia and the Balearic Islands by the Catalan-Aragonese crown under James I (the Conqueror), no independent dominions of Islam remained in Spain—with the exception of Granada, Minorca (until 1287), and the tiny area of Crevillente (Qirbilyān), which soon disappeared.

GRANADA

The Naṣrid dynasty, founded by Muḥammad ibn al-Aḥmar in Granada, endured for two and a half centuries. The Muslims of Granada lacked sufficient forces to constitute a genuine danger to the Christians, who limited themselves to collecting tribute and launching an attack against the Muslims from time to time, snatching from them some city or other. The people of Granada, for their part, always bore in mind what had happened in the cases of the Almoravids and the Almohads, who, having arrived from Africa as auxiliary troops, became masters in Al-Andalus. Vis-à-vis the new North African empires, particularly the empire of the Banū Marīns, they maintained a policy of balance of power. Although they permitted the influx of volunteers from Africa to enroll in their army to fight against the Christians, they never permitted the crossing of the Strait of Gibraltar by massive organized contingents. The years between 1302 and 1340 were extraordinarily complex both diplomatically and militarily. The Banū Marīns in both the western Maghrib and Castile vied for the possession of the Granadan ports of Tarifa (Jazīrat Ṭarīf) and Algeciras (Al-Jazīrah al-Khaḍraˇ), ports that controlled the strait. Granada, therefore, allied alternately with the Africans and the Christians, hoping thus to maintain the balance of power. A fourth state, Catalonia, called a Crusade; hoping to obtain a larger slice of the Reconquista, it intervened with its fleet and laid siege to Almería (Al-Marīyah) in 1309.

When Ismāʿīl I (1314–25) ascended the throne, another branch of the Naṣrid family gained power. Ismāʿīl checked the reconquest ambitions of Alfonso XI—who in 1340, with the aid of the Portuguese, won a decisive victory over the Maghribian army of Abū al-Ḥasan at the Battle of the Salado. The defeat of the Maghribians and the lack of interest in reconquest on the part of Alfonso's successors created a favourable climate for Granada, which found itself free from political pressures of both Maghribians and Castilians. During the reign of Muḥammad V (1354–59; 1362–91) Granada attained its greatest splendour; its ministers included some of the most learned men of the epoch, such as the polymath Abū ʿAbd Allāh ibn al-Khaṭīb, the physician Abū Jaʿfar ibn Khātima, and the poet Abū ʿAbd Allāh ibn Zamraq. Important figures from the Maghrib were in close touch with Granada.

During this long era there also developed the institution of the "judge of the frontier" (*juez de la frontera y de los fieles del rastro*); the judge was a Muslim official who heard Christian complaints against the Granadans. This procedure did much to reduce frontier incidents between Muslims and Christians.

Little is known about the decline of the Naṣrid dynasty, since with Ibn al-Khaṭīb died the last great Muslim historian of Al-Andalus. The extant records and reports from the 15th century are as a rule from Christian sources or from the tales of travelers. The narrative poems that are of the utmost interest as historic sources for other periods in Muslim history are completely lacking in this era. The conventional verses of the king-poet Yūsuf III (1408–17), of his court poet Ibn Farkūn, or of the anonymous Arab poet of the romance *Abenamar, Abenamar, moro de la morería*, do little to illuminate the history of this period. More illustrative, however, are the verses of ʿAbd al-Karīm al-Qaysī (*c.* 1485), an esteemed member of Granada's middle class, who eschewed classic themes and wrote of such mundane phenomena as the increase in the cost of living or the decline of Granada and its continuous territorial losses.

Foreign relations entered a long period of tranquillity as a result of the ghastly losses of life from the Black Death, which reached Spain in 1348, and afterward from the internal wars that weakened Christian Castile. Only an occasional confrontation served to remind the Muslims and Christians that their territorial struggle, considered by the latter as a reconquest, had not yet come to an end. In the 15th century, however, the Reconquista proceeded apace. The Castilian regent, Prince Ferdinand,

seized Antequera (Antaqīrah) in 1410; Jimena and Huéscar fell in 1435, Huelma in 1438, and Gibraltar in 1462. One result of these events was that the people of Granada became increasingly less tolerant of Christians, and the Granadan *faqīhs* professed the most extreme xenophobia. The policy of intolerance and xenophobia points to the existence of a Granadan school of law, which before long exerted an influence on the other side of the strait; the Maghribians—subjected to the constant pressure of the Portuguese, who had gained possession of their coastal areas (Ceuta first, in 1415)—realized, like the Granadans, that the only way to escape Christian hegemony was through the profession of the most rigorous Islamic ideals and the practice of the most extreme xenophobia. This policy, common to both sides of the Strait of Gibraltar, did not achieve equal results. It saved the Maghrib from its external enemies, but in Spain it became the *casus belli* for the "Granada War" (Guerra de Granada), which was to inaugurate the conclusion of the Reconquista.

The sultan Muley Hacén (Abū al-Ḥasan ʿAlī) refused to pay the annual tribute he owed to the Catholic Monarchs and seized the fortified town of Zahara (1481), thus launching hostilities that were destined to liquidate the last bastion of Andalusian Islam. The campaign proved difficult for the Christian army, despite the discord that split the royal family of Granada and was exploited in Machiavellian fashion by Ferdinand II (the Catholic): Muḥammad XI (Spanish:

Boabdil), son of Muley Hacén, rebelled in Guadix against his father and was recognized in Granada with the aid of the Abencerrajes, a powerful Granada family. Muley Hacén, however, who had taken refuge in Málaga, succeeded in recapturing the capital with the assistance of the Zegries family. Muley Hacén was successfully deposed by his brother, the Zagal (Abū ʿAbd Allāh Muḥammad al-Zaghall—the Valiant One), who was supported by the Venegas family.

Muḥammad XI was captured by the Catholic Monarchs during his attack at Lucena. In order to regain his freedom, he signed the Pact of Córdoba, in which he pledged himself to deliver the portion of the kingdom that was in the hands of the Zagal in exchange for help from the Castilians in recovering Granada, part of which (the Alhambra) was still in the hands of Muley Hacén. The latter and the Zagal allied themselves against Muḥammad XI, who fled and sought asylum in the court of the Catholic Monarchs. The death of Muley Hacén in 1485 enabled Muḥammad XI, with the help of the inhabitants of Albaicín, to occupy the Alhambra. The Zagal, who had been routed by the Christians before Vélez Málaga, retreated to Guadix in 1487 and, being incapable of further resistance, delivered his territories to the Catholic Monarchs and emigrated to Tlemcén (1491). Taking advantage of this civil war, the Christians seized Ronda, Marbella, Loja, and Málaga and were in a position to lay siege to Granada. When the siege began, the population divided

Court of the Myrtles in the Alhambra, Granada, Spain, 13th-14th century. Ardean Miller III/FPG

into factions: one consisted of pacifists and the other of belligerents who, despite their quarrels, fiercely defended the city.

By the end of 1491 the situation became desperate, and Muḥammad XI capitulated. But before making the news public, he brought a detachment of Castilian troops into the Alhambra on the night of January 1–2 for the purpose of avoiding a disturbance on the part of his vassals that might render it impossible for him to comply with the terms of the pact. The official surrender, and with it the end of Muslim political power on the Iberian Peninsula, took place the following day, January 2, 1492. Islamic

THE ALHAMBRA

The name Alhambra, signifying in Arabic "the red," is probably derived from the colour of the sun-dried *tapia*, or bricks made of fine gravel and clay, of which the outer walls of this famous fortress are built. Constructed on a plateau that overlooks the city of Granada, the palace was built chiefly between 1238 and 1358, in the reigns of Ibn al-Aḥmar, founder of the Naṣrid dynasty, and his successors. The splendid decorations of the interior are ascribed to Yusuf I (died 1354).

After the expulsion of the Moors in 1492, much of the interior was effaced and the furniture was ruined or removed. Charles V, who ruled in Spain as Charles I (1516–56), rebuilt portions in the Renaissance style and destroyed part of the Alhambra in order to build an Italianate palace designed by Pedro de Machuca in 1526. In 1812 some of the towers were blown up by the French during the War of Independence, and in 1821 an earthquake caused further damage to the structure. Restoration of the building was undertaken in 1828 and continued through the 20th century.

The Moorish portion of the Alhambra includes the Alcazaba, or citadel, which is the oldest part—only its massive outer walls, towers, and ramparts are left. Beyond the Alcazaba is the Alhambra palace, and beyond that the Alhambra Alta (Upper Alhambra), which was originally tenanted by officials and courtiers and was part of a royal city constituting a seat of government.

The principal courts of the palace are the Patio de los Arrayanes (Court of the Myrtles) and the Patio de los Leones (Court of the Lions), so named because in the centre is the Fuente de los Leones (Fountain of the Lions), an alabaster basin supported by the figures of 12 white marble lions, emblems of strength and courage. The most important rooms of the Alhambra are the Salón de los Embajadores (Hall of the Ambassadors), a spatially grand reception room; the Sala de los Abencerrajes (the name of this hall, also spelled "Abencerrages," was derived from a legend in which Boabdil, the last king of Granada, having invited the Abencerraje chiefs to a banquet in this room, there massacred them); and the Sala de las Dos Hermanas (Hall of the Two Sisters), with its outstanding example of stalactite work.

To the east on the Cerro del Sol ("Hill of the Sun") is the Generalife (from the Arabic Jannat al-ʿArif ["Garden of the Builder"]), constructed in the early 14th century as a summer palace. The complex is centred on picturesque courtyards such as the Patio del Ciprés de la Sultana (Court of the Sultana's Cypress). Terraced gardens, pools, and fountains combine to enchanting effect in La Acequia Courtyard, named for the canal that supplies its water. A theatre within the Generalife is the site of international performances of music and dance. The Alhambra and the Generalife were collectively designated a UNESCO World Heritage site in 1984 (expanded in 1994).

Alicatado, or mosaic, in the Tower of Comares, the Alhambra, Granada, Spain. Archivo Mas, Barcelona

minorities, such as submissive Mudéjars (later called Moriscos), remained in Spain until the 17th century.

SOCIETY

In discussing the influx of the Muslims into Spain, the various social groups into which the population was divided have already been pointed out: Arabs (*baladiyyūn* and Syrians), Imazighen, *muwallads*, Mozarabs, Jews, and slaves. The Muslim population continued to increase during the early centuries of the occupation because of the wave of conversions that markedly reduced the number of Christians. Precise figures cannot be given, but it is estimated that at the time of the conquest some 4,000,000 Spaniards inhabited the peninsula and that in the course of the 8th century the number of immigrant Arabs rose to about 50,000 and of Imazighen to about 250,000. The population was primarily rural, and large cities were few in number. At the end of the 10th century one can estimate the following urban populations: Córdoba, 250,000; Toledo, 37,000; Almería, 27,000; Granada, 26,000; Zaragoza, 17,000; Valencia, 15,000; and Málaga, 15,000.

At the peak of the administrative pyramid was the emir, caliph, sultan, or king, depending on the era. All the functionaries exercised their power by delegation from the sovereign, who embodied within himself all executive, legislative, and judicial authority, even though at times he delegated power to a *ḥājib* (chamberlain) or, after the 11th century, to a prime minister (*dhu al-wizāratayn*). In the discharge of his functions he was assisted by various viziers. At times there was, at the head of the various departments, a *kātib*, or official secretary. The provinces were governed by *wālīs* who enjoyed wide autonomy. Uniform municipal organization did not exist, and the duties fulfilled by some officials cannot be considered as representative; such officials included, for example, the chief of police (*ṣāḥib al-shurṭa*) and the market inspector (known until the 10th century as *ṣāḥib al-sūq* [*zabazoque*] and later as *muḥtasib*). The Muslim cities of Spain, with their baths, gardens, markets, mosques, and high cultural level, were quite different from and, some believe, superior to those of Christian Europe.

The army was based on the voluntary recruitment of soldiers or on contracts with soldiers from abroad. The units (*jund*), grouped according to the places of origin of their men, were deployed strategically along the borders and possessed extraordinary mobility at the time of the caliphate. Holding castles close to the enemy lands as their bases of operation, they were glad to welcome into their midst the Muslims, who were eager to die in combat in order thus to open for themselves the gates of paradise. These volunteers, who became more and more numerous with the passage of time and about whom many details are known, were frequently second-class soldiers, since they enrolled during years when they constituted a hindrance rather than a source of help. The navy and merchant marine, organized by ʿAbd al-Raḥmān II, remained an effective force until the middle of the 14th century.

The entire state structure rested, theoretically, on a foundation of the most rigid Islamic orthodoxy as interpreted by the Malikite (Mālikīyah) school, which in Al-Andalus manifested special characteristics of a hyperconservative nature. It is not known whether the school acquired these traits upon settling in the peninsula because intolerance was indigenous to the inhabitants there or whether it indoctrinated the Andalusian Muslims in this manner and they in turn transmitted it to the Christian states, their reconquerors.

THE ECONOMY

The Muslim conquerors divided the lands seized from the Christians by force of arms and operated them, as a general rule, by means of "tenant-farmer" leases. Possibly about the 10th century the woodlands achieved their widest expansion, and the cultivation of irrigated lands was encouraged by means of drastic regulations, which, however, were favourably received. Plants used in the manufacture of textiles (flax, cotton, esparto grass, and mulberry for silk) as well as those with medicinal properties were protected by the state.

In addition to agriculture, the raising of livestock (sheep and Arabian horses) occupied a central position in the peninsular economy. As in the Roman period, lead, iron, gold, and mercury were mined. Domestic industry, which never went beyond the handicraft stage, culminated in the production of luxury cloths such as silk (a state monopoly), in the tanning of hides (Córdoban leather), and in the export of ivory objects. Commerce was selective and carried on in products "of low weight and high value" that frequently reached the most remote regions of the known world. There are reports of Andalusian travelers as far as the Sudan, central Europe, and even China.

The evolution of economic life was conditioned by political events; as the productive centres passed into Christian hands, the commercial vigour of the Muslims kept diminishing proportionally. No phenomenon is more illustrative of this than the confidence placed in the currency. In the 11th century Barcelona was counterfeiting Muslim coins; in the 14th century Granada was doing the same with Barcelona's coins.

CULTURE OF MUSLIM SPAIN

Arab civilization in the peninsula reached its zenith when the political power of the Arabs began to decline. Immediately following the Muslim conquest in the 8th century, there were no traces of a cultural level higher than that attained by the Mozarabs who lived among the Arab conquerors. All available evidence points to the fact that in this period popular works of medicine, agriculture, astrology, and geography were translated from Latin into Arabic. Many of these texts must have been derived from the *Etymologies* of Isidore of Sevilla and from other Christian writers. In the 9th century the situation changed abruptly: the Andalusians, who traveled east in order to comply with the injunction to conduct a pilgrimage to Mecca at least once in their lifetimes, took advantage of their stay in those regions to enhance their knowledge, which they then introduced into their native country.

LITERATURE

In the 9th century there flourished such court poets as ʿAbbās ibn Nāṣiḥ, ʿAbbās ibn Firnās, Yaḥyā al-Ghazāl, and the knight Saʿīd ibn Jūdī. Towering above all these, however, was Muḥammad ibn Hāniˇ, nicknamed the "Mutanabbī of the West" (Abū al-Ṭayyib al-Mutanabbī was a 10th-century poet of Iraq), who by virtue of his religious ideas was obliged to forsake his native land and enter into the service of the Fāṭimid caliph al-Muʿizz. In the 10th century al-Manṣūr assembled in Córdoba a notable group of court poets.

Bards performed the functions of modern journalists, accompanying their protector on military expeditions and celebrating his exploits in verse, the singsong rhyme of which became engraved in the memory of the people of Al-Andalus. As al-Manṣūr chose the foremost talents of his time to serve as "poet-journalists"—men such as Ibn Darrāj al-Qaṣtallī, al-Ramādī, Ṣāʿid of Baghdad, al-Ṭalīq, and numerous others—this occasional poetry sometimes attained literary heights. In the 10th century Ibn Faraj of Jaén deemed himself to possess sufficient background to compose the *Kitāb al-Ḥadāˇiq* ("Book of Orchards")—the first anthology of Andalusian poets. This anthology was soon followed by one by the physician Ibn al-Kattānī.

The highest peak in Islamic literature in Spain was attained during the era of the *ṭāʾifas*, when the poet-king al-Muʿtamid established an embryo of an academy of belles lettres, which included the foremost Spanish intellects as well as Sicilians who emigrated from their native land before its conquest by

AL-MUʿTAMID

Muḥammad ibn ʿAbbād al-Muʿtaḍid (born 1027, Spain—died 1095, Aghmat, near Marrakech, Morocco) was the third and last member of the ʿAbbādid dynasty of Sevilla (Seville) and the epitome of the cultivated Muslim Spaniard of the Middle Ages—liberal, tolerant, and a patron of the arts.

At age 13 al-Muʿtamid commanded a military expedition that had been sent against the city of Silves. The venture was successful, and he was appointed governor of this and another district. In 1069 his father died, and al-Muʿtamid acceded to the throne of Sevilla. He was destined to rule in difficult times: neighbouring princes were resuming the inexorable advance that in time would bring all of Spain once again under Christian rule. Yet his first efforts were successful. In 1071 he conquered and annexed the principality of Córdoba, although his rule was not effectively secured until 1078. During that time he also brought the kingdom of Murcia under his rule.

In 1085 Alfonso VI, king of Leon and Castile, captured the city of Toledo. This was a crippling blow to Spanish Islam. Al-Muʿtamid had already been forced to pay tribute to Alfonso, and, when he dared to refuse a payment, Alfonso invaded his kingdom and sacked various towns. Soon Alfonso also began making demands for territorial concessions. Al-Muʿtamid recognized that he could not stay the Christian advance with his own resources, and, acting as leader of a number of Muslim princes, he reluctantly sought the aid of Yūsuf ibn Tāshufīn. The latter, as the reigning Almoravid sultan, had just conquered all of Morocco and had powerful military forces at his disposal. In 1086 Yūsuf crossed the Strait of Gibraltar and at Al-Zallāqah inflicted a crushing defeat upon the Christian forces. Yet he had to return to Morocco before he could follow up his victory. Al-Muʿtamid now had a respite from Christian military pressure but soon found himself again unable to defend his borders. This time he sought Yūsuf's aid in person, and in 1090 another Almoravid army invaded Spain. Now, however, Yūsuf decided to carry on the jihad ("holy war") in his own name and proceeded to dethrone those who had invited him. Sevilla was captured, and al-Muʿtamid was sent as a prisoner to Morocco, where he remained until his death.

the Normans. Other petty kings in the peninsula endeavoured to compete with al-Muʿtamid, but they were unable to assemble a constellation of writers of comparable stature.

Among the outstanding poets of the 12th century in eastern Andalusia (the Andalusian Levant) were Ibn Khafajā of Alcira and his nephew Ibn al-Zaqqāq. To the era of greatest decadence, in the 13th century, belonged Abū al-Baqāˇ of Ronda and Ibn Saʿīd. In the 14th century three court poets, Ibn al-Jayyāb, Ibn al-Khaṭīb, and Ibn Zamraq, preserved their verses by having them inscribed in the Alhambra.

In Arab literature, poetry possesses greater vitality than prose. Even so, there are several prose writers of importance. Ibn Shuhayd (c. 1035) was the author of a work that lent inspiration to Abū al-ʿAlāˇ al-Maʿarrī for his Risālat al-ghufrān ("Epistle of Pardon"). The prolific Ibn Ḥazm of Córdoba (died 1064) wrote the delightful Ṭawq al-ḥamāmah ("The Ring of the Dove"), which dealt with love and lovers and which is still popular today. The enormous output of Ibn Ḥazm includes Kitāb al-Fiṣal, a history of religions that was not surpassed by Western scholars until well into the 19th century. He also was a leading exponent of the Ẓāhirī school of jurisprudence, which stressed thorough knowledge of the Qurˇān and the Hadith. He applied the principles of Ẓāhirism to theology and denounced all non-literalist approaches to theology. Another polymath was the vizier-historian Ibn al-Khaṭīb (died 1375). Two 12th-century anthologies of historical and literary works by Ibn Bassām and Ibn Khāqān are excellent sources of information concerning the apogee of Andalusian letters. Often the best grammars and dictionaries of a language are written by authors living in peripheral zones who endeavour to prevent gross errors being committed by their countrymen in the region. This perhaps explains why Al-Andalus, located at the western fringe of the Muslim world, produced works that to this day are used as texts in some traditional Islamic universities. From among these grammarians al-Zubaydī, tutor of Hishām II and Ibn Maḍāhˇ of Córdoba, who proposed a drastic reform of grammatical methods, stands out. Ibn Mālik of Jaén's didactic poem *Alfiyya* ("The Thousand Verses") constitutes an excellent handbook of grammar; and Abū Ḥayyān of Granada (died 1344), who emigrated to the east, wrote an outstanding commentary on the Quˇrān as well as the first Turkish grammar. In the field of lexicology, the blind Ibn Sīda of Denia (died 1066) is preeminent, author of a sort of "dictionary of ideas."

Noteworthy in the field of Quˇrānic science are Abū ʿAmr of Denia and Ibn Fierro of Játiva, whose handbooks made possible the correct psalmodizing of the Quˇrān. In addition, various collections of hadiths (traditions referring to the Prophet) appeared, but none of these was of particular importance. In this area the Andalusians were imitators of the East, and figures such as Ibn ʿAbd al-Barr, Ibn Rushd (Averroës), and Ibn ʿĀṣim are of interest.

The first extant chronicles of Muslim Spain, such as the *Taˇrīkh iftitāḥ al-Andalus* ("History of the Conquest of Spain") by Ibn al-Qūṭiyyah, date back to the 10th century. In the *ṭāʾifa* era the preeminent Spanish historian is Ibn Ḥayyān of Córdoba (died 1076), whose mostly preserved *Muqtabis* is an anthology of historical texts collected from the works of his predecessors; however, he also wrote an original chronicle, the *Matīn*. Of human interest are the *Memoirs* of the king Zīrī ʿAbd Allāh, who was deposed by the Almoravids and who sought to justify in those memoirs his deeds as a statesman. In the Naṣrid era is found the aforementioned Ibn al-Khaṭīb. The works of the North African historians Ibn Khaldūn (died 1406) and al-Maqqarī (died 1631) supply much information concerning Al-Andalus.

PHILOSOPHY

Andalusia enjoyed a great tradition in philosophy, in part as a means to compete with the dynamic culture in Baghdad and also as a result of limitations placed on philosophic inquiry in the eastern Islamic world. As early as the 10th century, the caliph of Córdoba, al-Ḥakam II al-Mustanṣir, imported books from the east to build a great centre of learning in his city. His efforts bore fruit as Córdoba was graced by three great scholars in the 10th and 11th centuries—Ibn Masarrah (died 931), Maslama al-Majrīṭī (died 1008), and Kirmānī (died 1068)—all of whom were knowledgeable in philosophy, geometry, and other disciplines. The most important, however, was Ibn Masarrah, whose teachings drew from the 5th-century-BCE Greek philosopher Empedocles and laid the basis of later Andalusian mysticism.

The foundations of the study of philosophy, set in the 10th and 11th centuries, bore fruit in the 12th century when Neoplatonic thought flourished in Islamic Spain. This development is associated with two important figures: Avempace, known in Arabic as Ibn Bājjah, and Ibn Ṭufayl. Although Avempace, a physician who probably died by poisoning, wrote a number of commentaries on important works by Aristotle and al-Farabi, he is best known for his *Tadbir al-mutawah hid* ("The Regime of the Solitary"), which was influenced by Neoplatonism and commented on the corrupt nature of society. Avempace's later contemporary, Ibn Ṭufayl, court physician and adviser of the Almohad ruler Abū Yaʿqūb Yūsuf, offered a more-developed Neoplatonism in his philosophical novel, *Ḥayy ibn Yaqzān* ("Alive son of Awake"). It is the story of a man who lives the first 50 years of his life on a deserted island, develops his own philosophy, and learns the truth about God.

The greatest Andalusian philosopher, however, and arguably the most important Muslim philosopher, is Ibn Rushd—or, as he is commonly known in the West, Averroës. He represents the high point of the philosophic tradition in Islamic Spain. His commentaries on the works of Aristotle, which had been translated into Arabic in Spain, had great influence on Jewish and Christian thinkers, including Thomas Aquinas, Siger of Brabant, and Boethius of Dacia. From a prominent Córdoban family, Averroës enjoyed a career as a court physician and religious judge in Spain. In 1169 he was commissioned to write commentaries on Aristotle's works by Abū Yaʿqūb Yūsuf, who was introduced to Averroës by Ibn Ṭufayl. One of the greatest expositors of Aristotle, Averroës also wrote a commentary on Plato's *Republic*, in which he critiqued contemporary rulers and governments. Best known for his works on Aristotle, Averroës also wrote *The Incoherence of the Incoherence (Tahāfut al-Tahāfut)*, a spirited defense of philosophy against the theologian al-Ghazālī, and the *Decisive Treatise on the Agreement Between Religious Law and Philsophy (Faṣl al-Maḳāl)*, which argues for the fundamental agreement between religion and philosophy (he did not, however, advocate the doctrine of the double truth, which his Latin interpreters did).

SCIENCE

In the mid-11th century Ṣāʿid, a *qāḍī* of Toledo, composed a noteworthy handbook of the history of science that contained much information on technical subjects. Mathematical sciences received little attention, though Maslama al-Majrīṭī (died 1008), who probably took part in the translation of Ptolemy's *Planispherium* and made some contributions to pure mathematics, is particularly noteworthy. During the heyday of Granada, ʿAlī al-Qalaṣ ādī, commentator on Ibn al-Bannāˇ, did important work on fractions. Despite their lack of interest in the physical sciences, the Andalusians excelled in both theoretical and practical astronomy. A number of these scholars sought to simplify the astrolabe, and finally al-Zarqālī (Azarquiel; died 1100) achieved success by inventing the apparatus called the *azafea* (Arabic: *al-ṣafīḥa*), which was widely used by navigators until the 16th century. Al-Zarqālī also anticipated Johannes Kepler by suggesting that the orbits of the planets are not circular but ovoid. The Arab mathematician Jābir ibn Aflaḥ (12th century) was also notable for his criticism of the Ptolemaic system.

Astrology was popular in Muslim Spain, and after 788 the Umayyad rulers retained an official astrologer in their courts. The most widely used astrological treatises were those of the Tunisian ʿAlī ibn Abi al-Rijāl and another, anonymous scientist, who made a translation from Vulgar Latin into Arabic in the 8th century. This book was translated from Arabic into Spanish during the era of Alfonso the Learned under the title of *Libro de las Cruces* ("Book of the Crosses").

The treatises on esoteric or occult subjects attribute to Maslama al-Majrītī two works on natural science that are not properly his but may be ascribed to one of his pupils. They are *Ghāyat al-ḥakīm* ("The Goals of the Scholar"; also known as *Picatrix*) and *Rutbat al-ḥakīm* ("The Step of the Scholar"). Greater interest is merited by the *Materia medica*, a revision of the Eastern Arabic text of the 1st-century Greek physician Pedanius Dioscorides ordered by al-Naṣir, on which Jews, Arabs, and Christians collaborated. Gradually the Andalusian Arabs kept adding new medicinal "simples"—which described the properties of various medicinal plants—to those described by Dioscorides, and the last eminent essayist on the subject, Ibn al-Bayṭār (died 1248), describes more than 1,400 of these. The Andalusians were familiar with the texts of the great Latin classics relating to natural science, and Ibn Wāfid, Ibn Baṣṣāl, and Ibn al-ʿAwwām (11th and 12th centuries) quote Varro, Virgil, and others. The most notable geographers in Muslim Spain were Abū ʿUbayd al-Bakrī (died 1094), who wrote the *Kitāb al-masālik wa'l-mamālik* ("Book of Highways and of Kingdoms"), and al-Idrīsī (died 1166), who was in the service of Roger II of Sicily and is the author of the leading universal geography composed by the Arabs. Somewhat later (1323) there appeared the first Arabic nautical map, possibly of Granadan origin. In technology, Muslim Spain was noted for its windmills and for its manufacture of paper. The Jews who lived in Muslim Spain had become culturally Arabized. They also pursued their own religious studies; the works of Moses Maimonides (1135–1204) are a good example of the cultural brilliance of the Andalusian Jews.

CHAPTER 14

UNITED SPAIN UNDER THE CATHOLIC MONARCHS

When Ferdinand II (1479–1516; also known as Ferdinand V of Castile from 1474) succeeded to the Crown of Aragon in 1479, the union of Aragon (roughly eastern Spain) and Castile (roughly western Spain) was finally achieved, and the Trastámara became the second most powerful monarchs in Europe, after the Valois of France. The different royal houses of the Iberian Peninsula had long sought a union of their crowns and had practiced intermarriage for generations. Nevertheless, the union of the Crowns of Castile and Aragon was far from inevitable in the last quarter of the 15th century. A union between Castile and Portugal was equally feasible, and it has been argued that it would have made more sense, for it would have allowed the two western Hispanic kingdoms to concentrate on overseas exploration and expansion, and it would not have involved Castile in Aragon's traditional rivalry with France.

The reasons that led John II of Aragon to arrange the marriage of his son and heir, Ferdinand, with Isabella of Castile in 1469 were essentially tactical; he needed Castilian support against French aggression in the Pyrenees. In Castile an influential party of magnates, led by Alfonso Carillo, archbishop of Toledo (who later reversed himself) and opposed to King Henry IV, supported the succession claims of the princess Isabella, the king's half sister, against those of his daughter, Joan. They were anxious for the help and leadership of the Aragonese prince and content with the alliance of a country in which the magnates had such far-reaching privileges as the Aragonese nobility. It needed a forged papal dispensation for the marriage, the blackmailing of Henry IV into (wrongly) denying the paternity of his daughter (Joan), and, finally, several years of bitter civil war before Ferdinand and Isabella defeated Joan's Castilian supporters and her husband, Afonso V of Portugal.

ARAGON AND CATALONIA

Ferdinand and Isabella ruled jointly in both kingdoms and were known as the Catholic Monarchs (Reyes Católicos). It was, however, a union of crowns and not of kingdoms. In size, institutions, traditions, and, partly, even language, the two kingdoms differed greatly. Within the kingdom of Aragon, Aragon and Valencia each had about 270,000 inhabitants, of whom some 20 percent and more than 30 percent, respectively, were Muslims and Moriscos (Muslims officially converted to Christianity). Catalonia had about 300,000 inhabitants. In each of these kingdoms the powers of the crown were severely limited. The barons ruled their estates like kings, dispensing arbitrary justice over their peasants. In Catalonia they had the right to wage private war. In Aragon anyone arrested by order of the king could put himself under the jurisdiction of a *justicia* who held his office for life and was therefore independent of the king's pleasure. It was this highest judge who crowned the kneeling king and made him swear to observe the *fueros*, the laws and privileges, of the kingdom. The oath the king was compelled to forswear is commonly translated as:

We who are as good as you, swear to you, who are no better than we, to accept you as our king and sovereign lord, provided you accept all our liberties and laws; but if not, not.

Although it is now known that the formula is a forgery, most probably of the mid-16th century, the quotation does summarize succinctly the relations between the kings of Aragon and the Aragonese nobility.

Ferdinand made no attempt to change this position, nor did he do so in Catalonia, where the crown had just emerged successfully from a long and confused civil war. The nobility and the urban aristocracy of Barcelona had been faced with violent social movements of the peasants and the lower classes of the cities and were themselves riven by family and factional strife. The crown intervened, mainly on the side of the lower classes but, inevitably, in alliance with some of the noble factions and against the French who had taken the opportunity to occupy Cerdagne and Roussillon. In 1486 Ferdinand settled the Catalan problem by a compromise, the Sentencia de Guadalupe, which effectively abolished serfdom and the more-oppressive feudal obligations of the peasants in return for monetary payments to the lords. Otherwise, the political and legal privileges of the rural nobility and the urban aristocracy were left intact. Effectively, therefore, Ferdinand made no attempt to strengthen the powers of the crown and to give the principality a more efficient system of government. But Ferdinand had given Catalonia peace and the opportunity to make good the ravages of the civil wars and the losses of commercial markets to Italian competitors. This opportunity was only partially taken by the Catalans. They failed completely to prevent the Genoese from establishing a dominant position in the economy of Castile and, more especially, in the vital and rapidly expanding Atlantic trade of Sevilla. The union of the Crowns of Aragon and Castile therefore led to neither a political and institutional union nor to an economic integration of the Iberian Peninsula.

CASTILE

Castile, too, was a poor country. Much of its soil was arid, and its agriculture was undeveloped. The armed shepherds of the powerful sheep-owners' guild, the Mesta, drove their flocks over hundreds of miles, from summer to winter pastures and back again, spoiling much cultivated land. Despite the violent hostility of the landowners, the government upheld the Mesta privileges, since the guild paid generously for them and was supported by the merchants who exported the raw wool to the cloth industry of Flanders. The activities of the Mesta were undoubtedly harmful to the peasant economy of large parts of Castile and, by impoverishing the peasants, limited the markets for urban industries and thus the growth of some Castilian towns. A change,

however, occurred in the 16th century. Just as in the rest of Europe, the population of Spain grew, rising in Castile from about 4.25 million in 1528 to about 6.5 million after 1580. To meet the increasing demands for agricultural products, the peasants expanded the cultivation of grain and other foodstuffs, and the Mesta and its migratory flocks gradually lost their dominant position in the Castilian economy. Their contributions to government finances declined as a proportion of total government revenue. The growing market also stimulated urban industries. Segovia, Toledo, Córdoba, and other towns expanded their manufactures of textile and metal. The apex of this expansion was reached in the third quarter of the 16th century, but it never matched that of Flemish and northern Italian cities. Overall, Spain remained a country that exported raw materials and imported manufactures.

In the northern provinces of Castile there lived a large class of minor nobles, the hidalgos. The inhabitants of Guipúzcoa (by the westernmost French border) even claimed that they were all of noble birth. But the south, New Castile (southeast of Madrid), Extremadura (southwest of Madrid), and especially Andalusia—that is, those provinces most recently reconquered from the Muslims—were the domain of the great nobility. There the Enríquez, the Mendoza, and the Guzmán families and others owned vast estates, sometimes covering almost half a province. They had grown rich as a result of the boom in wool exports to

Flanders during the 15th-century, when there were more than 2.5 million sheep in Castile. It was they, with their hordes of vassals and retainers, who had attempted to dominate a constitutionally almost absolute, but politically weak, monarchy.

It was in this kingdom that the Catholic Monarchs determined to restore the power of the crown. Once this was achieved, or so it seemed, the liberties of the smaller kingdoms would become relatively minor problems. Like their contemporary Henry VII of England, they had the advantage of their subjects' yearning for strong and effective government after many years of civil war. Thus, they could count on the support of the cities in restoring law and order. During the civil wars the cities of northern Castile had formed leagues for self-defense against the aggressive magnates. A nationwide league, the *hermandad* ("brotherhood"), performed a wide range of police, financial, and other administrative functions. Isabella supported the *hermandad* but kept some control over it by the appointment of royal officials, the *corregidores*, to the town councils. At the same time, both municipal efficiency and civic pride were enhanced by the obligation imposed on all towns to build a town hall (*ayuntamiento*).

HERMANDADES

The *hermandades* emerged in 12th century Castile as unions of municipalities organized for specific ends—normally for police purposes or for defense against the aggressions of magnates. The associations were initially temporary but later became permanent. One of the most famous *hermandades* was that of Toledo, Talavera, and Villa Real. The mounted constables of the *hermandades* were known as *cuadrilleros*. Banditry and rural crime were their chief concern; they both apprehended and summarily tried suspects. Originally they were disliked by the crown, but Henry II accepted and regulated their organization and functions by royal decree (1370). During the reign of Henry IV the *hermandades* fell into decay, and the Catholic Monarchs suppressed them in 1476, substituting a highly organized constabulary for the whole kingdom, known as the Santa Hermandad, whose judicial powers were considerable and whose cost was borne only by nonnoble taxpayers. Discontent compelled the Catholic Monarchs to reduce the status and expense of the Santa Hermandad in 1498, but it survived as an inefficient rural police organization until the 18th century.

The famous Hermandad de las Marismas—a federation of northern Castilian and Basque ports—was concerned with protecting the trade and shipping of its members. It enjoyed wide powers from the end of the 13th century, negotiating directly with the kings of England and France as a diplomatic entity, but it was brought under royal control in 1490.

With the great nobles it was necessary to move more cautiously. The Catholic Monarchs revoked usurpations of land and revenues by the nobility if these had occurred since 1464, but most of the great noble estates had been built up before that date and were effectively left intact. From a contemporary chronicler, Hernán Pérez del Pulgar, historians know how they proceeded piecemeal but systematically against the magnates, sometimes using a nobleman's defiance of the law, sometimes a breach of the peace or of a pledge, to take over or destroy his castles and thus his independent military power. Even more effective in dealing with the nobility was the enormous increase in royal patronage. Isabella was stage manager to Ferdinand's election as grand master of one after another of the three great orders of knighthood: Santiago, Calatrava, and Alcántara. This position allowed the king to distribute several hundred commanderships with their attached income from the huge estates of the orders. Equally important was royal control over all important ecclesiastical appointments, which the Catholic Monarchs insisted upon with ruthless disregard of all papal claims to the contrary. In the Spanish dependencies in Italy, Ferdinand claimed the right of exequatur, according to which all papal bulls and breves (authorizing letters) could be published only with his permission. A letter from Ferdinand to his viceroy in Naples, written in 1510, upbraids the viceroy for permitting the pope to publish a brief in Naples, threatens that he will renounce his own and his kingdoms' allegiance to the Holy See, and orders the viceroy to arrest the papal messenger, force him to declare he never published the brief, and then hang him. In Spain the Catholic Monarchs had no formal right of exequatur, but they and their Habsburg successors behaved very much as if they did. From that time onward the Spanish clergy had to look to the crown and not to Rome for advancement, and so did the great nobles who traditionally claimed the richest ecclesiastical benefices for their younger sons.

Perhaps most effective of all in reducing the political power of the high nobility was their virtual exclusion from the royal administration. The old royal council, a council of great nobles advising the king, was transformed into a bureaucratic body for the execution of royal policy, staffed by a prelate, three nobles, and eight or nine lawyers. These lawyers, mostly drawn from the poor hidalgo class, were entirely dependent on the royal will and became willing instruments of a more efficient and powerful central government. The Catholic Monarchs established the Council of Finance (1480, but not fully developed until much later), the Council of the Hermandad (1476–98), the Council of the Inquisition (1483), and the Council of the Orders of Knighthood (for the administration of the property and patronage of the orders of Santiago, Calatrava, and Alcántara), and they reorganized the Council of Aragon. Charles I (Holy Roman emperor as Charles V) and Philip II were later to continue this work and to add further councils, notably those of the Indies (1524) and of Italy (1558).

After Isabella's death in 1504, the nobles appeared to be tamed and politically innocuous. In fact, their social position and its economic basis, their estates, had not been touched. The Laws of Toro (1505), which extended the right to entail family estates on the eldest child, further safeguarded the stability of noble property. In 1520 Charles I agreed to the nobles' demand for a fixed hierarchy of rank, from the 25 grandees of Spain through the rest of the titled nobility, down to some 60,000 hidalgos, or caballeros, and a similar number of urban nobility, all of them distinguished from the rest of the population, the *pecheros*, by far-reaching legal privileges and exemption from direct taxation. Thus, the Catholic Monarchs' antinoble policy was far from consistent. Having won the civil war, they needed the nobility for their campaigns against the kingdom of Granada and, later, the kingdoms in North Africa and Italy. They now favoured the nobles against the towns, allowing them to encroach on the territory around the cities and discouraging the *corregidores* and the royal courts from protecting the cities' interests. Thus, the seeds were sown for the development of the *comunero* movement of 1520.

THE SPANISH INQUISITION

With its large Muslim and Jewish populations, medieval Spain was the only multiracial and multireligious country in western Europe, and much of the development of Spanish civilization in religion, literature, art, and architecture during the later Middle Ages stemmed from this fact. The Jews had served Spain and its monarchs well, providing an active commercial class and an educated elite for many administrative posts.

By the late 14th century, however, the status of the Jews in Christian Spain began to change. Their former protectors, the monarchs in Spain, began to restrict the rights and privileges of the Jews, and the devastation caused by the Black Death led to increased popular hostility, as many believed that the plague was a plot devised by Jews to destroy Christianity. Animosity toward the Jews was stimulated further by Jewish converts to Christianity who issued polemics against their former coreligionists. Calls for the expulsion or persecution of the Jews were answered by anti-Jewish riots in 1348 and 1391. The pogroms of 1391 were especially significant because of the subsequent mass conversion of Jews to Christianity in response to the violence perpetrated against them.

The *conversos* and Marranos—the "new Christians"—became a highly controversial group throughout Spain. Many of these converted Jews and their descendants assumed important positions in government and society and associated themselves with powerful noble families. They also achieved economic power and prosperity, which inspired increasing hatred of them by the "old Christians," who already questioned the sincerity of their conversions. Indeed, although there were many devout Christians among the *conversos*, there were also those who were at most agnostic converts, and the Marranos secretly continued to practice Judaism.

The wealth of the *conversos* created jealousy and their uncertain conversions hatred in a population that traditionally saw itself as the defender of Christianity against the infidel. The Catholic Monarchs, ever good tacticians, profited from this feeling. In 1478 they first obtained a papal bull from Sixtus IV setting up the Inquisition to deal with the *conversos* whose conversions were thought to be insincere. Since the Spanish Inquisition was constituted as a royal court, all appointments were made by the crown. Sixtus IV realized too late the enormous ecclesiastical powers that he had given away and the moral dangers inherent in an institution the proceedings of which were secret and that did not allow appeals to Rome.

With its army of lay familiars, who were exempt from normal jurisdiction and who acted both as bodyguards and as informers for the inquisitors, and with its combination of civil and ecclesiastical powers, the Spanish Inquisition became a formidable weapon in the armory of royal absolutism. The Supreme Council of the Inquisition (or Suprema) was the only formal institution established by the Catholic Monarchs for all their kingdoms together. Nevertheless, they thought of it primarily in religious and not in political terms. The

Inquisition's secret procedures, its eagerness to accept denunciations, its use of torture, the absence of counsel for the accused, the lack of any right to confront hostile witnesses, and the practice of confiscating the property of those who were condemned and sharing it between the Inquisition, the crown, and the accusers—all this inspired great terror, as indeed it was meant to do. The number of those condemned for heresy was never very large and has often been exaggerated by Protestant writers. But during the reign of the Catholic Monarchs several thousand *conversos* were condemned and burned for Judaizing practices. The whole family of the philosopher and humanist Juan Luis Vives was wiped out in this way. Many more thousands of *conversos* escaped similar fates only by fleeing the country. Many Roman Catholics in Spain opposed the introduction of the Inquisition, and the Neapolitans and Milanese (who prided themselves on their Catholicism and who were supported by the popes) later successfully resisted the attempts by their Spanish rulers to impose the Spanish Inquisition on them. Even in Spain itself, it was the sumptuous autos-da-fé, the ceremonial sentencings and executions of heretics, rather than the institution and its members, that seem to have been popular. But most Spaniards seem never to have understood the horror and revulsion that this institution aroused in the rest of Europe.

The first inquisitor general, Tomás de Torquemada, himself from a *converso* family, at once started a propaganda

Court of the Inquisition, *by the Spanish painter Francisco de Goya. The Spanish Inquisition was an attempt to rid the country of those who were suspected of being disloyal to the Catholic Monarchs.* The Bridgeman Art Library/Getty Images

campaign against the Jews. In 1492 he persuaded the Catholic Monarchs to expel all Jews who refused to be baptized. Isabella and most of her contemporaries looked upon this expulsion of more than 160,000 of her subjects as a pious duty. At the moment when the country needed all its economic resources to sustain its new European position and its overseas empire, however, it was deprived of many of its most economically active citizens and was laid open to exploitation by German and Italian financiers.

TOMÁS DE TORQUEMADA

Tomás de Torquemada (born 1420, Valladolid, Castile [Spain]—died September 16, 1498, Ávila, Castile) was the first grand inquisitor in Spain. His name has become synonymous with the Christian Inquisition's horror, religious bigotry, and cruel fanaticism.

The nephew of a noted Dominican cardinal and theologian, Juan de Torquemada, the young Torquemada joined the Dominicans and in 1452 became prior of the monastery of Santa Cruz at Segovia, an office that he held for 22 years. He was closely associated with the religious policy of King Ferdinand II and Queen Isabella I, to whom he was both confessor and adviser (to Isabella, from her childhood). He was convinced that the existence of the Marranos (Jewish converts), Moriscos (Islamic converts), Jews, and Moors was a threat to the religious and social life of Spain, and his influence with the Catholic monarchs enabled him to affect their policies. In August 1483 he was appointed grand inquisitor for Castile and León, and on October 17 his powers were extended to Aragon, Catalonia, Valencia, and Majorca.

In his capacity as grand inquisitor, Torquemada reorganized the Spanish Inquisition, which had been set up in Castile in 1478, establishing tribunals at Sevilla (Seville), Jaén, Córdoba, Ciudad Real, and, later, Zaragoza. In 1484 he promulgated 28 articles for the guidance of inquisitors, whose competence was extended to include not only crimes of heresy and apostasy but also sorcery, sodomy, polygamy, blasphemy, usury, and other offenses; torture was authorized in order to obtain evidence. These articles were supplemented by others promulgated between 1484 and 1498. The number of burnings at the stake during Torquemada's tenure has been estimated at about 2,000.

Torquemada's implacable hostility to the Jews probably exercised an influence on the decision of Ferdinand and Isabella to expel from their dominions all Jews who had not embraced Christianity. Under the edict of March 31, 1492, more than 40,000 Jews left Spain.

In his private life Torquemada seems to have been pious and austere, but his official career as inquisitor was marked by a harsh intransigence, which nevertheless was generally supported by public opinion, at least in the early years. Within his own order he was influential as visitor of the reformed Dominican priories of Aragon (1481–88), and his interest in the arts is evidenced in the monastery of St. Thomas at Ávila, where he died. In his final years, Torquemada's health and age, coupled with widespread complaints, caused Pope Alexander VI to appoint four assistant inquisitors in June 1494 to restrain him.

THE *CONVERSOS*

The expulsion of the Jews in 1492 did not signify the end of Jewish influence on Spanish history, as was long thought. It is not, however, easy to establish a clear-cut direction or pattern of this influence. At the end of the 15th century there may have been up to 300,000 *conversos* in Spain, and the majority of these remained. They had constituted the educated urban bourgeoisie of Spain, and the richer families had frequently intermarried with the Spanish aristocracy and even with the royal family itself. After 1492 their position remained precarious. Some reacted by stressing their Christian orthodoxy and denouncing other *conversos* to the Inquisition for Judaizing practices. Others embraced some form of less conventional, more spiritualized Christianity. Thus the followers of Sister Isabel de la Cruz, a Franciscan, organized the centres of the Illuminists (Alumbrados), mystics who believed that through inner purification their souls should submit to God's will and thus enter into direct communication with him. While they counted some of the high aristocracy among their number, most of the Illuminists seem to have been *conversos*. Again, it was among the *conversos* that Erasmianism (named after the famous humanist Desiderius Erasmus), a more intellectual form of spiritualized Christianity, had its greatest successes in Spain. The Erasmians had powerful supporters at court in the early years of Charles I as emperor, when his policy was directed toward the healing of the religious schism by a general reform of the church. But in the 1530s and '40s the enemies of the Erasmians, especially the Dominican order, launched a systematic campaign against them. The Inquisition annihilated them or forced them to flee the country, just as it had done in the case of the Illuminists as early as the 1520s. Nevertheless, the influence of Erasmus did not completely disappear from Spanish intellectual life, and it has been traced into the latter part of the 16th century.

But the majority of the *conversos* and their descendants probably became and remained orthodox Roman Catholics, playing a prominent part in every aspect of Spanish religious and intellectual life. They range from such saints as Teresa of Ávila and St. John of God, one a mystical writer and founder of convents, the other an organizer of care for the sick, to Diego Laínez, a friend of St. Ignatius of Loyola and second general of the Jesuit order. They include Fernando de Rojas, author of *La Celestina*, the first great literary work of the Spanish Renaissance, and, two generations later, Mateo Alemán, who wrote a picaresque novel, *Guzmán de Alfarache*; Luis de León, a humanist and poet; a Dominican, Francisco de Vitoria, perhaps the greatest jurist of any country in the 16th century; and another famous Dominican, the defender of the American Indians and historian of the Indies, Bartolomé de Las Casas.

Along with Luis Vives (mentioned earlier), these are only the most famous among the many distinguished *conversos* who played such a central and varied role in creating the cultural splendours of Spain's "Golden Age." This extraordinary phenomenon had no parallel anywhere else in Europe before the 19th or even 20th century. Although any attempt at explanation is bound to be speculative, the following may be suggested. The Spanish Jews and *conversos* formed a comparatively large section of the relatively small educated elite of Spain who were primarily responsible for the cultural achievements of the period. Moreover, having deliberately broken with the Jewish tradition of Talmudic scholarship (from the Talmud, the body of Jewish civil and canonical law), the *conversos* found the glittering Renaissance world of Christian Spain ambivalently attractive and repellent but always stimulating. Their response to this stimulus was probably sharpened by the hostility that they continued to meet from the "old Christians," who were bitterly resentful and aware of the ubiquity of the *conversos*, however much the *conversos* assimilated into Spanish culture.

THE STATUTES OF LIMPIEZA

Religious, racial, and even anti-aristocratic class prejudices combined to create the obsession with "purity of blood" (*limpieza de sangre*) which became characteristic of the Spaniards in the 16th and 17th centuries. It first crystallized with a statute of *limpieza*, imposed in 1547 on the cathedral chapter of Toledo, by which purity of ancestry both from the "taint" of *converso* blood and from any accusations of heresy by the Inquisition was made a condition of all future ecclesiastical appointments. The author of this statute was Juan Martínez Siliceo, archbishop of Toledo, a man of humble and, hence, by definition, untainted origins who had found himself despised by the aristocratic canons, many of whom were of *converso* ancestry. In 1556 Philip II gave his royal approval to the statute on the grounds that "all the heresies in Germany, France, and Spain have been sown by descendants of Jews." This remark was sheer fantasy with regard to Germany and France, and it is especially ironic that Pope Paul IV, then at war with Spain, quite correctly described Philip II himself as a Marrano, or a descendant of Jews who had converted to Christianity.

Statutes of *limpieza* spread rapidly throughout Spain. The statutes helped to perpetuate a set of values that equated pure ancestry, orthodoxy, and personal honour. Although this certainly helped to prevent the spread of heresies in Spain, in the long run it had a blighting effect on Spanish society, especially because the statutes were linked so closely with the basically corrupt institution of the Inquisition and its encouragement of the inevitably corrupting and divisive practice of spying on and denouncing one's neighbours.

By the middle of the 16th century the Inquisition had largely run out of suspected heretics and Judaizers. Apart from its continued concern with the Moriscos, the Inquisition began to concentrate its efforts on the censorship of books and on enforcing correct religious beliefs and moral (i.e., mainly sexual) behaviour among the "old" Christians. As religious conflicts in Europe became sharper in the second half of the 16th century, such supervision came to be practiced in Protestant as well as in Catholic countries. It was in this respect that the Spanish Inquisition, spreading its network of courts and familiars from the towns to the countryside, could surpass even the strictest Calvinist-Puritan communities, even though the use of torture was no longer deemed necessary and death sentences had become rare. Taken together with a royal prohibition against students studying at foreign universities, even Catholic ones, the Inquisition tended to isolate Spanish intellectual life from that of the rest of Europe.

On the positive side there was the Inquisition's general unwillingness to join in the widespread mania of witch hunting that led to thousands of executions in other European countries, especially Protestant ones. Most Spanish theologians did not believe in the existence of witchcraft and held that spells and sorceries were only female vapourings that could be safely ignored or dealt with by shutting the witch-women up in convents.

THE CONQUEST OF GRANADA

The impact of the Muslims on Spanish life and traditions had been rather different from that of the Jews. It was most evident, perhaps, in the position of women in southern Spain, who long remained semiveiled and in much greater seclusion than elsewhere in Christian Europe. It was evident also where Jewish influence was practically nonexistent, in the visual arts and especially in architecture. Not only did houses in southern Spain for a long time continue to be built facing inward onto a patio, but a whole style of architecture, the Plateresque, derived from an imaginative fusion of the Moorish (Muslim) and the Christian: classic Renaissance structures were decorated with Gothic or Renaissance motifs but executed in the Moorish manner, as if a carpet had been hung over the outside wall of the building. This charming style, which was invented during the reign of the Catholic Monarchs, spread far and wide over Spain and eventually even to the New World.

To Ferdinand and Isabella, the Moorish problem presented itself in the first place in a political and military form, for the Muslims still ruled their independent kingdom of Granada. The Catholic Monarchs had to concentrate all their military resources and call on the enthusiastic support of their Castilian subjects to conquer the kingdom in a long and arduous campaign, which ended with the capture of Granada, the capital, in 1492. In this campaign Gonzalo Fernández de Córdoba, the "Great Captain," developed the tactics, training, and organization that made Spanish infantry almost unbeatable for 150 years.

The Muslims were granted generous terms and religious freedom. However, against the advice of the saintly Hernando de Talavera, the *converso* archbishop of Granada who was trying to convert the Muslims by precept and education, the queen's confessor, Francisco (later Cardinal) Jiménez de Cisneros, introduced forced mass conversions. The Muslims rebelled (1499–1500) and, after another defeat, were given the choice of conversion or expulsion. Jiménez and Isabella did not regard this new policy as a punishment of the Muslims for rebellion, for Christian baptism could never be that. It was rather that they considered themselves to have been released by the rebellion from their previous guarantees to the Muslims, which they had entered into only with misgivings. Although many Muslims chose conversion, the problem now became virtually insoluble. There were never enough Arabic-speaking priests or money for education to make outward conversion a religious reality. The Moriscos remained an alien community, suspicious of and suspect to the "old" Christians. There was very little intermarriage between Moriscos and Christians, and the Moriscos were less likely to accept Spanish Christianity than were the *conversos*, who, despite the statutes of *limpieza*, became an integral part of Spanish society.

Cardinal Jiménez and other Castilians wanted to follow up the conquest of Granada by invading North Africa. There were religious, strategic, and historical reasons for keeping the two shores of the western end of the Mediterranean under single political control, as indeed they had been since Roman times. But Ferdinand, thinking in dynastic and imperial rather than national terms, chose to concentrate his efforts and Spanish resources on the traditional Aragonese claims against France along the Pyrenees and in Italy.

Aragon still held Sicily and Sardinia from the much more extensive medieval Aragonese empire. French intervention in Italy from 1494 gave Ferdinand his chance. To secure his southern flank while he led his army into Italy, Charles VIII of France agreed to return to Ferdinand the counties of Cerdagne and Roussillon (Treaty of Barcelona, 1493), which Louis XI had seized during the Catalan civil wars in 1463. But it was through Ferdinand's own diplomacy and through the generalship of Gonzalo de Córdoba that he acquired the Kingdom of Naples (1503). For the first time the union of Aragon and Castile had shown its strength, and Spain now rivaled France as the most powerful state in Europe. Ferdinand had carefully arranged the marriage of his children to strengthen his diplomatic position against France by alliances with Portugal, England, and Burgundy (which ruled the Netherlands). The unexpected deaths of the two eldest and of their children, however, left the succession of Castile after Isabella's death (1504) to the third, Joan the Mad, and her husband, Philip I (the Handsome) of Castile, ruler of the Burgundian Netherlands. The Netherlands nobility were delighted to see this enormous accretion of power to their ruler and looked forward to the advantages that they might reap from it. They accompanied him to Castile, where a large section of the high nobility, in their turn, were anxious to acclaim him rather than the redoubtable Ferdinand. Ferdinand was therefore forced to recognize Philip's claims but, when Philip died in 1506, was left as uncontested ruler. Ferdinand's last great success was the annexation of the Spanish part of the kingdom of Navarre in 1512.

SPAIN AND THE NEW WORLD

While the exploration of the Atlantic coast of Africa had been mainly a Portuguese concern in the 15th century, the Castilians had not been entirely disinterested in such activities and had occupied the Canary Islands (off northwest Africa). In the Treaty of Alcáçovas (1479), Afonso V of Portugal renounced his claims to the Crown of Castile, and he also recognized Castilian possession of the Canaries in return for Spanish recognition of Portuguese possession of the Azores (in the Atlantic Ocean west of Portugal), the Cape Verde Islands (off West Africa), and Madeira (north of the Canaries). The conquest of Granada allowed Castile, for the first time, to concentrate major resources and effort on overseas exploration.

The support that Christopher Columbus received from Isabella was indicative of this new policy. In 1492 Columbus made his landfall in the West Indies, and over the next half century the Spaniards conquered huge empires in the Americas and made their first settlements in East Asia. From the beginning there were disputes with the Portuguese, who were establishing their own colonial empire. The Catholic Monarchs obtained a series of papal bulls (1493) from the Spanish pope Alexander VI, which eventually resulted in the Treaty of Tordesillas with Portugal (1494) to settle their respective claims. Everything west of an imaginary line 370 leagues (here, the league was just over three nautical miles) to the west of the Cape Verde Islands in the Atlantic was assigned to Spain; everything east went to Portugal. The rest of Europe saw no reason to accept the pope's decision, and the result was constant and brutal warfare in the overseas colonies, even when the European governments were officially at peace.

CONQUISTADORS

The conquistadors (Spanish: "conquerors") were the leaders in the Spanish conquest of America, especially of Mexico and Peru, in the 16th century. An expedition against Aztec Mexico was led by Hernán Cortés, who set up a base camp at Veracruz in 1519 to prepare for an advance inland. Cortés marched inland with about 400 men and secured an alliance with the independent city of Tlaxcala, with whose aid he conquered the Aztec capital of Tenochtitlán (now Mexico City). Between 1522 and 1524, Michoacán and the Pacific coastal regions were conquered, and in 1524, expeditions led by Pedro de Alvarado and Cristóbal de Olid, respectively, were sent to Mayan Guatemala and the Bay of Honduras.

Hernán Cortés, 18th-century engraving. Photos .com/Thinkstock

The conquest of Inca Peru was led by Francisco Pizarro and Diego de Almagro, adventurers from Spain who had originally settled in Panama. Pizarro departed for Peru in 1531 with 180 men and 37 horses. Taking advantage of a civil war among the natives, Pizarro captured the reigning Inca ruler, Atahualpa, and, when Almagro arrived from Panama, conquered the capital city of Cuzco in November 1533. Pizarro founded a new capital, Lima, in 1535. Meanwhile, Alvarado arrived from Guatemala with intent to capture Quito, but he was persuaded to sell his army and ships to Almagro and Pizarro. Later a quarrel between Almagro and Pizarro erupted in 1538 into a civil war, which Pizarro won. Pizarro himself was murdered in 1541.

Spanish dominion was extended by a number of expeditions from Peru, including one by Sebastián de Belalcázar to the present Colombia, whose rule he had to share with Gonzalo Jiménez de Quesada, who had marched inland from the Caribbean coast. Pedro de Valdivia explored Chile, founding the city of Santiago in 1541. The conquistadores, given more to fighting and the search for gold than to governance, were quickly replaced by administrators and settlers from Spain.

COLONIAL POLICY

Unlike the other European colonists of that age, the Spaniards were vitally concerned with the moral problems of the conquest, conversion, and government of so-called heathen peoples. If the great majority of conquistadores ruthlessly pursued gold, power, and status, they also took with them Dominican and Franciscan friars who set themselves to convert and educate the American Indians and, sometimes, to protect them from their Spanish masters. The Dominican Bartolomé de Las Casas fought long battles to modify at least the greatest evils of colonial exploitation. His debates with a theologian, Juan Ginés de Sepúlveda, and the writings of Francisco de Vitoria provide the first systematic discussions of the moral and legal problems of conquest and colonial rule. Their importance lay in their effects on Spanish colonial legislation. The Leyes Nuevas ("New Laws of the Indies") of 1542 were based largely on the arguments of Las Casas. While in the Spanish colonies these laws were breached more than observed, they provided at least some protection for the Indians, and there was nothing like them in any of the other European overseas colonies of the period. However, even Las Casas supported the transatlantic slave trade of black Africans until late in his career, when he began to recognize its evils.

THE ATLANTIC TRADE

The crown insisted that all trade with the colonies should be carried on through Sevilla and should be reserved for Castilians, on the argument that it was Castilian money and blood that had built the Spanish overseas empire. This trade was closely regulated by the Casa de Contratación (1503), or House of Commerce, in Sevilla. The city itself rapidly became one of the greatest trading centres in Europe, and its population rose from 25,000 in 1517 to 90,000 in 1594. Yet Castile was unable to supply all the manufactures that the colonists demanded and for which they paid in solid gold and silver. Far from seeing this trade as an opportunity for Castilian industry, the Cortes (parliament) actually petitioned the crown in 1548 to prohibit exports to the Indies, which, they claimed, were raising prices in Castile. The government did not accept this petition, but Castile had to import much of what its colonists needed from Italy and the Netherlands. The Castilian monopoly of trade with Spanish America had in practice only the effect of giving the rest of Europe the chance to compete on equal terms for the American trade with the monarchy's non-Castilian subjects. The organization and financing of the Spanish Atlantic trade was largely in the hands of Genoese and South German merchants.

From the 1540s, when a new method of extracting silver from ore with the use of mercury was discovered, silver mining became a major industry in both Mexico and Peru, and silver shipments in rapidly increasing quantities soon surpassed the earlier gold shipments in value. Precious metal was exported from the Indies to Spain, partly as the crown's right of one-fifth (*quinto real*) but, more important, as payment for imports. The average annual quantities, as registered by the Casa de Contratación (not counting the unknown quantities that were smuggled), rose rapidly from about 1 million pesos in the five-year period from 1526 to 1530 to 5 million from 1541 to 1554 and then to the peak of more than 35 million during the period from 1591 to 1595. The growth of overall trade between Sevilla and the New World followed a very similar pattern, rising until 1550, then stagnating until the early 1560s, and rising again to a peak in the last decade of the 16th century. Prices, especially of agricultural produce, had started to rise in Spain, as in the rest of Europe, long before American silver was imported in considerable quantities. Whatever the ultimate causes of the price revolution of the 16th century, there can be little doubt that American silver greatly aggravated the inflation in Spain in the second half of the 16th century. The theologians of the University of Salamanca (some 100 miles west-north-west of Madrid) in the 1550s were the first to see this connection and to formulate the earliest version of a quantity theory of money (in which money is worth more when scarce than when abundant). Very little of this American treasure seems to have been invested in economic production. Most of it was used for display by the court and ruling circles, to pay for Spanish imports, for the Spanish armies abroad, and to satisfy the government's German, Italian, and Netherlandish creditors. Thus Spain, with all the treasure of the New World at its command, remained a poor country.

CHAPTER 15

SPAIN UNDER THE HABSBURGS

Ferdinand died on January 23, 1516, and the crowns of the Spanish kingdoms devolved to his grandson, Charles I (1516–56), the ruler of the Netherlands and the heir to the Habsburg dominions in Austria and southern Germany. This new union had not been planned in Spain, and at first it was deeply resented. Francisco Cardinal Jiménez, the regent until Charles's arrival in Spain, had to battle the old antagonisms between nobles and towns that were flaring up again when the magnates took the opportunity of the regency to try to regain their old power. When Jiménez tried to raise a militia, the nobles and the towns both sabotaged the plan. The old hostilities between the different Spanish kingdoms were as bitter as ever, with the men of Navarre, for instance, claiming that they would rather accept a Turk than an Aragonese as governor of the fortress of Pamplona. Although the court at Brussels had been careful to hold its hand in the distribution of patronage, the Spaniards nevertheless accused the Netherlanders of greed and place hunting. It took Charles's Netherlandish ministers a year and a half to settle the Netherlandish government and to make agreements with France and England that would allow the boy king to take possession of his new kingdom without outside interference. It was a considerable achievement, but for Spain the time was still too long.

CHARLES I

When Charles finally arrived in Spain in September 1517, his supporters were already disillusioned, and the country was apprehensive of the rule of a foreigner. Ugly, inexperienced, speaking no Spanish, and surrounded by Burgundian councillors and courtiers, Charles did not initially make a good impression. The different Cortes of Castile, Aragon, and Catalonia granted his financial demands but attached to them much pointed advice and criticism

THE *COMUNERO* MOVEMENT

On June 28, 1519, Charles was elected Holy Roman emperor as Charles V and prepared to go to Germany. His chancellor, Mercurino Gattinara, summoned the Castilian Cortes to Santiago in northwestern Spain (April 1520) to demand more money, even though the former grant had not yet expired. The towns immediately made their displeasure apparent. The Toledans refused to appear; the others demanded the discussion of grievances before they would supply the funds. By a mixture of bribery and concessions, the government finally induced a majority of the delegates (who had transferred from Santiago to A Coruña [Spanish: La Coruña] on the northwest coast of Spain) to vote the new grant. Many of the delegates were immediately disowned in their hometowns, and one from Segovia was murdered by an enraged mob. As Charles set sail (May 20, 1520), the Castilian revolution had already begun.

The towns, led by Toledo, formed a league and set up a revolutionary government. They claimed—more boldly even than the Third Estate during the French Revolution in 1789—that they were the kingdom and that the Cortes had the right to assemble without a royal summons and to discuss all matters relating to the welfare of the realm. There was talk of dethroning Charles in favour of his mother, Joan the Mad. The *comunero* leader, Juan de Padilla, actually captured the castle of Tordesillas (100 miles northwest of Madrid), where Joan was kept as prisoner, but the queen, whether out of madness or calculation of the interests of the monarchy, would not commit herself to Padilla's proposals. The *comunero* movement spread rapidly through Castile, and the nobles did nothing to check it. They had not forgiven Charles for his quest to attain the imperial title (which they thought inferior to that of king of Castile) nor for his foreign councillors and courtiers. They resented above all his bestowal of the archbishopric of Toledo on a young Burgundian, Guillaume de Croy, and the appointment of his former tutor, Adrian of Utrecht (later Pope Adrian VI), as regent of Castile. Even the appointment of the admiral Fadrique Enríquez and the constable of Castile, Iñigo de Velasco, as Adrian's coregents did little to mollify the offended grandees. Only when the more radical and popular elements in the cities were gaining control of the *comunero* movement and beginning to spread it to the nobles' estates did the nobles combine to raise an army and defeat the *comunero* forces at Villalar (April 23, 1521).

The power of monarchy was thus restored in Castile, never to be seriously shaken again under the Habsburg kings.

Artist's depiction of the execution of Castillian comuneros *following a decisive battle at Villalar in 1521 that quashed the comunero movement for good.* Universal Images Group/Getty Images

But in practice it was far from absolute. The towns kept much of their autonomy, and the *corregidores* were often unable to exert effective royal control over determined town councils. The 18 "royal towns" that were summoned to the Cortes never again challenged the ultimate authority of the crown. However, they continued to quarrel with the king about their claim that they were entitled to delay granting taxes until after their grievances had been dealt with, and they frequently managed to sabotage the government's demand that their deputies be given full powers to vote on government proposals. Moreover, when the crown found it convenient to convert the *alcabala* (a medieval sales tax) into the *encabezamiento* (global sums agreed by the Cortes and raised by the individual towns as they wished), the towns achieved a great measure of control over the administration of parliamentary taxation. Nor did the estate of the nobles in the Cortes prove easier to handle. In 1538, when Charles proposed a tax from which the nobles should not be exempt, there were immediate rumblings of revolt. The king had to give way, but he never summoned the nobility again to the meetings of the Cortes. The monarchy had thus won its political victory in Castile only at the cost of letting the nobility contract out of the financial obligations to the state and the empire. The rising burden of taxes fell therefore on those least able to bear them and on the only classes whose activities and investments could have developed the Castilian economy.

THE NOBILITY

The traditions of the grandees and hidalgos, formed in the centuries of struggle against the Muslims, made them even more averse to economic activities than the rest of the European nobility. Many engaged in wholesale trade in wool and grain, and some profited from the American trade in Sevilla. But the majority invested their money in land—without, however, improving agriculture—and preferred careers in the army, the church, and the civil service to the ignoble occupations of commerce. In the long run, the economic weakness of Spain, aggravated by its social traditions and its system of taxation, proved a serious handicap in Spain's struggle with its western European rivals.

After Villalar, however, the Spanish nobility had come to accept Charles I.

His championing of Roman Catholic Christianity against the Muslim Turks and German heretics appealed to their own traditions of Christian warfare against the Muslims in the Iberian Peninsula and North Africa. While Charles kept the grandees out of the central government of Spain itself, he had many prizes to offer in military commands, provincial governorships, and even viceroyalties in Italy and Spanish America. The hidalgos, trained as lawyers at Salamanca or as theologians at Alcalá de Henares (just east of Madrid), could look forward to dazzling careers in the king's councils and in the Spanish church. Even though Charles spent only 16 of the 40 years of his reign in Spain, the Spanish upper classes were beginning to accept and enjoy their monarch's position as the greatest ruler in Europe.

CHARLES I'S FOREIGN POLICY

Because of Charles's role as Holy Roman emperor, Spain became involved in interminable wars. The necessity of defending southern Italy against the Turks brought Charles's empire into collision with the Ottoman Empire, with the central Mediterranean as the chief battleground. Ferdinand's failure to complete the conquest of North Africa now brought a bitter revenge. The corsair leader Khayr al-Dīn, known as Barbarossa, had made himself master of Algiers (1529) and acknowledged the suzerainty of the sultan of Constantinople. Thus, the purely local problem of the Muslim raids on the

Spanish south coast became merged into the much more formidable struggle with the Ottoman Empire. In 1535 Charles captured Tunis. In perhaps his most satisfying triumph, Charles appeared in his chosen role of, as he said himself, "God's standard-bearer." He now seriously considered carrying the war into the eastern Mediterranean, even conquering Constantinople itself. But in 1538 Barbarossa, with a Turkish fleet, defeated Charles's Genoese admiral, Andrea Doria, at Préveza (western Greece), and in 1541 the emperor himself failed against Algiers. At the end of the reign, the balance of the two great naval powers in the Mediterranean, the Spanish and the Turkish, was still even.

Rival claims to Naples by the Aragonese and the Angevins (cousins of the ruling French house) also brought conflict with the French kings, against whom Charles fought four wars. His armies conquered Milan (northern Italy) and reduced most of the still-independent Italian states to Spanish satellites. An increasing part of the burden of these wars fell on Spain and especially on Castile. The Spanish *tercios* (infantry regiments) were not only the emperor's best troops, but it was in Castile that he could raise the largest part of his imperial revenues—moreover, without having to account for the way he spent them, as he had to do with the taxes voted by the States General of the Netherlands. It is therefore not surprising that the empire in Europe with Charles V as head became gradually transformed into a Spanish—or, rather, Castilian—empire of Charles I. In the latter part of his reign, Spaniards and Hispanicized Italians monopolized all high positions in the empire south of the Alps and began to appear in Germany and the Netherlands. More and more they came to interpret the international and Roman Catholic ideals of the emperor in terms of the political predominance of Spain in Europe and overseas.

PHILIP II

When Charles abdicated his various lands (1555–56), Philip II (1556–98) succeeded to all his father's dominions except Germany. His empire in Europe, now without the imperial title, was still only a loose union of independent states recognizing the same head. Philip, a great traditionalist, was not the man to inspire his different subjects with a new unifying idea, though he improved the central administration of his empire by the creation of the Council of Italy (1558). But his own Castilian upbringing and preferences increased the tendency toward transforming the Holy Roman Empire into a Castilian empire. Six of the nine viceroys Philip appointed to govern Sicily were Spaniards, as were all those of Naples with the single exception of one, Antoine Cardinal Perrenot de Granvelle, and 10 out of 13 governors of Milan. In the Spanish viceroyalties of Aragon, Catalonia, Valencia, and Navarre and in those of Mexico and Peru, none but Spaniards, preferably Castilians, were ever thought of at all, with the exception of one or two Italians. These were the key figures in Philip II's empire, and they were backed by the commanders of the Spanish regiments. Fortresses were nearly always governed by Castilians. It was necessary to appoint natives to military commands only in the Low Countries (Belgium, Luxembourg, and the Netherlands).

When the viceroys and governors were appointed, they were given "secret" instructions—in short, ones not meant for purely propagandistic purposes. These instructions reflected the current commonplaces of Christian government that could be found in scores of "Mirrors of Princes" (handbooks of government popular at the time) published in the 16th century and that Philip had made his own. The governors were to represent the king—not the state or the Spanish empire—as if he were present in person; it was stressed that they were not appointed for their own benefit but for that of the community they were sent to govern; they were to watch so that the king's subjects might sleep in peace and quiet and to dispense equal justice to rich and poor.

Many of the Castilian grandees who were appointed to these high offices undoubtedly strove to live up to these precepts. In practice, however, their success depended largely on the strength of the local opposition they met: there was, for example, a great deal of local opposition in Sicily, which had gained the reputation of being "fatal to its viceroys," but very much less in Naples, about which at least one viceroy remarked that no one should wish to be viceroy there, because of the pain he would have to suffer when he had to leave that post at the end of his term. A great part of the viceroys' difficulties, however, stemmed from the unreliability of the king himself. Philip was always anxious to maintain the dignity of their office, but he encouraged the local ministers and officials to report on their viceroys behind their backs, and he had no compunction about recalling a viceroy, governor, or minister when it suited him in this way to appease local opposition.

The king kept control over his viceroys and governors by weekly, sometimes daily, correspondence, carried by the excellent postal service that the house of Austria had organized in Europe. All important political decisions were thus taken in Madrid, and there the king relied almost entirely on Spaniards for advice. Only one non-Spaniard, Cardinal Granvelle of Franche-Comté, was ever summoned to Madrid to play a leading role in the king's inner councils (1579–86). It was Granvelle who had earlier, as the king's chief minister in the Netherlands, reminded his master of the international character of his empire. He advised a more international dispensation of royal patronage, as, for instance, the appointment of the Prince of Orange (William I the Silent) to the viceroyalty of Sicily so that Netherlanders and Italians would no longer think that the king regarded only the Spaniards as his "legitimate subjects." But Philip had refused to listen, and the bitter Castilian hostility to Granvelle at court ended by making the cardinal's ministry in Madrid less and less effective in the last two or three years before his death in 1586.

FINANCE AND IMPERIAL POLICY

Philip II inherited from his predecessor an unfinished war with France and a debt of some 20 million ducats. While his ally England (to whose queen, Mary Tudor, Philip was married) lost Calais, Philip's own armies won considerable victories, and he was able to conclude the Peace of Cateau-Cambrésis with France (1559), which confirmed Spanish possessions and hegemony in Italy and which left the frontiers of the Netherlands intact. But the financial position had deteriorated irretrievably, and Philip's governments, both in Madrid and in Brussels, had to declare a moratorium on their debts, or rather a forcible lowering of the very high rates of interest on government loans and a rescheduling of the repayments of short-term loans. It was the first of three such moratoriums in Philip II's reign—the other two were declared in 1575 and 1596—and it set the tone for the remainder of Habsburg rule in Spain, marked by growing disparity between the monarchy's imperial policies and the financial resources at its disposal to carry out these policies.

For the rest of the 16th century this disparity was still largely masked by the fluctuating, but generally increasing, shipments of silver from the New World.

These shipments inspired both the king and his German and Genoese creditors with the perennial hope of new treasure to pay off ever growing debts. But the armies and navies continued to swallow up more than the stream of American silver. Much of the money was already spent in the ports and coastal areas where the troops assembled and waited for embarkation to Italy or the Netherlands. Moreover, successive naval building programs provided further economic stimulus to the peripheral areas of the peninsula rather than the centre, Castile—which, however, had the highest rates of taxation. Thus, the financial burden of empire fell more and more on Castile, and it was these conditions that did much to determine the course of Spanish history for the next 100 years.

When Philip II returned to Spain in 1559, he still faced a naval war with the Turks, and in the following year his galleys suffered a humiliating and costly defeat at the island of Jarbah (off Tunisia's east coast). In 1566 the steadily deepening crisis of the Netherlands came to a head when groups of radical Protestants ransacked Roman Catholic churches, desecrating hosts, smashing stained-glass windows, and breaking sacred images. In that year Sultan Süleyman I (the Magnificent) died, and for a time the Turkish danger faded into the background. Philip could therefore risk sending his commander Fernando Álvarez de Toledo y Pimentel, 3er duque de Alba, with his best Spanish and Italian troops to the Netherlands (1567) to settle the problems of that dominion once and

SPANISH NETHERLANDS

The Spanish-held provinces located in the southern part of the Low Countries (roughly corresponding to present Belgium and Luxembourg) are collectively referred to as the Spanish Netherlands. The area was in the unfortunate position of being a buffer between Protestant and Roman Catholic states. Consequently, after the Eighty Years' War, it was mercilessly carved up. Northern Brabant, Zeeland, and the region east of the Meuse River was ceded to the United Provinces (Dutch Republic) in 1648. The county of Artois was taken by France in 1659, to be followed later by large southern portions of Hainaut, Luxembourg, and Flanders.

Under these conditions, the territory began to decline. Spanish control was lost when Charles II of Spain died without issue (1700), naming Philip, duc d'Anjou of France as his successor (as Philip V). The Spanish Netherlands was ruled for six years by Bourbon France and occupied for another seven by British and Dutch troops. In 1713 the Treaties of Utrecht divided the Spanish inheritance, and rule of the Spanish Netherlands passed to the Holy Roman emperor Charles VI and the Austrian Habsburgs.

for all. Alba was to root out heresy, punish those responsible for the rebellion, and impose taxes sufficient to relieve Castile of the need to send any more financial help to the government in Brussels. It was the king's most terrible miscalculation, for rebellion now became revolt and involved Spain in the Eighty Years' War, 500 miles from its own borders (1568–1648). It was in the pursuit of this war that the Spanish empire in Europe eventually foundered.

The key to the strategic thinking of Philip II and his successors, however, was always France. This was reasonable, for France was potentially the strongest military power in Europe and its hostility to Spanish greatness was absolute, despite occasional short periods of rapprochement. But, until 1595, France was paralyzed by a long succession of civil wars. Much as Philip II hated and feared a possible Huguenot (French Protestant) victory in France, he was content to see the civil wars continue, anxious most often to intervene on the side of the Catholics yet sometimes covertly offering help to the Huguenots. Until the late 1570s the threat from the Turks rivaled in importance the problems of the Netherlands. Philip switched his limited resources from the Low Countries to the Mediterranean and back again, unable to achieve a decisive victory in either theatre. It was natural, therefore, that Spanish foreign policy remained on the defensive for 20 years after the Peace of Cateau-Cambrésis. There were, moreover, still formidable internal Iberian problems to be solved.

THE MORISCOS

The most immediate problem was that of the Moriscos of Granada. The attempt to Christianize and assimilate them had proceeded only very slowly. In the 1560s the ineptitude and the wrangling among the different public authorities in Andalusia brought government to a virtual standstill. The captain general of Granada, in charge of defense and internal security, was quarreling with the municipal council of Granada and with the *audiencia*, the supreme court for Andalusia, over precedence, rights of jurisdiction, and the ownership of some pastures. The *audiencia*, in its turn, quarreled with the Inquisition over disputed rights of jurisdiction, as did the captain general. He was supported by the archbishop of Granada, who was, however, involved in a lawsuit with his cathedral chapter.

Such disputes were typical of the Spanish system of government, and it was also characteristic that they became immediately involved in faction fights at Philip II's court. These were therefore rarely settled according to their merits but according to the prevailing political alignment at court. In this case the governor-general, who had usually acted as the protector of the Moriscos against exploitation by the Christians, lost. The government in Madrid first sent a commission to inquire into titles of land, and this commission confiscated mainly Morisco land. In 1567 a decree was published forbidding the Moriscos the use of their Muslim names and dress and even their Arabic language. Internal security was transferred from the governor-general to the *audiencia*. This decision meant that now there was no one to protect the peaceful Morisco farmers from the large number of outlaws in the Alpujarras mountains. On Christmas Day, 1568, they rose against the hated Christians. It took two years of ferocious campaigning, with dreadful atrocities committed by both sides, before the rebellion was put down. The Moriscos of Granada were then deported in small groups to different parts of Castile and settled in a last attempt to achieve assimilation. In the absence of systematic education and in the face of the hostility of the Christian population, this attempt was also doomed to failure.

PORTUGAL AND ARAGON

The question of the complete unification of the Iberian Peninsula remained. In the case of Portugal, Philip's opportunity came when his nephew, King Sebastian of Portugal, lost his life and a great Portuguese army in an ill-prepared Crusade at the Battle of the Three Kings in northern Morocco (1578). During the short reign of Sebastian's old uncle, King Henry (1578–80), Philip carefully prepared his ground in Portugal by intrigue and bribery. Nevertheless, when Henry died, the opposition to Castile was still so strong in Portugal and the attitude of France and England so threatening that it was necessary for Philip to send Alba with an army to conquer Portugal in 1580. Although Philip respected the laws and privileges of his new subjects and left them to administer their own colonial empire, the union increased rather than diminished the old hostility between the Castilians and the Portuguese.

Philip II's last action in the peninsula was against Aragon. It was precipitated by a court intrigue that led to the flight (1590) of the king's secretary, Antonio Pérez, to Aragon. Since Pérez was unlikely to be convicted in the *justicia*'s court there, the king demanded his transfer to the court of the Inquisition. The populace of Zaragoza (some 160 miles west of Barcelona) rioted, freed Pérez, and killed the king's special representative (1591). To the Aragonese this meant the defense of their liberties; to Philip it meant open rebellion. A Castilian army marched into Aragon (1591), and Philip made a number of constitutional changes. The *justicia* was from then on removable at royal pleasure; the viceroy could be a Castilian, and the principle of majority voting was substituted for that of unanimity in the Aragonese Cortes. These changes gave the crown the ultimate power of decision in Aragon but preserved the kingdom's autonomy.

LEPANTO

In the Mediterranean the Spanish fleet was inferior to that of the Turks, and Philip had to remain on the defensive, even when the Turks were besieging Malta (1565). However, the Turks' failure to capture the island from the Hospitallers, who had leased it from Charles V in his capacity as emperor, marked the end of their great offensive. Six years later the combined Spanish, Venetian, and papal fleets—in alliance the numerical equals of the Turks—virtually annihilated the Turkish fleet in the Battle of Lepanto (1571). The strategic effects of this great victory were negligible, but its moral effects were immense. It confirmed the Spaniards in their chosen role as champions of Christendom and explains much of their continued willingness to support their king's religious and imperial policies, even in the face of ruinous costs and mounting disasters. After Lepanto, however, it became clear that the stalemate in the Mediterranean could not be broken. In 1580 Spain signed a truce with the Sublime Porte (Ottoman government).

From about 1580 the Spanish government became convinced that the rebellion (1568–1609) and heresy in the Netherlands could not be crushed as long as the rebels received help from England and France. These countries, moreover, gave active support to the Portuguese pretender, António, prior of Crato (mid Portugal), and their privateers committed continual acts of piracy against Spanish trade in the Americas. Philip began to give financial aid to the Holy League, the ultra-Catholic party in France. From 1586 he prepared an invasion of England. The Armada, which set sail from Lisbon in May 1588 numbering about 130 ships and nearly 30,000 men, was commanded by Alonso Pérez de Guzmán, duque de Medina-Sidonia, in place of Alvaro de Bazán, marqués de Santa Cruz, who had died in February. Although a brave and resolute commander, Medina-Sidonia was given the impossible task of convoying the army under Alessandro Farnese, duke of Parma, from the Netherlands to

SPANISH ARMADA

Beginning on July 21, 1588, a great fleet of ships from Spain engaged English forces in combat in English waters. This was the Invincible Armada, sent by Philip II, king of Spain. The Armada was made up of 130 ships, though not more than 50 of them were real men-of-war. They carried 30,493 men, of whom 18,973 were soldiers.

Philip II had many reasons for attacking England. In part, his was a religious war against heretics. Mary Stuart, queen of Scotland and the Catholic hope for succession to the throne of England, had been executed. With her died the chance of defeating the Protestant Reformation. Pope Sixtus V urged Philip to the holy war, promising him financial aid.

Another reason for Philip's wrath was that English pirates, chartered by Queen Elizabeth I, had challenged Spain's dominions. English privateers captured Spanish ships carrying treasure from the New World and from Africa. This booty made up a large part of England's Royal Treasury. A climax was reached when Francis Drake sailed around the world, trading at will in Spanish territory, and was knighted by Elizabeth I on his return.

The original Spanish plan of attack was made by the foremost Spanish seaman of his time, Don Álvaro de Bazan, marquis of Santa Cruz. The plan, which called for an invading force of 556 ships and 94,222 men-at-arms, was spoiled by Drake's raids. Drake entered the harbor of Cádiz with 23 English vessels in April 1587 and destroyed or captured 38 of the Spanish ships that were to make up the Armada. He took still more ships at Cascaes Bay and off Cape St. Vincent, and Philip had to change his strategy.

The new Spanish plan of attack called for fewer ships and men. The land invasion was to be commanded by Alessandro Farnese, duke of Parma, an experienced soldier and the head of Philip's occupation army in the Netherlands. Santa Cruz opposed this selection, but his resistance ended with his death in January 1588. The Armada was then placed under the command of Don Alonso Pérez de Guzmán, duke of Medina-Sidonia, an inexperienced warrior.

The Armada sailed from Lisbon on May 20, 1588. After putting in at Coruña for repairs, it was sighted in the English Channel on July 19. The English fleet that met it had 197 ships; many were small coastal vessels, so the total tonnage of the two forces was about equal.

The battle was decided by the superior speed and maneuverability of the long, low English ships and by their long-range firepower. The Spanish were accustomed to the Mediterranean style of fighting, which called for ramming and boarding. The English raked the Spaniards with broadsides at long range. In the first engagement, near Eddystone, a Spanish flagship was destroyed and other vessels of the Armada were severely damaged. Other battles were fought off St. Alban's head on July 23 and off the Isle of Wight on July 25. The Armada retreated to Calais. Medina Sidonia sent a message requesting Parma's help. Blockaded, Parma was unable to aid him.

At midnight on July 28 eight fire ships drifted into the harbor of Calais and burst into flames. The Spaniards panicked, cut their anchor cables, and drifted near Gravelines. Attacked again, the Armada fled north, intending to sail around Ireland's west coast and return to Spain. Buffeted by gales, many ships sank or ran aground. In all, 63 Armada ships were lost. Only four had been sunk in battle.

England in the face of a better-armed English fleet and without control of a single deepwater channel port. The defeat of the Armada was probably inevitable but not dishonourable.

Spanish intervention in France from 1590 was equally doomed to failure. The duke of Parma, with his Spanish veterans, won great tactical victories, but Spain failed to prevent the succession of Henry of Navarre as Henry IV of France and the collapse of its ally, the Holy League, when Henry converted to Roman Catholicism in 1593.

Philip viewed his role and that of Spain essentially as that of defender of the Roman Catholic Church against the aggression of the heretics, an aggression that now seemed to have become mainly military and that consequently had to be met by military force. It was therefore essential that the king should safeguard and extend the power of Spain and the just claims of his house, such as those he made for his daughter for the throne of France. Every other consideration was subordinated to this obligation, even to the point at which the Spanish ambassador in Rome, Gaspar de Guzmán y Pimental, conde-duque de Olivares, intervened in three successive conclaves in order to assure, by a mixture of promises and threats, the election of popes congenial to his master (conclaves in 1590–91 of Urban VII, Gregory XIV, and Innocent IX). He just failed in the fourth, but crucial, election—of Clement VIII, who was to receive Henry IV back into the Catholic church (1595).

Although Philip II could thus justify his aggressive policies to himself, both Spain's enemies and its allies were convinced that they were witnessing the quest for Spanish dominance over Europe. Many Spaniards themselves believed this, and, as the war dragged on and the costs mounted, even the faithful Castilian Cortes began to question the king's policy. In 1574 Philip proposed tripling the value of the *encabezamiento*, which had remained fixed during the previous 20 years; however, the Cortes opposed this proposal and managed to achieve a considerable reduction. After 1580, silver shipments from the New World to Sevilla reached new record levels, and this undoubtedly helped to persuade Philip II to embark on his grandiose schemes against England and France. Yet this silver represented only a quarter of his annual revenues. The rest was derived from taxation and from loans for which future revenues were pledged. The Armada campaign was said to have cost 10 million ducats; the combined cost of the continuing naval war against England, the campaigns in the Netherlands, and the military intervention in France was even greater. In 1590 the Cortes accepted the royal demand for a new excise tax that was to raise eight million ducats in six years and that was appropriately nicknamed the *millones*. But by 1595 a deputy from Sevilla said bitterly that

the reason why taxes have been raised without noise is because they have not fallen on the rich who are those who have a voice... and the sweetness which they find, that is the blood of the poor.

The following year Philip II's government declared its third bankruptcy (moratorium) and failed to get the Cortes to agree to an increase or even the renewal of the *millones* before 1601.Spain had gambled its own prosperity and its American treasure, and with it its own hegemony over the European continent, on a decisive victory over the heretics in western Europe, and it had failed. Shortly before his death, Philip II concluded the Treaty of Vervins (1598) with France, which substantially reestablished the position of 1559. Yet, although Spain had failed in its highest ambitions, it remained the greatest power in Europe at the end of the 16th century. It had brought Christianity to millions overseas—which to most contemporaries, if they thought about it at all, seemed worth the appalling price paid in terms of the lives and freedom of non-European peoples—and Protestantism, though not destroyed, had been contained. Spanish monks and mystics had given Roman Catholicism a new content, and Spanish theologians and jurists had created the basis of international law. Spanish literature and art were only now entering their greatest period. Morally and economically, there were dark sides to the picture, but to the Spaniards the 16th and early 17th centuries have always been their "Golden Age."

SPAIN IN 1600

It is not surprising that the enormous exertions of the last quarter of the 16th century, with its mixture of triumphs, disappointments, and miseries, should have been followed by a general mood of introspection and even disenchantment. This was particularly evident in economic and social thinking. The *arbitristas* (literally, "projectors") were writers who combined an economic analysis of the social ills of Spain with projects for economic recovery and social and moral regeneration. They saw clearly the central weakness of Spain: the attitude of mind that despised productive work and those who engaged in it. Far too many strove to live the life of a hidalgo. The treasures of Mexico and Peru, so far from stimulating investment and industrial production, had only encouraged men to look for shortcuts to riches and to live the life of rentiers, investing their money in the *censos*, the government annuities. These *censos* were the greatest plague and perdition of Spain, wrote González de Cellorigo, perhaps the most acute of the *arbitristas* of 1600. "It seems," he concluded, "as if we had wanted to turn these kingdoms into a republic of enchanted men, living outside the natural order."

The positive plans (among many fantasies) advocated by the *arbitristas* included the drastic cutting of government expenditure, the reform of the tax system, the encouragement of immigration into Castile, systematic and extensive irrigation, protection of industry, improvement of transport, and, finally, the sharing of the cost of empire among the constituent kingdoms of the monarchy. These were reasonable proposals, not unlike those put forward by mercantilist writers in the rest of Europe who treated economic activity as a means of increasing the power of the state. But time would show that the Castilian ruling classes would be neither capable nor willing to act on them. Their attitudes were varied and often ambivalent, and this ambivalence is reflected in the imaginative literature of the period.

SPAIN'S GOLDEN AGE IN LITERATURE

At one extreme there was the picaresque novel, with its implicit satire of a society in which one could make one's way by cleverness and roguery rather than by honest work—that is, if one did not happen to be born a nobleman. Thus, the hidalgo in the *Lazarillo de Tormes* (published 1554; doubtfully attributed to Diego Hurtado de Mendoza), the first of the picaresque novels, is down and out but would rather starve than work, and he expects his servant, the boy Lazarillo, to scrounge for them both. In *Don Quixote* (published 1605 and 1615), Miguel de Cervantes raised the novel to a completely new level of social and psychological insight. It is, among other things, a parable of Cellorigo's "republic of enchanted men" living in a world of illusions and tilting at windmills.

At the other extreme, there was the drama from exponents such as Lope de Vega, Tirso de Molina, and Pedro Calderón de la Barca. As with the picaresque novel, the comedy of the Golden Age was concerned with the contemporary social scene. The psychological problems faced by its characters arose nearly always directly out of social conflicts. But the social purpose of these plays was essentially conservative, representing a defense of Spain's highly structured society. This was achieved by insisting on the special dignity and honour of all social ranks, from the king down to the peasants. Thus Lope introduced the common people as fully rounded characters on the stage, allowing, for instance, to the daughter of a blacksmith the emotions of love formerly reserved on the stage to aristocratic ladies. Heredity and blood are the principles of a social order that, in the comedies, may be threatened but is always reaffirmed in the end. There is perhaps a link here between the visual arts of the age and the Baroque style.

THE "GOLDEN AGE" IN ARCHITECTURE AND PAINTING

In the more severe artistic climate of the Catholic Reformation of the second half of the 16th century, the playful Plateresque style of buildings fell into disfavour. Philip II preferred the unornamented and monumental architecture of Juan de Herrera, the greatest Spanish architect of the century. It could be very effective, as in Philip's monastic palace of El Escorial (20 miles northwest of Madrid), which embodied the gloomy and ascetic spirit of the king and also blended with the stark and forbidding landscape of the Guadarrama mountain range northwest of Madrid. But too often the style produced only an ugly and pompous monumentality, such as not infrequently afflicts the architecture of countries at the height of their imperial periods. Yet, at the turn of the century, this style gave way to the Italian Baroque, which Spanish architects found no difficulty in acclimatizing to their country. The Baroque style could achieve monumentality without being pompous. It could display the grandeur of the church or the monarchy or anyone rich enough to build himself a palace. Perhaps most important of all, it was a style that, by its love of ornamentation and its essentially theatrical character, became immensely popular with the mass of the population.

The single most splendid monument in the Baroque style, the Buen Retiro Palace just outside Madrid, has not survived. Built in the 1630s, in the middle of the Thirty Years' War, at a time when Spain's military fortunes were beginning to decline, it was designed to reaffirm the greatness of the Spanish monarchy. Like El Escorial, it had a forbidding exterior; its interior decoration, however, like that of the splendid library of Philip II's monastery-palace, showed, literally or allegorically, Spain's victorious battles with the enemies of Catholic Christendom. Great numbers of paintings were bought in Spain and abroad, and Spanish courtiers were coerced to lend or even to make presents of their own paintings and other art objects. As in other courts of the period, splendid theatrical and musical entertainments were organized, mainly for the benefit of the court and the diplomatic corps, but occasionally the Madrid public was also invited or allowed to buy tickets. Perhaps it was symbolic of the Spanish monarchy in this period that such a grandiose vision and its overhasty construction should have produced rising and increasingly unacceptable maintenance costs.

The painting of the period does not lend itself as easily to a social interpretation, but certain patterns may still be observed. The greatest painter of the Spanish Counter-Reformation, El Greco (Doménikos Theotokópoulos, from Crete), made his home in Toledo, where the local aristocratic and ecclesiastical society (but not Philip II) seems to have fully appreciated his genius. El Greco's superb portraits, but, above all, his religious paintings, with their elongated figures rising like so many flames to heaven, seem like the embodiment of the most spiritual aspects of Spanish Catholicism.

El Greco left no school of painting. The painters of the following generation, especially Bartolomé Esteban Murillo, had a different religious sensibility, more naturalistic than that of El Greco, more personal, and more romantic; and again, as did Baroque architecture, they appealed successfully to a popular religiosity. But the greatest of them, Diego Velázquez, was hardly a religious painter at all. His subjects were the king with his family and court and, characteristic for the age and parallel with the drama of the period, the common people. All these he represented with a realism and psychological insight unmatched in the 17th century, except perhaps by Rembrandt.

THE REIGN OF PHILIP III

It was the tragedy of Spain that its ruling classes failed to respond to the social and political problems of the age as creatively as its writers and artists. For this failure there are at least some good reasons. In the first place, the system of royal government, as it was understood at the time, depended ultimately on the king's ability to lead and to make decisions. Philip II's very consciousness of his divinely imposed obligations, compounded by his almost pathological suspiciousness of the intentions and ambitions of other men, had led him to deprecate independent initiative by his ministers. He thus failed to educate an effective ruling class with a tradition of statesmanlike thinking and decision making

Devout but indolent and passive, Philip III (1598–1621) was incapable of carrying on his father's methods of personal government. He therefore had to have a minister (*privado*) who would do all his work for him. His choice, Francisco Gómez de Sandoval y Rojas, duque de Lerma, however, turned out to be a singularly unfortunate one. Amiable, incompetent, and, inevitably, under heavy attack from those who envied his position, Lerma strove to maintain himself by the lavish dispensation of royal patronage to the high nobility. He was unable to turn the schemes of the *arbitristas* into effective reforms. During the reign of Philip III the government of Spain either became the victim of events that it did not attempt to control or allowed its hand to be forced by outsiders.

Not all events could have been controlled. In 1599–1600 an epidemic plague claimed some 500,000 victims in Castile. This sudden decimation of the labour force caused a sharp rise in wages, which in turn acted as another disincentive to capital investment by Spaniards. Yet the advantages that the labourers had reaped from the rise in wages were quickly offset by renewed inflation, the result of the government's decision to solve its perennial financial problems by the massive minting of *vellón*, a debased copper coinage. Although this action did not prevent the need for another moratorium on government debts, in 1608 the king promised the Cortes of Castile that the government would not issue any more *vellón* money for 20 years. But in 1617 and 1621 he was forced to ask the Cortes to allow additional issues.

THE EXPULSION OF THE MORISCOS

The plight of the Moriscos was the most serious social crisis of the reign. The great majority of the Moriscos lived in the kingdom of Valencia. Like those of Andalusia, they had been forcibly but ineffectively converted to Christianity. Most of them were relatively poor farmers, agricultural labourers, or small tradesmen and hucksters. Although they were hated and despised by the poor Christian peasants, the Moriscos were protected by the landowners for whom they provided industrious tenants and labourers.

For many years a controversy raged between those who wanted to "solve" the Morisco problem by expulsion and those who pleaded for time and money to achieve the genuine assimilation and Christianization of the Moriscos. While the practical economic aspects of these two views were not neglected, it was characteristic of the Spain of the period that the main emphasis of the debate was on the religious and moral problems. In 1609 Lerma's government ordered the expulsion of the Moriscos. Lerma saw it as part of a policy of disengagement from "Castilian" power politics in central Europe—he himself was a Valencian—and a renewed shifting of Spanish energies toward North Africa and Islam. As a Valencian landowner, he also hoped for personal gain from the confiscation of Morisco land. By 1614 some 275,000 Moriscos had been forced to leave Spain. The majority of Spaniards undoubtedly approved of the expulsion.

The economic effects of the expulsion have generated considerable debate, both at the time and today. In Castile the effects were probably slight. In Aragon and Valencia, where the Moriscos had constituted between 20 and 30 percent of the population, they were certainly much greater. Some but by no means

all Morisco land was resettled by "old" Christians. There was a shift from labour-intensive sugar and rice production to mulberry cultivation for silk and viticulture. The greatest difficulties were caused by the indebtedness of the Morisco peasants and the consequent losses suffered by their urban creditors. An ironic footnote to the expulsion was the plight of the Aragonese and Valencian Inquisitions. Although they once favoured expulsion, they were now left without their major source of income, the composition fines for Moorish practices that they imposed on the Morisco villages.

SPAIN AND EUROPE

Neither Philip III nor Lerma was emotionally or intellectually capable of the fundamental reappraisal of foreign policy that Philip II's failures required. Very few even of the *arbitristas* had seen this need sufficiently clearly. The court, the nobility, and, above all, the clergy and the king's confessors remained caught in the now-hardening tradition of Spanish imperialism, simplistically interpreted as the cause of God. This attitude caused a serious misjudgment of the political forces in England, leading to the absurd hope of placing the infanta Isabella on the English throne upon the death of Elizabeth I. In 1601 a small Spanish force was disembarked at Kinsale, in Ireland, to cooperate with the Irish rebels. The English army had no difficulty in forcing it to surrender.

Fortunately for Spain, the new government of James I was anxious for peace. On the Spanish side, the Treaty of London (1604), which ended 16 years of Anglo-Spanish war, was negotiated on the initiative of Philip II's son-in-law, the archduke Albert, to whom Philip II in his last year had handed over the nominal sovereignty of the Spanish Netherlands. Albert and his Genoese general, Ambrogio Spinola, also urged the Spanish government to negotiate with the Dutch rebels. Between 1604 and 1607, Spain sent unprecedentedly large sums to Flanders. Spinola captured Ostend (on the coast of present-day Belgium) and won victories in Friesland (northern Holland). But, he wrote to Madrid, it would take 300,000 ducats a month to continue the war successfully. After the moratorium of 1607, Philip III was in no position to raise such sums. He and Lerma, but not the Castilian grandees in the Council of State, were prepared to recognize Dutch independence, but they insisted that the Dutch withdraw from their recent conquests in America and the East Indies. The Dutch refused to accept this as well as an alternative Spanish condition, the toleration of Roman Catholics in their state. As a compromise, the two sides concluded a 12-year truce, beginning in 1609.

In 1610 a new war with France threatened, but the French king Henry IV was assassinated, and for almost 20 years France, Spain's most formidable opponent in Europe, became preoccupied with its internal problems. The years from 1610 to 1630 were the last period in which Spain clearly dominated Europe. For the first of these two decades Europe enjoyed a kind of Pax Hispanica. Spanish armies controlled Italy, Flanders, and parts of the Rhineland. Spanish and Spanish-inclined Jesuits were confessors at the courts of the Austrian Habsburgs, Poland, Bavaria, and some of the minor German and Italian princes. Spanish subsidies, pensions, and bribes made clients even of Protestant politicians in England, Holland, and the Swiss cantons (although much less effectively so than Madrid hoped); and Spanish-paid spies fed the governments of Madrid and Brussels with valuable, if not always accurate, information about potential enemies in the United Provinces (Holland), England, and France. Yet, to a much greater degree than most contemporaries realized, this Spanish domination of Europe rested on default: the disunity and temporary weakness of Spain's political and religious opponents. The psychological effects of this position on Spain were wholly disastrous, for it confirmed the Castilian ruling classes in their imperialist attitudes.

For Philip III and Lerma this attitude led, for reasons of both finance and temperament, to a largely defensive stance, though its effect was quite the opposite for the Spanish representatives abroad. In the absence of an effective lead from Madrid, the Spanish grandees who were the king's viceroys and ambassadors in Europe took it upon themselves to advance Spanish interests as they saw them—that is, in terms of Spanish power. They fortified the route from Milan to the Tirol (western Austria) through the Valtellina, the vital link with the Austrian

Habsburgs; they annexed several small Italian lordships; they enticed Dalmatian pirates (operating from the eastern shore of the Adriatic), the Uskoks, to prey on the trade of Venice, and they even seem to have plotted the complete overthrow of that republic.

More fateful still were their activities in Prague and Brussels. At the courts of the emperors Rudolf II and Matthias, the ambassador Baltazar de Zúñiga organized an effective "Spanish" party. His successor, the conde de Oñate, negotiated the secret Treaty of Graz (1617) by which the Jesuit-educated archduke Ferdinand of Styria (later Emperor Ferdinand II) was designated as heir to Matthias. In return for giving up Philip III's claims to the Austrian succession, which Madrid had never seriously pursued in any case, Oñate obtained the promise of full Spanish sovereignty of the Tirol and Alsace (now in eastern France), the two German pillars of the "Spanish Road" between Italy and the Netherlands. At the same time, the "Spanish" party in Prague managed the preelection of Ferdinand as king of Bohemia in case of Matthias's death. Zúñiga and Oñate had undoubtedly strengthened Spain's strategic position in central Europe, but they had also, for the first time since the abdication of Charles V, involved Spain again in the local politics of the Holy Roman Empire. For Philip IV this involvement turned out to be even more disastrous than it had for Charles V. Spanish leadership, as practiced by the self-willed Castilian grandees abroad, had proved to be energetic and

clever, but it was ultimately as devoid of true statesmanship as the slackness of the king and his *privado*.

PHILIP IV'S REIGN

In 1618 Lerma's enemies at court finally managed to overthrow him. Zúñiga returned to Madrid and became the leading advocate of aggressive policies. Alonso de la Cueva, marqués de Bedmar, former Spanish ambassador to Venice and the organizer of the anti-Venetian conspiracy, went as ambassador to Brussels and immediately began to press for the reopening of the war against the United Provinces. In 1621 Philip III died, and with him disappeared the last restraints on the neoimperialists. Only 16 years of age, Philip IV left the effective powers of kingship in the hands of his former gentleman of the chamber, the conde-duque de Olivares. Olivares shared the political views of his uncle, Zúñiga, and he soon dominated the Council of State.

SPAIN AND THE THIRTY YEARS' WAR

In 1620, following the defeat of Frederick V (the elector palatine, or prince, from the Rhineland who had accepted the crown of Bohemia when it was offered to him in 1618) and the Bohemians, Spanish troops from the Netherlands entered the "Winter King's" hereditary dominions of the Rhenish Palatinate. Militarily, Spain was now in a favourable position to restart the war with the United Provinces at the expiration of the truce in 1621. The decision to do so was, however, taken on more general grounds. The Dutch had used the truce only to capture the carrying trade with Spain of western Europe and the Baltic, Zúñiga argued. On the oceans they had never observed the truce but continued their piracies against Spanish and Portuguese shipping. If they were allowed to continue, first the Indies would be lost, then the rest of Flanders, Italy, and, finally, Spain itself, for it would have lost the dominions that had made it great. These were very different grounds for resuming the war from those habitually advanced by Philip II. Little was said about religion or even the king's authority, while the protection of the overseas empire had become the central consideration in Spanish relations with the Dutch rebels. Olivares dismissed the counterarguments of the Council of Finance. The young king, content to be told that he was not responsible for the debts of his predecessors, piously declared his intention not to burden his subjects any further. Yet neither he nor his ministers could foresee that a recent slump in silver shipments from America was not a temporary setback but heralded a rapid, long-term decline. The Dutch were equally anxious for war—partly, at least, because of the vain hope that the Belgians would rebel against Spain and join the United Provinces.

Having decided on war, Olivares pursued a perfectly consistent strategy: communications between Spain and the Spanish Netherlands were to be kept open at all costs, and the Dutch were to be hit wherever they were most vulnerable. The first objective led Spain to build up a naval force in the Spanish Netherlands (Belgium) that preyed on Dutch shipping in the North Sea and, on the diplomatic front, to cultivate the friendship of James I of England and even to contemplate the restoration of Frederick V to the Palatinate and the marriage of Philip IV's devoutly Roman Catholic sister to the heretic prince of Wales (later Charles I). It led to very close cooperation with the Austrian branch of the Habsburgs and the need to fight for the control of the Valtellina. The second objective, which followed the advance of the imperial armies under Albrecht Wallenstein (an adventurer who made himself indispensable to the Habsburgs as a military organizer) to the Baltic, led to grandiose schemes of building an imperial Spanish fleet in the Baltic with Hanseatic (the Hanse towns on the Baltic were independent mercantile organizations) and Danish help in order to destroy the Dutch Baltic trade and with it the economic prosperity of the republic.

However rational and limited these aims and plans seemed in Spain, in the rest of Europe they appeared to show only too clearly the limitless ambitions of the house of Austria. The now habitual talk in Spanish court and military circles of restoring Spain's greatness did not help to persuade Europe otherwise. Spinola's and Wallenstein's victories in the mid-1620s convinced the Spanish Council of State that victory against the Dutch was possible and blinded them to the danger of raising up new and more powerful enemies. Thus, they let the last chances of a favourable peace slip away. Yet, despite enormous sums sent annually from Castile to Flanders, the Spanish armies could not break Dutch resistance. They could not even supply their own provisions and ammunition without the covert help of Dutch merchants, who, in their turn, argued that this trade with the mortal enemy brought in the money needed to pay for the troops fighting this enemy. From 1630, when Sweden and France actively intervened in the war, Spain rapidly lost the initiative. The war was fought on a global scale, in central Europe and from the Philippines to Brazil. Spanish armies could still win tactical victories in Italy and Germany, but the number and seriousness of Spanish reverses, especially at sea, were now steadily mounting.

THE GOVERNMENT OF OLIVARES

Olivares was undoubtedly the most able politician directing the Spanish government since Cardinal Granvelle. The Catholic Monarchs, the emperor, and Philip II had kept the high nobility, to a greater or lesser degree, out of the central government. Lerma had reversed this policy, and Olivares could not go back on this position, although he bitterly lamented the incompetence of his fellow aristocrats and sharply reduced the over-generous flow of royal patronage to them. He could—and did—develop a system of committees (juntas) of experts within the councils, which took over a great deal of government business and made its administration more efficient.

In 1623 and 1624 Olivares presented to the king and Council of State a number of memorandums that were nothing less than plans for a far-reaching reform of government and society on the lines advocated by the *arbitristas*. Like them, Olivares saw the need to change mental attitudes; in particular, he recognized the need for restraints on the aristocratic love of splendour and display, the need to appreciate the dignity of work and productive economic activity, and the need to end the economically harmful and morally indefensible mania for *limpieza de sangre* (Olivares himself, through his grandmother, was of *converso* ancestry). On the more immediately practical level, Olivares's memorandums were concerned principally with finance, for, with an annual expenditure of eight million ducats, there was a deficit of four million. The count-duke proposed the abolition of some of the most harmful taxes, the *millones* and the *alcabala*, and their substitution by simpler and more-equitable taxes. Finally, he argued that Castile should not be expected to continue to bear nearly the entire cost of the war. Like Granvelle, Olivares recognized that the king's non-Castilian dominions could be expected to share in the burdens of empire only if they could also enjoy its advantages—the honours, commands, and control over policy that had been all but completely reserved to the Castilians.

None of these plans was put into practice. The Spaniards were unwilling to change their mode of life and their ingrained beliefs at the behest of a royal favourite. Olivares did manage to arrange loans with a consortium of Portuguese Marrano (Christianized Jews) businessmen, but he was bitterly attacked for this action. The court itself gaily abandoned a short-lived austerity in the celebrations that followed the arrival of the prince of Wales in his romantic but abortive quest for a Spanish bride (1623). The financial reforms foundered on the opposition of vested interests to taxation by the Cortes and on the opposition of the whole Castilian ruling class to the plan for the decentralization of the empire. Just as had happened to Granvelle's proposals, there was not even any serious discussion of Olivares's plan. In the 1560s the result of this failure had left Philip II with no alternative but Alba's policy of repression, which caused the revolt of the Netherlands; in the 1620s it left Olivares with no alternative but his Union of Arms, which caused the revolts of Catalonia and Portugal. The Union of Arms was a scheme for the creation of a reserve army of 140,000 men that was to be paid for by the dominions of the Spanish empire in proportion to their estimated resources. But the non-Castilian dominions disliked this proposal because it infringed on their liberties. They also distrusted Castilian intentions—and with good reason, for in 1625 Olivares had advised the king in a secret memorandum to "secretly plan and work to reduce these kingdoms of which Spain is composed to the style and laws of Castile."

THE REVOLT OF CATALONIA

Apart from Portugal, Catalonia was the state with the greatest degree of autonomy. Its medieval form of government had not been changed since Ferdinand the Catholic had settled it in 1486. Its countryside, especially on the French border, was infested with smugglers and bandits and riven by local feuds. Its taxes were administered by the Diputació, a self-perpetuating and corrupt committee of the Catalan Corts that functioned during the long intervals between the meetings of that body. The viceroys, hemmed in on all sides by local privileges and without control over the finances of the province, were virtually powerless. In 1626 Philip IV summoned the Cortes of the realms of the Crown of Aragon. Aragon and Valencia reluctantly voted some money but refused conscription of troops. Catalonia refused everything. Nevertheless, Olivares published the royal decree for the Union of Arms. Subsequently relations between Madrid and Catalonia deteriorated rapidly.

As the costs of warfare mounted, the government resumed the inflationary minting of *vellón* coinage and had to declare yet another moratorium on its debts, in 1627. In 1628 the *vellón* coins were withdrawn, causing a collapse of prices and a recession. In the 1630s new taxes were instituted in Castile along with outright confiscations from private individuals, both of income from government annuities and of American silver imported in commercial transactions. Not surprisingly, Madrid was becoming obsessed with what it considered to be the injustice of Catalonia's immunity from taxation. In 1639 Olivares opened a campaign against southern France from Catalonia. It had no rational strategic objective except to pitchfork Catalonia into the war. If the Catalans had to defend their country, Olivares argued, they would have to support the army.

Olivares's logic was lost on the Catalans. The peasants, urged on by their clergy, refused to support the troops. During the winter the soldiers were quartered in the countryside. Soon there were clashes with the population, then riots and open rebellion. Too late, Olivares attempted to draw back and appease the Catalans. On June 7 the mob murdered the viceroy in Barcelona. The higher nobility and the urban aristocracies were still anxious for an accommodation, but the countryside was now completely out of control. The Diputació, which was the only remaining legal authority, was led by a strong-minded cleric named Pau Claris, canon of Urgel, located west of Barcelona, who was unwilling to make concessions. In the autumn of 1640 Olivares scraped together the last available troops and sent them against the Catalan rebels. Claris countered by transferring Catalan allegiance to the king of France, "as in the time of Charlemagne" (January 1641). French troops now entered Catalonia, and only after French forces withdrew with the renewed outbreak of the French civil wars (the Fronde) were the Castilians able to reconquer Catalonia (1652). The Catalan upper classes were relieved, for they had found the French even less congenial masters than the Castilians. Not repeating its previous mistakes, Madrid fully restored the liberties and privileges of Catalonia.

THE REVOLT OF PORTUGAL

The revolt of Catalonia gave the Portuguese their opportunity. The lower classes and the clergy had always hated the Castilians, and the Portuguese aristocracy and the commercial classes—previously content with the patronage and the economic opportunities that the union with Spain had provided—had become dissatisfied during the preceding 20 years. They resented the introduction of Castilians into their government (1634), the ineffectiveness of Spanish naval support in the defense of Brazil against the Dutch, and the growing reaction of the Spanish colonies against Portuguese economic penetration during this period of contracting economic activity. Rather than allow themselves to be sent to fight the Catalan rebels, the Portuguese nobility seized power in Lisbon and proclaimed the duque de Bragança as King John IV of Portugal (December 1640). Madrid, with an aristocratic conspiracy in Andalusia on its hands (1641), no longer had the means to react.

THE LAST YEARS OF PHILIP IV

The disasters on Spain's periphery were matched by continued mismanagement of Spanish finances at the centre. Once more the government tampered with the *vellón* coinage and then reversed course into a sudden and catastrophic deflation (1641–42). In January 1643 the Castilian grandees were finally able to force Philip IV to dismiss Olivares. The king now decided to run his own government. He dissolved the juntas, and the councils resumed their authority. Soon control of the government slipped into the hands of Olivares's nephew, Luis Méndez de Haro, a clever but colourless politician with neither his uncle's imperial vision nor his panache.

The defeats continued. In 1643 the French king's cousin, Louis II de Bourbon (the Great Condé), broke the Spanish *tercios* and their reputation for invincibility at the Battle of Rocroi in northeastern France. Popular revolutions broke out in Naples and Palermo (Sicily) in 1647, and soon both cities were controlled by revolutionary governments. The excessive taxation, imposed for Spain's war effort, had precipitated the rebellion, at least in Naples. The Spanish monarchy, wrote the Venetian ambassador to Madrid at the time, "... resembled that great colossus that during an earthquake had collapsed in a few moments while everyone hurried along to enrich himself with the fragments."

In fact, Spain survived and even managed to hold on to much of its empire. The revolts of Naples and Sicily, directed as much against the local nobility as against Spain, were suppressed in 1648. When the emperor conceded French claims to Alsace and the Rhine bridgeheads, the "Spanish Road" to the Netherlands was irrevocably cut, and the close alliance between the Spanish and the Austrian branches of the house of Habsburg came to an end. With Portugal in revolt and Brazil no longer an issue between the Dutch and the Spaniards, Philip IV drew the only possible conclusion from this situation and rapidly came to terms with the United Provinces, recognizing their full independence and agreeing to stop overseas trade on the Schelde, a river emptying into the North Sea west of Antwerp (Treaty of Münster, January 1648). But Philip IV had not changed his basic policy. He wanted to have his hands free for a final effort against France, even after Catalonia had surrendered. Once again the temporary weakness of France during the Fronde confirmed the Spanish court in its disastrous military policy. Haro passed up the chance of concluding a very favourable peace in 1656.

BATTLE OF THE DUNES

On June 14, 1658, during the Franco-Spanish War of 1648–59, French and British troops led by Henri de La Tour d'Auvergne, vicomte de Turenne, defeated Spanish forces near Dunkirk (then just north of the French frontier in the Spanish Netherlands) in the Battle of the Dunes. The victory led to the surrender of Dunkirk by Spain and eventually to the conclusion of the war with the Peace of the Pyrenees between France and Spain (1659).

The battle occurred during a siege of Spanish-held Dunkirk by French troops under Turenne. The British, to whom the French had promised Dunkirk in return for forming an alliance against Spain, blockaded the port with their warships by sea. In addition, Britain's lord protector, Oliver Cromwell, sent his envoy William Lockhart with 6,000 infantrymen, veterans of the English Civil Wars, to reinforce Turenne on land. On June 13, 1658, a Spanish force led by Juan José de Austria arrived to relieve Dunkirk. Under Juan José was a rebel French force commanded by the renowned fighter Louis II de Bourbon, 4th prince de Condé, and several regiments of English, Scottish, and Irish royalists commanded by the duke of York (later James II). Juan José had a strong superiority in cavalry, but he had left his artillery behind so as not to delay his advance. He took up a position on the dunes with his right on the sea and his left on the Bruges canal. Turenne at once understood the difficult ground that Juan José had occupied and attacked him.

The severest part of the fighting was borne by the British contingents on either side. In the centre, Lockhart's veterans directly assaulted a fortified dune held by the Spanish and succeeded in taking it after considerable losses. They then fended off counterattacks by their royalist foes. Meanwhile, Turenne's French cavalry swept around the Spanish right wing on firm sandy beach exposed by the ebb tide, while British warships bombarded the Spanish reserves from the sea. On the Spanish left wing, Condé's cavalry charged with great resolution and despite heavy losses gained the upper hand, but their success was nullified by the failure of the Spanish centre and right to resist the Anglo-French troops. When the rest of the Spanish army retreated, one small body of royalists, about 300 strong, held out stubbornly and laid down their arms only on terms that they be allowed to rejoin their king, Charles II, at Ypres. The surrender of Dunkirk by the Spanish quickly followed; it was presented to the British by France.

The war dragged on, with England joining France, capturing Jamaica, and contributing to the Spanish defeat in the Battle of the Dunes on the northern coast of France (1658). The Treaty of the Pyrenees (1659) cost Spain Artois (now northernmost France), Roussillon, and part of Cerdagne. More important than these relatively minor territorial losses was the realization throughout Europe that Spain's pretensions to hegemony had definitely and irremediably failed. The Spaniards themselves were slow to admit it. Philip IV had made concessions to France in order, once again, to have his hands free against the last unforgiven enemy, Portugal. There was no longer any rational basis for his hopes of success. All schemes for financial and tax reforms were still being blocked by vested interests, and the government again had declared bankruptcies in 1647 and 1653. Once more the Council of Finance issued a debased coinage to pay for the Portuguese campaign. But the Portuguese routed the last Spanish armies at Ameixial (1663) and at Villaviciosa on the northern coast of Spain (1665). Spain finally formally recognized Portugal's independence in 1668.

CHARLES II

For 10 years Philip IV's widow, Maria Anna of Austria, acted as regent for Charles II (1665–1700). She allowed her government to be dominated by her confessor, the Austrian Jesuit Johann Eberhard (Juan Everardo) Nithard. It was weakness, rather than strength, that prompted this government not to summon the Cortes any more. But this policy paved the way for the introduction of effective royal absolutism in the 18th century. In 1669 Nithard was overthrown by Juan José de Austria, an illegitimate son of Philip IV, but the regent still managed to keep him out of the central government. In 1677 Juan José led an army against Madrid and made himself Charles II's principal minister. This first *pronunciamiento*, or military coup, inaugurated a tradition that was to bear bitter fruit in the political life of Spain and Latin America in the 19th and 20th centuries. Juan José himself planned some promising reforms but died in 1679. Thereafter, the high nobility dominated the government as effectively as it had in the days of Philip III, playing court intrigues, first with the regent and later with the two successive wives of the incapable Charles II. The majority of these aristocrats were self-seeking and incompetent. Some, however—notably Manuel Joaquín Álvarez de Toledo y Portugal, the conde de Oropesa—had considerable ability. They finally restored the coinage in 1680, though not before they had caused another catastrophic deflation. They established a committee for commerce that pursued orthodox mercantilist policies, encouraging trade and industry. They even took the unprecedented step of investigating the Inquisition and recommending a right of appeal to the secular courts.

Even though the woolen industry of Segovia and some other towns expanded and the imports of American silver, now routed through Cadiz rather than Sevilla, recovered at least in some years to about their former levels, a broadly based economic recovery still lay in the future. Until the mid-1680s the Castilian economy declined at such a rate that the French ambassador claimed to see an appalling deterioration between his two visits, in 1668–69 and in 1671–73. In the 1690s the Venetian ambassador characterized the reign of Charles II as "an uninterrupted series of calamities." The population of Castile declined from about 6.5 million at the end of the 16th century to under 5 million about 1680. Figures for the whole of Spain followed a similar pattern, declining from 8.5 million to about 6.6 million. The reasons for this decline were not so much emigration to the overseas colonies, which averaged 4,000–5,000 per year in the 17th century, as military casualties from all causes, which averaged the frightening figure of 10,000–12,000 a year. More devastating still were the recurrent plagues and, perhaps, the sheer misery of the rural population, who lived on estates that their noble and ecclesiastical owners could not be bothered to manage with even a minimum of efficiency. The shortage of labour, especially skilled labour, and high wages attracted many foreign workers, perhaps as many as 70,000 Frenchmen. Nevertheless, Castilian industries continued to decline. The nadir was reached in the decade 1677–86 with crop failures, earthquakes, an epidemic that sharply reversed a slight upward trend in population dating from about 1650, and, on top of these natural disasters, the government's deflation of the coinage.

THE FRENCH WARS

In these circumstances it is not surprising that Spain now became the victim rather than the initiator of aggression. In three successive wars with France (1667–68, 1672–78, 1689–97), Spain lost Franche-Comté (Treaty of Nijmegen, 1678) and some Belgian frontier towns to France but still managed to hold on to the greater part of the southern Netherlands and the Italian dominions. The reason was less Spain's own military efforts, which were puny compared with those of the first half of the century, than the unwillingness of other European powers, especially the United Provinces, to see the Spanish dominions in Europe swallowed up by France. After the last and, for Spain, most disastrous of these wars, the War of the Grand Alliance (1689–97), Louis XIV himself restored Flanders and Catalonia, which his troops had occupied, for he now had his eye on the inheritance of the whole Spanish empire.

The last years of the childless and clearly dying Charles II were occupied by the maneuvers of the European powers for the Spanish succession or, alternatively, for the partition of the Spanish empire. Amid cabals, intrigues, exorcisms of evil spirits, and blood feuds at court, while riots were going on in the streets of Madrid, the rule of the house of Austria came to an end with the death of Charles II, on November 1, 1700.

THE DECLINE OF SPAIN

Although there is no doubt that Spain suffered economic and political decline in the 17th century, especially in its second half, it is not nearly as clear that there was also a comparable cultural decline or even decadence, as has sometimes been maintained. Certainly, Calderón, Velázquez, and Murillo had no successors of comparable stature. The court of Charles II was neither financially nor psychologically capable of playing the patronage role that Philip IV's court had played. Some of the supposed decline, however, may have been more a matter of changing styles in painting and architecture that did not please the more conservative contemporaries, nor many later historians. A good example is the architecture of the brothers Churriguera. Although it has often been dismissed as overly ornate, it has come to be appreciated as a delightful Mediterranean counterpart to the famous contemporary southern German Baroque-Rococo style.

The term *decadence*, except perhaps when applied to the person of Charles II himself, does not explain the timing of the economic and political decline nor its duration. In the first place, the economic decline was mainly a Castilian phenomenon and did not affect Catalonia or Valencia to anything near the same degree. For Castile, it is perhaps best to see the problem of decline as the *arbitristas* saw it: in the depreciation by Castilians of economic activity, an attitude that was rooted deeply in Castile's past history but that was particularly baleful in a period of general European economic depression, such as the 17th century. Moreover, the aggressive militarism that was central to the Castilian aristocratic tradition led to the political hubris of Spanish imperial policy, from Philip II to Philip IV. The Castilian ruling classes never produced, or perhaps gave no chance to, a leader who could break out of this tradition. Velázquez seems to have known it or felt it instinctively when he painted *The Surrender of Breda* as the beginning of a hoped-for reconciliation of enemies and when, in his portraits of Philip IV, he showed the pathos of a man half aware of his personal inadequacy for the role he was called upon to play. It was the wars, however, that devoured Castile, even though they were fought beyond its borders. They do not directly explain the end of the "Golden Age," but it may be suggested that a society that invests most of its energies and all of its pride in war, even though it may be ideal for war, is unable to provide a congenial ground for the exercise of creative genius when its ideal has failed and it is left with nothing but a now-hollow pride.

CHAPTER 16

Spain: From Bourbon Rule to the Second Republic

Although the wars of the 17th century had weakened Spain's power in Europe, the country still remained the world's greatest imperial power. Spain's central problem in the 17th century had been to maintain what remained of its European possessions and to retain control of its American empire. At the beginning of the 18th century, both tasks appeared to be beyond the military and economic resources of the monarchy. In the 17th century the greatest threat had come from a land power, France, jealous of Habsburg power in Europe; in the 18th it was to come from a sea power, England, while the Austrian Habsburgs became the main continental enemy of Spain.

THE WAR OF THE SPANISH SUCCESSION

In 1700 (by the will of the childless Charles II) the duc d'Anjou, grandson of Louis XIV of France, became Philip V of Spain. Austria refused to recognize Philip, a Bourbon, and thereby concede the defeat of its hopes of placing an Austrian candidate on the throne of Spain. To England, a Bourbon king in Spain would disrupt the balance of power in Europe in favour of French hegemony. Louis XIV conceived of Spain under a Bourbon king as a political and commercial appendage of France to be ruled by correspondence from Versailles. He wished to regenerate and strengthen his ally by a modern centralized administration, a task both complicated and facilitated by the War of the Spanish Succession (1701–14), wherein the allied armies of Britain and Austria invaded Spain in order to drive out Philip V and establish the "Austrian" candidate, the archduke Charles (later the Holy Roman emperor Charles VI), on the throne.

An efficient administration had to be created in order to extract resources from Spain for the war effort and thus relieve pressure on the French treasury; at the same time, financial shortages imperiled administrative reform, while war taxation and war levies drove Catalonia and Aragon to revolt against the demands of the Bourbon dynasty. The instruments of centralizing reform were French civil servants Jean-Jacques Amelot, Louis XIV's ambassador, and Jean-Henri-Louis Orry, a financial expert, and a handful of Spanish lawyer-administrators such as Melchor de Macanaz. They were supported by the queen, María Luisa of Savoy, and her friend the 60-year-old Marie-Anne de la Trémoille, princesse des Ursins.

The opponents of reform were those who suffered by it: the grandees who had dominated the cumbersome, inefficient councils; the councils themselves; the regions such as Catalonia, Aragon, and Valencia, in which the establishment of effective royal rule was seen as a Castilian centralizing imposition in conflict with the local privileges, or *fueros*; and the church, whose position was threatened by the ferocious and doctrinaire regalism of Macanaz, who wished to subject the independent jurisdictions of the church (especially of the papal nuncios and the Inquisition) to the absolute monarch. The disaffection of all these elements easily turned into opposition to Philip V as king. Opposition to the new

dynasty accentuated the determination of Bourbon civil servants to end special privileges that could serve as a cover for treasonable sympathy with the Austrian and English invaders.

Despite severe financial difficulties (owing to the loss of revenues from the Indies), Castile was ferociously loyal to the new dynasty throughout the war. The support of Castile and of France (until 1711) enabled Philip V to survive severe defeats and two occupations of Madrid. In 1705 the archduke Charles landed in Catalonia and took Barcelona. When Philip V tried to attack Catalonia through Aragon, the Aragonese, in the name of their *fueros*, revolted against the passage of Castilian troops. This revolt, backed by the local nobility, turned the king's advisers resolutely against local privileges and aristocratic treason. After the victory over the archduke Charles at Almansa (April 1707), the *fueros* of the kingdoms of Valencia and Aragon were abolished and the property of rebels confiscated. When the archbishop of Valencia resisted attempts to make priests of doubtful loyalty appear before civil courts, the regalism of Macanaz was given full course.

This was the last direct triumph of the reformers. With the death of Queen María Luisa in 1714 and the arrival of Philip's new wife, Isabella Farnese, court support for radical reform disappeared. Macanaz was condemned by the Inquisition, and a less rigid administration, more inclined to compromise with the church and the higher nobility, controlled the country's policy.

The last stages of the war were a Spanish concern. The allies deserted the archduke Charles; the French gave little help to Philip V. In 1714 Philip recaptured the archduke's capital, Barcelona. By the Decree of Nueva Planta (1716), the *fueros* were abolished and Catalonia was integrated into Spain. Integration, widely criticized by later generations of Catalans as the destruction of Catalan "nationality," was nevertheless a precondition for industrial revival; it gave Catalonia a domestic market in Spain and later an overseas market in America.

Paradoxically, a disastrous war had for the first time created a unitary Spanish state: except for the Basque provinces and Navarre, Spain was under direct royal administration.

Spain's defeat in war cost it many of its possessions outside Iberia. The treaties of Maastricht and Utrecht (1713) stripped it of its European possessions (Belgium, Luxembourg, Milan, Sardinia, Sicily, and Naples) and gave Britain Gibraltar and Minorca and the right to send one ship a year to trade with Spanish America.

TREATIES OF UTRECHT

The War of the Spanish Succession (1701–14) was concluded when France signed treaties of peace at Utrecht with other European powers. By the treaty with Britain (April 11, 1713), France recognized Queen Anne as the British sovereign and undertook to cease supporting James Edward, the son of the deposed king James II. France ceded Newfoundland, Nova Scotia, the Hudson Bay territory, and the island of St. Kitts to Britain and promised to demolish the fortifications at Dunkirk, which had been used as a base for attacks on English and Dutch shipping. In the treaty with the Dutch, France agreed that the United Provinces should annex part of Gelderland and should retain certain barrier fortresses in the Spanish Netherlands. In the treaty with Prussia, France acknowledged Frederick I's royal title (claimed in 1701) and recognized his claim to Neuchâtel (in present Switzerland) and southeast Gelderland. In return France received the principality of Orange from Prussia. In the treaty with Savoy, France recognized Victor Amadeus II, duke of Savoy, as king of Sicily and that he should rule Sicily and Nice. The treaty with Portugal recognized its sovereignty on both banks of the Amazon River. France's Guiana colony in South America was restricted in size.

The peace treaties involving Spain took longer to arrange. Spain's treaty with Britain (July 13, 1713) gave Gibraltar and Minorca to Britain. The treaty was preceded by the *asiento* agreement, by which Spain gave to Britain the exclusive right to supply the Spanish colonies with African slaves for the next 30 years. On August 13, 1713, the Spanish treaty with Savoy was concluded, ceding the former Spanish possession of Sicily to Victor Amadeus II as his share of the spoils of war. In return he renounced his claims upon the Spanish throne. The peace between Spain and the Dutch was delayed until June 26, 1714, and that between Spain and Portugal until the Treaty of Madrid (February 1715). *(continued on next page)*

(continued from previous page)

The Holy Roman emperor Charles VI, in what is considered the end of the War of the Spanish Succession, concluded peace with France in the Treaties of Rastatt and Baden (March 6, 1714 and September 7, 1714). Peace between the emperor and Spain was not concluded until the Treaty of The Hague (February 1720).

The question of the Spanish Succession was finally settled in favour of the Bourbon Philip V, grandson of France's Louis XIV. Britain received the largest portion of colonial and commercial spoils and took the leading position in world trade. In international politics the settlement at Utrecht established a pattern for the next 20 years.

"AMERICAN" AND "ITALIAN" POLICIES

Two tendencies can be discerned in Spanish policy until 1748: a desire for revenge and recovery in Italy and an "Atlantic" policy that sought to protect America from British incursions and to revive Spanish colonial rule. Both policies demanded a strong army and navy. The "Italian" tendency was influenced by Philip V's second wife, Isabella, and her desire to get Italian thrones for her sons. The instruments of her ambitions were two foreigners: the Italian cardinal Giulio Alberoni, the exiled son of an Italian gardener, and the Dutch-born adventurer Juan Guillermo Riperdá (Johan Willem Ripperda). The attempt to recover the possessions in Italy involved Spain in an unsuccessful war with Austria, which was now the great power in Italy. Spain suffered a serious naval defeat off Cape Passero, Sicily, in 1718. Nevertheless, Isabella's persistence was rewarded when her son, the future King Charles III of Spain, became the duke of Parma in 1731 and king of Naples in 1733, relinquishing his claims to Parma.

The American-Atlantic tendency was the work of Spanish ministers with a particular interest in the navy and foreign trade—José Patiño, Zenón de Somodevilla y Bengoechea, marqués de la Ensenada, and José de Carvajal y Lancáster. The "Italian" and "Atlantic" tendencies existed side by side in the late years of Philip V's reign. Atlantic rivalries in the form of a dispute over the interpretation of British trading privileges in Spanish America granted at Utrecht brought on the War of Jenkins' Ear (1739–43), during which the British sacked Porto Bello (now Portobelo) in the Caribbean. The Spanish fleet nevertheless was surprisingly effective and worsted Admiral Edward Vernon at Cartagena. The Italian-Mediterranean policy led directly to Spanish involvement in the War of the Austrian Succession (1740–48). It made possible an alliance of France and Spain against Austria, giving Isabella the opportunity to settle her second son, Philip, in an Italian duchy. In 1745 Spanish troops entered Milan.

Ferdinand VI (1746–59) was concerned with the domestic recovery of Spain rather than the extension of its power in Europe. He hoped to recover

Gibraltar at the general peace that ended the War of the Austrian Succession. But the Anglo-French rapprochement made recovery of Gibraltar an impossibility at the Treaty of Aix-la-Chapelle (1748); the treaty merely strengthened Spain's position in Italy when Philip became duke of Parma, Piacenza, and Guastalla. The Atlantic tendency became dominant under Ferdinand VI. Because Britain was Spain's most significant enemy in the Americas (as Austria had been in Italy), Spain's "natural" ally was France, as Ensenada and Carvajal had seen (hence a series of family pacts with France in 1733 and 1743). It was only in the last years of Ferdinand's reign that his minister, Ricardo Wall, attempted a policy of strict neutrality as the best means of saving Spain from the hostility of Britain, Austria, or France.

The American interest was reflected in increased trade (the old system of convoyed fleets was abandoned for individual sailings), the creation of privileged trading companies (1725), and the founding of new naval arsenals at Ferrol and Cartagena (1726). But Spain's central weakness as an imperial power remained; its economy could not supply America with the consumer goods it needed in return for its increased exports. Instead, these were supplied either by British merchants through the "legitimate" trade from Cadiz or by smuggling. Despite considerable efforts, the Spanish navy was unable to suppress a contraband trade that, from the colonists' point of view, was a necessity.

Ferdinand VI's ministers revived the reforming traditions weakened during the latter years of the rule of Philip V, whose lethargy had deepened into chronic melancholia. One of the most important imitations of French administrative practice was the use after 1749 of crown officers, or intendants, to rule in the provinces. The intendants strengthened royal control over local government, especially in its financial aspects; together with the captains general (established by Philip V), they were responsible for a renewal of provincial public works. Carvajal reorganized the postal system. Ensenada was a great road builder. He also opened the Sevilla tobacco factory, botanical gardens, and observatories, and he increased royal receipts through a rationalization of the tax structure. Charles III, Ferdinand's successor, implemented dramatic reforms that followed along the path set by Ferdinand.

THE REIGN OF CHARLES III, 1759–88

Two features distinguished the reforms of Charles III (the "Caroline" reforms) from those of the early Bourbons. First, Charles was a "reformer's king" in that he consistently supported reforming ministers. This was surprising in a monarch who had no great intellectual gifts, was obsessed by hunting, and whose court society was among the most boring in Europe. Second, the civil servants were distinguished from their predecessors by their adherence to a philosophy of government derived from the ideals of the European Enlightenment.

Nevertheless, there were sharp differences among the civil servants. Pedro Pablo Abarca de Bolea, conde de Aranda, and Pablo de Olavide y Jáuregui were influenced by the French philosophes; Gaspar Melchor de Jovellanos y Ramírez was a disciple of the Scottish political philosopher and economist Adam Smith; Pedro Rodríguez Campomanes drew more directly on Spanish reformers such as Macanaz; José Moñino y Redondo, conde de Floridablanca, was a professional administrator. All would have taken as their slogan "Felicidad" ("Felicity")—a well-ordered monarchy based directly on the productivity of people who are made happy by the intelligent application of the principles of political economy. There were, however, impediments (*estorbos*), such as traditional privileges (e.g., grazing rights held by the sheep-breeders' corporation, the Mesta) or attitudes (e.g., the prejudice of the nobility against the "mechanical trades"); they could not be allowed to stand in the way of greater prosperity and, therefore, of a higher tax income for the state.

ECONOMIC REVIVAL

After 1714 Spain experienced a gradual economic recovery, which became quite marked in the second half of the 18th century. It is doubtful that much of this revival was the work of conscious but often confused government policy. Thus, the famous decree (1783) "ennobling" the mechanical trades had little practical result; the attempt to establish government factories and replace religious charity by the productive employment of the poor was a relative failure. Government policy had little to do with the growth of population, which rose during the century from 8 million to 12 million. The increased demand for food and the consequent sharp rise in prices encouraged agriculture, benefiting the large landowners of the south and the small farmers near growing towns such as Barcelona. The most remarkable feature of this economic revival was the emergence in Catalonia after 1745 of a modern cotton-based textile industry. The industry benefited from a protected market in Spain and the colonies. In the Basque provinces the archaic iron industry began a slow process of modernization. In Galicia, Catalan immigrants established a flourishing fishing fleet. The brandy trade brought sudden prosperity to the ports of Catalonia and their hinterland. Nevertheless, government actions of earlier years, such as financial reforms and the abolition of internal customs duties, removed obstacles to the expansion of the internal market, and the opening of the American trade acted as a strong stimulant.

Most of these developments occurred not in the old Castilian core of the monarchy but in the peripheral regions and in the towns rather than in the countryside. Price rises were steepest on the periphery; in Barcelona, for example, they outstripped wages and thus created the beginnings of a social problem. The role of Catalans in the economic revival lies at the origins of the Castilian stereotype of the Catalans as selfish, thrusting businessmen, indifferent to traditional values and exploiting their fellow Spaniards.

IMPERIAL PROBLEMS

Charles III maintained that the key to Spain's prosperity lay in the development of an American market in the Indies. He saw clearly that Spain alone could not preserve an overseas market closed to the outside world against Britain. Ricardo Wall's policy of strict neutrality had allowed Britain to make gains in Canada that were bound to weaken France—the only other anti-British power in America. If Britain would respect Spain's possessions, or if Charles could mediate between France and Britain in such a way as to preserve the balance between them in America, then to commit Spain to the French alliance was a dynastic luxury. Once it was clear to Charles that British terms were nonnegotiable, then the Bourbon Family Compact of 1761, a mutual-defense treaty with France, was a piece of realpolitik, signed by the "Anglophile" Ricardo Wall.

The consequence of such an alliance was involvement in the Seven Years' War—too late to save France. In 1762 the British occupied Havana—the greatest single blow sustained by Spain in the war. Spain theoretically allowed no foreigners to share directly in the colonial trade, the effect of which was to starve the colonies of necessary imports and to encourage smuggling. In 1762, 15 ships entered the port of Havana; during the 11 months of British occupation, 700 did. This was a dramatic indication to the colonists of the drawbacks of the Spanish monopoly, especially when that monopoly was exercised by what was, in European terms, an underdeveloped country.

The Treaty of Paris (1763) concluded the Seven Years' War and destroyed France as an American power. Spain lost the territory between Florida and the Mississippi, in return gaining Louisiana from France. Spain also had to recognize Portuguese advances in the Río de la Plata (the fort of Sacramento) and the British right to cut mahogany in Central America. The Family Compact was therefore an immediate military failure, and it was only the revolt of the North American colonies against Britain that enabled Spain to recover the ground it had lost; the successful alliance with France to aid the colonists resulted in the Treaty of Versailles (1783), which gave back Sacramento, the two Floridas, and Minorca. Not until later did it become apparent that an alliance of revenge with colonial insurgents was a shortsighted policy for an imperial power.

Driven by fears of British and Russian expansion, Spain also undertook a more aggressive policy in the far north of its American possessions: California, New Mexico, Texas, and Arizona. These were reorganized into a single administrative unit, the Internal Provinces, under a unified military command. A string of missions was established in California to assert Spanish control.

The problems of imperial defense were thus temporarily solved by British weakness after 1765. The positive side of Charles III's imperial policy was an attempt to create an efficiently administered colonial empire that would provide the crown with increased revenues and with a closed market for the exports of an expanding Spanish economy, a program known as the "Bourbon Reforms."

The rationalization of the administration of the Indies had started before Charles III with the creation of a new viceroyalty at Santa Fé de Bogotá (present-day Colombia) in 1717. To protect the south against the British and against Portuguese incursions from Brazil, the Viceroyalty of the Río de la Plata was created in 1776. The centrepiece of Caroline reform was the introduction of the intendant system in the colonies to tighten up local administration. Most dramatic of all was the abolition of the monopoly of Cadiz, by which all trade to the colonies had to go through that port. Beginning in 1778, non-Castilian ports could trade directly with the colonies.

VICEROYALTY OF THE RÍO DE LA PLATA

The Viceroyalty of the Río de la Plata was the final of the four viceroyalties that Spain created during its colonization of Central and South America. Including the territory now comprising Argentina, Uruguay, Paraguay, and Bolivia, the new viceroyalty (established in 1776) controlled an area previously under the administration of the Viceroyalty of Peru. The decision to create a fourth viceroyalty was a result both of King Charles III's desire to decentralize the rule of his Spanish-American empire and of a recognition that the area south of Brazil required greater military defenses in view of Portuguese encroachments along the northern shore of the Río de la Plata. Spain also wanted to curtail contraband trade between Portuguese Brazil and Buenos Aires. In addition, by the 1760s the British had made clear their intention to take the Falkland (Malvinas) Islands. Although Spain pressured the British out of temporary possession of the islands, the need for greater military control of the South Atlantic region had become apparent.

In 1776 the first viceroy of Río de la Plata—Pedro de Cevallos—arrived in Montevideo with a large force of men and ships. Cevallos pushed the Portuguese back and organized a new government in Buenos Aires before being supplanted by another viceroy just a few months after taking office. The viceroys following Cevallos—Juan José de Vértiz y Salcedo (1778–84), Nicolás Francisco Cristóbal del Campo, marqués de Loreto (1784–89), and Nicolás de Arredondo (1789–95)—administered the region well, as did four others who served briefly between 1795 and 1804. During these years the viceroyalty in general and the city of Buenos Aires in particular became a flourishing outpost of the Spanish empire. Silver from the Potosí mines, previously exported via Peru, was sent through Buenos Aires. An enormous demand grew for salted meat—especially in Cuba and Brazil and other areas where slaves were fed cheaply—spurring an era of unprecedented prosperity for the cattle industry of the Pampas. Hides and other cattle products also brought wealth to Buenos Aires.

In 1804 Rafael, marqués de Sobremonte, assumed the viceregal post. Twice (1806, 1807) during his term the British invaded, and twice he fled. The Creole population of Buenos Aires successfully fought off the invaders on both occasions, in the process gaining confidence in their ability to govern and defend themselves. In 1810 the Creoles created a provisional junta and exiled the viceroy to the Canary Islands, thereby ending the Viceroyalty of the Río de la Plata and launching the independence movement.

The new policies brought some immediate and striking results. Energetic viceroys and ministers and ruthless intendants doubled or tripled imperial revenues. The volume of Spanish goods in the American trade increased 10-fold in 10 years, prompting British concern at the Spanish revival. But imperial free trade would not satisfy the growing demand from Creole producers for free trade with all nations. Nor did the colonial oligarchs desire efficient government and higher taxation; they preferred bad government that let them control their own affairs. They showed their discontent in a series of revolts in the 1780s; only the fear of the native Indians drove them back to allegiance to the Spanish crown.

DOMESTIC REFORMS

The domestic reforms of Charles III are more interesting for what they intended than for what they accomplished. They were not, as has often been maintained, directed at fostering a "bourgeois revolution." The middle classes were too weak, in a predominantly agrarian country, for the role of a modernizing elite; nor

did Charles III contemplate a frontal attack on the traditional nobility. The purpose of reform was to remove what seemed to civil servants to be "traditional" constrictions on economic growth and administrative anachronisms that prevented the efficient exercise of royal power. The reformers' view of the inadequacy of the existing system was well expressed by Pablo de Olavide, an active administrator who would later fall afoul of the Inquisition:

A body composed of other and smaller bodies, separated and in opposition to one another, which oppress and despise each other and are in a continuous state of war...Modern Spain can be considered a monstrous Republic of little republics which confront each other because the particular interest of each is in contradiction with the general interest.

Reorganizations of the machinery of central government made for greater executive efficiency, but complete rationalization was never achieved; the old machinery of the councils persisted, with the Council of Castile as the ultimate decision-making body. An attempt to establish royal control of municipalities (without which reforms could not get past the oligarchic councils) was likewise only a partial success. Most of the public works that characterized the late 18th century were the achievement of vigorous captains general. The extensive civil functions of these military officials were the first signs of a hybrid military-civilian government that, in another form, was to be developed in the 19th century.

Spain's agrarian economic structure also was not modified. All the chief reformers believed that the great and extensively cultivated estates, especially in Andalusia and Extremadura, constituted the greatest bar to agricultural prosperity. The landless underemployed proletariat who worked the large estates began to alarm reformers. The statesman and author Gaspar Melchor de Jovellanos asked:

> Why in our villages and towns are these men without land and in the countryside land without men? Bring them together and all will be served.

It was felt that property should be more widely distributed and that there should be a free market in land. Yet none of the reformers was radical enough to push through a wholesale assault on private property or on the civil entail (the juridical instrument by which the latifundios, or large estates, were preserved intact). Acts such as the limitation of future entail, which preserved great estates intact over generations (1789), the limitation of the privileges of the Mesta (1779), and the right to enclose olive groves and irrigated land (1788) showed that the reformers believed primarily in the right of private individuals to do what they liked with their own property; the unrestricted pursuit of private profit, they believed, would bring public prosperity. The enemy was corporate property. Hence, it was proposed that common lands owned by municipalities and the crown should be sold for individual cultivation and that ecclesiastical entail (mortmain) be ended.

The attack on the privileges of the greatest corporation in Spain, the church, was less radical than has sometimes been maintained. Charles III himself was a devoted Catholic who dedicated Spain to the Immaculate Conception. While some of his servants were fashionable anticlericals, most were regalists; that is, they asserted the right of the crown to control over the church in civil matters. In the extreme regalists' view, the state should take care of charity and education, and it should subject priests to civil jurisdiction for civil crimes and assert the traditional rights of the crown over church appointments.

The main attack of the regalists fell on the Jesuit order. In 1766 a serious riot in Madrid revealed some of the difficulties confronting the reformers. The abolition of fixed wheat prices during a bad harvest (a step that reflected the reformers' belief in the virtues of a free market) and an attempt to reform outlandish fashions in popular dress brought out the mob in Madrid. The Jesuits were alleged to have fostered the riot and were expelled from both Spain and America in 1767. The importance of this expulsion, however, has been overestimated. Already expelled from France and Portugal, the Jesuits were bitterly criticized by rival orders as well as by the secular clergy: 42 of the 56 bishops approved of the expulsion. Again, the expulsion was a negative achievement; more ambitious plans to establish a state university system and a state welfare organization failed.

The question arises of the extent to which the policies of Charles III resulted from the acceptance by his servants of the precepts of the Enlightenment. Certainly Aranda, the "Hammer of the Jesuits," and Olavide were what were called *esprits forts* ("strong spirits"; i.e., French-influenced radicals); their views gave a sharp edge to traditional regalism. Jovellanos was a disciple of Adam Smith. Although his famous *Informe sobre la ley agraria* ("Report on the Agrarian Law") is not original, the book is significant in that it attempts to apply dogmatic laissez-faire ideology to Spanish conditions and is one of the foundations of Spanish liberalism.

One of the aims of the Enlightenment was to produce a society in which no traditional prejudices or institutions should inhibit economic activity. This was the motive behind the attempt to encourage the nobility to engage in commerce by making it "honourable." Patriotic societies, organized with government encouragement from 1765 onward, were meant to provide the provincial basis for a progressive society and to familiarize Spaniards with European advances in technology and agriculture. However, this attempt did not progress much beyond the status of local reading rooms and debating societies.

Traditional Roman Catholic society was still strong, if under attack from a minority of intellectuals and civil servants. As the reaction of the countryside after 1808 was to show, the church was still a great social power. Arthur Wellesley, the duke of Wellington, observed that "the real power in Spain is in the clergy. They kept the people right against France." Although a number of bishops could be counted among the "enlightened" and supported much of the reform program, most of the clergy viewed the new ideas of the Enlightenment as "foreign" and dangerous. There could be no such thing as moderate progress encouraged by the king himself—the notion of a "revolution from above" that was to haunt subsequent Spanish history. Voltaire, John Locke, and Jean-Jacques Rousseau were quite simply dangerous heretics, though the Inquisition proved powerless to prevent the clandestine circulation of their works. It was the clerical attacks on heretics as much as the subversive works themselves that familiarized a narrow stratum of society with new ideas. When the French Revolution exposed the dangers of progressive thought, the traditionalist cause was immensely strengthened, and the Inquisition appeared to the crown itself to be a useful instrument to control the spread of dangerous ideas.

CHARLES IV AND THE FRENCH REVOLUTION

In 1788 Charles III, who had been the "nerve" of reform in the sense that he loyally supported able ministers, was succeeded by his son, Charles IV, a weak, amiable man dominated by a lascivious wife, María Luisa. Spain was ruled after 1792 by her favourite, Manuel de Godoy, a handsome, plump officer from the lower nobility. This choice was unfortunate not merely because Godoy was incompetent and self-seeking but also because the French revolutionary and Napoleonic wars put unbearable pressures on a weak power. Reform was now dangerous. Neutrality was impossible; alliance with either France or the anti-revolutionary coalitions engineered by Britain proved equally disastrous.José Moñino y Redondo, conde de Floridablanca, the prime minister, disliked both the internal effects of the French Revolution (the spread of radical as opposed to government-guided reform) and its external consequences (the weakening of the anti-British alliance). His hostility to France was the cause of his dismissal. Pedro Pablo Abarca de Bolea, conde de Aranda, a friend of France, was discredited by the excesses of the Revolution (1792). Godoy became prime minister at age 25 because the older ministers of Charles III

had failed to devise a foreign policy. In domestic affairs, Godoy supported a mild version of the enlightened reformism of his predecessors; like them, however, he failed to find a satisfactory place for Spain in the Europe of the French revolutionary and Napoleonic wars (1800–15).

Spain had no alternative but to declare war on France after the execution of Louis XVI in 1793. The war was popular but disastrous; in 1794 the French armies invaded Spain, taking Bilbao, San Sebastián (Donostia–San Sebastián), and Figueres (Figueras). Godoy feared the spread of revolutionary propaganda in the wake of the French armies in Catalonia and the north (there was a republican conspiracy in 1795). Above all, he was convinced that Britain was the true enemy of Spain. Thus, the Treaty of San Ildefonso (1796) represented a deliberate choice: the French alliance, irrespective of the nature of the French regime, was the only policy for a weak imperial power.

The consequences of this choice were disastrous. War with Britain became inevitable and cut off Spain from America, opening Spain's colonial markets to Britain and the United States. This development threatened complete bankruptcy of the royal finances, which Godoy attempted to alleviate by the issue of state bonds and the sale of church properties—a measure that alienated conservatives. Godoy invaded Portugal with success in the War of the Oranges (1801), but the defeat of the Franco-Spanish fleet by the British at Trafalgar in 1805 and the "selfishness" of Napoleon caused

Godoy to seek a rapprochement with the allies. Had Napoleon lost the Battle of Jena (1806) against the Prussians, Godoy would have joined the Fourth Coalition against him.

Godoy's position was now extremely weak. Disliked by the court aristocracy, who considered him an upstart, he was unpopular at home. In addition, severe inflation produced great hardship among the poorer classes, and a campaign of gossip was mounted against him by those intellectuals whom he did not patronize. He now hoped, with French help, to dismember Portugal and to secure personal salvation in a principality. This curious hope was the basis of the Treaty of Fontainebleau (1807), by which Napoleon and the Spanish government agreed upon the conquest and partition of Portugal. When French troops on the way to Portugal occupied the fortresses of northern and central Spain and when Napoleon demanded territorial gains in Spain itself, Godoy's policy was made bankrupt. It was obvious that Napoleon had lost all faith in Godoy and Spain as an ally; the "dirty intrigues" of Ferdinand, prince of Asturias and heir to the throne, against his father and Godoy led Napoleon to consider drastic intervention in Spanish affairs.

The opportunity for direct intervention by Napoleon was given by the Revolt of Aranjuez (March 17, 1808), in which the partisans of Ferdinand, an alliance of discontented aristocrats and others opposed to Godoy, compelled the abdication of Charles IV and the dismissal of Godoy. Napoleon summoned both the old king and Ferdinand VII to Bayonne, where both were compelled to abdicate. The Spanish throne was then offered to Joseph Bonaparte, Napoleon's brother.

WAR OF THE ORANGES

The War of the Oranges was a brief conflict in which France and Spain fought against Portugal. The war was brought about by Portugal's refusal in 1800 to accept Napoleon's demands to become a political and economic extension of France and to cede to France the major part of its national territory.

In April 1801, French troops arrived in Portugal, and on May 20 they were bolstered by Spanish troops under the command of Manuel de Godoy. In a battle that was disastrous for Portugal, Godoy took the town of Olivenza, near the Spanish frontier. Following his victory, Godoy picked oranges at nearby Elvas and sent them to the Queen of Spain with the message that he would proceed to Lisbon. Thus, the conflict became known as the War of the Oranges.

After Olivenza, Portugal negotiated a treaty with France and Spain—the Peace of Badajoz (June 1801)—ending the invasion. Portugal agreed to close its ports to English ships, to give commercial concessions to France, to cede Olivenza to Spain and part of Brazil to France, and to pay an indemnity.

THE FRENCH INVASION AND THE WAR OF INDEPENDENCE, 1808–14

Joseph could count on the support of cautious, legalistic administrators and soldiers, those who believed resistance to French power impossible, and those who considered that Napoleon might "regenerate" Spain by modern reforms. These groups became convinced *afrancesados*, as members of the pro-French party were pejoratively called. Relying on their support, Napoleon entirely underestimated the possibility of popular resistance to the occupation of Spain by French armies. Although the uprising of May 2, 1808, in Madrid was suppressed, local uprisings against the French were successful wherever French military power was weak.

THE WAR OF INDEPENDENCE

After the deposition of King Ferdinand, "patriot" Spain outside the control of the French armies split into a number of autonomous provinces. Resistance centred in provincial committees (juntas) that organized armies. A Central Junta at Aranjuez sought to control this nascent federalism and the local levies, and Spanish regular troops defeated a French army of inferior, ill-supplied troops under General Pierre Dupont de l'Étang at Bailén in July 1808. The French retired from Madrid. Napoleon then invaded Spain and by 1809 was in control of most of the peninsula. The Spanish regular army, led by incompetent generals, suffered defeat after defeat.

The War of Independence—or, as the English call it, the Peninsular War—became for Napoleon the "Spanish ulcer," and he attributed his defeat in Europe to its requirements for men and money. He was defeated not by the inefficient Spanish regular army but by British troops under the duke of Wellington advancing from Portugal with the aid of Spanish guerrillas. As the main battles—Talavera (July 1809) and Vitoria (June 1813)—were fought by Wellington, the guerrillas pinned down French garrisons, intercepted dispatches, and isolated convoys.

The term *guerrilla*, derived from the Spanish *guerra* (war), was first used during the Spanish War of Independence. The guerrillas were a complex phenomenon, and they did not share a single motivation for fighting the French. Some were patriotic liberals, and others were driven primarily by their attachment to the church and fought to defend traditional institutions against French-inspired reform.

THE CONSTITUTION OF CADIZ, 1812

The war years both recreated a patriotic spirit to cover the bare bones of Bourbon administrative centralism and resulted in the explicit formulation of a liberal ideology that was to be a dynamic factor in Spanish history. The Central Junta and its successor, the regency, were compelled to summon a Cortes in order to legitimize the situation created by the absence of Ferdinand VII, who was a prisoner in

France. Conservatives conceived of this task as the mere supply of the sinews of war on behalf of an absent king. However, the Cortes, when it met at Cadiz in 1810, was dominated by liberals who wished to go beyond the mere support of the war effort and establish a constitution that would make impossible the revival of rule by a favourite like Godoy. The constitution of 1812 was to become the "sacred codex" of Latin liberalism.

The Constitution of Cadiz gave Spain a strictly limited monarchy (the king must work through his responsible ministers), a single-chamber parliament with no special representation for the church or the nobility, and a modern centralized administrative system based on provinces and municipalities. All this had little basis in the medieval precedents quoted in the debates and was inspired by the 1791 constitution of Revolutionary France. Liberal individualism inspired legislation against entail, favouring instead the sale of common lands and the individual's right to dispose of his property as he might wish. The abolition of the Inquisition represented a mixture of historical regalism and modern anticlericalism. This measure produced a conservative reaction, as did all liberal anticlericalism through to the Second Republic in the 1930s. This reaction gave a popular underpinning to Ferdinand VII's destruction of liberalism and all its works in 1814.

In addition to initiating a liberal tradition, the War of Independence bequeathed two problems: first, generals chafed at control by civilian juntas and on occasion overthrew them, thus initiating the phenomenon of the *pronunciamiento*, or military revolution; second, the *afrancesados*, who were often of liberal inclination but were tarred with the accusation of collaborationism with the French, were left as an indigestible element within liberalism itself.

FERDINAND VII, 1814–33

With the help of an army corps and of conservative sentiment that had been outraged by the liberalism of 1812, Ferdinand returned from exile in France to rule Spain as an absolute monarch. In 1820 he was forced by military sedition to return to constitutionalism during the Liberal Triennium (1820–23). For the last, "ominous" decade of his reign, he returned to a relatively enlightened form of ministerial despotism. From 1814 to 1820 Spain attempted to reestablish its rule in America and to maintain an inflated wartime army with a permanent economic deficit.

THE FAILURE OF LIBERALISM

The solution of the Cadiz liberals to the imperial problem had been to make the colonies constitutionally part of metropolitan Spain by giving them representation in the Cortes. This did not stop the revolt of the colonies, where the Creoles wanted local self-government and free trade rather than liberal centralization. In 1814 it was not clear that the rebels under Simón Bolívar in the north and José de San Martín in the south would succeed; however, all Ferdinand's efforts to assemble a large army and a fleet to send to America failed. In 1820 the army that was to subdue the colonies revolted against the king in a *pronunciamiento* organized by Major Rafael de Riego y Núñez and supported by the local liberals organized in Masonic lodges.

The revolution of 1820 brought into power the "jailbirds"—liberals of the 1812 vintage who had been persecuted by Ferdinand VII. The constitution of 1812 was reestablished together with other liberal legislation, including the sale of monastic property.

The liberal system failed once more because it was a minority creed sustained by a section of the army—the military radicals such as Riego—against a mounting conservative reaction that had been fed by an attack on the church, especially the monasteries. The liberals themselves split. The more conservative wing (led by Francisco Martínez de la Rosa, a dramatist) wished for a more moderate constitution, based on the French Charter of 1814, which would give better representation to the upper classes and would not be totally unacceptable to the king, as was the "prison" of the constitution of 1812. The king gave no support to this movement and, in a cowardly fashion, disowned a rising of the guards' regiments that backed it. Thus, the extreme radicals (*exaltados*) gained control by means of demonstrations in the streets, organized by clubs run on the lines of the Jacobins of the French Revolution. The conservative reaction developed in the north around the regency set up at Seo de Urgel. Without French help, the movement would not have been successful, but when Louis XVIII sent French troops (the "Hundred Thousand Sons of St. Louis"), the liberal armies disintegrated and the liberal system fell.

Once more revolution at home favoured revolution in the colonies. Mexican conservatives, who had no desire to be ruled by Spanish anticlericals, successfully established an independent Mexico under Agustín de Iturbide (1822). Spanish military power in South America finally foundered in the decisive Battle of Ayacucho (1824). Of Spain's far-flung empire, only the islands of Cuba, Puerto Rico, and the Philippines remained.

THE "OMINOUS DECADE," 1823–33

The "ominous decade," as it was called by the persecuted liberals, began with a severe purge of liberals, but in its later stages the regime became increasingly unacceptable to extreme conservatives, who looked to the king's reactionary brother, Don Carlos (Carlos María Isidro de Borbón). Ferdinand had to rely either on inefficient traditionalists who could raise no money in the European money markets or on the more liberal ministers who were able financiers. Ministers such as Luis López Ballesteros, a friend of the *afrancesados*, set the tone with a serious attempt at a government-fostered economic revival.

The return to 18th-century "ministerial despotism" did not satisfy the liberal exiles, who mounted ineffective invasions in 1824 and 1830. More important, the conservatives of Don Carlos's court faction accepted Ferdinand VII's rule only on condition that Don Carlos would inherit the crown.

ISABELLA II, 1833–68

In 1829 Ferdinand married his niece María Cristina of Naples, who realized that her influence depended on the elimination of that of Don Carlos. In March 1830 her faction at court persuaded the king to exclude Don Carlos from the succession even if María Cristina produced a female heir. This attack on the rights of Don Carlos was the origin of the Carlist party and of the Carlist wars, which were to be a disrupting influence in Spain for more than a half century. After the defeat of an attempt to force María Cristina to recognize Don Carlos's rights during Ferdinand's illness (September 1832), María Cristina's faction became dominant at court. She succeeded in securing all important military commands in the hands of supporters of the claims of her daughter, Isabella. When, on September 29, 1833, Ferdinand died, Isabella was proclaimed queen, with María Cristina as regent, precipitating almost immediately the outbreak of the First Carlist War (1833–39).

THE CARLIST WARS

The dynastic war between Isabelline liberalism and Carlism was a savage civil war between urban liberalism and rural traditionalism, between the poorly paid and poorly equipped regular army of the liberal governments, supporting Isabella, and the semi-guerrilla forces of the Carlists. The Carlist strength lay in the north, especially in the Basque provinces and Navarre, where there was strong support for the *fueros* against liberal centralism and for the traditional Roman Catholic order represented by the religious bigotry of Don Carlos and his circle. But the Carlists could not break out of their bases in the north to capture an important city. The great Carlist leader Tomás Zumalacárregui y de Imaz was killed in an attempt to capture Bilbao, and Don Carlos's expedition to Madrid failed (1837). In 1839 Rafel Maroto, the Carlist commander, staged a mutiny against the clerical court of Don Carlos and came to terms with Baldomero Espartero, the most successful of Isabella's generals.

María Cristina allied with liberalism out of military necessity, not from conviction. She would have preferred to grant administrative reforms rather than consent that her daughter should become a constitutional monarch. But only the liberals could save her daughter's throne from the Carlists, and the minimum demand of all liberals was a constitution. As regent from 1833 to 1840, she therefore consistently supported conservative liberals against the radicals. The Royal Statute (1834) represented this alliance between respectable upper-middle-class liberals and the crown.

This conservative constitution, with its steep property franchise and the great powers it gave the crown in the choice of ministers, could not stop the drift toward the left implicit in liberalism itself. The radicals, who were the heirs of the *exaltados* of 1820–23, were installed in power first by a series of provincial town uprisings in 1835 and later, after a short-lived conservative reaction, by an army mutiny that forced María Cristina to accept the constitution of 1812. The radical politicians, however, accepted a more moderate compromise constitution—that of 1837. Of more enduring importance was the sale of church lands to finance the war. The great disentailment carried out by Prime Minister Juan Alvarez Mendizábal and his successors profoundly altered the social structure of Spain by putting on the market large quantities of land, most of which were bought by large landowners or prosperous peasants.

MODERATES, PROGRESSIVES, AND THE GENERALS

The Carlist wars left civilian politicians discredited, and generals became the arbiters of politics not, as in 1814–20, as intruders but as part of the political machinery. They became the "swords" of the two main political groups. The *moderados* (moderates), who were upper-middle-class oligarchic liberals fearful of democratic violence and upholders of the prerogatives of the crown, represented the conservative stream in liberalism. Their rivals, the *progresistas* (progressives), were the heirs of the *exaltados* and represented a lower stratum of the middle class; the *progresistas* were prepared to use the discontent of the urban masses in order to bring pressure on the crown to give them office. Their instrument was the Urban Militia. General Espartero used his military faction and his supporters among the younger *progresista* politicians and their artisan followers in the great cities to oust María Cristina and establish himself as regent (1841–43). Espartero proved a disappointment to the radical *progresistas*, who now allied with his conservative opponents under his military and political rival, Ramón María Narváez. In 1843 Espartero was ousted by a *pronunciamiento*.

Narváez jettisoned his *progresista* allies through a court intrigue, and between 1844 and 1854 he and his fellow generals dominated domestic politics as representatives of the *moderados*. Their administrative, educational, and financial measures and the formation of the Civil Guard were lasting achievements; however, the generals could not stabilize their rule on the basis of their constitution of 1845, a conservative revision of the constitution of 1837. The period was disturbed by a series of *progresista* military risings.

To the left of the *progresistas*, who were prepared to accept the monarchy if it gave them office, developed a Democratic Party, which was prepared to dethrone Isabella II, who was declared of age to rule in 1843. Never strong in numbers outside the towns, the Democrats radicalized politics. Orthodox *progresista* politicians were embarrassed by their extremist attitudes but could not neglect their potential role as urban revolutionaries.

It was not the Democrats but a group of discontented generals led by Leopoldo O'Donnell who successfully revolted in 1854. They were prepared to sacrifice the dynasty because the queen and her mother favoured a rigid court conservatism that effectively excluded them from influence. The rebellious military oligarchs were forced to call in civilian and radical support. This turned their *pronunciamiento* into a mild revolution. Isabella survived only through Espartero's political timidity. Unprepared to accept the backing of the Democrats as the "George Washington of Spain," he accepted an alliance with O'Donnell, who was determined to arrest the drift to radicalism. In 1856 he broke with Espartero, defeated a demonstration in his favour, and dissolved the National Militia, the instrument of the left-wing Progressives. The radical thrust was thus defeated.

ECONOMIC EXPANSION

The "revolutionary" period of 1854–56 saw no important constitutional change, but the further extension of disentailment to the lands belonging to the municipalities (the Land Reform of Madoz [1855]) and the new law for limited companies provided the legal structure for a rapid expansion of the economy. To promote this expansion, there were new injections of foreign credit—particularly French—and new banks. This capital allowed construction to begin on the railroad network that was to provide the transport infrastructure for a national market. The textile industry of Catalonia flourished as a modern wool manufacture grew up; in the Basque Country the second pole of an industrial economy developed slowly around iron. The still-dominant agricultural sector expanded as the church and common lands provided new fields for wheat, the easiest of cash crops; the growth of such towns as Barcelona created a market for vegetables, wines, and fruit.

Expansion resulted in the classic expression of 19th-century liberalism—the haute bourgeoisie of finance and industry. Members of this new class ranged from solid Catalan manufacturers demanding protective tariffs to safeguard their gains to daring speculators such as José, marqués de Salamanca, a railway financier who took an active part in political life and the urbanization of Madrid. It also included successful generals ready to forget their humble origins. Together with the large landowners, these groups formed the oligarchy of liberalism.

The government that presided over this prosperity was O'Donnell's Liberal Union, which was an attempt to fuse all dynastic parties in a broad-based coalition. It provided a long period of stable government (1856–63), and, had the Progressive politicians been less afraid of losing their left wing to the Democrats and had the queen been willing to grant Progressives power, the dynasty might have survived. Instead, she excluded the Progressives and forced them first to withdraw formally from political life and then to contemplate revolution. Their "sword," General Juan Prim y Prats (a pharmacist's grandson and a striking example of the social mobility of the liberal army), was a resolute conspirator and the ablest of the political generals of the 19th century. When Isabella's court ministers alienated O'Donnell's followers, a powerful coalition was formed, and Prim dropped his alliance with the Democrats. A series of mediocre ultraconservative governments, a growth in democratic agitation among university intellectuals (whose main concern was the hold of the church over education), and an economic slump caused by bad harvests gave wide support to the military rising against Isabella. Her armies would not defend her, and she was forced to leave for France in September 1868.

THE REVOLUTION OF 1868 AND THE REPUBLIC OF 1873

The revolution that led to the dethronement of Isabella was the work of army oligarchs led by Francisco Serrano y Domínguez and Progressive conspirators behind Prim. The Democrats became active in setting up juntas after the revolution; for the most part they rapidly became Federal Republicans under the influence of the theories of the French anarchist Pierre-Joseph Proudhon as presented by their leader, Francisco Pi i Margall. The Democratic intellectuals' main contribution was to add a radical democratic content to the demands of the military oligarchy.

The generals were determined to keep the leadership of the revolution in their own hands by channeling it into a constitutional monarchy. Although they had to concede universal male suffrage in the constitution of 1869, they ruthlessly suppressed republican risings in the summer of that year. Their problem was to find a constitutional monarch. Prim's attempt to persuade a Hohenzollern to accept the throne was opposed by France and set off the Franco-German War in 1870. In November 1870 Amadeo (Amadeus), second son of Victor Emmanuel, king of Italy, was elected king, and Prim, the kingmaker, was assassinated the day Amadeo entered Madrid.

Amadeo attempted to rule as a constitutional monarch. Opposed both by Republicans and by Carlists, he could form no stable government from the "September coalition" of former conservative Liberal Unionists, the ex-Progressives, and the moderate Democrats—now called Radicals. Once Amadeo called the Radicals to power, the conservatives deserted the dynasty. Amadeo abdicated after an attack by the Radicals on the army in February 1873, and subsequently the Cortes proclaimed Spain a republic.

The Republic of 1873 came into existence to fill the political vacuum created by Amadeo's abdication. The Republican Party was neither strong nor united. When the Republican leaders, on legal scruples, refused to declare for a federal republic, the provincial federal extremists revolted.

This Cantonalist revolt was serious in Cartagena, Alcoy, and Málaga. Simultaneously the authorities had to deal with a new uprising by the Carlists, the Second Carlist War (1873–76). The Republican leaders had allowed attacks on the army that had reduced it to impotence. To conservatives and other supporters of order, the country seemed on the verge of total dissolution; the Carlists were immensely strengthened by the "excesses" of the Cantonalists. Too late, Emilio Castelar y Ripoll, the last president of the republic, tried to recapture the loyalty of the army. In January 1874 General Manuel Pavía y Rodríguez de Alburquerque drove the Republican deputies from the Cortes building in the hope of creating a government of order. Pavía turned power over to General Francisco Serrano to form a coalition government.

General Serrano took over as president of a unitary republic ruled from Madrid. His main task was victory over the Carlists, now a strong force in northern Spain. In this he failed, and on December 29, 1874, a young brigadier, Arsenio Martínez Campos, "declared" for Alfonso XII, the son of Isabella.There was no resistance. The extreme threat of anarchy in 1873 had resulted in a strong conservative reaction, strengthened by the religious policies pursued since 1868. The constitution of 1869 for the first time had allowed complete freedom of religion. Despite its failure to deliver political stability, the Revolution of 1868 bequeathed to Spain the model of a modern secular state based on universal suffrage. Anarchism penetrated Spain's extreme left, especially in rural Andalusia and in industrial Catalonia, where the lower classes deserted a long tradition of political action via the Democratic and Republican parties and moderate unionism. Although anarchists were persecuted after 1873, the movement was kept alive by small groups of enthusiasts.

The independence movement in Cuba, which, along with Puerto Rico, was the last possession of Spain in America, posed the worst problem for Spain in the period 1868–75. Cubans had long resented the failure to reform rule by captains general, to grant some autonomy, and to ease the economic sacrifices that were imposed by the Spanish tariff system. The Ten Years' War that began in October 1868 made great demands on Spain both in terms of manpower (100,000 by 1870) and money. The war made difficulties for all governments in power in Spain after 1868 and forced abandonment of the most popular of the pledges made by the rebels in 1868: the abolition of the arbitrary and socially selective recruitment system. Like the Carlist wars, the war in Cuba tended to favour the monarchical reaction.

THE RESTORED MONARCHY, 1875–1923

Once the Carlists had been defeated and the Cubans had accepted the peace settlement of El Zanjón (1878), the restored monarchy provided the most stable government Spain had known since 1833. This stability was sustained by an uneven but respectable economic growth.

The architect of the restoration itself and of the constitution of 1876 was Antonio Cánovas del Castillo. A superb politician, Cánovas had hoped for a civilian restoration; he accepted Martínez Campos's coup but used the young Alfonso XII to keep the military out of politics.

The Canovite system was artificial in that it required the contrived rotation in office (*turno pacífico*) of a Liberal and a Conservative party; this in turn demanded governmental control of elections, which were run by *caciques*, or local political bosses, who controlled votes in their districts and delivered them in return for favours for themselves and their supporters. Only in this way could the government selected by the king and the politicians in Madrid obtain a parliamentary majority. Extensive corruption and the use of administrative pressures on electors were considered the only ways to make the parliamentary system work in an underdeveloped society. This system survived the death of Alfonso XII (1885) and began to falter only in the 1890s, toward the end of his wife's regency. The Carlist threat weakened with defeat, and the majority of Republicans in Spain were domesticated and reconciled to the use of "legal" means.

"Without being a rich country," wrote an economist in the early 1880s, "Spain has become comfortably off." This prosperity, untroubled by the claims of organized labour, was the result of the demand for iron ore after the invention of the Bessemer process (England and France invested heavily in mineral production), the demand for Spanish wine after the devastations by phylloxera in France, and the resumption of railway construction in Spain. The third largest wool industry in Europe grew up alongside the older cotton mills in Catalonia. The boom did not break until the late 1880s, when an agricultural depression set in. A wave of economic pessimism preceded the political and intellectual reaction of 1898.

The loss of Cuba, Puerto Rico, and the Philippines in 1898 following the Spanish-American War exposed the Spanish political system to severe criticism. No fiscal and political reform sufficient to satisfy Cuban demands could be effected within the framework of the monarchy, partly because of the pressure of the Spanish loyalist party in Cuba. A revolt in 1895 set off another costly war against Cuban guerrillas. The intervention of the United States could not be staved off by a last-minute grant of autonomy. Their humiliating and total naval defeat in 1898 became known to Spaniards as "the Disaster." Spain now lost the Philippines and the last of its possessions in the Americas at the very time when the great European powers were building their overseas empires. These events exacerbated an already existing pessimism among intellectuals about Spain's national and racial "degeneration."

OPPOSITION MOVEMENTS, 1898–1923

Criticism of the restoration monarchy came from the Catalan and Basque regionalists, a revived Republican Party, the proletarian parties, the army, the more forward-looking of the Spanish politicians, and intellectuals.

Basque regionalism, though more akin in its ideas to extreme nationalist movements, was less a challenge than Catalan regionalism. With their own language and a revived cultural tradition, known as the Renaixença, Catalan nationalists moved from a demand for protection of Catalan industry against "Castilian" free trade to a demand for political autonomy. The Regionalist League (Catalan: Lliga Regionalista), founded in 1901 and dominated by the Catalan industrialist Francesc Cambó

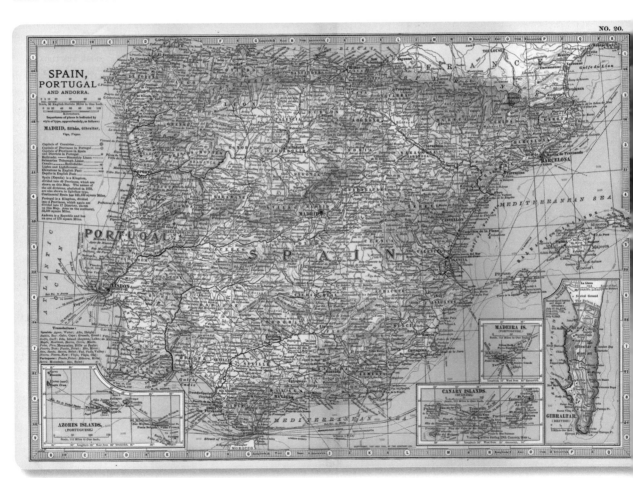

Map of the Iberian Peninsula, Andorra, and nearby islands (c. 1900) from the 10th edition of the Encyclopædia Britannica.

i Batlle and the theoretician of Catalan nationalism Enric Prat de la Riba, demanded the end of the *turno* and a revival of regionalism within a genuine party system. Cambó wished to solve the Catalan question "within Spain"—that is, by legal means and in cooperation with monarchist politicians. The revival of Catalanism, however, set off a "Castilian" reaction in which moderate Catalans were accused of selfishness or of hiding separatist aims under "respectable" regionalism.

Anti-Catalan sentiment was particularly strong among army officers, still smarting from the defeat of 1898. A string of antimilitary cartoons in Catalan periodicals led members of the Barcelona garrison to sack the offices of these publications (the *Cu-Cut!*) and demand the application of military law to insults against the military. The passage of the Law of Jurisdictions (1906), which largely met the officers' demands, led to the creation of Solidaridad Catalana, a united front of Catalanist parties.

In the 1907 election the Solidaridad Catalana defeated the establishment parties but then divided into a right wing (which accepted a solution within the monarchy) and a left wing (which was to drift to Republicanism). Cambó's cooperation with Madrid brought Catalonia no tangible concessions.

Republicanism, which had degenerated into local politicking and lived on its memories of 1873, was revived in a number of major cities: in Valencia by the novelist-politician Vicente Blasco Ibáñez, in Gijón by Melquíades Alvarez, and, most significantly, in Barcelona by the colourful demagogue and former journalist Alejandro Lerroux. Lerroux's Radical Party offered a program that appealed to the alienated working-class voter of Barcelona. Competing with a slow revival of anarchism, Lerroux veered between terrorism, educational propaganda, and union activity; the anarcho-syndicalist union, the National Confederation of Labour (Confederación Nacional del Trabajo; CNT), was founded in 1910. The socialist movement with its union (the General Union of Workers [Unión General de Trabajadores; UGT], founded 1888) was relatively weak except in the mining districts of the north and in Madrid, where it was dominated by its French-influenced founder, Pablo Iglesias. In 1909 the socialists abandoned their boycott of "bourgeois" politics and allied themselves with the Republicans. This alliance gave the party a political leverage in excess of its voting strength.

The intellectuals' protest embraced the writers of widely differing ideas collectively known as the Generation of '98. Joaquín Costa, a voluminous writer, was an especially harsh critic of *caciquismo* (the system of electoral manipulation on the local level by political bosses); he wanted a revived, effectively democratic, modernized Spain. Miguel de Unamuno saw regeneration in terms of a return to "pure" Spanish values. The Generation of '98 distrusted politics as managed by professional politicians, who, they said, were out of touch with the "real" Spain.

Although the defeat of 1898 loomed large in these intellectuals' thoughts, the cultural pessimism they expressed was far from a peculiarly Spanish affair. Rather, it was part of and shared many features with a more general European fin de siècle pessimism.

Among the politicians themselves, the conservative leaders Francisco Silvela and Antonio Maura and the democratic liberal José Canalejas sought to regenerate the system by widening the degree of political participation through "sincere" elections. Opposed by the professional party members, Maura only succeeded in confusing the party structure by splitting the Conservative Party. The danger of "sincere" elections to the political establishment was revealed by the Republican victories in 1903.

The call up of troops for Morocco, where Spanish troops were engaged in operations protecting the Spanish coastal possessions, set off the Tragic Week of 1909 in Barcelona. Public order collapsed, and anarchists and Radical Republicans burned churches and convents. Maura was driven from office because Alfonso XIII (who ruled in his own right from 1902) accepted the Liberals' estimate of the harm Maura's firm repression would inflict on the monarchy. Rather than resist a Liberal Party that had allied with the Republican parties, the king held that the Liberals were a useful "lightning conductor," protecting the monarchy from the threat on the left. Ever since Maura's fall, the king's diagnosis had been challenged by conservatives.

World War I produced increased strains. Real wages fell, making the unions restive, and in 1917 junior officers formed juntas and struck for better conditions. The ensuing crisis was exploited by Catalan politicians, who increasingly pressed for autonomy. The revolutionary coalition consisting of Radical Republicans and Catalan regionalists split, and a general strike frightened Cambó and the Catalans, who threatened to call a national convention that would unite all critics of the monarchy. The formation of a national government under Maura ended the last serious attempt to regenerate the political system and to make it respond to reformist and Catalan demands. No subsequent government was strong enough to face the anarchist agitation in Catalonia and the Moroccan War.

Spain, through negotiations with France, had obtained a protectorate in Morocco in 1912. In an effort to pacify Morocco, economizing politicians were ready for compromise with tribal leaders, but the generals saw conquest as the only solution. A bid by General Fernández Silvestre, reputedly backed by Alfonso XIII, for a crowning victory ended in the terrible massacre of Spanish troops at the Battle of Anual (Anwal) in 1921. Opposition politicians were determined to expose the king's action and criticize the army.

World War I had given the anarcho-syndicalist movement great power. At the same time there grew a terrorist fringe, which the leaders of the CNT could not control. Although CNT leaders Salvador

Seguí and Angel Pestaña shared the anarchist contempt for political action, they wished to build unions powerful enough to challenge the employers by direct action. They mistrusted the libertarian tradition of spontaneous revolution as a means of toppling the bourgeois state. The great Barcelona strike of 1919 was the most impressive in Spanish history. When the employers' violent reaction discredited the moderates in the CNT, it was followed by a wave of assassinations by gangsters employed by both the anarchists and the employers.

Thus, when General Miguel Primo de Rivera staged his *pronunciamiento* in September 1923, he received the support of the conservative classes fearful for social order. For example, the Lliga became more concerned about suppressing strikes than about Catalan autonomy, for which it had campaigned from 1915 to 1918. He also had a tacit alliance with Alfonso XIII, who was tired of politicians who could not provide him with effective governments and afraid of being blamed for the disaster at Anual by a parliamentary committee that was scheduled to report in the fall of 1923.

CHAPTER 17

SPAIN: FROM THE SECOND REPUBLIC TO THE BEGINNING OF THE 21ST CENTURY

Primo de Rivera was a political improviser who believed his mission was to save Spain from the old politicians and to hand over government (after an interval of personal rule) to "clean" patriots. He failed to complete the process because his rule became increasingly unpopular, especially among the intellectuals and Catalans. The September 1923 coup by which he had gained power had been widely welcomed in Catalonia, where, as captain general, Primo had listened sympathetically to Catalan demands. However, Primo soon became a Spanish patriot and permitted an "anti-Catalan crusade." His followers' attempts to build up a political party (the Patriotic Union) to run a regenerated Spain and provide it with an ideology collapsed.

At first Primo ruled via the army. In spite of initial quarrels with the African commanders, whom he forced to retreat in Morocco, the Military Directory was responsible for final victory in the protectorate. The Spanish, collaborating for the first time with the French, landed at Alhucemas (Al-Hoceima) in September 1925 and defeated the most successful tribal leader, Abd el-Krim. By 1927 the whole of the protectorate was successfully occupied.

The Civil Directory (1925–30) was responsible for a thorough overhaul of local government and for an ambitious public works program to increase irrigation, hydraulic power, and road building. Primo's economic nationalism entailed strict protectionist policies and an attack on foreign oil monopolies. The complicated bureaucratic control of industry did not endear him to capitalists after 1926; on the other hand, he collaborated successfully with the UGT while suppressing the CNT. The Civil Directory failed in its chief task, that of winning sufficient political support in the National Assembly summoned for 1928 to facilitate a return to quasi-constitutional government.

Primo oversaw an economic expansion based on favourable terms of trade for Spanish exports during the early years of his dictatorship. His governments carried out a policy of economic nationalism that included public works, the creation of numerous state regulatory agencies, the nationalization of foreign petroleum interests, and the establishment of a state-owned petroleum company. By 1929, however, the peseta (the Spanish currency) began to fall in value despite desperate measures to prop it up. Economic recession alone would not have forced the dictator from office, but he also lost the support of both the army and the king. The army turned against him as a result of his attempts to abolish the privileges of the artillery and engineer corps, and the king believed that student protests, the growing discontent in Catalonia, and the increasing conspiracies of the "old" politicians imperiled the dynasty.

On January 28, 1930, Alfonso forced Primo's resignation. However, the king acted too late. His earlier support of the dictatorship tarnished him in the eyes of the politicians and public. The weak governments of General Dámaso Berenguer and Admiral Juan Bautista Aznar could barely keep order. At San Sebastián (August 17, 1930) an alliance of former liberal monarchists, Catalan politicians, and Republicans agreed to overthrow the monarchy. The failure of a Republican military rising at Jaca (December 12, 1930) saved them from having to establish a republic by force. The municipal elections of April 12, 1931, proved that the great cities were overwhelmingly Republican. Rather than face civil war and street demonstrations in Madrid, Alfonso XIII left Spain.

THE SECOND REPUBLIC

The history of the Second Republic falls into four distinct phases: (1) the Provisional Government, which lasted until the religious issue forced its resignation in October 1931, (2) the governments of the Left Republicans and Socialists, which ruled from October 1931 and were defeated in the elections of November 1933, (3) the conservative government of the Radical Republicans and the Roman Catholic right from November 1933 to February 1936, which was punctuated by the revolution of October 1934 and ended with the electoral victory of the Popular Front in February 1936, and (4) the government of the Popular Front and "the descent into violence" that culminated in the military uprising of July 1936.

The Provisional Government was a coalition government presided over by Niceto Alcalá Zamora, a former monarchist converted to republicanism, whose Catholicism reassured moderate opinion. Another conservative Catholic, Miguel Maura, was minister of the interior. The coalition included all the groups represented at San Sebastián: Lerroux's Radicals, the Catalan left, the Socialists, and the Left Republicans dominated by Manuel Azaña y Díaz.

The elections to the Constituent Cortes strengthened the Socialists and Left Republicans and thus upset the parliamentary balance between moderate Catholic Republicans and the left. The left imprinted its views on the constitution, especially its religious clauses. Historically conditioned anticlericalism had already led the government to tolerate an outburst of church burning (May 1931). The Socialists and Left Republicans inserted in the constitution an attack on religious education and the regular orders, which forced the resignation of Alcalá Zamora and Maura.

This direct and ill-advised clash with Catholic sentiment provided a base for the formation of a right-wing party devoted to the reversal of the church settlement. This party, established by the Catholic politician José María Gil Robles, was known as Acción Popular and became the main component of the right-wing electoral grouping, the Spanish Confederation of Autonomous Rights (Confederación Española de Derechas Autónomas; CEDA). The left viewed CEDA's "accidentalism" (the doctrine that forms of government are irrelevant provided the church can fulfill its mission) as suspect, and these suspicions were only exacerbated by a proclivity among Gil Robles's followers, especially the youth wing, for fascist styles.

From October 1931 the government, with Azaña as premier, was controlled by Left Republicans and Socialists, with the Catholic right, the Basque Catholics, the Navarrese Carlists, and Lerroux's Radicals in opposition. Azaña aimed to create a modern democracy; labour legislation would be the work of the Socialists, with the UGT leader, Francisco Largo Caballero, as minister of labour.

In April 1931 there was a danger that Catalonia might declare its independence within a federal state. Overcoming conservative Republican opposition to limited home rule under the Generalitat, which was controlled by the Catalan left (Esquerra) under Lluis Companys, Azaña was able to settle the Catalan question—perhaps his greatest achievement. Largo Caballero's legislation provided labour with a strong negotiating position but could not in itself mitigate the mounting unemployment, which was particularly serious in the latifundios of the southwest. Because new machinery for the settlement of labour disputes was dominated by the UGT, it was opposed by the CNT, now influenced by the extreme revolutionary apoliticism of an anarchist group, the Iberian Anarchist Federation (Federación Anarquista Ibérica; FAI). Violent strikes were frequent.

Sedition from the right came to a head in General José Sanjurjo's pronunciamiento in Sevilla (August 10, 1932). Politically more dangerous than Sanjurjo's abortive coup, however, were the steady growth of Gil Robles's Acción Popular and the Socialists' desertion of the Azaña coalition, as Largo Caballero, influenced by increasing discontent with the slow pace of reform among Socialists, wearied of cooperation with "bourgeois" parties. In the elections of November 1933, therefore, the left was divided and the right relatively united behind CEDA. Given an electoral law that favoured electoral coalitions, the CEDA and Lerroux's Radicals, now a respectable middle-class party, triumphed. Although the CEDA had more seats than any other party, President Alcalá Zamora refused to call on Gil Robles to form a government and turned instead to Lerroux, who was unable to govern without the support of Gil Robles. With power in sight, Gil Robles accentuated his legalism, to the distaste of the militant monarchists among his supporters.

The election defeat further radicalized the Socialists, especially Largo Caballero, who was influenced by Luis Araquistaín, Spain's ambassador in Berlin when Adolf Hitler came to power in Germany in January 1933. Throughout 1934 the Socialists threatened an uprising should the CEDA, which they saw as a clearly fascist party, be invited to join the cabinet.

When four members of CEDA entered Lerroux's government in October 1934, the Socialists staged the revolution they had been threatening. Poorly planned, it was a total failure everywhere except the coalfields of Asturias, where the failure of the Republic to bring any improvement to their situation had a particularly radicalizing effect on the miners there. Revolutionary councils were established in the mining districts of Asturias, where there was considerable destruction of property. In Barcelona the revolution was led by Catalan nationalists, who believed autonomy was imperiled by the actions of the Madrid government in overruling an agrarian law passed by the Generalitat. Unsupported by the CNT, the revolution was quickly suppressed.

The October Revolution of 1934 was the dividing point in the Second Republic. The Socialists, fearing the fate of their Austrian and German brothers, had revolted against a legal government and thereby established in the minds of the right the fear of a "Red" rebellion. In the subsequent repression by the army lay the emotional origins of the Popular Front against "fascism"—a re-creation of the Azaña coalition of Left Republicans and Socialists.

When the Radicals collapsed in late 1935 following a series of scandals, Alcalá Zamora dissolved parliament and called new elections for February 1936. The campaign was violent, and the Popular Front won by a narrow majority. Spain was politically polarized, and this division intensified. The Popular Front government was exclusively Republican. Under Largo Caballero's leadership, the left Socialists put increasing pressure on the government, using revolutionary language if not intending revolution, and agricultural workers in the south and west staged a number of land seizures. Largo Caballero's revolutionary rhetoric concealed his hope that the orthodox Republicans could be eased from power, leaving the field open to a pure Socialist government, which his followers, using the language of Russian Communist Party founder and revolutionary Vladimir Lenin, chose to call the "dictatorship of the proletariat."

Just as the fears of the "fascism" of the right justified the defensive reaction of the Socialists, so the right argued that the Republican government was a prisoner of the revolutionary left. The Falange, a fascist party founded in 1933 by José Antonio Primo de Rivera, the son of the former dictator, grew significantly as the failure of Gil Robles's legalist strategy became clear. The Falange was primarily responsible for the marked increase in political street violence in the months after the 1936 election. Conservatives rallied behind the right-wing National Front, which openly appealed to the military to save Spain from Marxism.

FALANGE

The Falange Española ("Spanish Phalanx") or, as it was known from 1937–77, Falange Española Tradicionalista y de las Juntas de Ofensiva Nacional-Sindicalista ("Traditionalist Spanish Phalanx of the Juntas of the National Syndicalist Offensive"), was an extreme nationalist political group founded in Spain in 1933 by José Antonio Primo de Rivera, son of the former dictator Miguel Primo de Rivera. Influenced by Italian fascism, the Falange joined forces (February 1934) with a like-minded group, Juntas de Ofensiva Nacional Sindicalista, and issued a manifesto of 27 points repudiating the republican constitution, party politics, capitalism, Marxism, and clericalism, and proclaiming the necessity of a national-syndicalist state, a strong government and military, and Spanish imperialist expansion.

Despite parades and strident proclamations, the Falange made little headway in its first three years. In the election of February 1936, which brought the Popular Front to power, the Falange polled in Madrid only 5,000 votes out of a total right-wing vote of 180,000, and its only representative in the Cortes, Primo de Rivera himself, was defeated. With the coming to power of the Popular Front and the ensuing rapid polarization of Spanish politics, the Falangists gained increasing popularity at the expense of the conservatives and Roman Catholics of the right. Upon the military uprising against the Spanish Republic in July 1936, several of the Falange's principal leaders, including Primo de Rivera, were arrested and shot by Republican firing squads.

General Francisco Franco found in the Falange a potential political party and an explicit ideology at hand for his use. True, it had to be reconciled with traditionalist, clericalist, and monarchist elements within the Nationalist movement, but this was effected by the decree of April 19, 1937, whereby the Falange, the Carlists, and other right-wing factions were forcibly merged into one body with the cumbrous title of Falange Española Tradicionalista y de las Juntas de Ofensiva Nacional-Sindicalista. General Franco became the Falange's absolute chief and his brother-in-law Ramón Serrano Suñer its chief spokesman. The Falange's membership was over

250,000 when Franco seized control of it in 1937, and more than 150,000 Falangists served in Franco's armed forces during the Civil War.

After the victory of the Nationalists in 1939 and the end of the war, the Falange's radical fascist ideas were subordinated to the conservative and traditionalist values of Franco's regime. Membership in the Falange became indispensable to political advancement, but it gradually ceased to be identified with the original Falangist ideology as Franco's regime evolved during the late 1940s and '50s.

On January 12, 1975, prior to Franco's death, a law was passed permitting the establishment of other "political associations"; thereafter and especially after Franco's death in November, other political parties began to proliferate. The Falange itself had become utterly moribund by this time and was formally abolished on April 1, 1977.

The army played a decisive role. By the early summer of 1936 a young officers' conspiracy was backed by Generals Emilio Mola, Manuel Goded, and, finally, Francisco Franco. The murder of José Calvo Sotelo, the leader of the extreme right, with the connivance of government security forces, was the final outrage for the right and the army.

THE CIVIL WAR

The military uprising started in Morocco on July 17, 1936, and quickly spread to the garrisons of metropolitan Spain. The Civil War took place because the rising was successful only in Old Castile, in Navarra, where Carlist support was decisive, and, of the larger towns, in Zaragoza, Sevilla, Córdoba, Valladolid, and Cádiz. Galicia soon went over to the Nationalists, as did most of Andalusia. Catalonia and the Basque provinces were loyal to the government because the republic guaranteed their autonomy. In Madrid and Barcelona the security forces, aided by the workers who were armed belatedly by the government, defeated the officers. Thus, in broadest terms, the Republic held the centre, the Levant, Catalonia, and the Basque industrial zones; the Nationalists controlled the food-producing areas, which was to cause an increasingly acute food shortage in the Republican zone.

The role of the workers in defeating the rising made their organizations the power in the Republican zone. The legal government was bypassed or totally supplanted by local committees and trade unions; the workers' militia replaced the dissolved army. In many parts of Spain a social revolution took place in July 1936 as factories and farms were collectivized. The English novelist George Orwell described Barcelona, where the CNT was all-powerful, as "a town where the working class was in the saddle." The success of working-class control, in terms of increased production, is difficult to estimate.

The revolution was distasteful to the Left Republicans and to the Communist Party of Spain (Partido Comunista de España; PCE), the latter growing rapidly in number and in political influence because it controlled the supply of arms from the Soviet Union, which—given the refusal of Britain and France to support the legitimate and democratically elected Republican government or even to allow it to purchase arms—became the Republic's only significant ally. In the name of an efficient war effort and the preservation of "bourgeois" elements in the Popular Front, the communists pressed for a popular army and central government control. In September–November 1936, the CNT was brought into the government of Catalonia and into Largo Caballero's ministry in Madrid—an astonishing step for a movement that had consistently rejected "bourgeois" politics. The CNT militants did not approve the leaders' "surrender" and the dismantling of the militia-backed revolution.

A small Marxist revolutionary party, the Workers' Party of Marxist Unification (Partido Obrero de Unificación Marxista; POUM), which rejected the Popular Front in favour of a workers' government, set off a rebellion in Barcelona in May 1937. The communists, Republicans, and anti-Caballero socialists used this as an excuse to oust Largo Caballero, who proved insufficiently pliable to communist demands. The government led by the socialist doctor Juan Negrín was a coalition of Republicans, socialists, and communists. Thus, the UGT and CNT trade unions were replaced by the political parties.

The communists were correct in arguing that the committee-militia system was militarily ineffective. Ferried over from Morocco, General Franco's army cut through the militia and neared Madrid by November 1936. The successful resistance of the city, which was stiffened by the arrival of the International Brigades, organized by the Communist International, and by Soviet arms, prolonged the Civil War for two more years.

.Victory ultimately went to the Nationalists, who had a better army, unified political control, and an adequate arms supply. The core of the Nationalist army was the African army commanded by General Franco. Given the confused political control in Republican Spain, the secure military and political command of Franco (from October 1936) was decisive. In April 1937 he incorporated the Falange and the Carlists into a unified movement under his leadership. Franco also benefited from the support of the Roman Catholic Church, which proclaimed his cause a "Crusade."

The Nationalist zone saw the extensive use of terror against anyone suspected of being a "Red." The number of people killed for political reasons is unclear, but even conservative estimates put the figure at 80,000 between the outbreak of the war and 1943. The Republican zone also saw numerous political killings, including some 7,000 members of the clergy, but the circumstances were radically different. The vast majority of the executions in the Republican zone took place in the early months of the war when government authority had broken down. In contrast, the Nationalists consciously used terror as a policy, one that continued well after the war had ended.

INTERNATIONAL BRIGADES

The International Brigades were groups of foreign volunteers who fought on the Republican side against the Nationalist forces during the Spanish Civil War (1936–39). So called because their members (initially) came from some 50 countries, the International Brigades were recruited, organized, and directed by the Comintern (Communist International), with headquarters in Paris. A large number of the mostly young recruits were Communists before they became involved in the conflict; more joined the party during the course of the war. The French were the largest single foreign group (some 28,000); Germany, Austria, Poland, Italy, the United States, the United Kingdom, Yugoslavia, Czechoslovakia, Canada, Hungary, and Belgium were also represented by significant numbers of volunteers.

The first group of 500 trainees arrived in Albacete, Spain, on October 14, 1936. As other trainees and Soviet arms arrived, they were placed under the command of representatives of the Comintern. There were seven brigades in all, and each one was divided into battalions by nationality (e.g., the French-Belgian Commune de Paris Battalion, the American Abraham Lincoln Battalion, the British Battalion). The number of volunteers probably never exceeded 20,000 at any one time, but the total number of volunteers, including a small number of women, reached about 60,000.

From 1936 to 1938 the brigades, despite some difficulties, operated effectively on the Republican side, and their organization was imitated by other units of the Republican army. From 1937 on, recruits for the brigades diminished, and men lost in action or by desertion were replaced mainly by Spanish Communists. The brigades were formally withdrawn from Spain late in 1938 as part of Prime Minister Juan Negrín's attempt to win British and French support for his government. The last battle in which they participated was that of the Ebro. A farewell parade was held for the volunteers in Barcelona, Spain, on November 15, 1938.

"The Internationals—United with the Spaniards We Fight the Invader," poster by Parrilla, published by the International Brigades, 1936-37. Courtesy of the Abraham Lincoln Brigade Archives, Brandeis University Library

Gen. Francisco Franco's troops in Barcelona during the Spanish Civil War, late 1930s. Encyclopædia Britannica, Inc.

Both sides sought help from abroad. General Franco appealed immediately to Hitler in Germany and to Benito Mussolini in Italy, both of whom supplied aircraft early in the war. In return for mineral concessions, the Germans supplied the Condor Legion (100 combat planes), and the Italians sent some 70,000 ground troops; both supplied tanks and artillery. This support proved crucial to Franco's victory.

The Republic consistently hoped that France and Britain would allow them to acquire arms. Owing to fears of a general war and domestic pressures, however, both powers promoted a nonintervention agreement (August 1936), which committed 29 countries to refrain from selling war matériel to either side in the Spanish conflict. The agreement was supposed to be enforced by a London-based committee, but this turned out to be nothing more than a facade that did little to hinder the blatant violations by Germany and Italy.

The Soviet Union responded to the breakdown of nonintervention by supplying arms to the Republican side. Soviet supplies were of great importance (tanks, aircraft, and a military mission) after October 1936. Mexico also provided aid to the Republicans, though its support was very limited. Soviet supplies dropped off in 1938, and thereafter the balance of arms supply decisively favoured the Nationalists. Once the Popular Army replaced the militia, the Republic held Madrid and defeated two flanking attacks in the battles of Jarama (February 1937) and Guadalajara (March 1937), where the International Brigades decisively defeated a motorized Italian corps.

After his failure at Madrid, Franco transferred his effort to the north, where the bombing of Guernica (Gernika-Lumo) on April 26, 1937, by German planes outraged public opinion in the democracies. By October 1937 Franco had captured the industrial zone, shortened his front, and won a decisive advantage. When Franco concentrated again on Madrid, the Republican army staged its most effective offensive in the Battle of Teruel (launched December 15, 1937). Franco, however, recovered Teruel and drove to the sea, but he committed his one strategic error in deciding to launch a difficult attack on Valencia. To relieve Valencia, the Republicans attacked across the Ebro (July 24, 1938); once more they failed to exploit the breakthrough, and the bloody battle exhausted the Popular Army.

The final Nationalist campaign in Catalonia was relatively easy. On the Republican side, the question of the feasibility of continued resistance, which was supported by the communists and Negrín, caused acute political divisions. On March 7, 1939, a civil war broke out in Madrid between communists and anti-communists. On March 28 the Nationalist forces entered a starving capital.

FRANCO'S SPAIN, 1939–75

Throughout Franco's rule, his authoritarian regime was based on the emergency war powers granted him as head of state and of the government by his fellow generals in 1936. The first decade of his government saw harsh repression by military tribunals, political purges, and economic hardship. Economic recovery was made difficult by the destruction during the Civil War (especially of railway rolling stock and communications in general), a loss of skilled labour, a series of bad droughts, and a shortage of foreign exchange and the restriction on imports of capital goods imposed by World War II and its aftermath. These difficulties were increased by Franco's misguided policies of autarky, which aimed at economic self-sufficiency through the state control of prices and industrial development within a protected national economy cut off from the international market. The national income fell back to the levels of 1900, as industrial production and agricultural output stagnated and real wages dramatically fell. The near-famine years of the 1940s witnessed the rise of the black market and misery in rural areas that caused migration to the shantytowns of the cities. Given brutal repression and a controlled and censored press, sullen discontent could take no organized form. The regime maintained a division between the victors and the vanquished of the Civil War, with the vanquished excluded from public life.

Franco's sympathies in World War II lay with Germany and Italy, to whom he gave moral and material support. Nevertheless, Franco demanded France's North African colonies in compensation for military cooperation against the Western Allies, on whom Spain was dependent for food and oil imports. Hitler refused. When in 1943 it appeared that the Allies would win the war, Franco reaffirmed Spain's nominal neutrality without gaining their benevolence. The declared hostility of the great powers after 1945 and the diplomatic sanctions imposed by the United Nations (UN), from which Spain was excluded, gave Franco's opposition in Spain and in exile new life. Juan Carlos Teresa Silverio Alfonso de Borbón y Battenberg, conde de Barcelona (popularly known as Don Juan), heir of Alfonso XIII, presented the monarchy as something acceptable to the democratic powers and offered himself as king of all Spaniards, victors and vanquished alike. Because many of Franco's fellow generals were monarchists hostile to the Falange, demands for a restoration were parried only with difficulty. Valiant but futile guerrilla activities, inspired largely by the Communist Party (1944–48), were brutally suppressed.

Franco met these serious difficulties with success, shifting the balance of power among his supporters from the Falange to Catholics. The Fuero de los Españoles (1945), guaranteeing personal freedoms (provided no attack was made on the regime), was a cosmetic device that failed to establish Franco's democratic credentials with the Allies. More important for Franco was the support of the church, which was given control over education. The diplomatic ostracism imposed by the UN was skillfully turned into a means of rallying support for the regime in the name of national unity.

Franco's confidence came from his sense that, with the onset of the Cold War, the United States would come to consider Spain a valuable ally against the Soviet Union and that France and Britain, though declaring support for the democratic opposition, would not intervene directly to overthrow him at the cost of renewed civil war. Hence, the hopes of the opposition came to nothing. In 1953 an agreement with the United States gave Franco considerable financial aid in return for the establishment of four U.S. military bases in Spain; in the same year a concordat with the Vatican gave Spain added diplomatic respectability.

By 1955, when Spain was admitted to the UN, Franco's regime appeared secure. Internal political command remained in Franco's hands, ensured by his control of the armed forces and by his ability to play off the groups that supported him, in particular the Falange, the monarchists, and the church. Ultimately, the Falange lost power in the National Movement, the sole legal political organization; its attempts to create a Falangist one-party state were defeated in 1956, though tensions between the Falange and the conservative elements persisted.

Opposition to the regime took the form of student unrest, strikes, and the unsuccessful efforts of the Communist Party to forge a united front and challenge the regime (1958, 1959). The moderate opposition's attempt in 1962 to force a democratic opening in order to enter the European Economic Community (EEC) was dismissed by the regime as treason. More serious was the bankruptcy of autarky, evident in inflation, a growing deficit in the balance of payments, and strikes. This crisis was remedied by the technocrats of Opus Dei (a conservative Roman Catholic lay organization), a number of whose members were appointed to the cabinet in February 1957. The devaluation of the European currencies forced Franco to implement a stabilization plan in 1959, which provided a fierce dose of orthodox finance. Economic nationalism, protectionism, and the state intervention characteristic of autarky were abandoned in favour of a market economy and the opening of Spain to international trade and much-needed foreign investment. The stabilization plan was followed by a development plan in 1963, which was based on French indicative planning—i.e., the setting of targets for the public sector and encouragement of the private sector.

The new policies produced growth rates of more than 7 percent between 1962 and 1966, aided by a rapid increase in tourism, foreign investment, and the remittances of emigrants who, hard-hit by the immediate results of the 1959 stabilization policies, had sought employment in other European countries. There was a rural exodus from the impoverished countryside and a dramatic fall of the active population engaged in agriculture, from about two-fifths in 1960 to about one-fifth by 1976. Spain was rapidly becoming a modern industrialized country. However, the government's policies were fiercely resisted by the Falange, who claimed that the policies were a surrender to neocapitalism. All hopes of a limited liberalization of the regime by its reformist wing were blocked by conservative elements, with the exception of Manuel Fraga's Press Law of 1966, which gave the press greater freedom and influence.

Although the new prosperity brought a novel degree of social mobility and satisfied the enlarged middle class, the workers' movement revived. Workers, disillusioned with the "official" syndicates run by the Falange, set up Workers' Commissions (Confederación Sindical de Comisiones Obreras; CC.OO) to negotiate wage claims outside the official framework and called serious strikes. Sections of the church were sympathetic to claims for greater social justice and responsive to the recommendations of the Second Vatican Council. Indeed, many younger priests were sympathetic to the Workers' Commissions. Although the bishops generally felt that the church should support the regime, they were increasingly aware of the long-term dangers of such an alliance.

Peripheral nationalism constituted an intractable problem. In the Basque provinces the nationalists could count on the support of the clergy, and Basque nationalism developed a terrorist wing, ETA (Euskadi Ta Askatasuna; Basque: "Basque Homeland and Liberty"). The Burgos trials of Basque terrorists in 1970 discredited the regime abroad, and the following year the Assembly of Catalonia united the opposition with a demand for democratic institutions and the restoration of the Autonomy Statute of 1932.

In the 1960s elements in the regime were increasingly troubled by its lack of "institutionalization" and the problem of the succession, as Franco was in failing health and there was no designated successor. The Organic Law of 1969 gave the regime a cosmetic constitution, and in 1969 Franco finally recognized Juan Carlos, grandson of Alfonso XIII, as his successor as king and head of state; Juan Carlos's designation was rejected by the democratic opposition as a continuation of the regime. To secure continuity, in June 1973 Franco abandoned the premiership to Admiral Luis Carrero Blanco. However, in December Carrero Blanco was assassinated by ETA.

Carlos Arias Navarro, the former minister of the interior, was selected as the new premier. His government saw a fierce struggle between reformists, led by Manuel Fraga and the new foreign minister, José Maria de Areilza, who wished to "open" the regime by limited democratization from above, and the "bunker" mentality of nostalgic Francoists. Although Arias Navarro promised liberalization in a February 1974 speech, he eventually sided with the hard-line Francoists, and his Law of Associations proved to be completely unacceptable to the opposition and a defeat for the reformists. The government severely repressed ETA's terrorist activity in the Basque provinces, executing five terrorists in September 1975 despite international protests.

TRANSITION TO DEMOCRACY

After Franco's death on November 20, 1975, the accession of Juan Carlos as king opened a new era, which culminated in the peaceful transition to democracy by means of the legal instruments of Francoism. This strategy made it possible to avoid the perils of the "democratic rupture" advocated by the opposition, which had united, uneasily, on a common platform in July 1974. Arias Navarro, incapable of making the democratic transition supported by the king, was replaced in July 1976 by Adolfo Suárez González, a former Francoist minister. Suárez persuaded the Francoist right in the Cortes to pass the Law for Political Reform (November 1976), which paved the way for democratic elections. Suárez then convinced the opposition of his willingness to negotiate and his democratic intentions; in April 1977 he legalized the PCE against the wishes of the armed forces. In the elections of June 1977, Suárez's party, a coalition of centrist groups called the Union of the Democratic Centre (UCD), emerged as the strongest party, winning 165 seats in the Cortes, closely followed by the Spanish Socialist Workers' Party (PSOE), who captured 118 seats. It was a triumph for political moderation and the consensus politics of Suárez. The PCE gained 20 seats and the right-wing Popular Alliance 16.

JUAN CARLOS

Juan Carlos (born Juan Carlos Alfonso Victor María de Borbón y Borbón, January 5, 1938, Rome, Italy) acceded to the Spanish throne on November 22, 1975, two days after the death of Francisco Franco. He was instrumental in Spain's peaceful transition to democracy. Juan Carlos was the grandson of the last king, Alfonso XIII, who left Spain in 1931 and died in exile 10 years later, after renouncing his rights in favour of his third son, Juan Carlos Teresa Silverio Alfonso de Borbón y Battenberg, conde de Barcelona (1913–93), popularly known as Don Juan. (Alfonso's eldest son had been killed in an automobile accident, and his second son renounced his rights in 1933 for medical reasons.) Don Juan married María de las Mercedes de Borbón y Orleans, and their elder son was Juan Carlos.

Juan Carlos spent his early years in Italy and first came to Spain in 1947 for his education. After his father suggested in 1945 that Franco should step down as leader of the country and generally began opposing Falangist policies, Franco grew resentful and turned with increasing interest to Juan Carlos and his education, especially his military education. In 1955 Juan Carlos entered the General Military Academy at Zaragoza and later attended the Naval Military School at Marín in Pontevedra, the General Academy of the Air at San Javier in Murcia, and the University of Madrid.

Although a 1947 Francoist law abolished the republic and established Spain as a "representative monarchy," throughout Franco's lifetime Spain remained without a ruling monarch. On July 22, 1969, however, Franco presented to the Cortes (parliament) a law designating Juan Carlos the future king of Spain. The move was facilitated by two events: in December 1968 the Carlist pretender, Carlos Hugo de Borbón-Parma, had been expelled from the country; and on January 7, 1969, Juan Carlos said for the first time that he would accept the throne if offered (previously he had maintained that his father's claim preceded his own).

Although Juan Carlos swore loyalty to Franco's National Movement in 1969, he demonstrated far more liberal and democratic principles after his accession to the throne in 1975, appointing reformist prime minister Adolfo Suárez in 1976 and encouraging the revival of political parties and amnesty for political prisoners. In 1981 Juan Carlos underscored his democratic credentials by taking swift action to deflate a military coup that threatened to topple Spain's nascent democracy and return the government to Franconian reactionary lines; in doing so, he alienated the military sector but preserved the state of democracy that made possible the accession of a socialist government in late 1982. Also, a liberal divorce law was passed in 1981 and a law granting limited abortion rights in 1983.

In 1981 Juan Carlos became the first Spanish king to visit the Americas and was the first crowned monarch to make an official visit to China; in so doing, he became the first Spanish head of state to visit a communist country. Throughout his tenure as king, he traveled abroad on many goodwill missions, including a 1985 trip to France, where he and French Pres. François Mitterrand signed an accord calling for military and political cooperation between their two countries; a meeting with U.S. Pres. Bill Clinton in 2000; and a surprise visit to Spanish troops in Afghanistan on New Year's Eve 2007. The king remained popular with most Spaniards at home, but in the early 21st century, he was criticized by leftists who called for independence for Catalonia province.

Juan Carlos was married in Athens on May 14, 1962, to Princess Sophia of Greece, daughter of King Paul. They had two daughters, Elena and Christina, and a son, Felipe.

Suárez formed a minority government, and the political consensus held to pass the constitution of 1978. The new constitution, overwhelmingly ratified in a public referendum in December 1978, established Spain as a constitutional monarchy. Church and state were separated, and provisions were made for the creation of 17 autonomous communities throughout Spain, which extended regional autonomy beyond Euskadi (the Basque Country, encompassing the provinces of Viscaya, Guipúzcoa, and Álava) and Catalonia, both of which had already been given limited autonomy. Confronted by terrorism and economic recession, the UCD disintegrated into the factions of its "barons." After heavy defeats in local elections and fearing a possible military coup, Suárez resigned in January 1981.

The inauguration of Leopoldo Calvo Sotelo, also a member of the UCD, as prime minister was interrupted by the attempted military coup of Lieutenant Colonel Antonio Tejero, who occupied the Cortes (February 23, 1981) and held the government and the deputies captive for 18 hours. The coup attempt failed, however, because of King Juan Carlos's resolute support of the democratic constitution. Calvo Sotelo, who was left with the task of restoring confidence in democracy, successfully engineered Spain's entry into the North Atlantic Treaty Organization (NATO) in 1982.

THE ADMINISTRATION OF FELIPE GONZÁLEZ, 1982–96

The election of October 1982 marked the final break with the Francoist legacy, returning the PSOE under its leader, Felipe González, whose government was the first in which none of the members had served under Francoism. The PSOE won a solid majority (202 seats), while the UCD was annihilated, winning only 12 seats. The conservative Democratic

Coalition led by Manuel Fraga gained 106 seats and formed the official opposition.

A radical party in 1975 committed to the replacement of capitalism, the PSOE subsequently abandoned Marxism and accepted a market economy. The new government made its main concern the battle against inflation and the modernization of industry. González's policies were resisted by the unions (the socialist UGT and the CC.OO controlled by the PCE), which staged violent strikes against the closing of uneconomic steel plants and shipyards. The left was further alienated by the government's decision to continue NATO membership, despite the party's official opposition to membership during the 1982 election. To justify this radical departure from the PSOE's traditional neutralism, membership in NATO was submitted to a referendum and made dependent on a partial withdrawal of U.S. forces stationed in Spain under the 1953 agreements. Spain also was to make its contribution to collective defense outside the integrated military command of NATO. The government won the referendum of March 12, 1986—a triumph for González rather than evidence of understanding of or enthusiasm for NATO. González also secured Spain's entry into the EEC in January 1986 after prolonged and difficult negotiations.

The government lost some support on the left with the creation of the United Left (Izquierda Unida; IU), the core of which was remnants of the PCE, and the right capitalized on law-and-order issues, focusing on the fight against terrorism, disorder on the streets, the rise in crime, and the development of a serious drug problem. The government was accused of using its large majority to force through a major reform of university and secondary education and of abandoning socialist policies in the battle against inflation and in its support of a capitalist market economy. However, the government's control of the PSOE was ensured by its manipulation of political patronage. It was furthermore troubled by frictions created by the demands of Euskadi and Catalonia for greater autonomy. But the success of the government's economic policies (inflation fell and growth was resumed) and the popularity of González enabled the socialists in the election of June 1986 to retain their majority (184 seats), whereas Fraga's conservative Popular Coalition (105 seats) failed to make any gains and fell apart.

In its second term, the government's economic policies continued to provoke the hostility of the trade unions—unemployment ran at nearly 20 percent—and on December 14, 1988, the CC.OO and the socialist UGT staged a general strike. In foreign policy, all the major parties, with the exception of the United Left, supported the government's decision to offer logistical support to the United States and its allies in 1991 in the Persian Gulf War; however, massive demonstrations against the war revealed widespread neutralist sentiments. Tensions between the central government and the autonomous governments of Euskadi and Catalonia continued. Although ETA terrorists lost political support, the rise of nationalism in the disintegrating Soviet Union sparked outbursts of separatism in Spain. The Spanish government favoured greater political union with the EEC, the country's major trading partner. Following Spain's success in hosting football's (soccer's) World Cup a decade earlier, the country again achieved international prominence in 1992, when it hosted the Expo '92 world's fair in Sevilla and the Olympic Games in Barcelona.

Even before the glamour of those international events had faded, Spain entered a difficult period. The economy experienced a downturn, the government was rocked by a series of corruption scandals, and infighting within the PSOE reached intolerable levels. In these highly unfavourable circumstances, Felipe González called new elections for 1993. Surprisingly, the Socialists remained the largest party in the Cortes, though without an absolute majority; they were forced to rely upon the support of Catalan and Basque nationalists.

González's fourth term got off to a rocky start. Investigations led by judge Baltasar Garzón into the "dirty war" against ETA during the mid-1980s led to accusations that senior government officials had lent support to the Antiterrorist Liberation Groups (Grupos Antiterroristas de Liberación), whose activities included the kidnapping and murder of suspected ETA militants. Another scandal, involving missing security documents, led to the resignation of two ministers, including the deputy prime minister, Narcís Serra.

When Catalan leader Jordi Pujol withdrew his party's support for the government, González called new elections for March 1996, which were won by the conservative Popular Party (Partido Popular; PP), although by a much narrower margin than had been expected and without a parliamentary majority. Overall, the PP captured 156 of the Cortes' 350 seats, while the PSOE was reduced to 141 seats.

THE AZNAR REGIME

The new prime minister, José María Aznar, like González, depended on the support of Basque and Catalan nationalists (he also secured the support of the small Canary Coalition party), requiring him to alter the party's strident centralist rhetoric. Aznar's focus on deficit reduction provoked a wave of strikes and protests, including demonstrations by government workers, a two-week strike by truck drivers, and, in 1998, violent protests by Asturian coal miners. Nevertheless, Aznar's government reaped political benefits when Spain qualified to join the euro, the single currency of the European Union (in which the European Community [formerly EEC] was embedded in 1993); it did so by continuing many of the economic policies the Socialists had introduced to meet the Maastricht Treaty's terms for inclusion. It also benefited from a recovery in the late 1990s that put the economy on generally firm footing as Spain entered the new millennium.

Aznar's PP won a landslide election victory in April 2000, but it continued to face such intractable problems as the relationship between the regions and the state, Gibraltar's status as a British colony, and the seemingly eternal scourge of Basque terrorism. International affairs caused domestic political tensions to flare in 2003, when Aznar supported the U.S.- and British-led war to oust Ṣaddām Ḥussein's government in Iraq despite opposition by some 90 percent of Spain's citizens. On March 11, 2004, 10 bombs exploded on four trains in Madrid, killing some 200 people and injuring some 1,500 others in the worst terrorist incident in Europe since World War II. In elections held three days later, voters swept the governing PP from office in favour of the Socialist Party, led by José Luis Rodríguez Zapatero.

ZAPATERO AND A NEW GENERATION OF SOCIALIST LEADERSHIP

Zapatero had campaigned on ending Spain's participation in the Iraq War, a

MADRID TRAIN BOMBINGS OF 2004

Coordinated near-simultaneous attacks targeted commuter trains in Madrid on the morning of March 11, 2004. Beginning at 7:37 AM and continuing for several minutes, 10 bombs exploded on four trains in and around Atocha Station in the city's centre, leaving 191 dead and more than 1,800 injured. Occurring just three days before Spain's general elections, the attacks had major political consequences.

Both the Spanish government and the Spanish media immediately attributed the bombings to ETA, a Basque separatist organization whose campaign of violence over more than 30 years had claimed the lives of at least 800 people. Indeed, Ángel Acebes, the country's interior minister, claimed, "There is no doubt ETA is responsible." In an outpouring of grief and defiance, the following day an estimated 11 million Spaniards, including some 2.3 million in Madrid alone, participated in demonstrations against the violence and in support of the victims. This display of unity rapidly broke down, however, as the police investigation began to focus on the Islamist militant group al-Qaeda. On March 13, as the first arrests were being made, the government continued to blame ETA.

That evening spontaneous protests took place in Madrid, Barcelona, and other cities as demonstrators chanted, "We want to know the truth before we vote." With some 90 percent of Spaniards opposed to Prime Minister José María Aznar's support for the U.S.-led invasion of Iraq, the Islamic connection inevitably put Iraq back on top of the political agenda. This favoured the opposition PSOE, which had strongly opposed the war. On March 14 the PSOE scored an upset victory at the polls, and José Luis Rodríguez Zapatero was sworn in as prime minister three days later.

In October 2007, 18 Islamic fundamentalists of mainly North African origin and three Spanish accomplices were convicted of the bombings (seven others were acquitted), which were one of Europe's deadliest terrorist attacks in the years since World War II.

promise that he fulfilled immediately, though he also increased the number of Spanish troops serving in Afghanistan. Zapatero, who became prime minister at age 44, represented a new generation of Socialist leaders and brought a new type of progressive politics to government. Half his cabinet, including his deputy prime minister, were women, and his government passed a number of laws affecting private life—the most important of which were the legalization of same-sex marriage and the criminalization of domestic violence. Zapatero had long stressed the importance of the immigration issue for Spain, and his approach to it was very different from that of most other European governments; in 2005, for example, he implemented a program that enabled some 700,000 illegal immigrants to legalize their status. Zapatero also attempted to grapple with two long-standing issues: the status of Catalonia and of the Basque Country. He supported a reform of the autonomy statute for Catalonia in 2005 and the declaration, the following year, of that region as a nation. On the Basque question, Zapatero pledged not to yield to terrorism, though he hoped to arrive at a negotiated political solution with the Basque separatist organization ETA. The prospects for a settlement brightened in 2006 when ETA declared a "permanent" cease-fire, but it was broken off 14 months later.

ECONOMIC DOWNTURN

In March 2008 the PSOE triumphed again, in a hotly contested general election, although it failed to win an absolute majority; both the PSOE and the PP gained seats in the lower house of the Cortes (of which together they constituted 90 percent). Zapatero pledged to boost Spain's slumping economy and to continue his agenda of social and political reform. Zapatero's progressive policies had drawn criticism from conservatives and the Roman Catholic Church during his first term, and the PSOE's win widened the division between Spain's right and left.

The worldwide financial crisis that began later in 2008 contributed to the precipitous decline of Spain's already ailing economy in 2009. Of all the members of the European Union, Spain was one of the worst-affected by the recession; by early 2010 the unemployment rate had surpassed 20 percent. The administration initially responded with a hefty economic stimulus package, but in mid-2010 it was forced to implement unpopular cost-cutting measures to curb the swelling budget deficit.

In September 2010 the government met a cease-fire announcement by ETA with skepticism. Zapatero reiterated that the Spanish government would not negotiate with the Basque separatist group unless it renounced violence forever and that political parties with links to ETA—e.g., Batasuna—would continue to be banned.

A pair of earthquakes (the stronger of which was magnitude 5.1) that struck Lorca in southeastern Spain in May 2011 compounded the country's economic woes. At least 10 people were killed, and the city suffered extensive damage as a result of the deadliest earthquake to strike Spain in more than half a century. Later that month the PSOE suffered crushing losses in local elections as organized protests swept Spanish cities. Dubbed the *indignados* ("angry ones") by the media, the protesters were predominantly young people who were dissatisfied with the pace of economic and political reform. With the unemployment rate still topping 20 percent (more than 40 percent for job seekers under age 25) and the Spanish bond market ailing, Zapatero, who had already announced that he would not seek reelection, advanced the date of the next general election from March 2012 to November 2011. In the election on November 20, 2011, the PP swept the PSOE from power in convincing fashion, winning an overall majority of 186 seats in the 350-seat parliament. Zapatero remained prime minister of a caretaker administration, while PP leader Mariano Rajoy began the work of constructing a new government. Financial markets failed to respond positively to the results, however, and Spain's 10-year bond yield remained ominously close to the 7 percent threshold that had triggered bailouts for other countries embroiled in the euro-zone debt crisis. Rajoy was sworn in as prime minister on December 21, 2011, and he reaffirmed his commitment to cut spending and reduce Spain's deficit.

Throughout early 2012 credit agencies cut the Spanish debt rating numerous times, but markets seemed to respond positively to the adoption of a new EU fiscal discipline pact in March of that year. The return on Spanish 10-year bonds receded to 5 percent that month, but the respite was short-lived, as a power struggle erupted between Rajoy and EU ministers over the deficit target of Spain's 2012 budget. Labour unions organized a general strike on March 29, paralyzing transportation systems across the country as hundreds of thousands of demonstrators took to the streets in Barcelona and Madrid to protest the Rajoy government's austerity program.

The budget that Rajoy ultimately unveiled was characterized by his finance minister as the most austere since the reintroduction of democracy. It featured an array of public-sector wage freezes, cuts in social programs, and tax hikes, all aimed at Rajoy's ultimate goal of reducing government spending by €27 billion (about $36 billion). As 10-year Spanish bond yields continued to creep upward in April 2012, Rajoy introduced an additional €10 billion (about $13 billion) in budget cuts. The Spanish economy continued to struggle in spite of those measures, as regional governments faced unsustainable debt loads, and Bankia, Spain's largest mortgage lender, was nationalized. Rajoy's government spent billions to prop up Spain's ailing banks, and in June 2012 the finance ministers of the euro zone authorized a bailout of €100 billion (more than $125 billion) to recapitalize the Spanish banking sector.

CONCLUSION

Given their close proximity and their shared Celtic and Roman origins, Portugal and Spain have been deeply intertwined since their earliest days as independent political entities. Maritime prowess and colonial zeal placed each, for a time, among the greatest powers in Europe. The legacy of that period can be seen plainly in the cultures of Latin America.

The fortunes of both countries turned as their respective empires were stripped away, as the result of war or the rise of independence movements in the 18th and 19th centuries. Their political and economic power declined. In the 20th century, the histories of both Portugal and Spain can be defined largely by the dictatorships that rose to power in each; António de Oliveira Salazar in Portugal and Francisco Franco in Spain.

With the deaths of these strongmen in the 1970s, the two countries made terrific economic strides. Each saw closer integration with Europe as the path to the future. Portugal and Spain were founding members of the European Union in 1993. In the 21st century, challenges remained for both countries, but each was strongly committed to preserving its ties to the EU, and to Europe as a whole.

GLOSSARY

CHANCELLOR The secretary of a nobleman, prince, or king.

COMUNEROS Urban citizens of Spain dedicated to defending their rights against arbitrary government encroachment.

CONSECRATE To perform an act dedicated to ensuring a person's or object's sacred purpose.

CRUSADES Military expeditions undertaken by Christian powers in the 11th–13th centuries to win the Holy Land from the Muslims.

DISPENSATION An exemption from a law or from an impediment, vow, or oath.

EMIGRATE To leave one's native land in order to live elsewhere.

FLAGSHIP The ship that carries the commander of a fleet or subdivision of a fleet and flies the commander's flag.

GRANDEE A title of honour borne by the highest class of the Spanish nobility, first assumed during the late Middle Ages.

HIDALGO A large class of minor nobles in the northern provinces of Castile in 16th-century Spain.

IBERIAN Having to do with one or more peoples anciently inhabiting the Caucasus in Asia between the Black and Caspian seas.

LINGUISTIC Of or relating to language.

MONARCHIST One who supports a monarchial government, wherein a sovereign ruler such as a king or queen has preeminent power.

MOORISH Of or relating to the Moors, a Muslim people who invaded Spain in the 8th century and established a civilization in Andalusia that lasted until the late 15th century.

MUNICIPALITY A primarily urban political unit having corporate status and usually powers of self-government.

PAPAL BULL A formal, written proclamation made by the reigning pope of the Roman Catholic Church.

SECULAR Of or pertaining to the worldly, not the religious or spiritual.

SUBTROPICAL Of or relating to the regions bordering on the tropical zone.

SUCCESSOR One who follows, or takes over in a legal and expected manner a position of power.

TAPESTRY A heavy, handwoven, reversible textile typically used for hangings, characterized by complicated pictorial designs.

UBIQUITOUS Existing or being everywhere at the same time.

BIBLIOGRAPHY

PORTUGAL

Eric Solsten (ed.), *Portugal: A Country Study*, 2nd ed. (1994), contains chapters on the country's history, society, government and politics, economy, and national security. Walter C. Opello, Jr., *Portugal: From Monarchy to Pluralist Democracy* (1991), is a comprehensive overview of the Portuguese state from its founding through its democratic consolidation. The development of the cultural landscape, including a summary of the physical landscape, is provided in Jose Mattosé and Francisco Faria Paulino, *Portugal, Building up a Country* (1992). Marion Kaplan, *The Portuguese: The Land and Its People*, rev. ed. (2006), is a popular general work with illuminating glimpses of Portugal's long history. David Corkill, *The Development of the Portuguese Economy: A Case of Europeanization* (1999), charts Portugal's development within mainstream Europe.

Other general reference works on Portugal with an emphasis on its history include Douglas L. Wheeler, *Historical Dictionary of Portugal*, 3rd ed. (2010); and Iêda Wiarda (ed.), *The Handbook of Portuguese Studies* (1999). General historical works include Stanley G. Payne, *History of Spain and Portugal*, 2 vol. (1990); and A.H. de Oliveira Marques, *History of Portugal*, 2nd ed., 2 vol. (1991). More-specialized studies include Carl Hanson, *Atlantic Emporium: Portugal and the Wider World, 1147–1497* (2001); Glenn Joseph Ames, *Vasco da Gama: Renaissance Crusader* (2005); Malyn Newitt, *A History of Portuguese Overseas Expansion, 1400–1668* (2005); and Peter Russell, *Prince Henry "The Navigator": A Life* (2000). Combining a portrait of contemporary Portugal with insights into history is Paul Hyland, *Backwards out of the Big World: A Voyage into Portugal* (1996).

Discussions of the modern era of Portuguese history include Maria Filomena Mónica, *Eça de Queiroz*, trans. by Alison Aiken (2005); and Hugh Kay, *Salazar and Modern Portugal* (1970). The origins, course, and aftermath of the 1974 revolution are explored in Kenneth Maxwell, *The Making of Portuguese Democracy* (1995); Norrie MacQueen, *The Decolonization of Portuguese Africa: Metropolitan Revolution and the Dissolution of Empire* (1997); and *Contemporary Portugal: Politics, Society, and Culture* (2003).

SPAIN

Overviews of Spain include Adrian Shubert, *The Land and People of Spain* (1992); and Eric Solsten and Sandra W. Meditz, *Spain: A Country Study*, 2nd ed. (1990). Adrian Shubert, *A Social History of Modern Spain* (1990, reprinted 1992), examines Spanish society in the 19th and 20th centuries. William Chislett,

Spain (1992), provides a brief analysis of the Spanish economy with reference to its main regions. Paul Heywood, *The Government and Politics of Spain* (1995), presents a historical discussion of the modernization of the Spanish state. Frances Lannon, *Privilege, Persecution, and Prophecy: The Catholic Church in Spain, 1875–1975* (1987), provides a historical review of religion and church-state relations.

Richard E. Chandler and Kessel Schwartz, *A New History of Spanish Literature*, rev. ed. (1991), surveys the history of Spanish literature through the 1980s. John F. Moffitt, *The Arts in Spain* (1999), offers a balanced overview of the art history of Spain, with an emphasis on Spanish singularity and Spanish responses to international art trends. Emma Dent Coad, *Spanish Design and Architecture* (1990), covers fashion, interior and graphic design, and furniture, as well as architecture. Barry Jordan and Mark Allinson, *Spanish Cinema: A Student's Guide* (1999), offers a broad introductory survey of Spanish film.

A general book on Spain's early history is the richly illustrated Richard J. Harrison, *Spain at the Dawn of History: Iberians, Phoenicians, and Greeks* (1988). Works on Roman Spain include S.J. Keay, *Roman Spain* (1988); and J.S. Richardson, *The Romans in Spain* (1996, reissued 1998). Kenneth Baxter Wolf (trans. and ed.), *Conquerors and Chroniclers of Early Medieval Spain*, 2nd ed., trans. from Latin (1999); and the collection of essays in Edward James (ed.), *Visigothic Spain: New Approaches* (1980), are informative studies of the Visigothic period. Roger Collins, *Early Medieval Spain: Unity and Diversity, 400–1000*, 2nd ed. (1995); and Angus MacKay, *Spain in the Middle Ages: From Frontier to Empire, 1000–1500* (1977, reissued 1989), cover the medieval period.

Valuable treatments of Muslim Spain include Hugh Kennedy, *Muslim Spain and Portugal: A Political History of Al-Andalus* (1996); and Richard Fletcher, *Moorish Spain* (1992, reissued 1998). J.H. Elliott, *Imperial Spain, 1469–1716* (1963, reissued 1977), is the best single work covering this period. Treatments of the Inquisition include Norman Roth, *Conversos, Inquisition, and the Expulsion of the Jews from Spain* (1995); and Henry Kamen, *The Spanish Inquisition: An Historical Revision* (1997). John Lynch, *Spain Under the Habsburgs*, 2nd ed., 2 vol. (1981, reissued 1984), provides a good overview of early modern Spain. Antonio Domínguez Ortiz, *The Golden Age of Spain, 1516–1659* (1971), is a synthesis by one of the most distinguished Spanish scholars. John Lynch, *Bourbon Spain, 1700–1808* (1989, reprinted 1993), is an excellent survey of that period. General histories of political, economic, and social developments in modern Spain include José Alvarez Junco and Adrian Shubert (eds.), *Spanish History since 1808* (2000). *Burnett Bolloten, The Spanish Civil War: Revolution and Counterrevolution* (1991), is an encyclopaedic account of the conflict. The standard work on Francoism is Stanley

G. Payne, *The Franco Regime, 1936–1975* (1987, reissued 2000). Paul Preston, *Franco: A Biography* (1993, reissued 1995), is the definitive account of the dictator's life. Sources on the period of political transition include Paul Preston, *The Triumph of Democracy in Spain* (1986, reissued 1990). Among the many studies of regional nationalism, the most important include Daniele Conversi, *The Basques, the Catalans, and Spain: Alternative Routes to Nationalist Mobilisation* (1997, reissued 2000); and Juan Díez Medrano, *Divided Nations: Class, Politics, and Nationalism in the Basque Country and Catalonia* (1995).

Index